Radicalization
The Life Writings of Political Prisoners

Expanding the influence of auto/biography studies into cultural criminology, *Radicalization: The Life Writings of Political Prisoners* addresses the origins, processes and cultures of terrorist criminality and political resistance in a globalized world.

Criminologists and penologists have long been aware of the sheer volume of autobiography emerging from our prisons. Political prisoners, POWs, freedom fighters and terrorists have been consistently and strongly represented in this corpus of work, including such authors as Bobby Sands, Wole Soyinka, Nelson Mandela, Moazzam Begg, Ngugi wa Thiong'o, Angela Davis, George Jackson and Aung San Suu Kyi, among others. For many of those who have been detained for ostensibly politically motivated crimes, life writing has proved to be indispensable in explaining the reasons and processes which account for their situation. Embedded with these life writings are narratives of radicalization or resistance. Melissa Dearey here undertakes an international and comparative analysis of such narratives, where the 'life story' is considered as a mode of expressing and transmitting 'radical' cultural values.

Melissa Dearey is a Lecturer in Criminology at the University of Hull.

Radicalization

The Life Writings of Political Prisoners

Melissa Dearey

Routledge
Taylor & Francis Group

a GlassHouse book

First published 2010
by Routledge
2 Park Square, Milton Park, Abingdon, Oxfordshire OX14 4RN

Simultaneously published in the USA and Canada
by Routledge
711 Third Avenue, New York, NY 10017

A GlassHouse book

First issued in paperback 2014

Routledge is an imprint of the Taylor & Francis Group, an informa business

© 2010 Melissa Dearey

Typeset in TimesNewRoman by Taylor & Francis

British Library Cataloguing in Publication Data
A catalogue record for this book is available from the British Library

Library of Congress Cataloguing in Publication Data
Dearey, Melissa.
  Radicalization : the life writings of political prisoners / Melissa Dearey.
    p. cm.
  Includes bibliographical references.
  1. Radicalism. 2. Political crimes and offenses. 3. Terrorism. 4. Political
prisoners' writings. I. Title.
  HN49.R33D43 2010
  303.48′4–dc22
                    2009026908

ISBN 978-0-415-46772-8 (hbk)

ISBN 978-0-415-68569-6 (pbk)

ISBN 978-0-203-86450-0 (ebk)

To my family, Paul, Sam, Luke, Greta, Genevieve and Stan, with all my love.

Contents

Acknowledgements

There are many people to whom I owe a debt of gratitude for their contribution to the research that resulted in this book. First of all, I acknowledge the financial support provided by the ESRC in conjunction with the UK Ministry of Defence, grant number RES-000-22-3078, and the staff at the Defence Science and Technology Laboratory who helped make this project possible. I would also like to thank my colleagues at the University of Hull who have, through their kind support and immense generosity with their time and advice, helped me when I needed it most. Those to whom I am most indebted are Dr Mark Johnson, Professor Peter Young, Professor Keith Tester, Professor Paul Gilbert and Professor Majid Yar, who all read and commented helpfully and incisively on early draft chapters. Each of you in your own way epitomize the spirit of collegiality, and I have benefited greatly from your advice and your good company. I would also express my gratitude to the staff at Routledge who offered their kind, generous and patient support, particularly Colin Perrin, Holly Davis and especially Dan Benton. While all of you have undoubtedly helped improve the quality of the final book, you are of course not to blame for any of the errors inevitably present despite my best efforts, whether by omission or commission – that buck rests squarely with me.

On a more personal note, I would like to acknowledge the very important role played by my friends and fellow book group members who provided a uniquely accommodating and loving place for me to let off steam, with wine and nibbles (my favourite way). Cate, Keri and Annette, to you I owe a great debt of thanks, I only hope to pay off over many long years of enduring friendship.

And finally to my family, to whom I dedicate this book. To my husband Paul, I have really tried (though not very successfully) not to breach the moratorium on the subject of political prisoner life writing, which I know too well I thoroughly exhausted years ago. To my children Sam, Luke, Greta and Genevieve, I owe you the deepest gratitude and the most irreparable debt – I only hope all the time I spent on this instead of other things was worth it. And finally, to my puppy Stan, the stalwart who loyally slept alongside me while I worked through all the long months and helped perfect the peripatetic method of research with all those walks.

Chapter 1

What is radicalization?

From the civil society to the enemy within

Radicalization is a term that is used within many political and cultural discourses about important areas of modern life as diverse as disability, 'race', gender, economics, human/animal rights and crime – but what precisely is 'radicalization'? While its more infamous analogue 'terrorism' has been on the receiving end of considerable effort by a number of commentators with a view to achieving a sufficiently rigorous definition (Crenshaw 2004; Milton-Edwards 2005; Schmid and Jongman 2005; Hoffman 2006; Nielsen 2007; Abbas 2007a; Bhatia, 2008), a review of the existing research literature reveals that there has not yet been any such compulsion to define radicalization. However, this lack of definition and conceptual understanding has not lessened its appeal as a focal point for current strategic policy-making in counter-terrorism and security – if anything, just the opposite:

> Radicalisation is one of the four strategic drivers for terrorism identified in the first part of this strategy: in the context of this strategy radicalisation refers to the process by which people come to support terrorism and violent extremism and, in some cases, then to join terrorist groups. The aim of the *Prevent* workstream is to stop radicalisation, reducing support for terrorism and discouraging people from becoming terrorists. In 2003, this part of CONTEST was the least developed.
>
> (Home Office, 2009: 82)

In place of a definition, as with so many formative concepts shaping the everyday culture of modern life, the assumption appears to be that everyone knows it when they see it, and so we are able to proceed with the tasks in hand while awaiting further conceptual clarification. Despite our admitted lack of understanding of radicalization, it has emerged as a phenomenon that has displayed substantial 'epistemological creep' into contemporary discourses about freedom, security, identity, crime and deviance, covering a wide spectrum from the deeply personal issues of identity faced by individuals in their everyday lives to the global politics of terrorism and threats to human and animal rights, the environment and the nation state. In this chapter, I will investigate what radicalization is, in terms of how it has been used by various commentators and within a variety of discourses in public policy, the media and academia; and who are the sorts of people susceptible to radicalization, how and why, where does radicalization lead, and how might it be conceptualized as a topic for research in criminology and beyond.

This review of the literature includes an analysis of the methodological foundations underpinning current policy and political discourses of radicalization, as well as some proposed alternatives from other scholarly and/or professional disciplines. This is followed in Chapter 2 by a further detailed examination of one such alternative interdisciplinary methodology: auto/biographical studies. Here I make the case for consideration of this interpretive or qualitative method as applied to another 'alternative' and underestimated data set: the life writings of radicalized actors who are among the most 'fully radicalized' of radical actors, and who have reached at least one possible and common destination in the radicalization 'process', prison. The following chapters take a more in-depth view of these life writings to explore a range of key themes and patterns that emerge from a micro analysis based on my reading of these and many other such texts over the years. These cover the influence on the radicalization narratives of these writers that originate in the diverse experiences of gender, sexuality and the body (the subject of Chapter 3), children and childhood (Chapter 4) and family life and kinship relationships (Chapter 5). While this is in no way intended to represent a comprehensive list of the key variables influencing radicalization, they do, in my view, constitute a list of hugely significant aspects of modern life that, according to this particular data source, are highlighted as being elemental to what made these writers become radicalized in the first place. These factors should therefore be of interest to those who adopt a 'crime' as opposed to a 'war' paradigm of counter-terrorism that seeks to prioritize prevention over military or other ad hoc forms of intervention by force. This selection of themes also offers the advantage of concentrating on variables that represent those which have been identified by experts in counter-terrorism as being significant but little understood (e.g. family, gender, prison), while others have thus far have gone relatively unmarked (e.g. sexuality, the body, childhood), but are still important for gaining a fuller understanding of the phenomenon of radicalization.

What is radicalization?

Radicalization as a modern social phenomenon has displayed a substantial presence, complexity and malleability as an emergent concept within expert subject disciplines such as political science, law, sociology, security studies, medicine, social work, gender studies and forensic psychology. These discourses cover a wide spectrum of individual, collective, national and global experience, including politics, education, environmentalism, feminism, class, employment and the range of social movements including the women's, civil rights, animal rights and disability movements. Immediately we encounter the problem of devising a sufficiently focused yet generically inclusive definition to cover all instances of such a broadly polymorphous, fluid and complex phenomenon as conceptualised within such diverse disciplinary frameworks, while at the same time retaining a sense of distinctiveness and meaning. In a recent essay, Tarik Fraihi provides this elegant yet succinct generic definition:

> Radicalization is a process in which an individual's convictions and willingness to seek for deep and serious changes in the society increase. Radicalism and radicalization are not necessarily negative. Moreover, different forms of radicalization exist.
>
> (Fraihi, 2008: 135)

As this definition suggests, radicalization can be characterized generically by its intentional situating of the individual actively pursuing 'serious' or 'deep' change at the wider social level in an intense manner. This concentration on the individual is indicative of the focus of expert and governmental concern, as reiterated by Jenkins: 'jihadists recruit one person at a time. The message from the global jihad is aimed directly at the individual' (Jenkins 2007: 3). Radicalization is by implication thus regarded as a matter of potency on the part of the individual, and is frequently spoken of in terms of extending and penetrating the social body in order to substantially alter its material or organizational form. In itself, as we will see over the course of this chapter, this does not necessitate a pernicious, dangerous or destructive way of achieving social change, either on the part of society or of the individuals or collectives of like-minded persons who opt for this form of politically orien-ted activism. Indeed, in a great number of cases, radicalization has yielded many positive and dramatic transformations in areas of social life that, in hindsight, have been acknowledged as having required such 'conviction' vis-à-vis individually motivated efforts in the face of a widespread culture of ignorance, apathy or passivity. This includes radical changes to social atti-tudes and practices concerning areas such as disability, gender equality, sexuality and the natural world, to name but a few. Modern history regards radicals as heroes as well as villains, and at least one European former prime minister, the Dutch premier Ruud Lubbers, has openly identified himself as an erstwhile radical (Lubbers, 2007: 7).

Even with this focus on the individual, however, for many contemporary commentators and decision-makers, definitions such as Fraihi's are too vague and generic to be of much use as the basis of empirical study and policy formation. Many opt for a narrower perspective, defining radicaliza-tion in terms of what it is, how to recognize it, what 'causes' it, who is sus-ceptible to it, and (ideally) how to predict and pre-empt, 'counter' or even reverse it (the much sought 'de-radicalization' strategy). The emphasis is thus on radicalization as a *process*: while it is often linked to a single manifest act or event, it is regarded as taking place over time in the ordinary course of the daily life of the individual in question. What is more, this is a process that represents an anomalous or pathological deviation of the usual course of normal historical progression (both individual and social). Radicalization itself is thus regarded as an intrinsic or even essential, but nonetheless anomalous, part of the broader socio-historical narrative arc of modernity – something akin perhaps to dissonance or counterpoint in music – which can, in its most extreme or advanced forms, result in the type of terrorist action that has the capacity to destroy the overall cohesion or thematic unity of the (socio-political) whole. According to this view, radicalization represents a phenomenon with the momentous coalescence of the terrorist action or *event* at its heart, while at the same time comprising qualities that are the just opposite of episodic, i.e. that are developmental or evolutionary in character and thus *cyclical*; in Jenkins's words, radicalization is the 'front end' of the 'jihadist cycle' (Jenkins, 2007: 1).

The tensions between event-based theorizing and the aberration of terrorism in relation to 'normal' historical progression have been noted in scholarly research on terrorism (e.g. Crenshaw, 2008). This is an approach that would seem to be most notable in the field of security studies, law enforcement and public policy-making, where the analytic focus is directed towards the nexus of the *individual* and his or her own personal *experience* of the radicalization process itself, and the impact this has on his or her *intentions* (Kelly in Silber and Bhatt, 2007: 2) as a social actor, as opposed to taking into consideration the wider historical perspective that incorporates the process of social change. In other words, some commentators are increasingly directing their concerns not at the social aims or teleologies of radicalization, but at the particular type of deep personal change that takes place within the radicalized individual, and subsequently the outcomes of these individuals' actions on the existing social order. This perspective on the radicalized or radicalizing agent, who exists in opposition to 'the social' and foregrounds the need to actively preserve the status quo, emphasizes the *normative* aspects of radicalization as an immoderate and thus aberrant mechanism for the pursuit of social change, with the deviant individual as lone wolf or member of an extremist sub-group at its core. Radicalization is thus usually characterized in contemporary policy discourse by its 'extreme' and potentially 'violent' nature, as opposed to its capacities as one among other possible mechanisms for agitating for social change. It is in this spirit that attention is more often than not directed at the need to isolate and actively address certain belief systems, subcultures or personality types that are identified as seeking to engage in such seminal changes to socio-political norms, rather than acknowledging the relativistic and normative character of radicalization itself:

The word 'radicalization' (used interchangeably in this report with 'radicalized' and 'radicalizing') is frequently used to describe the process whereby individuals transform their worldview over time from a range that society tends to consider to be normal into a range that society tends to consider to be extreme. In some cases these individuals may then take a further step and involve themselves in acts of violence. However, it is not the case that those who embark on such a transformation do so solely as a consequence of their interpretation of Islam.

(Hannah, Clutterbuck and Rubin, 2008: 2)

While the authors of this statement rightly point out that this worldview transformation is not always due solely to the influence of Islam, the mention of this particular religious ideology as a relevant factor is nevertheless notable (see Abbas, 2007b). In his expert testimony to the US House Homeland Security Committee, Jenkins (2007) shifts the discursive focus from a military to a religious paradigm – an ideological framing of radicalization in which jihadists become the self-styled moral and political entrepreneurs of the contemporary modern global age, proselytizing a new 'mindset' as part of the spoils of agitating for a new world order:

More than a military contest, the jihadist campaign is above all a missionary enterprise. Jihadist terrorist operations are intended to attract attention, demonstrate capability, and harm the jihadists' enemies, but they are also aimed at galvanizing the Muslim community and, above all, inciting and attracting recruits to the cause. Recruiting is not merely meant to fill operational needs. It is an end in itself: It aims at creating a new mindset.

(Jenkins, 2007: 2)

The themes of the individual, socio-cultural norms, social change and the 'process' view of radicalization will be further interrogated in the following chapters. For now, let us turn our attention to the issue of religious ideology, in particular the role of Islam in radicalization.

Radicalization and religion: does Islam cause radicalization?

At this point, it is worth pointing out that contributors to the debate on radicalization or parties with a vested interest in defining and responding to the 'problem' of radicalization differ with respect to the focus on the individual or religious ideologies. In the case of religion, there is a detectable reticence among some western academics and policy-makers to stipulate directly Islamic religious ideology as the object of official concern, though others have shown little or no hesitation about where to point the finger. There has been some criticism of this 'naïve' approach to demure from religion whether based on an ethos of 'political correctness' or a more pervasive ignorance of religion or theology predominating in the secular west. Abuza (2006) shows no such hesitation in making his point about the influence of religious ideology on radicalization, and the subsequent need for political and security analysts in the west to understand it and discuss it in an informed way that resists anxieties about being politically correct:

> Western analysts of terrorism tend to discount the 'religious' nature of terrorists' struggle. We cannot make this mistake; we need to bring the religion back in. This will be all the more difficult because political and security analysts have little religious understanding or training. But groups like JI [Jemaah Islamiyah] base their membership on religious conviction. They will want their leaders not only to have technical or operational know-how, but also to be steeped in religious understanding.
>
> (Abuza, 2006: 76)

Instead, western governmental approaches (with the notable exception of the US, and other states such as the Netherlands and occasionally the UK) tend toward the position adopted by the different arms of the European Union, where a comparatively more open, broadly construed, and complex set of factors and methodologies are invoked from the outset as objects of institutional concern, as well as potential resources for understanding the issues and devising appropriate responses or solutions to the problem of radicalization. Generally speaking, religious ideology tends to come well down the list of variables, or is otherwise clustered together with other 'narratives' or ideologies of 'belief':

> In 2006 the Commission contracted out three studies on violent radicalisation that encourage a multi-disciplinary and comparative approach to analysis of the phenomenon, based on fieldwork. The studies cover (i) the factors that may trigger or affect violent radicalisation processes, particularly among youth; (ii) the beliefs, ideologies and narrative of violent radicals; and (iii) the methods through which violent radicals mobilise support for terrorism and find new recruits.
>
> (Council of the European Union, 2007: 16)

What is needed, according to the Council of the European Union, is not a greater concentration on, or engagement in, the areas of traditional life as represented by, for example, theological issues or debates, but rather the need to embark on new strategic thinking about the problem of radicalization and recruitment from a 'fresh' (but not yet worked out) perspective:

> If the European Union wishes to supplement Member States' efforts in the field of prevention, then fresh ideas for implementation of the

Strategy for Combating Radicalisation and Recruitment need to be developed.

(ibid.: 2)

The objective is thus to take a 'cautious, modest and well-thought' view, in order to devise appropriate and effective 'long-term' strategies for dealing with the issue of *violent* radicalization,[1] an issue of huge complexity and a project that requires fresh thinking based on in-depth and multidisciplinary analysis in combination with past historical experiences of dealing with extremist groups in Europe:

> Interest in this subject has increased in recent years. It is admittedly a very complex question with no simple answers and which requires a cautious, modest and well-thought approach. In this Communication, the Commission reports on its ongoing work in this area and proposes possible ways in which work in various fields within its competence could be channelled more effectively into addressing the issue. The Annex to the Communication merely provides a preliminary analysis of the possible factors contributing to violent radicalization and terrorist recruitment. Certainly, more in-depth research and analysis into the phenomenon is required.
>
> As specifically requested by the Hague Programme[2] ... this document is the Commission's initial contribution to the development of an EU long-term strategy (whose presentation by the Council is foreseen for the end of 2005) to address the factors which contribute to radicalization and recruitment to terrorist activities. The actions and recommendations presented in this document are a combination of soft (e.g. intercultural exchanges among youth) and hard (e.g. prohibition of satellite broadcasts inciting terrorism) measures and are to be viewed as complementary to, and in support of, current national efforts. The Commission however believes that the EU, with its span of policies in various areas that could be used to address violent radicalization, is well placed to gather and spread at European level the relevant expertise that is being acquired by the Member States in addressing this problem. ...
>
> The core areas of immediate focus are broadcast media, the Internet, education, youth engagement, employment, social exclusion and integration issues, equal opportunities and non-discrimination and intercultural dialogue. Furthermore, in order to acquire greater knowledge in the field, the Commission will support more extensive analysis of violent radicalization that will serve as a basis for better policy-making in the future. Finally, the external relations component to tackling the problem is a crucial aspect of a future EU strategy in this area.
>
> (Commission to the European Parliament and the Council, 2005: sections 1 and 2)

Reference to any specific religious ideology or ethnic group recedes into the distance with such a 'long' view, or are otherwise considered one among many complexly related but generic (i.e. not linked to any particular religious affiliation or orientation) factors:

> Violent Radicalisation is defined under section 1, above. In order to understand its historical and psychological roots one needs to look at a wide range of movements, organisations and struggles, with political, religious, national and ethnic motivations, or combinations of these. Radicalisation has become a particular area of focus due to its link with combating terrorism. Europe has a long experience of fighting terrorism. Examples such as the ETA, the IRA and the Brigate Rosse come to mind. Terrorists under many guises and invoking different ideologies and motives have claimed victims in many Member States. The ideologies and propaganda have varied and included extremism of different types – whether from the extreme left or right, anarchist and religious or in many cases nationalist. All these groups have tried to terrorise democratic societies to concede political transformations by non-democratic means. While they sometimes invoked aspirations shared by wider parts of the population, the use of terrorism has always been rejected both by societies as a whole and by the very groups whose interests the groups purportedly sought to promote.
>
> (Commission to the European Parliament and the Council, 2005: annex)

Though there is evidence to suggest an underlying philosophical difference between European and American conceptualizations of radicalization and hence strategic responses to it, it is important not to overstate this supposed division or the homogeneity of any particular regional or geographic view. As we will see over the course of this chapter, focusing on the individual and/ or Islam is not exclusive to the American approach, nor does it characterize it entirely, but is also detectable in many British and Dutch contributions; similarly, French commentators have taken either position at different times over a long period of debate on terrorism. Neither a historical or composite approach leaves the individual or religion out of the equation. In addition, it is important to recognize that the presence of the individual and/or religion in these debates can signal important conceptual and philosophical shifts, not just regarding the individual–society or secular–religious dichotomies, but also the incursion of methodological individualism (of more later).

Notwithstanding the breadth of analytic scope for research in this area, references to historical experiences of extremism and terrorism as cited by the Council of Europe and the European Parliament often invariably lead again to the question of the radicalized individual. Indeed, historical research shows that the types of individuals who are or have been perceived to be especially prone to radicalization, and their relationship to the social body, has changed significantly over time. Whereas in the past, those who emerged into the public eye as figures who were noted for their capacity to achieve such seminal social change were generally regarded as truly exceptional in some way (e.g. Martin Luther King, Sylvia and Christabel Pankhurst, Mahatma Gandhi, and so forth), the focus on celebrated individuals as the drivers of social change has for many academic historians gone very much out of fashion. This can be seen in the many emerging revisions over the last decade or so of the histories of the women's movement, the civil rights movement and the Black Power movements (e.g. Collier-Thomas and Franklin, 2001; Nasstrom, 2003; Patton, 2004; Payne, 1996; Tyson, 1998; Dittmer, 1994; Horowitz, 1998). The turn to the 'ordinary' person and the sphere of everyday life is also observable in the current focus on a particularly urgent form of radicalization, that of the 'homegrown' variety. This pertains to ordinary, 'unremarkable' people who live among us and who represent a more or less undifferentiated part of the social mass; these are the terrorists-in-waiting who are characterised by their potential to pose a threat, who may not even be actively planning terrorist attacks, but nevertheless occupy what is increasingly regarded as the latent sphere of collective and daily modern life pervaded by risk:

> Where once we would have defined the initial indicator of the threat at the point where a terrorist or group of terrorists would actually plan an attack, we now have shifted our focus to a much earlier point—a point where we believe the potential terrorist or group of terrorists begin and progress through a process of radicalization. The culmination of this process is a terrorist attack.
>
> Understanding this trend and the radicalization process in the west that drives 'unremarkable' people to become terrorists is vital for developing effective counter-strategies and has special importance for the NYPD and the City of New York.
>
> (Silber and Bhatt, 2007: 5)

The urgency of the threat presented by these 'ordinary', 'homegrown' and potentially violent radicals in our midst has encouraged some commentators to conflate 'radicalization' with a certain type of 'extremism' that is conditioned by the very proximity of the Other within the social body based on alternative and aggressively pathological ideologies of belief. This perspective has led to the identification of a particularly virulent source of extremism variously labelled as violent Islamic, Islamist, or jihadi (e.g. NCTb, 2007; Council of the European Union, 2007; Jenkins, 2007) originating from a particular community group commonly identified as the Muslim diaspora, and within this the sub-group of major concern, mainly young Muslim men. Contrary to the rhetoric of radicalization adopted by these groups, the emphasis here is not on political agency or the potency of the radicalized individual, but rather the weakness and fragmentation of their communities that makes them vulnerable to such outside influences or external social circumstance:

> In the European diaspora, Muslim immigrant youths are vulnerable to radicalization and crime ... because they feel excluded from hope and opportunities, and because their own communities are weak and plagued by multiple social problems.
>
> (Benard, 2005: 162)

While other commentators do not specify Muslims per se, along with Abuza (2006) cited previously, 'sets of belief' relating to jihadi or Islamist ideologies are again singled out as objects of official concern:

> Radicalization comprises internalizing a set of beliefs, a militant mindset that embraces violent jihad as the paramount test of one's conviction. It is the mental prerequisite to recruitment.
>
> (Jenkins, 2007: 2)

> The disruption of terrorist plots in the United Kingdom, Canada and the United States, as well as the July 2005 attacks in London, generated significant attention to the concept of homegrown radicalization. But this term does not define the real focus of concern—violent Islamic extremism ...

Once again, however, as Dyer *et al.* (2007) point out, while these ideological or religious foci provide a target area or indicate the identification of discrete group(s), they also give rise to new problems of definition:

> Before finding an effective solution to this problem, law enforcement first must understand and define it. What is Islamic extremism? Do radical beliefs always lead to terrorist activity?
>
> (Dyer *et al.*, 2007: 3–4)

By way of improving expert knowledge of Islamism, Milton-Edwards (2005) offers the following contribution by concentrating on Islamic fundamentalism in terms of its intrinsically volatile and violent influence as a primarily *political* and only secondarily spiritual or religious aspect of contemporary social life, to the extent that the terms 'Islamism' and 'fundamentalism' are practically interchangeable. What is more, history shows that while Islamic fundamentalisms have displayed a capacity to be extremely complex and malleable, nonetheless what has endured more or less as a constant has been their essentially gendered nature, particularly their propensity to be shaped by shifting patterns of Muslim masculinities. The cultural repercussions of masculinities are made all the more urgent in the contemporary context due to the rise of violence carried out mainly by young men in modern western society (Spierenburg, 2008).

> The analytic perspective ... centres on Islam as a political experience. This is not to say that the religious/spiritual dimension of Islam is ignored but instead it is to say that ... I will concentrate on the political manifestation of Islam in the late twentieth century. Moreover, Islam [for these purposes] is defined as a fundamentalist phenomenon. Although this implies a singular unitary entity, as the historical account that unfolds in these pages reveals the reality is rich in diversity, context and response. Suffice to say, then, the term Islamic fundamentalism is employed loosely ... in respect more generally of a variety of impulses, movements, ideas, thinkers and groups that are active across the globe. In one respect, the term is employed this way because there is in fact little agreement of what fundamentalism strictly constitutes. Scholars can agree to nothing more than the assertion that the term refers to 'family resemblances' between a variety of monotheistic faiths and includes characteristics such as: religious idealism, cosmic struggle, demonising the opponent, reactionary thinking, and envy of modernist hegemony and the revolutionary overthrow of power. Moreover, fundamentalism is not gender-neutral but is represented as a specifically male business. Fundamentalism is also interchangeable with the term Islamism—this underlines the political emphasis that is attached to expressions of Muslim religiosity in specific contexts.
>
> (Milton-Edwards, 2005: 2)

Others have seized on the reactionary qualities of radicalization suggested by Milton-Edwards, as in the case of Ruud Lubbers' (2007: 11) statement on the resurgence of violent extremism and fundamentalism, that it represents a 'rebound' by anti-globalization groups against the benefits of globalization and/or 'American hegemony', which in turn have been met by the 'rebound' of non-government organizations (NGOs) and corporate social responsibility (CSR). This, along with consideration of other forms of violent radicalization such as those carried out by Loyalist paramilitary groups in Northern Ireland or anti-abortion groups in the US, significantly problematizes the notion of radicalization as pertaining exclusively to the teleology of social change. Some radical groups are more conservatively oriented, and hence their radicalization praxes are intrinsically shaped by the intention to frustrate, disrupt or even reverse immanent or established trends of social transformation. Even groups such as al-Qaeda, while advocating radical social change on a global level, hark back to a 'golden age' for many of their rhetorical justifications.

Suffice to say that these attempts at definition give rise to a number of serious issues with respect to the reciprocal impact that they are likely to have upon the members of the groups or communities who have become identified as the object of such suspicion or concern. We may ask if this contraction of the definitional scope to fundamentalist Muslims, the Muslim diaspora or young Muslim males is warranted, or if this is an example of creating a deviant sub-group, potentially denoting a process of criminalization rather than mapping the process of radicalization. To this end, I will now broaden the conceptual lens and consider the development of radicalization as a cultural and political phenomenon generally, in the first instance conducting a brief review of some of the scholarly literature on radicalization in a range of social contexts in post-war western society, concentrating on how the term has been used, who it has been attached to, and what the consequences for these definitional discourses have been with respect to politics, policy-making and public opinion on radicalization. In line with the scope of this book, particular attention will be given to the representation of these aspects in auto/biographical forms, or otherwise represented via the individual experience of radicalization. We will return to the issue of religion in the section on preradicalization (pg 38).

Disability

Tom Shakespeare (1998) traces the emergence of radicalization in relation to disability to the era of the 1960s and 1970s. As with the women's movement and the civil rights movement, which were similarly experiencing resurgence during this period, the radicalization of disabled people has been interpreted as a reaction to the consensus politics and functionalism that dominated western societies until and including the immediate post-Second World War period. In this context, Shakespeare refers specifically to the radicalization of young American disabled people in the Independent Living Movement (ILM), and their demand for a complete reconsideration of the concept of disability and its association with obsolete social norms in the wake of new theoretical models of deviance such as labelling theory, in addition to the impending crisis of the welfare state. Of particular concern to many 'radical' reformers was the need to critique the medical model of disability, arguing that disability is in many ways (if not completely) a product of social construction whereby society disables people through its unreflective and exclusionary social norms, practices and institutional structures, which can be prejudicial, stigmatizing and oppressive for those who do not fit such restrictive models of normality (Goffman, 1963).

As Groch (2001) explains, it is against this growing awareness of institutionalized, systematic and historical injustice that what she terms 'oppositional consciousness' has taken shape among disabled people. 'Oppositional consciousness' is used here as an 'umbrella' phrase to denote a spectrum of collective responses by:

> members of a group that others have traditionally treated as subordinate or deviant ... when they claim their previously subordinate identity as a

positive identification, identify injustices done to their group, demand changes in the polity, economy or society to rectify those injustices, and see other members of their group as sharing an interest in rectifying those injustices.

(Mansbridge, 2001a: 1)

Importantly, the spectrum of what constitutes oppositional consciousness is extremely wide and varied, as illustrated by the range of disability activist (as well as other) groups. Some groups, such as those representing the mobility impaired, have been the least radical, promoting integrationist and reformist policies in favour of more blatantly oppositional stances. Others, notably the deaf, tend to be the most radical in their approach, adopting a distinctive culture of 'deaf consciousness' based on their own language and symbols, demanding social change on their own terms, exclusive from those of other disabled groups, and embracing segregationist lifestyles. Groups representing the blind tend to fall somewhere in the middle – some pursuing alliances with other types of disability rights groups, others refusing to embrace such a generic political agenda based on disability as opposed to one founded exclusively on promoting the interests of blind people (Groch, 2001).

Central to this and other social movements based on the new identity politics of this era (e.g. the women's movement, the civil rights movement, the Black Power movement) was the radicalization of substantial numbers of disabled people, although as Couser (1997: 5) justifiably points out, for this group, the gap between bodily dysfunction and personal narrative in the form of life writing has until relatively recently proved to be a particularly difficult one to bridge. This gap is likely to account for the notable absence of a corpus of 'classic' life writings by disabled people until the 1990s.[3] However, there is ample evidence that this is changing, and that disabled people are increasingly regarding their own life experiences as appropriate not just for public dissemination but also as the basis of radical argument for widespread social change. As Nancy Mairs (1997) writes, for many people disabled by the onset of chronic illness (in her case, multiple sclerosis), the need to articulate a new life narrative often originates from a particular space which is for many ' … a tiny, probably white [room], probably without windows … ' (Mairs, 1997: ix) where, if you're lucky, you may have the luxury of wearing your own clothes or at least having them back on soon, and where the voices and noises of other anonymous individuals filter in. Here she refers of course to the quintessential doctor's office, but implies that the feeling is not wholly different from a prison cell, where the devastating (at least to previous identity narratives) medical diagnosis is delivered and its digestion by the now permanently identified 'patient' begins. From within this space, Mairs notes the dreadful feeling of solitude and abjection, even for those who were prepared enough to be accompanied by a loved one for support. The response for many is typical: 'Then, if you're a writer, you start to scribble' (ibid.: ix), accounting for the considerable and growing corpus of life writings by disabled people that comprises a rich data set from which to study any number of phenomena associated with it, including radicalization.

Economics, class and employment

In their survey of radicalism and radicalization during the 1980s in the UK, Edgell and Duke (1986) trace the formative influence of production and consumption in the battle between public and private sectors with respect to their competing models of capitalism. They argue that radicalization as a process should be distinguished from the structural qualities of radicalism, and warn that the factors that explain one do not necessarily explain the other. They argue that radicalism as a structuring device characterized the leadership of public sector workers during the recession of the 1980s; radicalization mainly manifested itself in the increasingly divided and divisive culture of partisanship of party politics developed in the UK and beyond, albeit one that was not attached to any particular political ideology or group. Henceforth, the structures of radicalism and the processes of radicalization should both be regarded as features of established and legitimate politics within the public sphere, and thus important points of contention in the struggle over control of a 'free' democratic society by a variety of competing political actors – in the sense that the politics of contemporary capitalism are both 'free' from totalitarianism and (just as importantly) 'free' to consume. In their survey of attitudes and behaviours, Edgell and Duke found that public sector 'controllers' were most likely to be at the 'vanguard' of radicalism, and that the issue of radical versus 'dominant values' is firmly rooted in partisanship, which is in turn affected by variables such as labour and class (Edgell and Duke, 1986: 479). Their findings concerning the often contradictory tensions brought about by the complexities of the new market state (Bobbitt, 2008) and consumerism can be regarded as relevant in the ensuing period of globalization, as witnessed in the recent UK example of a brief series of 'wildcat strikes' initiated by British oil refinery workers in Lincolnshire in protest at the employment of foreign (EU) workers in 2009. In many instances, these strikes were undertaken without recourse to, or even in contravention of, established trade union leadership or structural protest mechanisms; moreover, they facilitated the incursion of extremist political elements into the ensuing radicalization of the workers, as influenced by the extremist and race-based politics of the far right, notably the British Nationalist Party (BNP).

Radicalization and the media

From the current media-dominated perspective, radicalization seems to fuel a now-familiar sense of 'moral panic' based on the emergence of a new breed of 'folk devils' (Cohen, 1980) from whatever part of the political spectrum.

Despite frequent demands for government policy-makers to be more 'radical' in their approaches to entrenched social and political problems, radicalization of and by non-state actors is increasingly seen as intrinsically worrying if not downright dangerous. But the question constantly arises: how 'radical' should states be in their efforts to combat terrorism and/or its 'precursor', radicalization? Is it legitimate or counter-productive to suspend or violate principles of law, human and/or civil rights in the effort to make society safe from the terrorist threat?

The scholarly literature reiterates the crucial importance of the propaganda and PR value not only of politically motivated violence but also of responses to it by the state in a media-dominated society. The research shows that campaigns of armed resistance undertaken by extremist factions can be about both promoting radicalization among the general populace and also expressing and enhancing the radicalization bonds within these groups, for example by attacking the state in the hopes of provoking an overly reactive counter-response that will polarize the population, hence reducing or precluding the efficacy of more moderate political interventions (de Mesquita and Dickson, 2007). In this scenario, de Mesquita and Dickson describe how radicalization can occur as a result of state action incited by terrorist insurgency, which from the outset is knowingly doomed to failure – as with the Provisional IRA campaign in the 1970s against a greatly superior military force, which the IRA itself recognized it did not have a hope of vanquishing on the terms of conventional military warfare. Nonetheless, military failure can offer the opportunity for political victory in reality, either as a result of the economic damage caused by counter-terrorism operations or by the way in which such operations alter public perceptions of the government based on considerations of the proportionality and/or effectiveness of state response. This is an important and interesting contribution to the current security debate, as it highlights how even terrorist campaigns that lack any realistic prospect of military success in the 'war on terror' can exhibit genuine potency in advancing extremist ideologies within the current political context, with the media playing a highly influential role in this distinctively collective radicalization process. Indeed, we have seen high-profile examples in the media of radicalized individuals or groups who claim that they had no ability or intention of engaging in actual terrorist activity, but rather sought to influence public opinion by goading the state into an overreaction (e.g. the Glasgow airport and London nightclub bombers). Recognition of this factor arguably exacerbates the complexity and breadth of effective governmental responses to radicalization linked to extremist activism and ideologies, but in another sense it simplifies the need for states to 'stick to their guns' when it comes to resisting the temptation to violate the very freedoms they claim to defend, as well as the inviolability of the law and human rights in the fight against terrorism.

But what part does the media play in radicalizing individuals, i.e. how does it contribute to, or facilitate, the radicalization process? A relatively rare example of early research in this area carried out in Canada by Woelfel *et al.* (1974) offers suggestions. Their survey of 412 adult education students in Montreal revealed that attitudes towards French-Canadian separatism within this sample population are ' ... well explained (R^2 = .64) by a weighted average of the information they received from interpersonal and media sources' (Woelfel *et al.*, 1974: 243), and that the evidence showed that the resultant attitudes substantially affected subsequent behaviours related to the engagement in separatist activities. More recently, Awan (2007a, b) has conducted research on one of the most significant media influences: the use of the Internet in Islamist radicalization. Among his findings is that the Internet, among all form of the new media, is increasingly becoming the medium of choice for radical jihadists through a proliferation of dedicated websites, forums and blogs. Among the advantages of the Internet as a source of radicalization are its accessibility and low cost, anonymity and lack of censorship, speed and immediacy of contact, scope and audience reach (importantly overcoming potentially exclusionary issues such as class, geographical and gender divides), ease of communication and interactivity, and attractive multimedia environment (Awan, undated). While Awan admits that the precise role of the Internet in the radicalization process is difficult to quantify, at the same time he contends that it is possible to identity its function in four key and interrelated areas: the provision of an alternative source of news; the effective and timely dissemination of propaganda (both of which are frequently backed up by crudely modified photographic 'evidence'); the capacity to advertise, recruit and collect funds for paramilitary training and technical and financial support; and the expression of emotion and catharsis. Interestingly, Awan highlights the increasing reliance on visual media communicated via the Internet for propaganda, indoctrination and publicity purposes in the interests of radicalization, for instance by providing visual images of the Madrid train bombings, the failed 21 July London bomb plot, and the rise of 'gore sites' with extreme audio-visual content. He also stresses the nature of the Internet as an as yet 'elective' medium, meaning that people must in some sense actively choose to visit one these sites, thus implying that they provide more of a reinforcement to radicalization – or at most an initial impetus – than a more substantial and pivotal motivational role. Awan thus points to the significance of the new media in the radicalization process, but with the proviso that it is essential to resist the reductive conclusion that such 'surfing' activities actually 'cause' radicalization. This is, he rightly states, a much more complex and nuanced process.

Social policy and professional practice

Beyond the realm of academia, the correlation of radicalization with the everyday social construction of identity converging on the 'Other', often with respect to issues of 'race', class and gender extends even to professional work practices, as for example in nursing – here we can cite the examples of Linda Gustafson's (2007) critical reflections on her own personal professional practice as a white nurse in relation to the ongoing issues of race and power in the care professions, and in society more generally; and Sue Middleton's equally critical and reflective remarks on the radicalizing influence of education on teachers and students in schools. Using life history methods, both Gustafson and Middleton refer to the 'radicalizing' influence of working and learning in such vital social institutions, and specifically how they were able to recreate for themselves a durable professional biography while also recognizing the significance of radical activism on their own part and those of others with respect to how nursing and teaching are actually done. Such life histories demonstrate very effectively how, even in some of the most regulated and socially conservative (small 'c') or 'total' institutions devoted to the task of social control, individuals do not carry out their roles passively, but actively shape, change and resist the various contradictory, unjust or obsolete systems they encounter, and are reciprocally shaped by these same efforts of regulation, negotiation and resistance, as are the institutions they inhabit (e.g. Foucault, 1977; Cohen, 1985; Goffman, 1972).

The research literature in the area of the professional practice reiterates the tensions introduced by radicalization as some sort of aspirational principle for reflective practice and reflexive capacity within what are often very large and unwieldy institutional structures. As a way of measuring the convergence of the daily realities of one's job with the principles underlying its foundational justification as something worth doing, by offering some kind of benefit to society or reinforcing a sense of self-belief, radicalization extends to more than just earnest individual practitioners 'who care'. As Lynne M. Healy remarks in her book *International Social Work: Professional Action in an Independent World* (2001), while the development of social work as a profession has been significantly shaped by the notion of radicalization, in terms of its substance as an 'action agenda' (Healy 2001: 38) item as opposed to simply a topic of discussion radicalization remains relatively inert. In social work, she argues that radicalization has functioned mainly as a symbolic designator with respect to delineating on which side of the state/social divide members of the social work profession reside, a kind of totem through which individual social workers display their tribal membership, rather than a mechanism for seeking institutional or cultural change.

In the field of medicine and bioethics, radicalization has also been experienced as a tension-producing influence, giving rise to significant ethical and professional problems in the wake of new cultural discourses regarding individual well-being and agency within existing structures of professional disciplines, alongside new developments in medical science and technology. According to Almeida and Schramm (1999), the impact of radicalization in medicine is especially evident in the introduction of bioethics and the new principle of informed consent by the patient on professional practice, representing a paradigm shift in medical ethics in response to the contemporary crisis in the Hippocratic ethical code. The radicalizing influence of bioethics as a result of informed consent and the derivative principle of autonomy, they argue, has caused the greatest changes to the modern patient–physician relationship, and therefore the greatest challenge to hierarchical power structures that were previously foundational to professional medical practice. This has been at the heart of the shift in power that previously dominated what was a rather paternalistic relationship, ushering in a dramatically new paradigm of medical care – a true 'radicalization' in the sense of interrupting previous traditions and inaugurating significant change with the needs of the individual at its heart, while at the same time accomplishing this by harking back to aspects of core values ascribed to ancient times.

A similar trend regarding the radicalization of psychiatry has also been noted. At the forefront of this was the so-called 'anti-psychiatry' movement of the 1960s and 1970s, which included R. D. Laing, David G. Cooper, Thomas Szasz and Michel Foucault. These thinkers and practitioners advocated a radical critique of the existing hierarchical power structures of orthodox psychiatry as an 'enlightened' medical science, arguing that it was these very social and political institutional structures that were not only responsible for 'obscuring' the mental patient, but made it impossible for psychiatrists to 'cure' mental illness, and moreover were responsible for generating mental illness itself. What was required was the total reconstruction of psychiatry itself, with the voice of the 'patient' at its foundation. For psychiatrists like Cooper, the fundamentally social nature of mental illness meant that its 'cure' lay in the therapeutic 'treatment' of political revolution. For Laing, the need to listen to the experiences of those diagnosed with mental illness was based on his view of the fundamental intelligibility of psychotic experience over diagnostic taxonomies of psychiatry, which were arbitrary and ambiguous (Reed, 2009). Similarly, Foucault pointed to the fundamental issue of power in the social construction of mental illness and the oppression of 'patients', arguing that the history of madness charts the silencing and exclusion of 'other(ed)' voices in what he calls the 'monologue' of rational science (Foucault et al., 2006: xxviii). The resulting institutional power structures of psychiatry are inherently shaped by the interests of the capitalist market economy, represented for example by the pharmaceutical industry. However, the therapeutic responses to mental illness should be much more inclusive, taking in the cultural and political dynamics of society at large, and incorporating other, less 'scientific' theoretical models, such as philosophy and literature, which can receive the existentialist message about the human condition that mentally ill people have to tell (Reed, 2009).

Others in the medical and healthcare professions in the UK have concentrated on the effects of radicalization not in terms of rethinking or critiquing existing institutional structures, but rather of how these very same power structures are open to exploitation by radicalized agents with alternative political agendas. There has therefore been a growing commentary of concern in public and media discourses regarding accusations of 'infiltration' (Holyoake, 2007: 27) of the National Health Service (NHS) by terrorists, as a consequence of the fact that some of the most notorious terrorists of recent times have also been doctors employed by the NHS. Some healthcare professionals have subsequently called for more determined and directed efforts to fortify barriers to NHS employment by 'rooting out' radicals from the NHS through, for example, the enhancement of Criminal Records Bureau (CRB) and other background checks, recruiting more British-born and UK-educated medical professionals, and pulling UK troops out of Iraq and Afghanistan (Wheatley, 2007). Others have pointed out the subtlety of committed radicals and the inherent difficulty of detecting radicalized individuals or unearthing radical views, because the only practicable way that the NHS could realistically prevent the recruitment of radicalized staff would be if they expressed extremist views during their interviews, which is unlikely (Arif, 2007).

This leads us to consider other more practical and empirical issues such as social and public policy formation in relation to radicalization, whatever it turns out to be, and social institutions. Is it to do with things like social inequalities based on collective experiences of variables like 'race', gender, religion, politics or ethnicity, as some of the above would suggest, or is it about something much more intimately personal and ephemeral in the form of aspects of daily life and livelihood, as much of the above concentration on the day-to-day experience of work – as opposed to the more abstract arena of employment and economics (the domain of radicalism) – would seem to indicate? Or is it something that shakes up the previously cherished historical notions of legitimacy and power, making way for pivotal cultural changes in the wake of new conceptions of the individual, agency and human rights within institutional structures that are organized or overseen by the state? Or is it just an aspirational notion, which enables individuals to feel a subjective sense of legitimacy and reflexivity while in practice exerting little evidence of change in terms of materially altering existing organizational structures, cultures or behaviours? As we will see in the following chapters, relationships, social interaction, and subjectivity play a key role in the phenomenon of radicalization; this extends not just to employment, health, education and other institutional networks, but also to the more intimate domains of sexual, filial and kinship bonds.

Environmentalism

In his article 'The Politics of Environmental Discourse: Ecological Modernization and the Policy Process' (1995), Maarten A. Hajer links radicalization with Ulrich Beck's thesis on the new societal patterns of organization based on the sociological concept of risk. Hajer regards this link between society and risk as key to explaining and understanding modernization in terms of the shifting patterns of social and economic realities that exist in relation to nature and traditional human interaction with the natural world in the wake of industrialization. In contrast to some of the previous usages of the term, in this radicalization discourse, the consequences of modernization tend to be presented pejoratively in the form of 'dangers' or 'threats' to the stability of the various socio-economic systems of the state. These require fundamentally managerial solutions, hence we no longer speak of the chronic social 'evils' such as poverty, unemployment, inebriation or infant mortality that issue from the new practices of industrialization, nor do we seek to address their underlying social causes as sociologists and philanthropists of the late nineteenth and early twentieth centuries did. Rather, we expect our political and institutional leaders to attend to the more organizational problem of dealing with these new social evils vis-à-vis addressing the acute 'risks' they present as and when they emerge. These social evils are now regarded as unfortunate yet inevitable byproducts of modernization, rather than the consequence of human vice coupled with faulty or obsolete institutional structures. Hence, the project of the 'risk society' is to concentrate not on the fair and equal distribution of 'goods' within a post-industrial context, but rather to attend to the efficient distribution of 'bads' among sections of the general populace: the negative aspects of a modern way of life are now accepted as a new normative or reality principle, viewed somewhat impassively as the unintended consequences or the 'flip-side of progress' (Hajer, 1995: 36). The new modern culture of increased individualization – and its manifestation in emergent social phenomena like radicalization – is accommodated therefore through the systematic dispersal of collective risk. Hajer describes his reading of Beck as itself a 'radicalization' (ibid.: 36) of Perrow's normal accidents theory, which argues that catastrophes (including those involving the environment) are to be regarded as unintended yet unavoidable consequences of human progress and economic modernization – potentially disastrous, but eminently manageable with the potential remedies offered by developments in science and technology.

Alongside Beck (1992) and Giddens and Pierson (1998), Hajer (1995) associates the phenomenon of radicalization in the environmental movement with the macro orientations of the relationship of society to the state. Also in agreement with Seippel (2001), Hajer identifies radicalization in the field of environmental activism as intrinsically linked to one specific historical era, the 1970s – a time when the political discourse around the environment was undergoing significant change with respect to the demise of prophetic declarations of 'global doom' and the emergence of new and equally if not more focused and urgent concerns to do with the emblematic threat posed by nuclear energy (Hajer, 1995: 89–90). Radicalization in environmental activism during the 1970s converged both in a new wave of mass political protests and in the institutionalization of environmental politics in a number of emerging, expert-based organizations devoted to the cause of environmentalism.

These organizations included established institutional bodies such as the Organization for Economic Co-operation and Development (OECD) and the United Nations Environment Programme (UNEP), in addition to more grass-roots organizations like Greenpeace, Friends of the Earth and the Campaign for Nuclear Disarmament (CND). The result was the creation of new domains of expertise with their own neologisms and conceptual and institutional frameworks within which to discuss the 'problem' of the environment in a society irretrievably dominated by risk, in tandem with the newly constructed dramaturgical public spaces for the performances of acts of protest or civil concern. Hajer claims that a convergence of these two discursive spheres has taken place in the public debate on environmentalism, reinforcing the new institutional languages and cultures of expertise, while at the same time (generally) diffusing the radical character of civilian environmental protest. As Seippel (2001) warns, it is important to resist a simplistic or deterministic view of the extremely complex nature of this institutionalization of social movement activism during and after the 1970s; notwithstanding this proviso, Hajer's thesis is supported by a wealth of evidence from the proliferation of lobbying and interest-group-based political strategizing by independent environmentalist organizations at the expense of widespread and discrete 'direct action' campaigns.

This line of analysis leads to another neologism in the study of radicalization – *de-radicalization*. In their study of environmental protest movements in Italy, Diani and Forno (2003) note what they call the 'de-radicalization' of environmental protest movements across the range of social movements in the early 1980s, characterized by the adoption of more moderate and non-confrontational repertoires of political activism. Hajer (1995) thus concentrates on the influence of institutionalism in this convergence of interests and interest groups over individual activism, and Michael Mason (1999) focuses on the union of the twin ideologies of democracy and environmentalism. While Hajer (1995) emphasizes the influence of institutionalism in this convergence of political interests and interest groups over individual activism or 'direct action', Mason concentrates on the union of the twin ideologies of democracy and environmentalism as justifying a set of mutually held concerns about improving the general quality of life through care of the environment, underscored by democratic participative communication and decision-making processes that are analogously energized by the radicalization of political liberalism. Though admittedly vulnerable to the contradictions arising between the ideologies of liberal democracy and environmentalism, such reformist approaches have – until quite recently at least – retained a basic allure, not least due to their appeal to the Enlightenment civic virtues of moderation, tolerance and pragmatism.

According to these accounts, radicalization represents a seminal discursive ideal, albeit one that is attenuated by the dynamic forces of

liberal-democratic political structures, cultures and decision-making practices that tend towards the forces of consensus politics, as opposed to the
politics of violent or confrontational conflict. It would seem, in this context, that the term 'radicalization' is meant to imply an intensification of
the commitment to inherently *democratic* political values as a strategy for
influencing environmental policy-making, as opposed to questioning or
challenging (let alone resisting) the democratic institutions of liberal politics as a means of affecting social change. On the face of it, this represents a very different manifestation of radicalization – one that is
subservient to the principles of liberal democracy. Radicalization in less
democratically oriented organizations is thus perhaps more prone to embracing conflict and violence, and therefore apparently more disposed to prioritize the ethos of radicalization over democratization. However, it is
important to recognize that it is not unheard of for radicalization to function
alongside the democratic institutions of political liberalism, and therefore
not to give in to the temptation to demonize it as a political ethos or concept
in contemporary political ideology, even in western democratic capitalist
societies.

An example of this in the context of environmental protest is represented
by the actions of four citizens in the Republic of Ireland who, unable to
achieve their aims to challenge what they regarded as the unacceptable
threat to public health posed by nuclear reprocessing in the UK to people
living on the east coast of Ireland through the usual democratic channels
(by for instance lobbying their political representatives or writing letters to
the press), in 1994 took legal action against British Nuclear Fuels Limited
(BNFL) and the Irish Government. While their actions have yet to result in
the fulfilment of their political objectives through the courts, the symbolic
impact of their rather audacious protest has resulted in the amassing of not
inconsiderable political capital, due in part to the 'David and Goliath' character of this protest, in which the individuals involved took on such
powerful adversaries and the real financial risk of being potentially liable for
huge legal costs to all parties concerned. This political capital is evidenced in the first instance by the emergence of a grass-roots community
organization called Stop Thorp Alliance Dundalk (*STAD*) to support the
litigants. While *STAD* has over the years become relatively inactive as a
political organization, and while some of the original litigants have
expressed their regrets over becoming involved in what has turned out to be
such a personally costly and drawn-out protest action, other litigants have
used the political capital gained from their legal action to embark on
more reformist careers as activists, one by becoming an elected member
of local government as a Green Party member and the other by developing private business interests in eco-waste systems. This example shows
how the paths into and out of political activism can over time shift
between reformist/collective/consensual and more 'direct'/confrontational/

radical manifestations – or indeed can dissipate altogether. It also demonstrates the possibilities for 'ordinary' citizens to mount 'radical' challenges to the state through the innovative use of institutional democratic systems (such as the courts), exposing the potential for public embarrassment to governments and industry to be sure, but at the same time and more importantly putting the credibility of democratic institutions to the test by way of challenging their legitimacy via the pursuit by concerned citizens of social change in the public interest through the 'system'. Hence the need to remember that radicalization should not be conflated with criminality; on the contrary, such challenges to political hegemonies are at times entirely consistent with the ideals of (western) citizenship and the common good.

Even so, clearly not all activists' concerns can be accommodated within the politics of moderation, negotiation and compromise (however intensively felt or believed in), nor with the promise of incremental progress based on the principles of consensus or collusion with the state or its organs. For a core 'radical' group of environmentalists, this type of activism is to be resisted at all costs. Instead, a confrontational and adversarial relationship with the state is actively sought as a primary strategic and legitimating ethos. Thus, conflict – as opposed to consensus – functions as a paradigm model for constructing the collective and exclusionary political agenda.

> The new social movements thought in terms of sharp antinomies such as yes–no, them–us, the desirable and the intolerable, etc. Especially in continental Europe, the environmental movement in fact constituted an independent discourse-coalition complete with alternative life-styles and new structures of organization embracing alternative communicative practices such as mass demonstrations, and separate newspapers and radio stations.[4] Its actions were typically supported by slogans starting with 'stop', 'ban' or 'freeze' and its concern was formulated in exclusionary terms: 'no part of it [could] be meaningfully sacrificed … without negating the concern itself'.
>
> (Hajer, 1995: 90–1)

According to this type of radicalized environmental discourse (in which the ideologies of democracy or liberalism are secondary or opposed to that of radicalization), the very survival of life itself is at stake, and hence there is no allowance for 'exchange or trade off' (Hajer, 1995: 91), whether with governments or NGOs – which these radicals considered to be 'toothless' organizations in any case (Rootes, 2003: 18). On the contrary, radicalized environmentalists of the 1970s considered the common cause of human survival to be justifiably fundamental to unitary human interest, and thus more legitimate as an object for collective concern that the technocratic discourse or structures of

the state. More recently, O'Keeffe (2006) notes that the rising profile of environmentalism on the (governmental) political agenda, in response to warnings
presented in the Stern Review Report on the Economics of Climate Change
(2006) regarding the potential 'catastrophe' of climate change, has presented
radical environmental protest groups with a dilemma: while there are signs that
significant shifts in political will are taking place among national governments
and NGOs, there is still the underlying sense that this is too little, too late.
Radical environmental groups such as Plane Stupid are increasingly preferring a
diverse range of 'direct action' to political lobbying, considering the reformist
politics of liberalism unfit for the urgency and seriousness of the problem at
hand.

> I hear the government talking a lot of hot air about climate change, but
> I look around and there's still nothing actually happening. We haven't
> got the time to waste. Making changes in our own lives is important but
> it isn't going to make the difference. We have five, ten, maybe 15 years to
> implement massive changes to the way everyone lives. That requires fast
> and wide-reaching government action.
>
> (in O'Keeffe, 2006: 13)

What is more, this new generation of radical environmentalists – many of
whom include among their membership a large proportion of young, educated, middle-class, white and women members who embrace their task with
a sense of heady enthusiasm – have been energized by the protests against
the war in Iraq and Afghanistan. Like their radical predecessors (e.g. the
Baader-Meinhof Group or Red Army Faction in Germany (Becker, 1978)),
in the light of the failure of previous generations to deal effectively with the
problem, they consider it their duty to reject the non-violent liberal approach
and act instead (sometimes but not always violently) against the institutions
of state capitalism on behalf of 'powerless' others from 'developing countries' in order to finally solve the problem.

> 'The responsibility is all on our generation, here and now,' says Murray.
> The people of the past didn't know what the problem was. For the
> people of the future it's going to be too late. People in developing
> countries are powerless to do anything about it. If we don't do this, it's
> not going to get done.
>
> (in O'Keeffe, 2006: 13)

This quote reflects one version of the appropriation of the 'third world' in the
rhetoric of (often) violent political resistance by white, western and middle-
class radical groups, reacting to what is perceived to be an unjust war against
a much weaker adversary identified by Trnka (2003), combining the irrational
and rampant culture of consumption which is exploitative to workers,

destructive of natural resources and damaging to the environment (Becker, 1978). Added to this is the empowerment of 'finding a voice':

> 'While we were sitting on that runway, it was amazing to think that, right then, we were stopping carbon emissions,' says Garman. 'People are so used to feeling completely helpless on this issue. But in that moment, we felt that we had the power.'
>
> (in O'Keeffe, 2006: 15)

While some characterize this as a new innovation in radical (environmental) protest, history suggests that this is not the case. Notwithstanding the strong trend represented by the streaming of environmental activism towards the moderate forces of political liberalism noted by Hajer, the durability of environmentalism on this more radicalized model is remarkable. In their 10-year study of environmental radicalism in Germany (1988–97), Rucht and Roose (2003) found that the stability of radical environmentalist groups in terms of their numbers, demographics and policies was notable, particularly when compared with other radical movements. They surmise that this is due not so much to any ideological so-called 'de-radicalization' campaign on the part of the government, but rather to the durability and potency of single-issue politics such as the anti-nuclear campaign to absorb any dynamic fluctuations in group demographics or individual ideologies of members. Single-issue politics thus remains a relatively constant and consistent beacon for radical activism over the course of decades marked by turbulent change. In other words, while the individuals constituting the membership of these more radicalized groups might leave as they aged and were obliged to take on other responsibilities and concerns, the number of members and organizational infrastructure remained remarkably stable as other young people arrived on the scene to take their place. This intergenerational trend towards a cycle of 'natural' attrition and renewal is a key factor in the durability and resilience of radicalization, and among other things places the de-radicalization strategies of the state under a burden of proof in terms of their capacity to claim success with regard to desistance (cf. Bjorgo and Horgan, 2008).

Animal rights

In his book, *The Case for Animal Rights* (2004), Tom Regan expands on the 'radical' nature of the animal rights movement. For example, they have been unwilling to compromise with industry on issues such as larger cages for farmed animals, and insisted on the abolition of such industries and industrial practices, '"Not larger cages", we declare, "empty cages"' (Regan, 2004: xiv). In this respect, radicalism in the animal rights movement is similar to that of the more radicalized spectrum of the environmental movement and other radical social movements (notably radical feminism): they resist compromise and remain determined to eliminate the structures, institutions and practices associated with the targeted organizational hegemony (in this instance, the capitalist market in farmed animals) rather than seeking to reform them from within. Interestingly, Regan goes further by referring to the 'radicalizing' character of religion, referencing Jesus's message that there are only two laws: to love God and to love one's neighbour as we love ourselves. For Regan, this is radical in that it summarizes and encapsulates more than 200 laws of the Pharisees into two simple and basic maxims, each of these rooted in a singular and undeniably good ethical principle. This type of recourse to basic philosophical maxims founded, as in this instance, on principles of religious morality enables some radical activists to evade the prevarications of utilitarian and consequentialist ethical debates on issues like animal versus human rights. In practice, this sort of reductive approach offers an accessible route for individuals to undertake immediate protest action based entirely on the grounds of reductive principle interpreted as a matter of individual conscience, without the need for expert, rhetorical or propagandist intervention by third parties (except in order to periodically reinforce the basic principle, in the case that they do).

There is a considerable research literature on animal rights activism – far too extensive to summarize here – but most of it traces similar lines of engagement as Regan's between the 'radical' and the 'moderate' – or alternatively the 'reformist' or 'abolitionist'. In his review of Harold Guither's *Animal Rights: History and Scope of a Radical Social Movement* (1998), Julian McAllister Groves endorses the widely agreed historical thesis, outlined by Guither, of the emergence of the animal rights movement in the nineteenth century. This was a campaign spearheaded by mainly white, educated, middle-class New England women who were motivated by the desire to protect animals from undue suffering and harm. It was in the 1960s and 1970s that animal rights activism departed from this agenda of reducing pain and discomfort, and invested animals with fundamental and inalienable rights similar to if not the same as those extended to humans. Denial of this view led to accusations of 'speciesism', a social evil regarded by radicalized animal rights activists as being analogous to 'racism' in human society. For our purposes, Groves' commentary is interesting in that he bemoans the extension of social movement theory to the study of the animal rights movement, as well as the usage of the terms 'radical' and 'extreme' being applied to animal rights activism, considering these to be far too pejorative in the normative sense, as well as concealing an intrinsically *ad hominem* argument against animal rights activists. 'As one of my seemingly sociologically informed interviewees in the animal rights movement explained to me, "the term radical tells us more about its user, than the person against whom it is used"' (Groves, 1999: 348). It is interesting that radicalization in this context is considered an evaluative if not morally dubious designation, at least as perceived by those like Groves who are arguing for a more universally acceptable and less self-destructive political agenda in the articulation of radical discourse around animal rights. In this respect, it is questionable whether Groves' rejection of the negative terms of moral ascription can still be congruent with Regan's insistence on the roots of animal rights radicalism in moral – as opposed to ethical or political – territory whereby animal rights activists are the heroes rather than the villains, or the suggestion that this type of language should not be used at all.

This focus on 'the radical' as a divisive, negative, and/or potentially destructive normative term is echoed by Ted Benton (1993), who begins his study of the animal rights and environmentalist movements with a reflection on the inherent paradox underpinning radical subcultures:

> Politically, the paradox consists in the mutual suspicion, hostility, or, at best, indifference which has pervaded the relations between radical social movements (primarily socialist in orientation) and those which campaign for radical changes in our relations to non-human nature, despite evident complimentarities or outright convergences in values and policies ... As to the political paradox, there is no special reason to expect friendliness between political movements to increase with the similarity of their values and policies: precisely the reverse often happens.
>
> (Benton, 1993: 1)

Nor indeed is this antipathy among radical groups necessarily restricted to inter-group – as opposed to intra-group – relations. In this particular discourse, the issue of radicalism gives rise to insistently emotive, speculative and ultimately divisive arguments over the applicability of the essentially transcendental or metaphysical language of rights and moral language of value norms to both human and non-human creatures (see Benton, 1993: 124). The irony is that human rights and contemporary moral philosophy (after Kant) are both facets of a modern philosophical discourse emanating from Enlightenment thinking, which was in turn initially based on the difference between humans and other types of natural organisms. We can think here of Descartes' rewriting of Aristotle's *De Anima* and his reconsideration of animals (and indeed human bodies) as automata – mechanical objects which operate not by gears and levers but by 'flows and resistances' (Des Chene in Sutton, 2003) – distinct from the operation of the mind. There is also the need to situate these modern discourses outside the speculative realm of religion, scholasticism and metaphysics. Radicalism and radicalization, it would seem, represent (among other things) a discomforting reminder of the intransigence of modern humanist philosophies, the failure of the abstract logic of human rationality to correspond to the moral and felt realities of lived experience, and their ability to be represent within a single harmonious, coherent meta-narrative. What is more, failures to live up to the abstract demands of such 'principled' human-rights based political discourse by powerful western states when dealing with hostile and hated enemies in practice substantially erodes the legitimacy of such ideological regimes, often creating the very conditions of marginalization, oppression, exploitation and occupation that are themselves at least partially responsible for the resurgence of fundamentalism and extremism founded on a sense of grievance, and the subsequent generation of radicalization on a massive scale, (Berger, 2007).

Political science theory: from civil society to the evil within

Some academics and other commentators have approached radicalization by recourse to the existing corpus of political science theory, arguing for example that radicalization is elemental to the dichotomous ideological construction of the recently rediscovered paradigm of the civil society in Western European political thought (Mabogunje 2000; Voglis 2002; Adekson 2004; Ellner 2005; Dyer *et al.* 2007). According to this approach, the radicalized 'Other' is characterized by his or her association with the 'Oriental-East', and thus imbued with the qualities of backwardness, exoticism, traditionalism and strangeness, rendering it by its nature the source of antipathy, suspicion and fear (Adekson, 2004; Said [1981] 1997); alternatively, it is discernible by its exemption from, retardation or refusal of what Elias called the 'civilizing process' (Voglis 2002).

Some political scientists observe a strong, and growing, tendency to regard radicalization as a product of an 'evil ideology' (Chan, 2005; Jervis, 2003), fuelled by Islamaphobia and what Tahir Abbas (2007a) terms 'Occidentalist sensationalism'. Here, citizens and nation states are encouraged to locate themselves within a political landscape mapped in negative binary terms, in order 'to see themselves as engaged in a battle that pits "good" against "evil"' (Abbas 2007a). This reference to evil – a term usually associated with the normative domains of theology, morals or metaphysics – as a meaningful concept within contemporary political discourse is revealing, in terms of how and why radicalization has emerged as a core area of concern. As the following section sets out in more detail, I argue that the subsequent failure of the politics of evil with respect to the 'war on terror' represents a significant precursor to the current refocusing on radicalization as a determining causal process that underpins the contemporary understanding of terrorism. As a result of its implicit dualistic, transcendental and religious connotations, the failure of the politics of evil as a basis for understanding and dealing with the threat of terrorism (the culmination of the radicalization 'process') has ceded to the demand for more decidedly humanistic discursive concepts. These concepts are more consistent with the principles of political liberalism and its existing rationalistic theoretical frameworks – a concept such as radicalization fits the bill. Evil as a designator of danger within modern society does not disappear entirely; however, its use to evoke a metaphysical battlefield on which current political conflicts are played out in a sort of transcendent war of good against evil gives way to a greater concentration on the situated, embodied, emotional, cultural and quotidian social processes – like radicalization – that are seen as posing a threat to the institutional political status quo, and moreover one that can be dealt with in the human realm of the here and now.

Let's pause here for just a moment to take stock. First, on the basis of these various readings, we can see that radicalization as a cultural phenomenon has for some time been deeply embedded in modern society, as evidenced in colonial and also post-war identity, economic and social movement politics; it is thus a durable and enduring social concept. Second, radicalization is a feature of modern life that does not necessarily culminate in 'extremism', let alone 'terrorism', but can apparently be quite easily accommodated within the processes of ordinary, everyday life as a way of motivating people to become politically active to try to make life better for themselves and others like them (or others who are perceived as unable to do this for themselves) or alternatively as a reaction to draconian changes to civil law and criminality by the state. In this context, as will be investigated throughout the remainder of this book, radicalization in the form of a diverse range of life narrative accounts is significant in that it provides a necessary cultural space within which to (re)imagine and (re)consider the utopian possibilities of liberation discourses and future social worlds.

Radical feminism

Generally speaking, radical feminists denote radicalization as an epipheno-menon of the 'consciousness-raising' process embedded in post-war social movements and identity politics. Consciousness-raising as a radicalization technique is often generated by the sharing in small group discussions or via private reading/reflection of women's intimate personal experiences of oppression and exploitation. It is argued that this leads to feelings of collec-tive solidarity and political activism fuelled by the discovery of the structural socio-political origins of what were formally deemed to be isolated, private or personal problems (Ward 2006). For radical feminists, consciousness-raising is crucial to the phenomenon of radicalization. This fundamental link is clearly expressed in the opening lines of Kathie Sarachild's landmark paper 'Consciousness-Raising: A Radical Weapon': 'To be able to under-stand what feminist consciousness-raising is all about, it is important to remember that it began as a program among women who all considered themselves radicals' (Sarachild 1978: 1).

Other feminists take a 'radical' line on the structural and philosophical workings of patriarchy as a primary organizational system in capitalist mod-ernity, criticizing its fundamental reliance on conflict, inequality, alienation and domination. The feminist political philosopher Kathy Ferguson (1993) analyzes the epistemological link between the political and the individual with respect to meta-theoretical claims about 'truth' and 'reality' as the basis for this sort of phallocentric 'conflict-and-conquer' political praxis. In her book *The Man Question: Visions of Subjectivity in Feminist Theory* (1993), she examines how the Hegelian 'philosophy of right' is predicated on a 'hidden order' of reality apprehended through the exercise of rationalist cognition, marshalling for its cause a distinctly masculinist 'hermeneutics of doubt'. Such a hermeneutics of doubt is modelled on the dual social traits of suspicion and conflict, constituting a distinctively adversarial system for exposing the true and undistorted representation of the 'real' phenomenal world, within which power hierarchies are ordered according to these same values, each claiming legitimacy in their use of force in the interests of pursuing 'freedom'. Such conflict-and-conquer thinking underpins the politics of the modern capitalist hegemony, as well the extremist discourses advocating the universal usurpation of state power.

With respect to a radical feminist critique of terrorist and/or politically motivated violence, it is worth examining in depth a particular interpretation of the relationship between evil and the state developed by Andrea Dworkin (1946–2005). Dworkin wrote extensively on physical and sexual violence against women, and was deeply committed to radical social change of the current patriarchal social order. Her works are extremely interesting, but also very provocative and controversial. Here we will concentrate on her polemical argument against the violent militancy and sexism of the Israeli state developed in her book *Scapegoat: The Jews, Israel and Women's Liberation* (2000).

Dworkin begins her critique of the modern nation state by attacking the ideology of nationalism in its entirety. She is particularly critical of the seminal link between nationalism and sexism in the modern age – it is the case, she argues, that the modern capitalist nation state is built upon the largely unpaid and undervalued work of women. Nationalism is also closely associated with feelings of romance, obsession, infatuation, love without condition and blind loyalty to one's fellows. This is the basis of patriotism and citizenship upon which the modern nation state is built – all elements of nationalism and proto-terrorist radicalization as described by Dyer *et al.* (2007), as well as emotions that have been at the heart of the systematic exploitation and abuse of women, children and less socially enfranchised men. In particular, Dworkin points out the pitfalls of Jewish nationalism in the aftermath of the Eichmann trial, i.e. the establishment in the public mind of the connection between the (Jewish) diaspora, the Holocaust (*Shoah*) and the state of Israel. This constellation of dispersal, trauma and emotion in post-war international relations has given rise to a new and strong sense of the collective identity among Jews in global contemporary society; it has also exacerbated the feeling that they are constantly in peril, subject to the ongoing and palpable danger of great evil, and under siege no matter where they live, as the Holocaust has proven to still be the case. As in the case of the Muslim *umma*, Jewish feelings of nationhood spread beyond national borders and the state, to the extent that these feelings on the part of the Jewish diaspora have begun to influence the national policies of other nation states, particularly those with a sizable Jewish population (e.g. USA). Consequently, the realities and experiences of Arab and Palestinian suffering have generally (or until recently) taken on a much less urgent tone in the public consciousness, resulting in a reduced appetite internationally for subjecting the Israeli military machine to public criticism for the suffering inflicted on the Arab 'other'. The priority has become defending the state of Israel, at any and all cost. In the unfortunate instances where Israeli soldiers inflict suffering on the Palestinian people, they are excused from moral culpability because they are, in Dworkin's phrase, 'just following orders'. As a Jewish woman in the aftermath of the Holocaust, Dworkin is deeply disturbed by this infliction of great suffering on a 'people' and the resultant indifference to it, as well as the ease with which Jewish soldiers are able to divest themselves of moral responsibility using the same excuses as the Nazi war criminals did. Paraphrasing Paul Breines (in Dworkin, 2000: 71), Dworkin stresses the ways in which nationalism breeds conformity, an ideology of toughness, violence and paranoia in the face of difference. These constitute feelings and an ethos towards other nations that Dworkin considers highly dangerous and hypocritical.

However, although Dworkin's book is mainly concerned with Israeli nationalism, other modern states are not immune from the same basic faults. In Ireland, Algeria or France, as well as Israel, Palestine, etc., where women support liberation movements, women are immediately re-subordinated after the dissident leadership comes into power; the suffering of women (on both sides) that took place during the conflict is immediately devalued. While women's complicity is typically lionized, and they are typically promised the world during resistance struggles, these promises tend to come to nothing when the fight is over, and they are simply told to get back into the home and back to their unpaid work.

Dworkin insists that this phenomenon extends not only to periods of violent political conflict, but also to the everyday lives of many women in peacetime. For women, the family is the ideological equivalent of the state: 'All power and authority traditionally reside in the head of the family, male; and religion, culture, art, and money delineate and reinforce his sovereignty over women and children' (Dworkin, 2000: 73). In the family, women are accorded the domain of 'love' as the source of meaning (not real, reciprocal love, but the 'love' of subordination and servitude); her work is unpaid and usually seen as valueless. Her other main duty is to reproduce and to socialize her daughters to fulfil similarly subordinate and often exploitative roles. In many cultures, the woman of the family is subordinate even to her own sons. For Dworkin, the family constitutes the physical and social site of women's captivity. This accords with what Betty Friedan, another Jewish feminist intellectual of the mid- to late twentieth century, argued, branding the family home the 'comfortable concentration camp' (Friedan, [1963] 1992). At the same time, the family is the site of men's absence, as they occupy other and more powerful, and more politically meaningful, places in the public sphere. In the aftermath of the Second World War where everyone, women included, were promised so many freedoms, the modern nuclear family is the central carceral institution delimiting the power of women for participation in the public sphere and also their potential for self-realization in the private sphere.

Dworkin points out the fact, backed up by generations of crime statistics, that women (and children for that matter) are more likely to be violently abused in the home than they are on the street. This division between the public and the private sphere, in which violence against women and children remains largely hidden and under-addressed, is a major issue for Dworkin and other feminists and non-feminists, radical or otherwise, and reflects the intrinsic imbalance of gender power relations in the modern nation state. This is the real truth behind the 'freedom' of the modern nation state, one built upon conflict and violence that often disproportionately affects women and children.

Dworkin goes on to link the systematic correlation between relations that are characterized by conflict and violence in the home with those at the level of the state on the international stage. Like their male counterparts, states as actors are able to manifest their will in the global arena by adversarial politics backed up by military power, which constantly generates conflicts and then seeks to remedy these conflicts through the use of force, often violent. This is the real history of the modern age, and it seems to get more violent and atrocity ridden as it 'progresses'. There is little or no real effort or confidence invested in more consensual means of conflict resolution – which Dworkin associates with the (social) aspects of femininity – or the divestment of power from the top-to-bottom hierarchical structures of modern society. In other words, it's a man's world at the public and private level, and at the family and state level, and it operates according to very masculine principles of 'power over' and conflict. This is rooted in the Hegelian politics of right (Ferguson, 1993).

This is a political reality that is emotionally energized by a potent mythical discourse, rooted in the ancient and religious past, and shaped by gender. Dworkin develops her thesis implicating the modern nation state in the systematic abuse and suffering of women by drawing attention to the link between the historical and mythical suffering of the Jewish people and their status as God's 'Chosen' people. This, she says, provides a strong cultural model that legitimizes the infliction of sometimes great and even undeserved suffering on 'loved ones' or intimates. The wielding of great power is accompanied by emotions of jealousy and anger, both in the relationship between God and his people, and also between man and his 'chosen' woman, which equates to a spiritual paradigm that lends itself to sadomasochism and the equivalence between being 'chosen' and suffering. Both are extremely influential in women's experience of the state.

Throughout history, the Jews as the 'Chosen' people have been regularly subjected to jealousy and envy, including among modern men. Dworkin argues that Hitler was in part motivated by this 'Chosen' status; like other anti-Semitic leaders, he sought to appropriate this title from the Jews as the narrative template for the new Master Race, hence the need to destroy the Jews, rather than just subjugating or humiliating them. This response to being 'Chosen' has led to even more suffering by the Jewish people. Consider also, according to Dworkin, the symbolic influence of the body in this context: the mark of this 'Chosenness' and the Covenant among Jews in the practice of circumcising their men. Even though it has become a widespread practice among some non-Jewish populations in the interests of 'hygiene', circumcision still carries a specific symbolic meaning for Jews. Dworkin argues that this particular practice marks Jewish men in a very special way, as it gives rise to huge if latent anxiety among other men (i.e. the cutting off of the penis) and symbolically links them with women (as penis-less and bleeding beings). Chosenness equates to the strong racial and more recently national sense of superiority, but also leads to the identification of the 'Other' as those who are not Chosen (or those who are, depending upon your perspective). This is a very potent and dangerous status in a political context dominated by conflict and violence. In accordance with Dworkin, George Steiner has argued that the symbol of the Chosen race served Hitler not only as a marker of historical esteem but also as a model for Aryan racial superiority. However, Dworkin is more interested in the phenomenon of linking Chosenness with femininity and masculinity in a world dominated by violence, and the struggle for legitimacy and dominance through radical or resistance movements.

Here we encounter in Dworkin's work the discomfiting figure of the 'menstruating male': the bleeding and emasculated man as a symbol of both Chosenness and submission, linked by great and undeserved suffering. 'The chosenness antagonizes; the submission feminizes' (Dworkin, 2000: 115); both are extremely sinister and the source of overwhelming anxiety and fear among men. They have generated massive amounts of hostility and resentment against the Jews as 'feminized' men for millennia. However, as with many such seminal myths, part of its immensely disruptive potential is the assimilation of the 'Other', which is foundational to such narratives; another example of the menstruating male is the figure of the crucified Jesus. Symbolically, for Dworkin, one of the central strengths of this New Testament Christian myth is its power to supplant the Hebrew God with a new figure of the divine that similarly links Chosenness and suffering in a new covenantal relationship, not least one forged under the occupation of an oppressive colonial power. Take away the narrative conclusion of resurrection, however, and what you have in the Christian story, Dworkin contends, is a paradigm case of the historical suffering of the Jewish people epitomized in the figure of the crucified Christ. This constitutes a brutal and violent attack on an innocent and defenceless person, whose body as a Jewish male was further feminized by the piercing of Jesus's body by the centurion's spear (a symbolic act of rape foretold by prophesy). Dworkin offers this version of the Christ story as a possible source of reflection by Christians on the Jewishness of their Saviour, and a way of perceiving the great historical suffering of blameless and nameless peoples (men, women and children) at the hands of the state. This alternative retelling of the story of Jesus's passion could be put forward as an another version of the 'good news'.

The relevance of Dworkin's thesis to the topic of radicalization in the contemporary international context is instructive. What her analysis indicates is that the phenomenon of modern political violence is deeply embedded in religious myth and memory, and that it is mistaken to try to delimit the meaning of these mythical stories to any particular political group, ideology, religious doctrine or sect. Rather, these seminal mythological narratives permeate and elide all such boundaries of identity, be they nationalist, sectarian, ethnic or biological. What is more, the suffering inflicted and directed largely upon the 'innocent' (to use the term most often cited within the political rhetoric of counter-terrorism), defenceless or undeserving populations is fundamentally gendered in character – it is mainly visited on women, but also children and the disempowered (and thereby symbolically feminized), such as older people, the mentally or physically infirm, and men, often in their homes or in the course of their daily lives carried out in mainly in the private sphere. The cultural phenomena of 'Chosenness' and 'Otherness' or deviance are consequential in the emergent social patterning of interpersonal violence resulting in severe injury or death in the modern age. As Spierenburg (2008) has found, since the Middle Ages in Europe, the trend has been a rapid decline in overall levels of serious interpersonal violence, notably between male strangers in public places; however, since approximately the 1970s, coincidentally the same decade that witnessed the rise in extremism and terrorism, this long-term trend has begun to reverse, showing a proportionate rise in interpersonal violence leading to serious injury or death, especially in private or domestic spaces between male and female intimates. This chimes with Dworkin's thesis regarding the potential for the nearest and dearest or 'Chosen' to be the victims of domestic violence. Spierenburg's other main finding is the simultaneous rise in street violence between young men (and less often, though on the increase, among or involving young women) using weapons such as knives, which he hypothesizes marks a resurgence of violent interpersonal conflict, influenced by what he calls the 'spiritualization' of honour based not on material wealth or physical strength, but on distinctively modern codes of civility or 'respect'. This, along with the notion of 'Chosenness' could explain why so many young men are potentially attracted to the recruitment strategies of terrorist groups that focus on their special status as among the 'chosen' – as for example in the case those selected for suicide missions (e.g. Pedahzur and Perliger, 2006) – and also why it is considered such an intensely emotional (as opposed to simply an operational) betrayal for members to try to resist, contest or leave these groups, as so many of the autobiographical records show.

Taking all of these aspects into consideration, Dworkin's argument implies that the phenomenon of radicalization as a precursor to terrorism is not to be perceived as a distinct or discrete process linked exclusively to subcultural extremist groups or actors. Instead, this propensity towards widespread, continuous and indiscriminate violence in the name of political progress, power dynamics between nation states and those with aspirations directed towards usurping their hegemony, is embedded in the very infrastructure of the patriarchal state. In this context, it is mainly women and children who are the victims. Without addressing this evil and its consequent inequalities, trauma and paranoia, a viable solution (as opposed to serial historical examples of 'final solutions') to political violence is a virtual impossibility.

By way of an interim summary, it would appear that radicalization is a phenomenon that has its roots in contemporary discourses of politics, violence, conflict and the evil Other – as well as the daily negotiation of social interaction, identity norms and felt experiences about areas such as work, gender, care, disability, medicine, race, the natural world, religion and social work. However, in the social sciences and law enforcement research literatures, the emphasis is on metacontext (history, politics, society and language), arguably influenced by Kant's rejection of metaphysical notions of evil in his seminal work *Religion Within the Limts of Reason Alone* (1960) in the nineteenth century. Kant recommended a study of evil in the modern world as the object of humanist and historical–political discourse and a social–collective phenomenon. More recently, many others including philosophers, cultural theorists and feminists argue instead for a fuller and more embracing reconsideration of traditional understanding of evil (including religious spirituality, Manicheanism, myth, symbol, etc.), which are in any case still a disruptive presence in the emerging 'scientific' discourses of radicalization and terrorism. Such analyses promise a greater capacity to understand the narratives of the 'far enemy' and the 'home-grown' or 'evil within', specifically in the latter case the proximity and intimacy of the radicalized terrorist Other in public and private life in a globalized world. In 1945, Hannah Arendt declared that The problem of *evil* will be the fundamental question of *post-war* intellectual life in Europe (Arendt, 1993: 134). Perhaps the incursion of evil and the demonic in modern discourses around knowledge, security, morality and risk offer an opportunity for a fuller appreciation of human experience, including the religious, sexual and embodied. It would seem that the problem of evil, in terms of its impact on these elemental areas of modern life, is nowhere more urgent than in the secular culture of western modernity:

> If demonic work is the mark of an incomplete appreciation in human beings of the workings of the divine, then the demon is the sign of

all human activity and the notion of evil becomes indistinguishable from a non-communication between the human and the divine. Such a separation is marked up by Heidegger in his diagnosis of the modern age as one in which the gods have departed, in which a relation between the mortal and the immortal is unthinkable. His diagnosis of a resulting destitution has implications also for theories of knowledge, with a contrast between an epistemology, as veridical theory of knowledge, available to the divine or the immortal, distinct from the partiality arising from the specific location of the human, as divided from the universal, from divinity and immortality. Thus there emerges a distinction between an epistemology as such and the partial epistemologies of the human.

(Hodge, 2000: 25)

Hence evil will figure as an orienting point of reference throughout this study, not least as a basis for understanding one of the most immanent and threatening forms of radicalization, the 'homegrown' terrorist or the 'enemy within', and the 'process(es)' by which he or she becomes radicalized in a local embodied and emotional context.

'Homegrown' radicalization: causes and prevention

With the ostensive demise of the 'war on terror' and its replacement by a criminological paradigm model based on risk management and prevention, the attention of policy-makers has turned to the strategy of identifying 'homegrown' radicalization and pre-empting or even preventing it as early in the 'process' as possible. This strategy is much in evidence in recent government-sponsored reports on counter-terrorism, such as for instance the recent FBI Counterterrorism Division-generated report 'Countering Violent Islamic Extremism: A Community Response' (Dyer et al. 2007). The authors open by recognizing that the shift from the 'war on terror' to 'homegrown radicalization' represents a new focal point for law enforcement which is superseded only by concern about 'violent Islamic extremism' or global terrorism[5] (Dyer et al. 2007: 3). They begin by posing the important definitional questions of what radicalization and Islamic extremism are, and if they always result in terrorist activity. Practical solutions to this newly perceived problem of radicalization, shaped by western codes of principle and conduct, are an immediate priority. In deference to First Amendment rights to free speech, indicators other than statements of hostility to the West and admiration of extremist leaders like Bin Laden are sought by law enforcement agencies in the first instance, in order to be able to ' … identify individuals with the most potential to effect immediate harm, thereby controlling the operating environment and designating time to address the larger issues underlying violent Islamic extremism' (ibid.: 4). This is accomplished through a two-pronged strategy to first identity these individuals at an early stage and second to engage Muslim communities in outreach programmes designed to 'dispel misconceptions that may foster extremism' (ibid.: 4). Despite the potential hazards of engaging with a worrying population, the strategy emphatically remains one of *risk management* and *social control* (Feeley and Simon, 1992). This strategy relinquishes the Bush agenda to resolve the problem of terrorism at the metaphysical level through mor(t)al combat in favour of a battle on the terrain of ordinary everyday life, where potential enemies can be individually identified, neutralized, incapacitated and (where appropriate) expunged and/or punished before they can act, preferably within the ordinary, everyday operation of the security and criminal justice systems. To put it another way, the metaphysical plane of eternal battle is replaced by the local and quotidian terrain of surveillance, community policing, the legal–judicial system and risk management.

This shift to more managerial, quotidian response to radicalization as a main driver of counter-terrorism policy (see also CONTEST2, (Home Office, 2009)) has resulted in a focused concentration on the key variables that lead up to and thus 'cause' terrorist action, specifically its presumed seminal precursor, radicalization (without radicalization, there are no terrorists and hence no terrorism). Hence radicalization is increasingly being viewed as a significant and discrete preliminary stage in what is deemed to be a temporal and progressive evolutionary *process* (e.g. NCTb, 2007) with its distinctive causes rooted in the sequential cadences of daily life, a profoundly inter- and intrapersonal phenomenon that takes place within the ordinary social interaction of an individual's everyday life over a period of time culminating in the eventual (though by no means inevitable) terrorist act.

While research on radicalization in the USA, the UK and the Netherlands draws similar conclusions regarding the causal influence of issues such as the search for identity and feelings of marginalization and frustration, American law enforcement agencies tend to take a more distinctively individualistic view of the radicalizing actor.[6] He or she is perceived to be affected not so much (if at all) by the external or 'push' influences of society at large but instead by the 'pull' factors of internalizing beliefs and practices of discrete extremist subcultural groups (likening entrance into radical groups to those of street gangs, neo-Nazi movements, or cults (Kay, 2005)) or, if there are external influences, these coalesce in the equally subjective and individualistic 'push' factors such as of wanting to get away from a dysfunctional family (Jenkins, 2007). Other contributors to US-based research on radicalization (e.g. Benard, 2005), focus on the individual using positivist research methodologies like Rational Choice Theory (e.g. Landi and Colucci, 2008) and/or offender profiling (e.g. Nesser, 2005), thus leaving aside any implicit or explicit critique of democracy, unemployment or other social structures, and highlighting the increasing influence of (positivist) criminology. Along these lines, the FBI report by Dyer *et al.* (2007) identifies four stages in the radicalization process comprising (in ascending order): pre-radicalization, identification, indoctrination and action. Each stage is considered to be distinct, and in itself a potential end point of the radicalization process, signalling that even a radicalized or radicalizing individual need not necessarily reach the final stage of acting on the basis of their experience of the previous formative stages. Individuals often drop out at particular stages, or are obliged to recalibrate their commitment in response to other factors in their lives (Jenkins, 2007). Each of these stages and their underlying methodological foundations (vis-à-vis Durkheim's functionalist typology) will now be examined in turn.

Pre-radicalization

Pre-radicalization is characterized by Dyer *et al.* (2007) as linked to the conversion experience, either to a religion or some other form of personal or group commitment (often claiming to be based on a religious orientation). While the latter type of pre-radicalization is observable in terrorist groups such as the Weathermen or later Weather Underground Organization, for the most part, the current concentration on Islamist or jihadist terrorism clearly favours the former conversion experience based on religion. Indeed, notwithstanding the demise of the politics of evil, this is in many ways apropos the Bush doctrine's evocation of (quasi-)religious experience as a focal point of concern previously cited. But this reference to religious conversion need not necessarily be perceived as in essence a reactionary political step; we can also recall here Žižek's (2008: 70) pronouncement of religion as among the last possible sites for the critique and resistance of modern society, indicating once again that radicalization in itself (even of a religious variety) need not necessarily be a bad thing for society at large or for social cohesion. Whether a force for good or evil, Abbas (2007a) reiterates the rise of religion as a key focus of attention in a post-9/11 age:

> One of the major shifts in thinking in recent years has seen the move from a focus on race to a focus on religion. Since the events of 9/11, and more recently 7/7, there has been a perceptible shift in relation to the major 'race relations' problems in Britain.
>
> (Abbas, 2007a: 7).

While the nefarious influence of Islamism is clearly of key concern, the confluence of religious conversion and political radicalization is not perceived to be about the finer points of theological debate, the assignation of religious heresy or traded accusations of apostasy. According to Dyer *et al.*, this initial conversion experience can display dynamic qualities, in that the group or outlook originally converted to can change during this phase. The pre-radical conversion experience is motivated by the felt (inter)personal need for change or perceived need for reinterpretation of or reidentification with other groups or other ways of life. It can be a result of internal introspection or external acceptance-seeking by proximate social others, but in any case it is often driven by a respected and usually older extremist who provides stimulus and opportunity for furthering the radicalization process. This can take place in mosques, prisons, universities, businesses or Internet chatrooms, all identified by the authors as places that provide hospitable environments for private meetings and consultations with individuals who are prone to question society and/or feel disaffected by it. In Durkheimian terms, this stage has distinctively integrative and regulatory overtones: the individual develops the initial sense of identification and belonging with the group and starts to become knowledgeable about its rules and regulatory strategies for ensuring that collective practices are obeyed and any infractions discouraged or duly punished, and thereby the rules are reinforced for the entire group. This initial stage is thus about the identification and formation of shared values and collective cohesion.

Identification

Identification, the second stage, is about further accepting and internalizing one's identification with a particular extremist cause, ideology or sub-group. The binary 'us–them' mentality is fully adopted in this phase, enabling the individual to exclusively identify him/herself with a particular group, cause or ideology, and also to recognize outsiders or dissenters as the 'enemy'. This identification increases the sense of isolation from the individual's former identity, social ties and lifestyle. Guidance from superiors in the minutiae of daily life, and encouragement to socialize and bond with other like-minded individuals, reinforces the new sense of identity and commitment. Investment by means of financial, material and other displays of confidence through networking and training (often obtained through travel) enhance this stage of self-commitment, encourage a sense of personal obligation and facilitate the possibility of future action. This represents a further strengthening of the altruistic phenomenon of excessive integration and overidentification with others at the expense of a sense of individuality or self (from the perspective of Durkheim's typology). Hence, as in the most extreme case of altruistic suicide, the individual's needs and wants are increasingly sublimated to those of the collective, whose perceived needs and aspirations form the basis upon which the individual is now obliged to act, even if this means the death of the individual actor.

Indoctrination

Indoctrination furthers this propensity or readiness for action. During this stage, group bonds are intensified and more strongly forged. A recruit's potential as a fully radicalized extremist are explored by the leadership, commitment is tested and significant roles are parsed accordingly, with increasing demands made on the convert/recruit to prove their loyalty. The knowledge, skills, leadership and charisma of senior figures (such as extremist Imams) play a vital role in transforming recruits into active service during this phase. This is a highly volatile and emotional stage. Dyer *et al.* (2007) do not explore the situations in which this pivotal stage occurs, e.g. in prison, or the other social or cultural factors that facilitate this seminal transitional stage possible; this question will form an elemental part of this book: to work out and interrogate in further detail the personal, social and political domain within which this stage and the knowledges and skills associated with it takes place.

Action

Action is the operational final stage, consisting of actively supporting or engaging in terrorist activities, which include planning, financing, preparing and executing terrorist actions. During this stage, role identification can be so strong as to completely erase a sense of individuation, thereby preventing the possibility of the individual acting in their own self-interest by leaving the group. Here the sense of overidentification with the group is at its most extreme and total, buttressed by (in Durkheimian terms) the fatalistic notion that any attempts to leave the group or resist such action are impossible, or would at best be futile.

According to Jenkins (2007), the radicalization process can take months or even years, although he claims that it has been accelerated in the wake of 9/11 (but without explaining how or why). While he does not adopt the specific taxonomy devised by Dyer *et al.* (2007), like others (e.g. Weimann, 2006) Jenkins nonetheless identifies a similar process in which indoctrination by 'self-selection' and continuous recommitment are crucial throughout, processes that are characterized by the lack of explicit coercion by leaders, although the implied force of peer pressure is hugely influential:

> Submission is voluntary. Not all recruits complete the journey. Commitment is constantly calibrated and re-recalibrated. Some drop out along the way. A component of our counter-recruiting strategy must be to always offer a safe way back from the edge.
>
> (Jenkins, 2007: 4)

Conclusion

So what are we to conclude from the previous disparate usages and discourses of radicals, radicalism and radicalization? Taking all of the above policy and scholarly literature reviews into consideration, we find that generally speaking:

- Radicalization is about *rootedness*: about establishing some sort of foothold or recovering a sense of stability in a fast-paced, ever-changing globalized world, or 'rooting out' the causes of social evils and injustice (whether through the newly found relationships of 'sisterhood' or reconnecting to the original lives/texts of religious movements or nature); it is often described in terms of being a conscious, if not also conscientious, effort to halt or redirect the seemingly relentless or (in Giddens' memorable phrase) Juggernaut-like quality of 'progress' of capitalist modernity on its own predetermined course over the subjective desires, wishes and beliefs of individual citizens, returning to a social order based on something other and presumably more substantial and enduring than monetary exchange value. It can thus be linked variously to 'radical', conservative or perhaps even moderate political ideologies (e.g. to be 'radical' about pursuing liberal reform).
- Radicalization is a *normative* concept: it represents a term of moral valuation in a contemporary modern world that in many respects *claims* to have divested its political discourses from such normative influences, while invoking such archaic ontological concepts such as evil as foundational to many of its most consequential acts of 'rationalization' or 'final solution'; it shares and overlaps discursive boundaries with good and evil, while at the same time functioning in contemporary political discourses as an acceptably secular alternative to a discursive realm deemed to be too rooted in theology–metaphysics; from the perspective of radicalized individuals and the resistance culture of radicalized groups, it tends to be associated with the ancient heroic values of courage, martyrdom and sacrifice ascribed to pre-modern warrior cultures, adopting these over the more moderate civic values of civil justice, tolerance and temperance associated with the logocentric and reflexive culture of modernity (see MacIntyre, 1981).
- Radicalization is *pejorative*, or it can be, at least as viewed from the perspective of current public and policy discourses. With respect to the Muslim community, radicalization constitutes a label of deviance, a way of identifying real or potential enemies whose belief systems, cultural practices and even physical presence is anathema to western modernity generally and the nation state in particular. To extend the previous designation of radicalization as a concept with intrinsic normative dimensions, to be 'radicalized' is to deviate from the normal hegemony of political liberalism by adopting a disruptive or even violent means of social change and political activism. From this perspective, it represents the volatile and potentially violent forces of chaos that make it inconsistent with the organizational management of contemporary social movements that seek to shape or reform the political status quo from within, e.g. the environmental movement or the women's movement.
- Radicalization is *conflict oriented*: in its extreme forms it is dualistic and adversarial in character, marked by the rejection of activism within

institutions to effect reform in favour of a political agenda based on conflict and sometimes (but not necessarily) violence and destruction (vis-à-vis revolutionary change, insurgency, sedition or the rejection of social labels and roles, conventional political hierarchies, or recognizable organizational structures) as a preferred way of achieving political aims. Based on the Weberian notion that the state has a moral monopoly on the legitimate use of violence, it adopts the attitude that such a quasi-capitalist market economic notion on monopoly should either be broken or is open to contestation by other political actors/groups. Also founded on a Hegelian 'philosophy of right' model of politics, which prioritizes a 'conflict-and-conquer' mode of engagement over more consensual, inclusive, dialogical and diplomatic methods (Ferguson, 1993).

- Radicalization is particularly amenable to *single-issue* politics: it is able to display a remarkable consistency and stability as a discrete social phenomenon when it is attached to simple, or reductive political agendas, especially those which can be boiled down to one core issue, e.g. anti-nuclear, anti-global-warming, anti-vivisectionist, pro-woman, sectarian, etc. In the domain of religion, this is reflected in the dominance of fundamentalism and literalism, and the perception of secondary institutional structures, authorities, hierarchies or commentators, based on tradition or hermeneutic interpretation, to act as barriers to religious authenticity and the individual's access to the 'truth' as the basis of a deeply political spiritual pursuit. In more current research, this is reflected in references to al-Qaeda (as a pertinent example of a radical–extremist group) as an organization bereft of structure, doctrine or ideology and more of a 'brand' (Dyer *et al.*, 2007), emphasizing that at least part of its attractiveness emanates from its simple yet vague, ambiguous and loosely connected yet reductive set of ideas, combined with a strong symbolic identity as a focus for projecting anger and directing activism in response to feelings of disillusionment with, and alienation from, western capitalism. Part of its appeal is its almost naïve simplicity and resulting capacity for projecting the detailed experiences of potential sympathizers upon this basic framework, while at the same time eliding the need to learn complex or intellectually demanding theory or engage in time-consuming and distracting doctrinal debate instead of action.

- Radicalization is *dualistic*: it is generally predicated on the various dichotomies (masculine/feminine, master/slave, black/white, capitalist/proletariat, religious/secular, public/private, etc.) that pertain to the politics of modernity and the political hegemony of the capitalist nation state (and its perceived threats, risks, or enemies). This exacerbates its conflict-oriented character, by virtue of the predominance of 'us-versus-them' rhetoric. Many commentators reiterate the need for the security and police forces of the state to be restrained and proportionate in their responses to radical activity in order to avoid the escalation of conflict; at the same time, however, there is an underlying desire to see more decisive 'confrontational' dealings with radical groups by the police as a desirable way of pre-empting terrorist activity (e.g. Hegghammer, 2006: 54). Radicalized actors often view their activism as a response to antagonism rather than an invitation to engage in consensus-oriented politics, a view typically also reflected by the state institutions that occupy the role of the target and the other side of the conflict. Just as importantly, radicalization is about not being passive and running away from a fight, but rather confronting conflict full on and resolving it through either victory or death, with no room for negotiation or compromise. As stated previously by Dworkin (2000) and Ferguson (1993), it is intrinsically gendered, with its origins in extreme versions of masculinity and patriarchy that fundamentally deride more feminine and matriarchal forms of identity and socialization. This is not to say, as will be shown in the remainder of the book, that women are not susceptible to radicalization.

- Radicalization is about *action*: it stresses and draws upon the agency of individuals as single actors who more often than not belong to their own distinctive collectives or cultural sub-groups that are in some way either excluded (e.g. banned) or considered to be exclusive to broader society (i.e. secretive, hidden or subversive). The strength of this ideological link between the individual and his/her potential as an agent-member of a cell or group capable of bringing about widespread social change is of key importance to understanding radicalization and its appeal to those who feel otherwise disempowered or marginalized. It also emphasizes the close link between radicalization and the culture of individualism in western modernity, ironically implicating the cultural hegemony of capitalist modernity as an originary source. The complexities of global and local power struggles highlights important questions about identify and belonging for many individuals in a globalized and multicultural world as Berger (2007) rightly points out; it also brings into the equation passionate sentiments and potent emotions about being the victims of globalization and the global hegemony of those who do not count you among them or do not value your cultural ways (whether or not these feelings are based on reality or perceptions), and hence is about more than just rational or intellectual positioning on issues of political ideology. We may think of Durkheim's theory of effervescence here: action, passion, collective agency, emotions, individual representations and the past emerge into contemporary social life as an upsetting 'radical' mode of social change (e.g. Jones, 2001).
- Radicalization is a *process* (or is generally considered to be) taking place over time, whether in the form of a series of progressively reinforcing causal stages, or as a result of a more ephemeral influence impacting the otherwise normal and ordinary temporal progression of daily life or the life stages. It is narratively construed (whether retrospectively

by former extremists or in the form of prediction by law enforcement and policy-makers) in distinctly teleological terms, most specifically as a prerequisite, if not also a cause, for extremism and terrorism (often interpreted by institutional agencies in hindsight – though also – and sometimes very problematically – as a predictor of eventual terrorist activity). Though its processual aspect has received prominent attention, it is important not to reify, overstate or fetishize its temporality at the expense of its other equally important dimensions, e.g. cultural, spatial, symbolic and embodied, etc. This notion of process, and its consequences on expert and policy discourses, will be subject to further examination in this study.

- Radicalization is *cultural*: it (and its potential remedies and responses) is deeply embedded in the diverse and complex convergence of language, symbols, legal–moral and gender norms, relationship bonds, social patterns of interaction, consumption practices, embodiment, sexuality, ethnicity, belief systems, and other aspects of identity and everyday life. Radicalization is thus not a straightforward matter subject to a menu of pre-emptive or ad hoc responses by the security services, the military, the police or the law, though at times these may be appropriate, depending on context. The importance of context reinforces the importance of culture in understanding the concept of radicalization. Culture is frequently identified within the extant research literature on radicalization as playing an important role, but has as yet received comparatively little attention by researchers or policy-makers. Additionally, few contributors on the subject have made use of cultural studies or other humanities-based theories or methodologies to explore or analyse radicalization, nor have they sampled the wealth of available cultural data sets (e.g. art, fiction, resistance literature, life writing, etc.) with the exception of a considerable amount of research on the Internet and the media, and to a much lesser extent some forms of popular culture – e.g. film (Croft, 2006), hip-hop music and videogames (Gruen, 2006). Concentration on the influence of culture and the importation of cultural theories and methodologies applied to the considerable data set of political prisoner auto/biography will also form a pivotal part of this study.

- Radicalization is *spatial, temporal* and *biological*: it is specifically rooted in the 'organic' system or cluster of 'master metaphors' (to use Silber's (1995) terminology) of time, space and biology/body. Interestingly, given the meaning of *radic-* as 'root', many of these metaphors are similarly organic, geographical or otherwise terrestrially oriented; others relate to the human body or biological organism itself. Consider the language of radicalization in terms of 'networks', 'cells', 'sleeper cells' or 'nodes'. Similarly, radicalization is explained in terms of 'routes/pathways' to terrorism, defence of the 'homeland' or 'holyland', 'underground' or 'grassroots' organisations, the 'seeds' of radicalization, locating the 'fertile ground' or 'breeding ground' (Communication from the Commission to the European Parliament and the Council, 2005) for recruitment; the meaning of al-Qaeda, itself translates as 'base or 'foundation' (another form of 'ground'), and the emergence of neologisms such as the renaming of the former site of the Twin Towers of the World Trade Center in New York as 'Ground Zero'. Threats emanate from the 'near' (local/national) or 'far enemy' (global) (Gerges, 2005); these enemies are 'subversives' – the subterranean and underhand nature of whose activities accounts at once for the secrecy and lack of transparency sets them against the principles of enlightened democratic government and for the difficulty for these same governments to 'see', recognize or even find them. The 'enemy within' narrative foregrounds its spatial and geopolitical orientations not only on a global but also on an intimate domestic front (Eagleton, 2005; Dworkin, 2000), hence the fear and anxiety generated in the modern global environment in relation to the viability of the nation state as well as the fears and anxieties emanating from the close physical proximity of those with whom we share our homes and local communities within a globalized world. Time is also important. De Figueiredo and Weingast (2001) highlight the distinctive temporality of nation states susceptible to terrorism, listing among their temporal characteristics the sporadic nature of violence, long periods of peace interrupted by extended episodes of violence or peaceful bargaining. Similarly, observable differences in strategic decision-making by terrorist groups, with respect to cost–benefit analysis of engaging in violence, suggest that their perceptions of incentives and deterrents change over time; this is mainly in line with the perceived levels of support or sympathy from 'moderate' social groups, but also takes into account the need to avoid total suppression by the state and (on the part of the state) full-scale civil war.

- Radicalization is amenable to *positivism*: there are contingent positivistic connotations in the treatment of radicalization in the research literature with respect to prioritizing certain externally observable – if more subterranean than (pan)optical – phenomena that are capturable by modern technology and that enable and reinforce the predictive powers of the nation state (Lyons, 2006). Narrative metaphors also feature prominently, e.g. terrorist 'plots' and 'frames'. Explanatory discourses focus on the influence of information 'networks', which in other sociological discourses form the basis of the institutionalization of unequal power structures in the information age (e.g. Castells, 2000). The radicalization process – from 'pre-radicalization' to 'self-selection', 'indoctrination' and 'action' – takes place through the temporal phenomenon of *intensification* (Silber and Bhatt, 2007). In their discussion of what makes some people proceed from pre-radicalization to terrorist action, they use the images of a 'funnel' (which would seem to suggest that everyone who starts off on the process arrives at the end, though they acknowledge that that isn't the case) and 'incubators'. However, elements of the supposed radicalization process time and again incorporate or comprise aspects of ordinary social life (such as leisure activities, socializing in small groups, travel, reading, watching videos, engaging in minor criminal activities to obtain money, hanging around at bookshops, joining Internet chatrooms and youth centres, etc.) that many if not most people engage in with no ill effects; this in itself suggests that radicalization is the manifestation of some sort of predisposition or 'tendency', a quasi biological concept applied to deviant groups like homosexuals (see Brown (2000)). Narratives of the state, security and criminology mirror these metaphorical narratives and concepts, for example the nation is often referred to as the 'motherland' or 'fatherland' (suggesting close proximity between the individual and the state, a relationship of emotion and intimacy, but also one founded on conflict (Dworkin, 2000); the 'rhizomatic' nature of contemporary technological surveillance (Lyons, 2006) and Stan Cohen's (1985) famous 'master patterns' thesis of social control modelled on the metaphor of the 'net', whereby historical narratives of the transformation of deviancy and control can be told through tropes such as 'net-widening', 'mesh-refining', etc. While these constellations of narratives clearly echo one another in their use of metaphor, at the same time one cluster is intended to communicate the sociological/criminological phenomenon that we are all becoming increasingly subject to the penetrating surveillance gaze of the state, while the other tends to focus its attention on the empirical identification of particular group(s) of deviants (in the current circumstances, mostly immigrant or young male Muslims).

In response to the complexity and malleability of radicalization, its link to the emergent self and shifting patterns of culture and identity, and the need to extend analysis beyond positivist methodologies, the next chapter is devoted to one qualitative alternative, the interpretivist and interdisciplinary approach and data set of auto/biography.

Chapter 2

Using auto/biographical methodologies to analyze radicalization

The purpose of this chapter is to give a more expanded and detailed historical, theoretical and methodological positioning of the problem of radicalization as a precursor to terrorist crime and criminality, and the significance of political prisoner life writing in extremist subcultures and in culture generally. It also examines the role and function of prisoner auto/biography in the social construction and individual manifestation of radicalization, and the multiple ways in which prisoner writing has influenced modern culture. The main themes covered in this chapter are: the case for using interpretive or qualitative methods such as auto/biography and its history and foundations in hermeneutics and cultural studies, sociology and criminology.

Making the case

In his speech to the Royal United Securities Institute (RUSI) in 2006, the then Chancellor of the Exchequer and later British Prime Minister Gordon Brown stressed the paradoxical character of modern life, with specific reference to the role of globalization and technology in facilitating the new threats to national security posed by terrorism worldwide. In this speech, Brown articulated what is increasingly becoming the expressed view that – to some extent or on some abstract or macro level – the ongoing threat of terrorism is not just a familiar feature of our modern way of life, it is somehow elemental to it: in criminological terms, terrorism (and hence radicalization) is 'criminogenic' to modernity. Other more recent commentators have expressed the same sentiment in even starker terms, surmising that global terrorism is to be properly understood as a *product* of modern life: 'The very success of the parliamentary democracies in the Long War of the twentieth century has created the conditions for a new kind of conflict', and furthermore contemporary terrorism actually mirrors the globalized consumerism of the emergent 'market state' (Bobbitt, 2008: 11). As will be shown in more detail in the chapters that follow, both points are well taken, not least with respect to the ubiquitous influence of modern Enlightenment values and consumerism on the life stories of radicalized actors. Neither take any particular interest in developing or exploring these cultural links between the life writings of radicalized actors and globalization, however, but launch straight into what is to be done about this disruptive and destructive by-product of modern life.

For Brown, the priority in dealing with the threat posed by terrorism and extremism is to strengthen military and security responses:

> To root [it] out ... [hence] we are rightly investing in increased military and security forces, and policing. And after yesterday's photographs [of the abuse of prisoners by coalition forces at Abu Ghraib Prison in Iraq] let us remember it is incumbent upon all of us to ensure discipline at all times and to root out indiscipline.
>
> (Brown, 2006 [online])

For contributors such as Bobbitt (2008), the solution consists of a total rethinking of the problem of terrorism, and a subsequent revision of military strategy and renewed commitment to (inter)national law. For the most part, there has for some time been a general consensus among policy- and decision-makers concerning these generic assessments of the problem of terrorism as an unintended consequence of global capitalism and technological development and the need for more robust strategic responses, mainly in the form of military intervention, policing and/or legislation. However, in the wake of notable failures in military and intelligence-based responses to deal with the problem, there are signs that this generic view is changing, and that alternative strategies are being considered for combating terrorism using other more culturally embedded means, such as:

> through newspapers, journals, culture, the arts, literature. [As in the Cold War, the battle against fascism in the twentieth century] ... was fought not just through governments but through foundations, trusts, civil society and civic organizations. Indeed we talked of a cultural Cold War – a Cold War of ideas and values – and one which the best ideas and values eventually triumphed.
>
> And it is by power of argument, by debate and by dialogue that we will, in the long term, expose and defeat this extremist threat and we will have to argue not just against terrorism and terrorists but openly argue against the violent perversion of a peaceful religious faith.
>
> (Brown, 2006)

Only two years after giving this speech, in the aftermath of the bombings on 7 July 2005 and Brown's elevation to prime minister, a senior minister in his government, Hazel Blears, gave a speech to the same body, saying that the priority is now for the government to tackle 'violent extremism ... on the ground' in order to deal with the 'challenge of radicalization' by countering

and rebutting historical, theological and political 'narratives' of organizations like al-Qaeda (Blears, 2008). Though military and law enforcement are
mentioned, their role has been (so it is claimed) demoted in favour of com-
munity-based strategies that are based on prevention through the promotion
of dialogue, cohesion, inclusion and debate (e.g. Wheeler, 2008). Blears
describes the government's strategy as one aimed at prevention (indeed it is
code-named PREVENT).[1] She represents it as a fundamentally 'rhetorical'
task, reiterating Gordon Brown's earlier call to ' ... use a range of cultural,
academic and intellectual arguments, including arguing against what he
called "the violent perversion of a peaceful religious faith"' (Blears, 2008).
To this end, in her role as the Secretary for State for Communities and Local
Government, Blears concludes that 'nationally we need a clearer understanding of the groups we are funding through better on-the-ground intelligence ... ' (Blears, 2008). It is becoming clear in the research literature that
the type of 'intelligence' that is called for, and its analysis, are qualitatively
different from the narrowly construed conventions of military or police
investigation that have dominated until now, in favour of a more inclusive
and contextually rich scope (it is another matter whether or not the local
communities in question actually regard such 'intelligence gathering' exercises as qualitatively different).

What this shift in political rhetoric and strategy demonstrates it is neither
simply the new information and communication technologies of the Internet
and mobile telephones, nor the impact of the global economics that are 'paradoxically' useful to insurgent groups or otherwise causally responsible for the
emerging threat of terrorism. Cultural factors such as ideology, religion, kinship
and friendship relations, history, education, mythology and identity (among
others) are also of key concern in making sense of the phenomena of terrorism,
extremism and radicalization – equal or possibly even greater than the factors
of information technology and economics. Another important concern is, as
Sayigh puts it, the need to avoid what has become the habitual 'blindness
towards ourselves' (Sayigh, 2008: 43) in the study of terrorism and radicalization: the jettisoning of a normative approach to the problem of terrorism or the
nature of global conflict that somehow obviates the need to examine our own
part and interests in the material and cultural processes from which these
threats emerge. The point has been repeatedly made that we live in a violent
society (Palmer, 1972; Moonman, 2005; Žižek, 2008b), though the claim of
comparatively high levels of violence in modern western societies has been
contested (cf. Spierenburg, 2008). What is more, throughout the modern period
it is more common than not for modern nation states to emerge from an episode of violent conflict or revolution, and thereafter to occasionally counter
rebellious activity through violent means. Hence violence, protest, sedition and
insurrection form an integral part of the history and everyday life of the modern
nation state. It is therefore imperative for governments and other international
bodies not to overstate the presumed antipathy between politically oriented

violence and the modern nation state by demonizing or criminalizing such activities out of hand or – to paraphrase Žižek – to condone our political leaders when they indulge in a meaningless 'gesture of fetishist disavowal' (Žižek 2008b: 45) by constantly referring to a fundamental contradiction between violence and the state. Hence political rhetoric that is reliant on an absolute dichotomy or dualistic representation of conflict, in which one side is violent (evil, seditious) and the other non-violent (good, consensual), should be used extremely cautiously, if at all. This includes declarations by western political leaders of the supposedly total commitment by national governments to the 'shared values' of democratic pluralism and non-violence (e.g. Blears, 2008) when this is patently not (always) the case. Perhaps it is time for governments to recognize that '[i]t is rare for an outside actor other than the United Nations (UN) to be completely honest, neutral, and even-handed' (Sayigh, 2008: 43) in their assessment of, and response to, conflicts in which they are involved. Instead, strident efforts should be made to inculcate a more moderate, reflexive, self-critical and inclusive approach from the outset, in order to promote a strategy of honesty, transparency, realism and pragmatism – all of which are presumably resonant with the values of freedom and democracy, at least in the long run.

To this end, the reconceptualization of what constitutes 'intelligence' and 'knowledge', with respect to the problem of terrorism or radicalization on a broader and more inclusive and culturally oriented basis, requires a rethinking of methodology in the first instance. This consists first of a critical review of previous epistemologies in terms of what constitutes explanations of the phenomena in question, and second a review of how existing cultural methodologies from other disciplinary and interdisciplinary fields can be most effectively incorporated and adapted for the task at hand. This is the dual objective of the following sections of this chapter.

Redirecting the critical focus to the individual

In a recent, high-profile international conference devoted to the topic of radicalization and political violence, 'individualization' or consideration of 'the issue of radicalization at the level of the individual' (Roy, 2008: 12, 10) was listed as one of the critical factors in understanding radicalization. Thus far, this has been variously examined by considering the individual's relationship to *external* factors such as the modus operandi of specific organizations (e.g. al-Qaeda), the 'fit' of their profiles to pre-established categories of offending behaviour, the part they play in the forensic reconstruction of specific terrorist events or their disposition in relation to the broadly historical metanarratives or 'forces' of civilization, political ideologies and/or macroeconomics. Little, if any, credence is given to the investigation of subjective or personal influences, what we may generically label the questions about 'who' radicalized actors are and 'why' someone becomes radicalized. Among other criticisms, such 'who' questions have been derided as providing too little by way of answers, but instead by providing too much: 'The "who?" questions – who are the attackers, who joins the global *jihad* against the west, what typology do they exhibit? – produce too many answers to be useful' (Munthe, 2005: 1). Instead, the concentration here is usually phrased in terms of 'how' or 'what' questions, and thereafter focuses on *process* (as observed in the review of the literature on radicalization undertaken in Chapter 1), i.e. how *individuals become radicalized*, differing from previous approaches that tend to concentrate solely on the individual or terrorism in abstraction development. The claim is that

> acknowledging that involvement and engagement in terrorism is best thought of as a *process* brings fresh perspectives via critical distinctions that enable us to understand the reality of involvement in terrorism as well as provide a conceptual base from which we might develop beneficial analysis. By considering involvement in terrorism in terms of *process*, we also help to move aspects of these debates away from complex but essentially sterile discussions that postulate terrorism as some sort of abstract event. This allows us instead to focus on identifiable behaviors and their antecedents, and on expected consequences and outcomes that are associated with terrorism.
>
> (Horgan, 2005: 66, original emphasis)

Horgan's contrast between 'process' and 'event', and their tendency to be interpreted in abstraction in their conceptualization (as opposed to alternative formulations of other research questions that embrace the 'abstraction' of the radicalized subject as potentially 'becoming' or 'being' a terrorist from very different philosophical perspectives), and the proposition that other more subjectively oriented foci are 'sterile' in terms of what they offer by way of explanation (or at least better understanding) are highly suggestive and will be further investigated in this study. For the moment, the salient point is that the attention is continually directed back onto the individual, whose involvement or engagement in terrorism does not necessarily reflect a neatly unfolding process of 'becoming', then 'being', then possibly 'disengaging' from terrorism (as implied for example by Dyer *et al.*, 2007). Instead Horgan envisages this as a messier 'process' whereby

> the factors that impinge upon the individual at each of these phases [i.e. 'becoming', 'being' and then 'disengaging' from terrorism] a) may not be necessarily related to each other, and b) may not necessarily reflect each other. In other words, answering the call of one of these phases of the process may not reveal anything useful or insightful about the other.
>
> (Horgan, 2005: 67)

Horgan raises a very interesting and important point here, with respect to the lack of interrelatedness or cogency of any potential underlying 'process' as a causal series of linked events, albeit one that raises as many new questions as it might answer, particularly in relation to the possibility of any ostensibly *narrative* (and therefore comprehensible or explanatory) representation of radicalization as a contiguous unity (I will return to the notion of the 'event' as a factor in explaining radicalization later). However, it is not to narrative methodologies that Horgan then turns for his theoretical framing, but rather to the positivist 'logic' offered by rational choice theory (RCT),[2] which, to put it bluntly, takes a very dim view from the outset of trying to answer questions about *why* people become involved in terrorist activity:

> This logic is consistent with Rational Choice perspectives in criminology. The implications of thinking about terrorism in such a way are essentially a recognition that answering questions about why people may wish to become involved in terrorism then may have little bearing on the answers that explain what they do (or are allowed to do) as terrorists (or something else) or how they actually become and remain involved in specific terrorist operations. Similarly, answering questions about what keeps people involved with a terrorist movement may have surprisingly little if any bearing on what subsequently sees them disengaging from terrorist operations or from the organization (and/or broader movement) altogether.
>
> (Horgan, 2005: 67)

Not all analysts take such an unreconstructedly positivist view. The return to the individual by other security analysts, such as for example Thomas Hegghammer (2006), is in comparison increasingly accompanied by a call for a more thorough understanding of *narrative* and its role in the radicalization process (see also Neumann *et al.*, 2008) and indeed in global politics and dissent more generally. This dual invocation of the *individual* and *narrative* gives rise to the articulation of new and innovative questions that in themselves represent a rethinking of the previous assumptions about, and approaches to, studying the radicalized actor. Until very recently, as we have seen, this project has been dominated by the pursuit of pragmatic or 'practical', empirical, 'outcomes'-based approaches (shaped by theoretical frameworks such as RTC (e.g. Horgan, 2005) or game theory (Enders and Sandler, 2006; de Figueiredo and Weingast, 2001)) that prioritize 'how' and/or 'what' over 'who' and/or 'why' questions:

> [I]dentifying issues as to 'how' people become involved [as maybe] more valuable than attempting to arrive at answers 'why' people become involved ... essentially ... we need to shift our expectations away from

the goal of arriving at a simple, and probably naïve, answer about terrorist motivation.

(Horgan, 2005: 68).

And

I believe we are misguided to ask only, 'Who are the terrorists, and why do they hate us?' Rather we should ask, 'Who are we and how have we organized ourselves such that terror could become an historical inevitability?'

(Bobbitt, 2008: 18)

According to the approaches adopted by these two distinguished contributors, the 'how' questions conform quite adroitly to the search for causal explanation – i.e. how does someone become radicalized, turn into or desist from being a terrorist (Horgan's question) – or functional explanation, i.e. how are our social systems constructed so as to allow or even encourage terrorism (Bobbitt's). In contrast, the 'why' questions tend to receive short shrift, whether because of the fear of association or contamination that is potentially posed by such exercises in sympathy or empathy. This latent anxiety is evidenced by the recent high-profile withdrawal of the educational pack devised for use in schools in West Yorkshire, which included an exercise designed to encourage the children to imagine the events of the London '7/7' terrorist atrocity from the perspective of the bombers (Suleman, 2009), and the equally palpable anxiety that such endeavours will merely descend into a mire of subjective emotions and generate little by way of rational, objective and actionable findings. Of course, however, the 'why' questions that may be posed are not merely limited to the 'why do they hate us?' or 'why did they bomb that train?' variety, nor do the possible answers merely provide 'oxygen' that facilitates the pointless grandstanding of self-righteous and deluded evil thugs. It is entirely legitimate for people to seek to understand why people become radicalized in order to find out what the motivations and reasons behind these actions actually are as the basis of prevention, rather than sticking to the more action-oriented, problem-solving and mainly reactive investigations into 'what' or 'how'. Increasingly, contributions to discussions on terrorism and radicalization would seem to indicate that the 'why' questions are not just coming back onto the agenda, but indeed moving up the agenda, and not as replacements for but as augmentations to the 'how' questions so favoured by pragmatists, empiricists, strategists and positivists (see Neumann *et al.*, 2008). This opens up new questions about the articulation of research questions, but it also expands the potential use of new data sets, theories and methods of analysis.

In social scientific methodology, articulating and answering such 'why' questions usually means incorporating qualitative research methods, such as interviews, open (as opposed to 'closed' multiple-choice) questionnaires, ethnographic observation and discourse analysis into research design. With respect to the study of radicalization, certain issues emerge from the outset that tend to impact strongly on the range of options available to researchers working outside of the security services who must rely upon 'open-source' data, i.e. information that is publicly available and not subject to restrictions on the basis of national security (Bobbitt, 2008). Contrary to general opinion, as Bobbitt contends, open-source data comprises an extremely rich, ample, challenging and under-utilized resource for information and analysis.[3] These diverse data sources are much more prolific and (given the proper treatment) are perhaps less problematic than the highly restricted, closed-source intelligence data that pose their own difficulties, primarily with access to those who are, have been or are suspected to be in the process of being 'radicalized' due to legal and security restraints. Realistically, this immediately forecloses the options of research interviews and ethnographical observation of these radicalized individuals. Of course there are other publicly available resources for researchers who are not allowed access to secret, restricted or classified information (on or off the record). These include the sorts of data either produced by radical groups or individuals that are created for the purposes of public or semi-public dissemination (e.g. for recruitment or reinforcement of group members) or else 'leaked' into the public domain (e.g. by correspondents, comrades or confidants). Such a rich and under-scrutinized data source is represented by the great array of life writings – autobiographies, biographies, letters, diaries, notebooks, etc. – written by or about notable radicals, which constitute what the professor of English literature Barbara Harlow (1987) calls the immense and ever-growing canon of 'resistance literature'. These writings proliferate in and among radicalized groups nationally and internationally and have done so throughout the modern period, potentially containing important information concerning the implicit and explicit reasons 'why' and indeed (in many instances) also 'who' and 'how' individual actors became involved in, and stay with, or perhaps eventually break from, radical, extremist or terrorist organizations. While it is, from a certain perspective, surprising that so little attention has as yet been devoted to this particular cultural data source, given the overwhelming predominance of quantitative and positivist research in the study of terrorism and (by association) radicalization, this is quite understandable. The good news is that, among sociologists, cultural theorists and literary critics, the analysis of these types of life narrative texts has been well under way for more than a generation, and the benefits of their insights are beginning to be incorporated into criminological and related areas of research.[4]

An additional justification for the incorporation of auto/biographical research methodologies into security studies and counter-terrorism research on radicalization is that it helps illuminate the cultural 'technologies of the self' – to use Foucault's (Foucault and Martin, 1998) expression. These are represented by a variety of cultural forms within the genre of resistance literatures, including but not limited to forms such as novels, poems, short stories, films, plays, etc. As many security analysts will know, the life writings of radicalized actors who are or have been imprisoned at some point for their political activities are particularly notable among the forms of resistance literature currently available to potential recruits. Their predominance in the communication and dissemination of resistance cultures means that these life writings from prison deserve special attention in understanding the nature of the current threat to national and international security. It is the painstaking analysis of these texts as cultural products and thereby data sets linked to the overall phenomenon of radicalization, and its meaning as a distinctively modern form of criminality and source of fear and anxiety, which fires what C. Wright Mills calls 'the sociological imagination'. While such biographical research is unlikely to produce the so-called 'silver bullet' that will solve the problem of radicalization leading to terrorist action in one shot, it might be useful in clarifying the problems and central issues that are currently at stake – as qualitative research is meant to do. This can be accomplished, as mentioned before, as a complement to existing quantitative research methodologies, for instance by exploring the meaning of terms used by radicalized actors and groups that form the concepts which are then used to construct survey questions or do statistical analysis: are these still meaningful or valid? Do they relate to the sense-making processes and shifting interpretations as used by these groups? While this may be frustrating in the short term, the painstaking work of clarification can only be a good and useful thing in the long term.

In the next section, I will set out the case in more depth for the incorporation of qualitative, but specifically auto/biographical, research methods in the study of radicalization, by first scrutinizing the types of research methodologies that currently predominate in this area and the types of explanations that have been produced, and how this alternative methodology can help address the existing lacunae in research about radicalization.

What would a cultural or sociological explanation of radicalization look like: functional, causal or something else?

The turn to radicalization is a very recent innovation in the study of terrorism: prior to the early 2000s, the term 'radicalization' was scarcely to be found in the research literature on terrorism and political violence (Neumann, 2008). Even now, few texts produced by academics and other public experts on terrorism contain much by way of reference to radicalization, although, for reasons discussed in the previous and present chapter, this is changing. In Chapter 1, we saw that one of the advantages offered by the current concentration on radicalization (as opposed to the 'war on terror') is its correlation to an evidence-based approach that boasts the added advantage of presenting an alternative to the more evaluative normative ontologies underpinning the political rhetoric of the 'axis of evil'. It relocates the study of terrorism according to a rational and empirical scientific paradigm, modelled on the natural or 'hard' sciences. This renewed and optimistic commitment to evidenced-based policy-making, geared towards generating 'solutions' in the form of 'concrete outcomes' (Neumann *et al.*, 2008), seamlessly linking the work of academics, governments and industry, is strengthened by this empirical focus. At the same time, there is an abiding discomfort with the complete jettisoning of the norms of 'principle' from the equation, as any political speech on the subject of radicalization and terrorism will demonstrate (e.g. Blears, 2008; Brown, 2006). One facet of this uneasiness resides in the very task of analysis and the possibility of explanation itself. At some level, there is the latent anxiety that even attempting to understand or represent (let alone enter dialogue or – even worse – 'negotiation' with) the radicalized 'enemy' is to somehow become complicit in making excuses for their heinous acts (Neumann, 2008) – to furnish them with the 'oxygen of publicity', in Mrs Thatcher's memorable phrase, or to simply suffer the contagion of guilt by association, as has been noted previously.

It would seem that part of the work of being a politician, public servant or policy-maker in the global media age is the need to broadcast in no uncertain terms a deeply felt abhorrence and total rejection of the ideologies, activities and personal motivations associated with any kind of political extremism. As with the despised figure of the paedophile[5] and (lately) the banking executive, the ready public display of disgust, denunciation and desire to expunge these enemies of society from the public civil sphere offers a cathartic balm for the collective majority of incomprehension of and remoteness from these people and their atrocious acts based on their anti-social ethos. For most people, engagement through seeking to *understand* the motivations, intentions and personal qualities of such individuals is a distinctly distasteful proposition. It is important that this sense of anxiety and discomfiture should not be lightly dismissed or uncritically denounced as naïve or counter-productive. In fact, these feelings can reveal important insights into the ways in which such topics have been studied thus far. Consider the observations of the French sociologist Émile Durkheim over a century ago in *The Rules of Sociological Method* (1938). Durkheim found that such cultural attitudes towards criminality are significant, in that they serve to inhibit intolerance, prevent the ossification of moral codes and simultaneously reinforce social bonds of moral solidarity through the act of collective condemnation, in the face of the suffering of the unfortunate victims. For Durkheim, such periodic expressions of collective moral outrage and experiences of moral solidarity are essential for the 'healthy functioning' of any society, particularly as they are engaged in the process of encountering and trying to make sense of that which they abhor.

This thesis represents an example of Durkheim's *functional* explanation of the nature of crime and punishment, in which the focus is on the broader questions of 'why' or 'what for' of deviant or criminal phenomena. This is not to be confused with internal subjective 'intention' or 'purpose' of specific individuals, but rather refers in Durkheim's work to the general *needs* of the social organism in order to maintain itself.[6] By focusing on the systematic or organizational 'needs' of the collective organism of society and the overall impact of the 'pathology' of crime upon the entire social system, Durkheim promotes the seemingly paradoxical notion that a certain level – not too much, not too little – of crime is actually good for society: that some good can come from even the most terrible crimes. A certain level of crime is thus to be tolerated, as long as it does not reach such excessive levels that it compromises the moral fabric of society (or in the more familiar parlance of New Labour, 'community cohesion'), i.e. that destroys the prevailing sense of moral solidarity and encourages apathy or fatalism among the general populace in relation to their ability to withstand or deal with the problem of crime. This is illustrated by Bobbitt's statement that 'Americans are willing to pay this price [i.e. retention of civil liberties in favour of the rolling back of privacy and human rights for the purposes of more trenchant though more effective law enforcement] in part because the cost of ordinary crime does not *cripple* their society' (Bobbitt, 2008: 299, emphasis added). This thesis also contains something like the position referred to by Gordon Brown at the beginning of this chapter: the implicit recognition that crime (even terrorist crime) in modern society has a paradoxical character, that the very fabric and systems of society somehow also generate the types of crime and criminality pertaining to a specific society. (This is the notion of a 'criminogenic' society, i.e. that societies actually produce or generate their particular types of crime, e.g. through the use and availability of information and communication technologies, patterns of social interaction, the availability of travel, porous or open national borders, the flow of people and money, etc.) Also, in modern societies, the *law* represents the prevailing moral code (hence the need for legal codes to change in order to accommodate transformations in the moral sentiments of the social collective). This type of functional explanation is detectable in very recent and distinguished studies, like law professor and security analyst Philip Bobbitt in his book *Terror and Consent: The Wars for the Twenty-First Century* (2008), in which he concentrates on the important notion of *consent* as an expression of the perceived moral legitimacy of the state in relation to the perceptions of those who are governed, and the subsequent need for states to legitimize their strategic responses to crime and emerging threats to national security through a reinforced commitment to updated legal (and hence collective moral) norms.

As Durkheim pointed out, crime exists in every society, and it is a relative concept: there is no crime (not even mass murder) that is absolutely determined to be criminal by its nature (consider the act of killing during military campaigns in wartime – not only possible but even highly noble and desirable depending upon circumstances). Hence we must to some extent come to terms with the reality of crime, and deal with the particular sort of criminogenic nature of crime for our times as best we can, reflecting the prevalent idea that the sort of terrorist crime currently in evidence in modern society in some way is created by, or 'mirrors', the prevailing social organization and techno-economic systems.

While this may be an unpalatable and even alarming prospect, at the same time it is founded upon what is at least intended to be the reassurance of a supposedly durable and substantial social consensus among the majority of the members of society. In practice, this type of functional thesis tends to shift the emphasis away from the individual offender and/or criminal event and onto the overall capacity of society to not only survive the onslaughts posed by crime and deviance (which society itself is implicated in producing), but moreover to benefit by the periodic response to the need for collective social bonding. This affords an occasion for ensuring the durability of the social, but also for celebrating society's ability to weather the damaging effects of crime; it is a theoretical impulse that is still recognizable in recent analyses of terrorism and radicalization today. Without seeking to oversimplify, this type of functional theorizing is developed along the lines of 'what doesn't kill us makes us stronger', focusing on the durability of societal bonds rather than the destructive potential of discrete instances of crime and criminality, which is particularly useful given that the many 'dangers' facing society on this premise are themselves perceived to be generated by the prevailing modes of social organization. This thesis forms the basis of emergent concepts such as *resilience* (e.g. Durodie, 2004), as well as the significance of collective *emotions* or affective *networks* within the cultures of politics (including political resistance groups) (e.g. Sageman, 2004; Hill, 2003; Mansbridge, 2001b). This type of functionalist theory also informs the analogous focus on *risk* in current thinking on radicalization and terrorism as a determinant of social cohesion (e.g. Beck, 1992) and a way of *managing* (by way of predicting or 'policing') potential harms (e.g. Ericson and Haggerty, 1997) as opposed to 'curing' or 'fixing' damaged criminals (Garland, 2001) or the 'broken society'. It also emphasizes the functionality implicit in the creation of 'moral panics' (Cohen, 1987) as mechanism for 'moralization' which in turn forms a 'common feature of contemporary political discourse' (Hier, 2008: 174). This drive towards functionalism can also be read into some recent thinking in criminology, such as the concept of 'the new penology' developed by Feeley and Simon (1994), which is predicated on the notion that crime is ultimately an unsolvable social problem, and the best that can be done is to come to terms with this reality and manage it as well as possible; this approach gives rise to the much-flaunted and contemporary response to crime and criminality, which is that policy-makers should attend to the job of quantifying 'risk' through the quantitative and positivistic analysis of actuarial data, and that its pernicious effects are subject to the machinations of moral entrepreneurs.

However, as Durkheim himself stipulated, such functional arguments are insufficient in themselves as complete explanations of criminality (or indeed potentially dangerous or criminogenic phenomena like radicalization). *Causality* must also be explicated in order to fully understand social phenomenon. Durkheim's functional explanation of crime differs from, but is augmented by, his later theory, which is more recognizably empirical in character (although it is important to stress that in Durkheim's work both approaches are modelled on distinctively positivistic scientific epistemological frameworks). In his land-mark study *Suicide: A Study in Sociology* (1952), which developed his early work *The Division of Labour in Society* (1960), Durkheim directs his attention at the question of 'how', which involves above all the identification of universal *laws* capable of explaining the succession of social phenomena, particularly those implicated in the manifestation of social change, like radicalization. An example of these laws that Durkheim uses is his explanation of the causal relationship between moral density and the growth of the division of labour from simple to more complex societies, which is developed in *The Division of Labour in Society*, or alternatively his causal thesis concerning the incidence of suicide in relation to the relative levels of social integration and/or regulation of individuals in *Suicide*. Durkheim observed, for example, that excessive levels of integration of the individual into the collective can result in what he termed altruistic suicide – a type of self-imposed death, in which the individual sub-verts his or her own self-interest to the extent that they are willing to give their own life in the interests of others. In itself, the presence of this type of suicide does not necessarily indicate pathology in the social organism as a whole; this type of suicide can be quite beneficial for society, for instance, during wartime. However, altruistic suicide can be pathological when it does not facilitate any inherently functional role in maintaining social cohesion, or when it reaches excessively high or low levels,[7] or occurs in certain intrinsically antisocial cir-cumstances (e.g. suicide bombers).[8] Here the *cause* of a social phenomenon (in this case, overidentification with the collective at the expense of individual self-interest) must be isolated from the *function* it fulfils (e.g. moral solidarity, social resilience, collective conscience, etc.), although it is essential that both have to be present for an adequate sociological explanation to exist. Such a sociological theory stipulates that the 'causes' or 'needs' in question are not those of an individual person, or even an atomistic cluster of individuals, but of *society as a whole*. 'Collective beliefs, emotions and tendencies are not caused by certain states of consciousness of individuals but by the conditions in which the social group in its totality is placed' (Durkheim, 1938: 106). In other words, internal states of mind, personal intentions or subjective motivations are, strictly speaking, irrelevant (as in the example of church attendance). Indeed, this rather derogatory attitude regarding individual feelings, intentions or personal motivations within certain strata of academic disciplines such as psychology is still much in evidence today (for examples relating specifically to the individual and radicalization, see Neumann (2008: 4); Horgan, 2005)). This is an attitude that could at least partially account for the notable lack of research methodol-ogies that take such subjective and intentional issues into consideration. What is more, the same assumptions concerning the importance of social consensus or equilibrium in the modelling and representation of political realities that are characteristic of functionalism (e.g. de Figueiredo and Weingast, 2001) persist in many areas of current theorizing on radicalization and terrorism (e.g. Markel, 2006–7; Durodie, 2004, 2006a, 2006b), a situation that has endured more or less intact since the post-war period, despite recurrent attacks upon it by feminists, postmodernists, and others.

These two types of explanation – functional and causal – must be present to adequately explain social phenomena and/or mechanisms of social change, but they should be clearly distinguished. Both types of explanatory arguments have been strongly represented in the positivist theoretical analysis of terrorism and latterly radicalization cited in Chapter 1, though not always together or in tandem. These theses are exemplified by the explicit or implicit assumption about the *function* of radicalization: that is to say, is it *good* (e.g. in the case of radicalization of suffragists, at least in hindsight) or *bad* (e.g. in the case of Islamist radicalization, for the foreseeable future) for society? Is it a mode of social change that (in the long run, at least) assures the continuity of social progress, legitimacy of social consensus, and thereby the stability of society through the disruption of social stasis (albeit not always without suffering or disharmony), or is its function always to be the source of conflict and discord, and thus perceived as intrinsically a social evil? The predisposition towards functionalism in explaining and even defining radicalization is exemplified by the enduring paradox cited by Markel: ' … some explicitly conflate insurgency with terrorism, operationalizing the adage that "one man's terrorist is another man's freedom fighter." Objectively this may be true, but US joint doctrine distinguishes the two *functionally*' (Markel, 2006–7: 133, emphasis added). Here functions are primarily distinguished in relation to the contextualization of action within political doctrine, e.g. whether the main function is to depose a political regime through subversion or engagement with state militia, or to achieve the same or similar objectives by targeting civilian or non-combatant populations. This is related to the distinction between insurgency and terrorism which, as Markel notes, are both highly contextual as indicated by the adage 'one man's terrorist is another man's freedom fighter', but at the same time are commonly conflated (ibid.:133–4). Aside from the discovery of universal, abstract laws that claim to offer the advantage of making identification and prediction of threats possible (e.g. de Figueiredo and Weingast, 2001), the proliferation of functionalism in security studies nevertheless indicates that *context* matters. This is a significant point, and again indicates the appropriateness of qualitative research methods, which are highly cognizant of meanings and actions embedded in their local contexts, irrespective of the deriding of subjectivity in classical functionalism.

As also noted in Chapter 1, causal theses pertaining to explain radicalization abound. Consider the examples discussed in the previous chapter represented by the frequently cited four-stage process comprising the progression from pre-radicalization, identification, indoctrination, to (possibly) action (e.g. Dyer *et al.*, 2007: 3–4) currently favoured by law enforcement agencies in the US and elsewhere or the more controversial and ambiguous citation of religious ideology as a cause of radicalization. On closer inspection, the commonality of this type of explanation is probably not very surprising, since there is a fundamental correspondence between the notions of *process* and *causality*, i.e. the idea that one thing not only follows another in a particular order but also that this happens in a way in which there is a triggering effect that then impacts on any potential, if not inevitable, outcome. This implicit yet fundamental relationship underscores one of the strongest and most compelling attractions of any positivist methodology: the ability to articulate *laws* that provide an abstract and universal mechanism for making sense of a series of events and their outcomes, and also help with the generation of hypotheses in order to ensure the replicability of findings; and hence the power to *predict* when something is in the process of unfolding, and thereby to create a window of opportunity to do something about it. Where theses are presented in the form of abstracted, process-oriented phenomena or stages that claim to apply to all cases in a law-like manner, they can be said to be modelled on the type of causal positivism advocated by Durkheim. Currently in the frame as causal arguments for radicalization are the range of 'extremist' ideologies represented by nationalism, Marxism, animal rights, racism, religion, etc. (Forest, 2005; Benton, 1993); the emotional influence of friendship and kinship networks (Sageman, 2004); youthful rebellion against family and religious tradition (Husain, 2007); education (especially higher education) (Abuza, 2006; Kapcia, 2005; Chauvin, 1998; Wonmo, 1987); youth and/or gang cultures (Young, 2007; Rand, 2007; McEvoy-Levy, 2006; Carey, 2007; Gruen, 2006); poverty, poor housing, unemployment or underemployment, alienation (Rand, 2007; Jones, 2005; Tobin, 1985; Videla, 2006; Edgell and Duke, 1986; Benard, 2005); or a combination of some or all of these elements, and more. Such a tendency towards causal argumentation is also prominent in many emergent theories of 'de-radicalization', which claim to set out once again the basic universal conditions for interrupting or reversing the causal progression of the radicalization process, for instance by constructing and broadcasting 'counter-narratives' as a way of combating terrorism by preventing or pre-empting radicalization in the first instance (e.g. Blears, 2008), or offering other incentives for desistance (e.g. Bjorgo and Horgan, 2008). However, as security analysts are aware, the causal link identifiable between any or all of these key factors as precursors to radicalization is extremely weak, and in some cases negligible or even counter-intuitive: clearly, the hypothesis that going to university 'causes' someone to become a terrorist is strongly rebutted by the reality that so many people who go to university do not become radicalized in any perceivable, let alone negative, way. Additionally, there is a growing body of evidence that suggests that radicalization is very much a malady affecting members of the middle classes, and not a product of poverty (e.g. Gamage, 1994; Tosh, 1997). Once again, as in the case of the various functionalist theses, what we can see here is that *context* is key, and the contextual influence of cultural influences (including class) will feature in the chapters that follow. While the complexity of the task in hand is admittedly daunting, this should not be regarded as an occasion for giving into despair, as some commentators have been tempted to do, but rather as an opportunity to incorporate other less familiar but more appropriate methodologies for the study and analysis of such deeply context-dependent and cultural phenomena.

The aim of this section has been to attempt to provide a sociological analysis of the explanatory models with respect to currently held methodologies in the study of terrorism and/or radicalization within policy-making and security studies circles, and their implicit epistemological foundations. The predominance of empirical, functional, pragmatic and/or quantitative methodologies that are modelled upon positivist scientific paradigms is commonplace as the basis for policy-making, and are themselves insufficient for making sense of phenomena such as radicalization. What is very important, however, is that policy-makers and others who have an interest in these sensitive and volatile areas of modern social life should be as informed as possible about the limitations of such methodologies, so that the best possible decisions can be made about what to research when, and how and why this should be done. There is no doubt that function and causation are key aspects for explaining any particular social phenomenon; however, it is also essential to listen to what the literature on research methods tells us about the inherent limitations of such positivist approaches, particularly in areas of social life that we are becoming increasingly aware are very subjectively and culturally oriented, with respect to the motivations and intentions of the individual actor, and also extremely context dependent in relation to how such actors behave in their everyday environments and interact in their own groups and with others.

Like all methodologies, such positivist research methodologies have their advantages and disadvantages. Advocates of empirical and/or quantitative research argue that it guarantees greater representativeness and generates information that is reliable, consistent, accurate and comparable, and that, unlike qualitative methods, generalizations can be made from these data, making it a valuable research technique. They claim that quantitative research is objective, and that to some extent even feelings and attitudes can be reliably represented numerically (for example, by the use of Likert scales). As Bryman (1996: 94) puts it, quantitative research data is characteristically *hard and reliable*. The objectivity and comparability of these research methods makes them very attractive to funding bodies and other organizations that regularly commission research (such as private corporations, think-tanks, governments or political parties). Unlike subjective data, which are strongly culturally influenced, numbers are an international language, and data that can be represented in this way are commonly endowed with considerable credibility as an unbiased non-partisan view on social reality. Despite some researchers' dissatisfaction with the positivistic connotations of empirical research and its limited perspective on the social world, others embrace its emphasis on the scientific nature of subject disciplines such as sociology and criminology as an enhancement to their status in the academy and in the more general hierarchy of knowledge. However, such positivist methodologies have their limitations and, in some instances, even their drawbacks. They can be quite complex, and require considerable effort to properly understand and use. For instance, audiences may 'tune out' elaborate statistics, thereby creating difficulties in making the most effective use of the products of research or even misinterpreting them. Critics have also commented that it is difficult to get the 'real meaning' of an issue by looking at numbers or generating universal, abstract laws, where the absence of context can generate conclusions that appeal to common sense, but are in practical terms biased, tautological or self-evident and hence fairly meaningless (as for instance in the findings that radicalized actors are 'evil' or that the cause of terrorism is a sense of grievance or 'discontent'). Despite the claim to objective neutrality, even statistical information needs translating and interpreting into a form that is comprehensible to target audiences, so, strictly speaking, it is not just qualitative methods which are open to the claim of interpretation and hence cultural or theoretical bias.

Having considered the epistemological foundations underscoring many of the approaches to radicalization and/or terrorism in the research literature, let us now turn our attention to qualitative methods, specifically auto/biographical research. The question now is: why should other, less positivist and more individual oriented analyses of radicalization be pursued? Isn't the concentration on the individual represented by auto/biographical or life narrative methodologies relating to life writing contrary to Durkheim's directive on the adequacy of sociological explanation (i.e. cause and function)? What is the case and possible repercussions for incorporating such an unconventional methodology into this important area of social life and government policy? And considering that we do answer these questions and take the subjective life stories of radicalized individuals seriously, how do we know that they are worth the toilet paper that many such works emerging from prison are written on? How do we know these prisoners are telling the truth, and is this even an important or meaningful question? Are they even aware of their own motivations, and if so, do they seek to distort them after the fact, and what does this mean in terms of the capacity of auto/biographical methods to analyse these texts? How should we regard political prisoner life writings? And how are auto/biographical methodologies positioned to meet the current needs of evidence-based policy-makers, social scientists and criminologists? It is to these types of questions which we now turn.

Qualitative and cultural methodologies – a historical and epistemological justification for doing this type of research in the study of radicalization

In the extensive research literature on qualitative and quantitative research paradigms, what basically distinguishes qualitative methodologies from quantitative is that they seek to understand the underlying reasons for people's *attitudes*, *beliefs*, *feelings* and/or *motivations* for the ways in which they *act*. This accords with the philosopher and cultural theorist Wilhelm

Dilthey's emphasis on understanding (*Verstehen*), which was further expanded by the sociologist Max Weber in his dual emphasis on *Verstehen* and *action* as the main conveyors of social meaning. The focus of qualitative research is thus on capturing how people make sense of the social world of which they are a part through their patterns of interaction in everyday life. This fundamental shift in approach should be useful in seeking to make sense of the thought processes, subjective states of mind and personal motivations of those who are, become or cease to be radicalized.

Qualitative methods are usually associated with *interpretive* epistemologies (or theories of knowledge), and tend to adopt forms of data collection and analysis which rely primarily on *understanding* or *sense-making* processes with a particular emphasis on the creation of cultural symbols, norms, patterns of interaction and shared *meanings*. It is also about situating this (or more appropriately these) understandings within their localized contexts, and also about acknowledging the position of the researcher as a formative influence in this dynamic process. In comparison to positivist methodologies, there is less an aim to achieve high levels of objectivity, abstraction or universality in order to discern laws and more a desire to embrace these very contextually embedded processes in the task of generating possible explanations.

The emphasis on meaning in qualitative research is paralleled by a concentration on the depth and texture of everyday social life. This type of methodology is often utilized within exploratory, descriptive or in-depth studies where familiarity with or 'immersion' in the subject is considered more important than objective quantification (Silverman, 2005). Accordingly, the overt emphasis on the positioning of the researcher with respect to the research process and those being researched (and the ensuing power imbalances) assume a higher profile (Richie and Lewis, 2005). In addition, there is also a significant emphasis on *context*, rather than on universality, representativeness or viewing phenomena in abstraction (Richie and Lewis, 2005). These elements have led to qualitative methods being labelled 'unscientific', as they often seek to identify long descriptive narratives rather than produce statistical tables, which can lead to problems with reliability and accusations of anecdotalism, i.e. focusing on one or few samples which may or may not be representative (Silverman, 2005: 33–4). In practical terms, this means that qualitative research is therefore usually confined to relatively small sample of individual cases, in comparison to quantitative studies. Because they embrace subjective experience as a focal point of the research process (on the parts of both researched and researcher) they are regarded as fundamentally *interpretive* in their analytical approach (as opposed to objective or getting at the 'truth' represented as a singular and universal law or principle which would normally be the aim of a positivist researcher).

The techniques adopted for qualitative research include one-to-one interviews (mainly semi-structured or unstructured), participant or non-participant observation (ethnographies), group interviews (e.g. focus groups), oral histories or life narratives. But qualitative methods are not all just about talk. Other techniques include the systematic collection and analysis of texts (e.g. diaries, newspapers, novels, government reports, etc); visual data (e.g. official photographs, films, family snapshots, paintings); and even spatial forms (e.g. buildings and other architectural structures) and the body (e.g. other sensual or physical experiences of being in the social world – such as the concept of personal body space or the various meanings of actions such as holding hands). As Bryman (1996: 94) notes, in contrast to quantitative research methods and positivist methodologies, while quantitative research is regarded as being *hard* and *reliable*, qualitative research is characterized by being both *rich* and *deep*.

These differences between approaches extend to modes of coding and analysis, where quantitative researchers will typically refer to extant theoretical concepts, laws and/or hypotheses (deductive reasoning), whereas qualitative researchers, though also but not always guided explicitly by theory, will seek to identify these categories as emerging from within the data themselves (inductive reasoning). But it is important not to overstate the differences between the two methodologies, as in practice there is usually a bit of each in both methodologies.

Taking the narrative turn: a brief history of auto/biographical methodology

There is a substantial and growing research literature on what Brian Roberts (2002) refers to generically as biographical research methods, which according to his typology includes biographical, life history, auto/biography, oral history, life narrative and ethnography all under this one umbrella term. From the outset, it is important to stress that the objective of this study is not to comprehensively cover or summarize the scholarly literature on this rich and diverse methodology, as this task would be well beyond the scope of this book. What I will attempt to do is provide a brief introduction to this research method and set out the case for how and why it should be used to study radicalization, and why this should happen now, leading finally to examples of how this could be done in the remaining chapters. Readers who would like to investigate biographical research further will find additional references in the bibliography.

First to attend to the usual task of definition. 'Life writing' is a term that has been adopted by scholars working in this area to designate an inclusive and varied array of 'texts' (which can strictly speaking be spoken, written, performed, and in any other way 'inscribed'); it has since the eighteenth century historically comprised biography and autobiography but has since come to incorporate other more personal and less formal types of writing such as letters, diaries, notebooks, curriculum vitae and even shopping lists (Parr, 1992). Though this study will occasionally reference sources such as published letters and diaries and very occasionally the life history interview, by far the majority of the sample comprises published auto/biographies[9] by writers who were serving or former prisoners, and who were or considered themselves to be or have been incarcerated for political offences. I will turn to the issue of political prisoners and prison life writing later in this chapter. In the next section, I will specifically address the topic of auto/biographical research method.

Historical background and literature review of auto/biographical methods

By way of a very brief review of the historical literature on auto/biographical research, we may first document its rise in the nineteenth and early twentieth centuries, fall from favour in the interwar years, and eventual restitution as an influential presence in the human sciences following the so-called post-structuralist or 'narrative' or 'cultural turn' of the 1960s. From its zenith in the nineteenth-century hermeneutic theories of Wilhelm Dilthey and Friedrich Schliermacher, auto/biography enjoyed a prominent position as a key concept for interpreting modern culture. With the ascent of structuralism and the domination of methods of literary criticism such as Russian Formalism and the American New Criticism in literary studies in the early to mid-twentieth century, the critical emphasis on the internally generated world of the text necessitated an almost total disregard for the text's historical or biographical circumstances of origin, thereby leaving auto/biography as a critical idiom somewhat out in the cold (linked as it was to the real, often living, subject/author). Once even the most sophisticated attempts at 'disciplining' autobiography by literary structuralists Tzvetan Todorov (1990) and Philippe Lejeune [1973] (1982) had so consummately failed to render it amenable to the values and practices of the new 'science of literature' even by way of establishing a sufficiently rigorous definition, the way was open for deconstructionists like the philosopher and literary critic Paul de Man (1984) to deliver the final blow to auto/biography, and (so he claimed) to write its final epitaph.

Notwithstanding de Man's final act of 'de-facement' (de Man, 1984) – and not to mention the posthumous damage wreaked by the emergence of his own life history as a reporter in occupied Belgium would eventually take on his own reputation – others have been less keen to consent to the 'death' of the subject/author, particularly those who are interested in preserving auto/biography for the purposes of recovering the feminine, suffering, embodied, oppressed, resisting and/or post-colonial subject. This can be observed in the re-emergence of hermeneutics in the twentieth century, particularly in the works of theorists such as Georg Gusdorf, Hans-Georg Gadamer and Paul Ricœur, whose philosophies have rekindled interest in auto/biography as a site for cultural analysis, an interest which has also increased in the wake of the so-called 'narrative turn' in the human sciences (Andrews, Day Schlater *et al.*, 2000). Other commentators in the field, notably Ken Plummer (2001), have built upon this distinguished hermeneutic tradition of life narrative scholarship to emphasize its distinctly *humanistic* qualities as a research methodology, and moreover its potential as a corrective to what are regarded as previous positivist excesses in social scientific research. Plummer's work on narrative and life stories (specifically in relation to the telling of sexual stories (Plummer, 1995) will inform the analysis of sexuality in the auto/biographical narratives of radicalization and resistance cultures undertaken in Chapter 3). In addition, with the appearance in the academy of the various 'area studies' (e.g. women's studies, ethnic studies, American studies, and so forth) has come the resurgence of the auto/biographical text in its full and disruptive glory, powerfully influencing current ways of thinking about and formulating appropriately relevant questions for academic research, fuelled by the demands of students and other 'ordinary' readers from a broader range of social backgrounds for such texts (Olney, 1980). Against this cultural background, auto/biography has not only provided access to a hidden or previously ignored canon of literature, it has moreover opened the way for a future literature of *re*storation, *re*membering and *re*covery of diverse and previously hidden or secreted experience (Gilmore, 1994), such as those who, as seen in Chapter 1, have been especially prone to radicalization, including women, disabled people, revolutionaries, (care) workers and indeed political prisoners. This recapturing of the past and laying claim to the future through autobiography as an as yet undisciplined presence in the academy – a 'literature of resistance' (Harlow, 1987) – has been at the heart of recent interdisciplinary/transdisciplinary attempts to harness its distinctive qualities for the purposes of academic research. Thus from the shaping of the subject disciplines to the formation of research questions, as a creative, transgressive and cross-fertilizing method for reinvigorating the research process, the scholarly analysis of auto/biography has gained in prominence and become a fixture in the research community in academia and beyond, due to in large part to its capacity to help recover lost or silenced voices and hidden life stories, and to interpret them in terms of the dialogical influence of both humanist and societal forces.

Certainly subjectivity, representation and truth in autobiography have consistently posed problems for the dominant analytical models in human sciences research, not least from the positivist or empirical perspective which prizes the discovery of universal and monolithic 'truth'. The sociologist Norman Denzin (1989) was among the pioneers of the new generation of sociologists (after the Chicago School in the 1930s) to identify two general uses of the auto/biographical or 'life history' research method in sociology, first, advocating it for its aim to provide an 'objective' account of a 'life' as story or personal journey at a particular time and place, revealed through the given subjective meanings of personal experience attached to these historical narratives. This method links a 'life' with the particular overarching social structures and processes of social change operative at the time. Such an approach is commonly used to map new fields of sociological inquiry or to further support the findings of existing statistical or general quantitative studies. However, the main problem with this approach is the typically unreflexive theoretical and methodological treatment of these materials in light of what we know about life narrative storytelling and its complex relationship to 'the truth' or indeed any objective or mutually recognizable social or political 'reality' as something physically tangible, empirically verifiable or otherwise capable of being explained by a positivist methodology that can capture and deal with bits of reality 'out there'. Hence there have been unfortunate but nonetheless observable instances of some rather naïve treatments of life narrative or auto/biographical texts as transparently and unproblematically 'true'.

Where these instances occur, sociologists are usually quick to seize on such faults in the application of auto/biographical methodology. In her article 'On Auto/biography in Sociology' (1993), Liz Stanley is critical of sociological research where these 'documents of life' are accepted as a relatively straightforward resource or 'data set' like any other, purporting to tell us something factual and generally applicable about 'life out there' in the 'real' world (Stanley, 1993: 41). Stanley argues that the problem with life history research, as exposure to these documents quickly reveals, is that the 'life history' they relate is in actuality composed of a number of histories, many of them contradictory or in complex social competition with each other. Strictly speaking, all life histories are a form of historiography as well as autobiography, and as such they each represent particular written *versions* of the past and the self rather than objective historical 'slices' of the past as it 'really was' (Stanley, 1993).

Thus, to return also to Denzin (1989), the second and more recent approach to autobiographical methodology focusing prominently on the interpretive procedures utilized in auto/biographical research itself and the analysis of life-history production, following and developing the generic principles of reflexive sociology (Denzin, 1989; Stanley, 1992, 1993). Here auto/biography as a form of life narrative or life history methodology is characterized by the multiplicity and mutability of its truth claim and its ethnographic accessibility in terms of *who* is able to use the auto/biographical voice. Therefore auto/biography warrants sociological analysis not as an unproblematic straightforward data resource, but as an object of inquiry in its own right in terms of analysing *who* speaks, in addition to how, when, from where and why and listening to what they have to say about the world as they encounter it and (possibly) try to change or guide its course – all pertinent to the present study. In the scholarly research literature on life writing, the concentration with respect to the question of *who* in the auto/biographical text has overwhelmingly been directed towards the experiences and construction of gender in the text; while other forms of social privilege, e.g. 'race' and class have also featured in these critiques, they have been more or less adjuncts to the generally phallocentric nature of (conventional, traditional) auto/biographical writing. The question of how such issues of 'race', class, ethnicity and religion affect the auto/bio-graphical 'I' from alternative subject positions – such as those of radical actors in prison – has received comparatively less attention. This is all the more regrettable given the massive and growing corpus of prisoner auto/biography and its exposure of prison as, among other things, a remarkable space for the construction of alternate subjectivities and life narrative routes (Morgan, 1999; Nellis, 2002) as well as aesthetic spaces for reimagining the self and the world (Carnochan, 1995).

With respect to mapping the output of autobiography by gender and class, Martin Danahay's (1993) study of nineteenth-century autobiographies demon-strates the identification of conventional autobiography (i.e. celebrating the accomplishments and social autonomy of the sovereign individual) with bour-geois culture, typically identifiable with male writers who were either of the very wealthy classes and/or members of the social elite (see also Sturrock, 1993). During the late nineteenth and early twentieth centuries, however, the public dissatisfaction with biography was due in no small part to what was increasingly regarded as its anachronistic concentration on the exemplary lives of extraordinary male figures (e.g. Disraeli, Johnson, Wordsworth, de Quincy, Hazlett, Gosse, etc.) whose lives were perceived by many of those living in a newly and fully industrial capitalist social order to be too esoteric and distant from the lives of ordinary people. A taste was developing among the reading public for (1) more 'ordinary' life narratives of people who readers could identify with more easily; (2) more intimate and deeply revealing, personal, spiritual and latterly even sexual (Evans, 1998) accounts; and (3) a greater variety of life narratives from those who might not otherwise be recognized as worthy enough to attract the attentions of a biographer.

This demand for ordinary-life writing has been put down to a number of factors. According to the cultural theorist Michael Mascush (1997), the reinvention and democratization of autobiography in the twentieth century emanates from its roots in hagiography and working-class culture in eighteenth century England, traceable to the high market demand for the published lives of John Wesley following his death in 1791, combined with a growing public taste for the gallows confessions of the notorious 'London Hanged'. The social significance of the lives of the 'London Hanged' has also formed a pivotal role in Peter Linebaugh's (1993) historical thesis concerning the rise of capitalism and social purpose of the spectacle of punishment on the poor population of London, a practice that he argues forced the community to accept the criminalization of what were previously customary rights, and also to acknowledge new forms of private property. This was predicated on the utilization by the state of what Foucault calls 'spectacular' forms of punish-ment in order to press upon the public consciousness a refiguring of what were previously held to be legitimate interpretations of civil rights. This is instruc-tive in the present context of the various 'extraordinary' penal strategies to a population of radicalized 'criminals' whose official biographies play a not inconsiderable role in the new discourse on crime and punishment as well as human and civil rights in the wake of the 'war on terror'. These personal auto/ biographies remain generally unread,[10] retaining an air of mystery and/or suspicion, neither of which adds to the public understanding of radicalization or reduces the sometimes irrational fear of these 'extraordinary' or evil 'others'.

In the historical context, arguments have been put forward regarding the drive by the reading public at large to gain a glimpse of the realities of conflict, crime and war through the recapturing of 'ordinary' life stories. Along these lines, the sociologist Mary Evans (1998) argues that the interest in ordinary lives was initially a consequence of the First World War and the demand that it created for published accounts of life in the trenches as experienced by a growing number of ordinary young men who were neither officers, authors nor of any other high social rank. This afforded the reading public a new, and in many ways much more realistic and disturbing, depiction of the realities and consequences of war, while also changing prevailing attitudes about who could legitimately write auto/biography. As Evans (1998) points out, however, with the increase of autobiographical texts written by members of the working classes during the interwar years (specifically those written by First World War soldiers returning from the front) came a greater diversification of the form, with respect to both reading and writing practices, winning a broader popular audience for autobiography, and hence greater market demand.

The subsequent growth in the division of labour in the post-Second World War years in the wake of the feminist second wave resulted in a remarkable increase in the production of autobiographies, those written by women in particular. This created an explosion of interest and demand for auto-biographical writings by those in the academic community and beyond, which is similarly explicable by a complex and reciprocal interplay of economic, political and aesthetic factors (Smith and Watson, 1998: 5) largely contingent on class, and the prospect of class consciousness and/or social mobility. The dialogical impact of autobiography on contemporary modern culture, in terms of its expression of more diverse class interests, is reflected in the increasing access by so-called non-traditional groups to social institutions that were once the preserve of the middle and upper classes, notably the higher education system. In itself, this has stimulated an economic demand for, and inclusion of, texts into the curriculum that express more diverse and wide-ranging life experiences, issues and points of view than ever before, with which to study a greater range of contemporary social, cultural and political phenomena. To this end, women's autobiographies and those written by people from a variety of classes, cultures, 'races', ethnicities and sexualities produce empowering narratives of self-discovery, and experiences of community and identity, in both the 'literature of emancipation' and the 'literature of resistance' modes, mirroring and reinforcing the widespread experiences and broadened horizons of self and identity politics in a post-traditional or postmodern age. While this demand for ever more diverse and innovative auto/biography informs the expansion of the social agency of the individual via autobiography in contemporary cultural life, these texts also reiterate the continuing potency of social structural/ideological frameworks like class, 'race', gender, religion, age, nationality and dis/ability on emergent models of self, and the reciprocal influence of these cultural representations on these same structural and ideological institutions that are often linked to the state. What is more, it is noteworthy how deviance, criminalization and stigma play a significant role in this 'opening up', and in recovery and resistance processes, as the experience of the 'pains of imprisonment' (Sykes, 1958) seem inexorably to rely on the testimony and witness of autobiography as a literature of (political) trauma (Millett, 1994).

Post-colonialism: 'race', diaspora, exploitation and the life journey

While it has been argued that changes to subjective/autobiographical forms of writing have been linked to prevailing cultural models of the individual in terms of class and gender, others contend that discursive constructions of 'race' have also exerted a significant influence on the culture and forms of life writing. As the writer and commentator on black auto/biography Kenneth Mostern (1999) observes, this view can be attributed to the growing disaffection among theorists in identity politics who throughout the 1980s were frustrated by the limitations of Marxian economic determinism and its vague, reductionist accounts of the individual and his/her experiences of socio-political life (Laclau and Mouffe, 1985). This disaffection led to a gradual move away from 'determination' as a primary stratagem for modelling individual experiences of identity and towards the more agentive notion of 'articulation', a transformation most identifiable with the work of Stuart Hall.

The significance of this shift in interpretive strategy for auto/biography studies is difficult to overstate. This is attributable to Hall's influential work in race theory, and specifically his attack on both structuralism and essentialism, which can be broken down into four main constitutive elements: articulation, process, culture and fragmentation (Mostern, 1999: 6). The focus of these elements is on the 'incompleteness' of identity as experienced by real, living individuals in the context of their everyday lives, in response to the 'structural' influence of enforced migration, oppression and exploitation that are endemic to capitalism in general and colonialism (and indeed radicalization) in particular. These experiences are discernible in the reciprocal burden that is placed upon individuals who are compelled to live under these conditions to continually manage and negotiate a sense of their own identities, without being disabled or overwhelmed by broader positive social structures. The very idea of the post-colonial subject thus suggests an intimate imbrication of discursive positions and material locations, albeit one that does not form a coherent, unified identity, nor a relationship with place that is ever unambiguously fixed, finished or complete (Anderson, 2001).

As post-colonial thought is centrally (though by no means exclusively) concerned with the nature and construction of 'black' identities and the experience of slavery, the very notion of 'place' assumes numerous dimensions and dislocated meanings, which makes the concept of hybridity central to the post-colonial exploration of the crossings, migration and diaspora generated by colonial capitalism. This is especially evident in the work of Paul Gilroy (1993), who argues that the trans-Atlantic displacement of black peoples has produced new diasporic cultures that have rendered the notion of the 'purity' and also the 'difference' of colonizing cultures nonsensical. Gilroy argues that these migrations have produced, among other things, new models of identity that are now dislocated from previously stable notions of ethnicity and nationhood, introducing aspects such as 'creolization' and other hybrid influences into the 'host' cultures. These hybrid influences are detectable in the various cultural products of 'host' cultures, including auto/biography.

This presence can be observed in Hall's concentration on the language of *dispersal* in post-colonial representations of identity, where the inbuilt resistance to unity, fixity and essentialism does not rule out a position from which to speak. On the contrary, such discourses typically construct

> 'arbitrary closures', points at which the infinite flux of differences is brought to a halt temporarily as a condition of speech. This moment of stasis is a kind of stake, a kind of wager. It says, 'I need to say something, something ... just now.'
>
> (Hall in Anderson, 2001: 115).

Introducing the language of 'stakes' and 'wagers' as conditions of identity speech is reminiscent of Derrida's (Bennington and Derrida, 1999) autobiographical exploration of his own identity as a French/African/Jew, as well as Lejeune's later musings on autobiography as a discursive 'wager' on the part of the writer as opposed to a legalistic 'pact' with the reader. It also echoes the dominance of risk as the trope according to which much of the current sociological and political discourse and decision-making praxes are perhaps modelled, in addition to (as will be explored in the next chapter) the prominence of the language of gaming in political prisoner life writing. For Hall, the recovery of these 'arbitrary closings' by post-colonial writers as temporary platforms from which to speak are themselves the necessary fictions required to make identity and political positioning/stand-taking possible. While the significance of displacement and dispersal makes the symbolic language of the 'rootedness' (*radic-*) of identity in blood, nationality or soil less meaningful in post-colonial societies, the resulting narratives of contingency, fragmentation, conflict and oppression that are characteristic of these types of radical autobiographies make the concept of the life journey, which was once understood as a kind of Cartesian travelogue through the subjective domain, exceedingly problematic.

The post-colonial revision of the life journey incorporates within it a comprehensive critique of the contingent discourses of freedom, tolerance, progress, fraternity and equality that are foundational to modernity. It is these critical aspects of the texts that will be of particular concern in this study.

This assortment of theoretical responses indicates not only the distinctive presence of autobiography in modern culture but also its commitment to the individual as a primary social constituent. In addition, the growing literature on auto/biography maps the ways in which it has influenced and been influenced by writing practices in response to the social construction of identity politics and the polarization of the public and private spheres of everyday and historical life. What emerges is a landscape of the modern subject rendered via the highly public celebration of the life of the great man of letters in the canonical autobiographies of the nineteenth century, and its subsequent dissemination into the writings the more obscure, private and unorthodox life narratives of those such as prisoners, women, slaves and criminals. While the former reflects the social institution and expansion of the egocentric, anti-altruistic, normatively male subject as individual social unit, the latter reflects a more genuinely autobiographical ethos in their exposure of the real lives of other identity groups who make up modern social life. In contrast to the canonical examples, these texts are typically imbued with the rich textures of what were previously hidden, shameful, deviant or unremarked details of private life, many of which are externally shaped by the socialization processes of gender, intimacy, sexuality and the body.

From these observations and analyses, it is apparent that autobiography (and life writing more generally) displays a cultural relativity and fluidity that changes with political, historical and literary movements, whether or not it actually dictates these changes or is determined by them (or indeed if the direction of causality is unclear). From the range of theoretical perspectives, most literary critics of life writing in general and autobiography in particular would endorse this dialogical relativity as more or less axiomatic (Gusdorf, 1956; Bruss, 1976; Lejeune, 1971; Weintraub, 1978; Spengemann, 1980; McDonald in Derrida, 1985; Eagleton in Wolfreys, 1999; Stanley, 1992). The ultimately unsuccessful attempts by structuralist literary theorists to adequately define and thus to effectively bring autobiography into line with the other rules and conventions of (formalist or structuralist) literary theory may have rendered it problematic or inoperative as a 'scientific' methodology, but at the same time, its very cultural relativity and fluidity recommends it both as a core object for understanding and interpreting the highly individualistic culture of modernity from a hermeneutic perspective. In light of recent developments in feminist, post-structuralist and post-colonial thought, the methodical working out of these implications with respect to the auto/biographical text takes on a new sense of urgency.

Auto/biography and sociology: an intimate social and life history

Its ostensible links to the individual as opposed to the social has done little to temper the sharp rise in sociological interest in auto/biography, particularly over the last generation. From the perspective of the 'long' twentieth century, this is perhaps not as remarkable as it might at first appear, especially in light of sociology's extended and intimate history with the auto/biographical text. Even before C. Wright Mills' [1959] (1970) much-cited location of the sociological imagination in the conceptual space between biography and history, auto/biography has maintained a notable and recurrent (if not always quite celebrated) presence in the sociological literature. This presence extends all the way back to sociology's so-called 'classical' period in the mid to late nineteenth century. Working back, this lineage is traceable from Erving Goffman's dramaturgical analysis of the autobiographical works of writers such as Brendan Behan, T. E. Lawrence, George Orwell, Thomas Merton and others in his landmark *Asylums: Essays on the Social Situation of Mental Patients and Other Inmates* (1968) in the post-war period, to the fascination with oral life histories in the Chicago School (e.g. Clifford Shaw's celebrated *The Jack Roller* (1966), and the lesser known *The Natural History of a Delinquent Career* (1931) and *Brothers in Crime* (2005)) in the interwar years. These works were strongly influenced in turn by the sociological research of other members of the Chicago School, which was itself heavily reliant upon Thomas and Znaniecki's landmark study of immigration and urbanization at the turn of the twentieth century *The Polish Peasant in Europe and America* ([1918] 1984). In addition to these works, Max Weber made substantial use in his detailed qualitative analysis of *The Autobiography of Benjamin Franklin* (1964) in his seminal *The Protestant Ethic and the Spirit of Capitalism* ([1930] 1992). Even Karl Marx's theory of political economy developed in *Capital: A Critique of Political Economy* ([1867] 1972) was partially drawn from an interpretation of Daniel Defoe's fictionalized auto/biography of Alexander Selkirk in *Robinson Crusoe* ([1719] 1985). As this brief but impressive list indicates, auto/biographical texts have been influential throughout the history of social sciences in shaping some of their most distinguished works and seminal theses, which were developed to creatively explore and indeed scientifically explain the nature of capitalist modernity. As in the hermeneutic and cultural theory traditions, the recurring presence of auto/biography in sociology's canon suggests that there is something intrinsically sociological about auto/biography, and that it offers an innovative if sometimes troublesomely subjective way of exploring contemporary social life.

At the same time, embedding auto/biography in the sociological canon has resulted in a tendency – especially noticeable in the anglophone tradition – to view this type of discourse as relatively unproblematic, comprising simply another methodological resource in the form of a more or less straightforward data set like any other, as we have seen (Stanley, 1992). As Kenneth Mostern

(1999) has cautioned, however, such a simplistic perception of auto/biography is extremely naïve, as auto/biographical texts do not 'speak for themselves', but rather require a large degree of awareness of their rhetorical construction in order to be appropriately interpreted (cf. de Man, 1984). In recent years, this methodological naïveté has been countered by increasingly sophisticated views of auto/biography and its potential for the purposes of sociological theorizing, beginning, for example, with Robert K. Merton's (1988) reflections on the functional qualities of autobiography. Merton drew upon Durkheim's study of what would appear on the surface to be distinctively individualistic if not wholly private social products or acts (e.g. suicide), but for which the under-lying sociological motivations, symptoms and causal processes are more often than not unknown or inaccessible at a conscious level to the individual who acts in this way. Nevertheless, as Atkinson's (1982) subsequent research on suicide has reiterated, the 'relic' of the text (in this instance, usually the suicide note) is a vital part of reconstructing the narrative or 'psychological autopsy' in expert discourses (e.g. coroner's courts); the relic is a way of making sense of these actions in the context of other functional and contextual influences, dis-courses and events, without the false supposition that the writer is or was (with respect to motives, identity or knowledge) fully 'transparent' to him/herself at the time of writing. Such a stance has been augmented by the growing aware-ness of the social (de)construction of the subject in feminist social theory (e.g. Jelinek, 1980, 1986; Mason, 1980; Brée, 1988; Stanton, 1998; Spacks, 1988; Steedman, 1986; Felski, 1989; Nussbaum, 1989), all of which will influence the analysis undertaken in the following chapters of this book.

Apart from the substantial feminist analyses of autobiography undertaken throughout the 1990s and beyond (e.g. Stanley, 1992, 1993; Gagnier, [1990] 1998, 1991; Gilmore, 1994; Heller, 1992; Marcus, 1994; Miller, 1994, 1995; Steedman, 1992, 1995; Swindells, 1995; Smith and Watson, 1998), it is impor-tant to note that considerable work has also been carried out in this area of research throughout the 1990s in other less obvious quarters. This includes, for example, Anthony Giddens' appeal to self-representative discourses like auto/biography as a way of resolving the fundamental structure–action dichotomy within his general structuration theory (1990, 1991), which focused on the 'plasticity' of self in late modernity, and personal freedom of choice in the wake of 'detraditionalization' (Heelas *et al.*, 1996). Others view auto/biography from a different perspective, as exemplifying the semiotic 'regimes of signification' which characterize the distinctive social realism foundational to contemporary social epistemology (Friedman and Lash, 1992). Still others suggest that such explicitly self-referential discourses offer a means for developing an unprece-dentedly thorough-going and reflexive critique of social theory itself (e.g. Sandywell, 1996). While these lines of argument represent rich alternatives to what have in the past been either dismissive, naïve or uncritical views of auto/biography, there is still considerable work to be done in this area, not least in the expansion of this methodology to other fields, such as the study of (counter)terrorism and radicalization. The sophistication of responses such as those previously listed, by a range of scholars over the last generation, to auto/ biography represents a dynamic and fruitful engagement with these important and distinctive texts as cultural products. This in itself augurs well for the development of a more nuanced theoretical understanding of the increasingly individualistic culture of modernity.

Autobiography and sociological methodology

Though these are generally positive signs from a methodological standpoint, how is auto/biography's potential to be realized with respect to the analysis of radicalization, and what assurances are there that it will be worth it? Considering past engagements with the individual in the history of sociology, how should the systematic study of auto/biography be approached from the standpoint of social theory and research methodology? To start with, it is worth remembering that the emergence and development of the social sciences – particularly at the height of the general theories of history and economics in the nineteenth century – came out of the general project to identify and explain the causal mechanisms of society and social change. This was itself a part of the (social) scientific response to the implicit limitations of individual knowledge and subjective experience. In hindsight, this attitude has led sociology to be conspicuously neglectful of the individual in society and his/her role as an agent in social change manifested in the real, historical, living (latterly termed 'embodied') person. In many ways, this failure was later exacerbated by the perceived need to distance social theory from the individual following the disintegration of the historical metanarrative in the wake of the poststructuralist critique or the linguistic, narrative or cultural turn. This is understandable in the context of the historical period that saw the rise of the modern nation state, the conglomeration of the masses into cities, and the resulting establishment of sociology as a uniquely inclusive discipline with which to study the workings of society as essentially an essentially urbanized (and latterly globalized) collective. However, perhaps now is the time for sociology to own up to its limitations in terms of fully engaging with the individual experience of modern social life beyond the generic framework of role theory or alternative the (very) micro-level theorizing of phenomenological sociology and ethnomethodology. Auto/ biographical methodologies constitute an important meso-level methodology – not too abstracted from social or collective influences, but also not totally rooted in the individual or personal realm.

Against this background, and given the intense concentration on the auto/ biographical text over the last twenty to thirty years, what would a specifically auto/biography methodology look like from the area studies perspective? Should it replicate what the literary theorist John Sturrock (1993) describes as the 'punishing' project of theorizing auto/biography developed within literary studies – which comprises reading great numbers of autobiographies and drawing general conclusions about the 'genre' from these examples – and then subject this 'knowledge' to the hypothetical–deductive methodology of modern science? Is this the type of work that experts in counter-terrorism and security studies are letting themselves in for? Or should they look elsewhere for thematic models and conceptual paradigms?

For an insight into how this type of methodological issue has been approached in the research literature on radicalization, let us return to a recent article by the Norwegian political scientist Thomas Hegghammer:

> One of the main objectives of this article is to fill an empirical gap in the growing corpus of profile-based studies of Islamist militancy. The individual-oriented approach to terrorism studies, which fell out of fashion in the mid-1980s, has regained popularity since 9/11 and has yielded significant new insights into the causes of Islamist violence.
>
> (Hegghammer, 2006: 39)

Hegghammer's data set comprises some 240 biographies of Saudi militants, recovered from a range of primary and secondary (mainly Arabic) sources:

> In addition to international and local press reports, I have made extensive use of the militants' own publications, which contain a wealth of biographical information [identified in a footnote as QAP magazines, statements, films, and radical Internet message boards ... in addition to] numerous interviews with former radicals as well as families and acquaintances of militants.
>
> (ibid.: 40)

Hegghammer recognizes the advantages and limitations involved in using such biographical data, as well as the issues that arise in terms of access to militants who, as Curcio (2005) also finds, typically end up either in high-security prisons or dead:

> There are undoubtedly certain problems with this material. For a start, the information may not always be one hundred percent accurate. Regrettably, I have not had the chance to interview the militants themselves, because most are dead or in high-security prisons. Most biographical details come from jihadist publications and Interior Ministry statements that were produced in a context of intense mutual conflict and information warfare. Another problem is that the militants portrayed here may not be entirely representative of all the followers of the QAP [al-Qaeda on the Arabian Peninsula]. While the exact total number of QAP-related individuals is unclear, we know that Saudi authorities have arrested between 500 and 1000 suspected militants, while around

150 have been killed in attacks and shootouts. Having said this, our core sample of 70 is likely to include most of the prominent and active members of the QAP. These are, after all, the most relevant for understanding the organization.

(Hegghammer, 2006: 40)

Within such nascent studies of terrorism using biographical data, Hegghammer's brief remarks on the nature and limitations of this sort of data is unusually insightful and frank. He is right also to quantify the weaknesses of this sort of data and its analysis, alongside its unique strengths. His analysis conforms generally to other such studies, in that it is presented in mainly statistical form, comparing 'biographical' details such as age, socio-economic class, educational attainment, gender (almost exclusively male), geographical region, tribal identity, criminal and prison records among these militants, and also in relation to known data about militants from other countries, using devices like maps, bar graphs and pie charts to represent this information. There is no attention devoted to the scholarly literature on biography, however, nor to the meaning or use of biographical narratives within these militant subcultures. What does this imply in terms of the shape and quality of the resulting analysis? While it is certainly interesting and revealing to map details concerning the various demographics of these militants, the establishment of causality and sequencing of phenomena is perhaps less satisfactory, as are some of the emergent identities such as 'lifestyle jihadists', 'passive Islamists', etc. in terms of their conceptual capacity as identity models, in what context they convey meaningful information, and for what purpose. Similarly, while the well-known link between attendance at training camps, combat experience and radicalization is reaffirmed, the order of causation is somewhat less clear:

It is commonly accepted that the training camps in Afghanistan played an extraordinarily important role in the operationalization of al-Qaeda's recruits in the 1996–2001 period. Recruits who attended these camps underwent four important interlinked processes: violence acculturation, indoctrination, training and relations-building. These processes are the key to understanding the extremism, ideology, abilities and intra-group loyalty of the militants who returned from Afghanistan to Saudi Arabia in late 2001.

(ibid.: 46).

Again, we detect the familiar 'four step' process outlining the causal process of radicalization, which is common within empirical research. But is this what we mean by 'radicalization', we may ask, i.e. what happens to militants once they have already embarked on a course of military training and active combat? Don't most people think of radicalization as being about what leads up to this type of action in the first instance, albeit one that in all likelihood requires continual reinforcement through these subsequent processes? This constitutes as much a methodological and conceptual problem for carrying out research on radicalization. What about the meaning or salience of other more 'subjective' auto/biographical accounts that pre-empt such activities and choices?

Considering the flaws, contradictions and anachronisms enshrined in literary and social theory and its obsession with genre in respect of the auto/biographical text, there are many good reasons to opt for – or at least incorporate – alternative qualitative or interpretive approaches that are specifically amenable to the auto/biographical text. For one thing, as Sturrock (1993) rightly observes, there is a substantial ethical conflict underlying the genre-based approach, and other such formalist or 'scientific' theoretical approaches, whereby a consciousness of the intrinsic singularity and difference manifested in the autobiographical text diminishes 'the theoretical need ... to locate generic sameness in a kind of writing which aims at imposing difference' (Sturrock 1993: 3). Even literary theorists admit that this type of 'scientific' methodological reading contrasts starkly with the 'ordinary' reader's typical engagement with these texts. In practice, such indiscriminate and extensive reading of many auto/biographies, and the subsequent extrapolation of their meaning from this broad reading is not the norm for the ordinary reading public; readers of auto/biography are not generally in the habit of consuming numerous works written by authors who they have never heard of in order to gain a comprehensive knowledge of the form for its own sake – neither to improve their knowledge of the 'genre' nor to enhance their reading experience. In fact, as Sturrock admits, not only is expert or theoretical knowledge of this sort unnecessary for the ('ordinary') reading of auto/biography, it may actually be detrimental to the understanding and interpretation of these texts, at least in the way in which the author intended. It is worth bearing in mind that this is a matter of some considerable significance, taking into account the potency of authorial intentionality to this form of writing and the residual 'real life' presence of the author (again, something that runs counter to post-structuralist approaches to the text). If Sturrock's assertion is accurate, one wonders whether this mode of reading should be the central focus of auto/biography methodology adopted in this and other similar studies – in the sociological, criminological, counter-terrorist, or any other context. At the same time, however, it is imperative that social scientists retain some measure of critical distance to both authorial intentionality and ordinary reading practices; making such major concessions to these elemental aspects of the auto/biographical text at such an early stage could seriously threaten any subsequent capacity to recover a sufficiently objective yet still reflexively substantial analytical position. It is imperative for those who deal with these kinds of materials to attempt a balance between this search for sufficiently critical distance and the commendable ethical motives underlying such a trusting approach, which tries to recognize the credibility of auto/biography without erring on the side of naïveté. In other words, while it is not strictly necessary to read *all* auto/biographies written by or about radicalized actors (probably an impossible task anyway), it is highly recommended to read and compare a number of examples, and also to 'enter into' the world of the text as constructed by each individual author. For those who work in counter-terrorism, it is probably not a bad idea to become familiar with this corpus of life writing, as a way of gaining a more nuanced and fuller understanding of the history of radicalization, its development and general trends, and the ability to be able to recognize what are new or innovative manifestations of this phenomenon in other self-representative discourses (e.g. investigative interviews).

How to read auto/biography in order to theorize about it, how auto/biography changes in relation to its reception by its readers, how it has been read historically, and the way this has instigated changes in its production and interpolation of the self, are in themselves important sociological issues throughout the modern period (Baumeister, 1986). While it is easy to sympathize with the theoretical perspective that eschews the methodical reading and analysis of autobiography associated with formalist/structuralist analysis for its positivistic connotations, solving this methodological problem by going to the other extreme and jettisoning the intertextual reading of autobiography is also deeply counter-intuitive – not least because of the unwarranted political advantage it affords (some) authors by effectively endorsing the authenticity of their individual position and derivative sovereign social status. Clearly, to recognize auto/biographers as absolutely and uniquely individual – as they often claim to be – would mean recognizing a social category of discreteness that is wholly untenable, as it subverts sociology's broader conceptualization of the individual as existing *in* (if not also *of* and *for*) society. It is extremely difficult to see how such a concession to the singularity of the auto/biographical text could possibly benefit the sociological study of the individual/self via its ostensibly subjective representations. Such a position would moreover ignore the devastating polemics against auto/biography by literary critics – here I have in mind Paul de Man (1984) in particular, who severely castigates the form for its rhetorical and tropological character, and the ways in which these serve the partial, biased and self-interested concerns of the socially privileged (read: elite white male) individual (a polemical position on auto/biography that is not without its own ironies and paradoxes (see Derrida, 1986)).

It is probably the case that most 'ordinary' readers of autobiography lack an encyclopaedic knowledge of the wider corpus of auto/biographical writing, and neither are they usually acquainted with the work of its Demanian deconstruction (by which I mean that readers are very likely fully au fait with the general construction of auto/biographical discourse and its employment of partiality, deception and selective disclosure, as its identification relies so strongly upon its common-sense character). Although the scholarly literature on auto/biography reveals that it is extremely difficult to define (as indeed are 'terrorism' and 'radicalization'), it can nevertheless in practice be easily identified, not only by a formal disclosure by the real, named author, but also from the presence of the major autobiographical tropes (notably the life as a *journey* or a *struggle*, characterized by the long and temporally linear and progressive developmental path to maturity which can include such narrative tropes as the rags to riches, triumph over adversity, rebellion against the world, recovery from notoriety and/or infamy to respectability, etc.). These are often conveyed narratively through the various rites of passage from infancy to childhood, followed in succession by education, adolescence, sexual awakening, productive adulthood, marriage, parenthood, old age and decline. In other words, there is a strongly *Bildungsroman* quality to autobiography, perhaps even more so than in the classic modern novel. Indeed, in the following chapters, we will see that this *Bildungsroman* influence is often very evident – though in perhaps unexpected ways – in the life writings of radicalized individuals, not least in their narrative reconstruction of what *caused* them to become what they are and do the things they do as a process embedded in their own personal life course (often originating in childhood experiences or initiated by sexual relationships or experimentation or family life). At the same time, these life writings very much disrupt, and call for the reconsideration of, *process*, as has already been noted and will be shown in the following chapters. Indeed, this is consistent with the influence of prisoner life writing on the literary tradition of the modern age that has been substantial and fundamental, such as the emergence of the picaresque novel (e.g. Franklin, 1978). The transgression and disruption of the linear contiguous narrative associated with conventional or classic autobiography in favour of more determinedly disjointed and synchronic narrative, as can be found in prisoner life writing, provides a source of inspiration to other writers generally, and also offers great insights into the nature of modern society and mechanisms of social change themselves. These life writings cast a fascinating light on the nature of contemporary society and cultural change, especially in terms of the involvement and agency of the radicalized individual and emergent discourses of freedom, power and dissent. In the words of the South African Communist, anti-apartheid activist, auto/biographer and one time political prisoner Ruth First, the intellectual journey and life history of political radicals 'necessarily combines both biography and bibliography' (in Harlow, 2002: 152), i.e. the singular life story presented in auto/biography and the interplay of intertextuality.

Given the previously stated misgivings concerning overly positivistic readings of auto/biography as capturing the image of life as lived 'out there' in the real world, the wealth of common-sense knowledge among the reading public concerning the rhetorical construction of autobiography must, to some degree, justify and allow for comparative intertextual reading and analysis of these texts on a relatively modest scale. The question now is how and to what extent should intertextuality be used, i.e. how many texts are required to ensure methodological adequacy and allow for sufficiently authoritative theoretical conclusions to be drawn.

Small case studies and discourse analysis

This leads into not unfamiliar methodological territory for sociology and the other social sciences. As a focal point for social theorizing over the last half century, as we have seen, sociology can boast a distinguished and sustained encounter with what can be broadly described as textual representations of self and everyday life (e.g. Goffman, 1972; Giddens, 1991; Sandywell, 1996, 2004). Such a long-standing tradition informing sociological method in this area is represented, among others, by the interactionist traditions of discourse and conversation analysis, which specifically recommend the closely detailed analysis of single cases, excerpts or texts (Wooffitt, 1992: 72) – a method that will be adopted, or at least adapted, and indeed recommended, in this study.

For the specific purposes of analysing political prisoner auto/biography, this strand of sociology has the added advantage of drawing upon useful inferential links between the representation of unconventional, damaged, stigmatized or deviant identities, and the indirect, implicit and high-profile nature of *description* in these discourses, in the absence of familiar or generic narrative tropes. According to discourse analyst Jonathan Potter (1996), the reason people resort to description in these kinds of discourses and in these sorts of texts is that in a majority of unusual situations, the type of action required by the narrator is often of a sensitive or difficult nature, so the recovery of agency by individual speakers/writers through indirect or detailed descriptions offers certain advantages over more direct or conventional narrative methods. It is often the case that in such uncomfortable circumstances, the straightforward use of more conventional narrative stratagems can result in a negative impact on the image or identity of the narrator, as it indicates to the reader/listener that the writer/ speaker is either unaware of, or otherwise unconcerned about, the difficulty of his/her current situation. This impression itself can cause a negative impact on the writer/speaker to accrue. On the contrary, what we find in real interactional situations is that those instigating the discourse need to carefully management *what* is said and *how* it is formulated, in order to construct first an adequate sense of self, and second to recover a sense of agency sufficient to convey this under constrained or difficult circumstances. This can be observed in the cases of the political prisoner auto/biographies examined in the following chapters, in which the writers strongly convey their eagerness to eschew identification as criminal deviants, passive victims or complacent bystanders with respect to their own personal choices and life histories. Similarly, they are often (to differing degrees of conscious awareness) not averse to using narrative devices – or telling the sorts of stories – that they think people want to hear, and thus are more likely to foster a sense of empathy or (failing this) at least to make themselves more attractive and thus draw the reader into their world. The ability to accomplish this with some basic level of success is vital for ordinary readers and the writers who seek to influence them – whether by trying to get them to support or follow their example (as in the case of Sayyid Qtub (2006)), to reject of desist from the path they once took (e.g. Ed Husain (2007)), or a shifting or uncertain mix of the two (e.g. Malcolm X (1965) and Jane Alpert (1981)). Hence the kinds of stories they tell are of crucial importance in tracing the cultural and evolutionary development of radicalization, as is their dissemination in wider (popular) cultural media as expressions of formative narratives of identity, security and captivity (see Namias, 1993), as in the example of Steve McQueen's recent film *Hunger*, which is based on the prison life writings of Bobby Sands.

The main point to stress here is that descriptive discourse displays numerous qualities implicit in the type of action orientation to which such prison auto/biographers aspire. From the discourse analysis perspective, these descriptions are strongly bound up with the creation of *action* in the text, almost to the point of being inseparable from it. The problematization by prison auto/biographers of action or agency in self-representative discourse is a key focal point in this study. As we will see in the following chapters, for many prison writers, this is accomplished vis-à-vis the reconstruction of the self in auto/biography as a form of active participation in social and cultural life, which is directed at conscious and indeed radical cultural change in circumstances where access to the normal routes facilitating individual autonomy are systematically denied. Given this take on the auto/biographical text by such demonized prison writers, it is perhaps not surprising that their reception, interpretation and use by their intended audiences often encourage identification with them to subsequently instigate similar action.

The discourse analysis perspective on auto/biography offers a number of clear advantages over the traditional structuralist sociological and historicist accounts that tend to portray the individual (on its rare appearance) as a nonparticipant in the social events going on around them, and reduce their life narratives either to simply by-products of events played out around them according to the macro forces of history or politics, or to profile of empirical 'facts'. So, as has been acknowledged, a sociological analysis of auto/biography must resist the temptation to overly individualize or valorize the auto/biographical subject as either a simplistic mode of evidence or social agency; at the same time, as Durkheim himself recognized, it is nevertheless abhorrent for sociology to regard the individual as simply the docile object of the macro forces shaping his or her life world, a composite of externally oriented empirical facts, or indeed the passive observer of the times through which they live(d).

While Potter (1996) stresses that ' ... descriptions are closely bound up with the idiosyncratic particulars of settings' (111), making generalizations problematic nevertheless, to some extent, observable common features among singular but similar descriptive texts make some limited generalizations possible. This alternative position offered by discourse analysis highlights the necessity and legitimacy of focusing on a small number of individual texts or case studies, recognizing the validity of highly descriptive idiosyncratic discourse for the purposes of sociological analysis, while remaining open to the possibility of drawing qualified generalizations about such texts. Together, these principles constitute a viable take on the conceptual gap that is perceived to exist between the individual and the social as portrayed for instance in cultural forms like auto/biography. In addition, discourse analysis offers the possibility of traversing the diachronic and synchronic dichotomy of Saussurean structural linguistics that is the focal point of much of literary studies and narratology; this represents a distinct advantage in dealing with auto/biographical texts, in terms of resisting getting bogged down in the problems of subjectivism or memory in either the technical usage of historical language that changes over a span of time (diachronic) or the use of language as a more or less complete system of representation at a given moment in time (synchronic) (Baldick, 1996).

Technical issues concerning the problematics of synchronic and diachronic micro-usage of language are marginalized in such discourses; however, as we will see, apertures are opened up with respect to exploring the impact of synchronic and diachronic aspects of everyday life on the macro-narrative structures of life writing more generally. This is manifested, for example, in the concentration on the synchronic qualities of prisoner life writing where, from a normative 'outsider' perspective, 'nothing' seems to happen, and consequently everyday life is emptied of its normative (diachronic) narrative capacity (see Cohen and Taylor, 1990). On the contrary, as will be shown, prison writers are often compelled to depart from the conventional attachment to the life understood as a progressive and coherent diachronic history. Instead they focus more on the extended present as a richly synchronous resource for examining and representing the self, and indeed for imagining a radically different collective future. This enhanced concentration on synchronic narrative and descriptive writing represents an innovative and transformative influence on the comparatively static and predictable conventions of generic life narrative writing, which is utterly reliant upon a contiguous and coherent narrative structure characterized by the diachronic movement of 'progress', 'profile' or 'career'. What is more, such challenging life narrative texts disrupt stock modes of reading auto/biography, shifting the focus of the auto/biographical 'I' from the sovereign individual to the communal/interpersonal and the detailed textures of everyday social life. Similarly, as will also be shown in the following chapters, the innovative usage of synchronic narrative and other narratological devices such as diegesis by these prison writers gives rise to many interesting insights and challenging questions concerning the nature and meaning of extremely pertinent concepts regarding the study of terrorism and radicalization. Among these, again as will be shown, is a deconstruction of the conceptualization of 'process' (which as we have seen is prioritized by experts in the field of terrorism) versus 'event' (which tends to be decried by these same experts as something which has an unfortunate tendency to 'drive' the study of terrorism (Coolsaet, 2008)). An analysis of the available life writings of these radical actors and groups suggests that the priority given to these seminal concepts is well placed, but might currently be in the wrong order – i.e. radicalization may turn out to be more oriented towards 'event' than 'process', and its study could perhaps more fruitfully be approached by a more thorough attention to social 'processes', as opposed to terrorist events.

Another major element of these texts that will be closely examined in the following chapters is the notion of *agency*, and its role in the (re)construction and/or recovery of subjectivity by political prisoners, and subsequently on new mechanisms of social change. With respect to investigating these issues, it is beneficial to adapt the position on the text that is taken by discourse analysts who base their analysis of text(s) on a hierarchy and framework of description through which action orientation (agency) is rendered meaningful and explicable. This is an elemental component of everyday or ordinary social life, as opposed to being regarded in some deeper sense as antithetical to the diachronic history of the contiguous life story, and thus seen as simply occasional, trivial, irrelevant, extraordinary, idiosyncratic or anecdotal. However, this does not necessarily relegate theory to the area of micro-sociological investigation, as in the case of ethnomethodology. Insofar as these other 'idiosyncratic' aspects of the text can be rendered explicable, this is accomplished by reading these texts in the context of their specific macro-social structures or meta-historical forces, in order to be able to identify if not the universal abstract *laws* sought by positivists, then the *patterns* that emerge from the texts themselves. The aim is that this may offer a more fruitful approach to analyzing these challenging texts, while also helping to further incorporate qualitative and interdisciplinary methodologies in security and terrorism studies. From the discourse analysis point of view, we can begin to appreciate the indelibly sociological qualities of auto/biography as an unapologetically individual form of discourse that is embedded within and playing off the socially encoded practices of self-representation prevalent at any given time or in any set of cultural circumstances. To use the common cartographic method often applied to the modern subject, discourse analysis attempts to 'map' in a detailed manner the directions or individual discursive 'pathways' out of which action orientation and individual agency emerges, rather than following other more generic or ethnomethodological treatments of the quotidian to achieve the same outcome, as for example in literary theory or conversation analysis. Again, this offers the possibility of drawing more general (and hence potentially more comparative) conclusions by way of discerning general patterns, even at the expense of more specialist readings of texts that relate exclusively to a specific group or context (an approach that is not only possible but wholly justified, albeit one which I do not adopt in this particular instance). My contention is that, at this stage, the case for a more comparative study is justified, not just to try to establish general patterns in radicalization stories (if and where they exist), but also to illustrate how auto/biographical methodologies can be used in relation to a diversity of texts and extremist groups, and how this might be used in policy-making.

Given these considerations, it is my contention that in the case of socio-logical analysis of auto/biographical texts for the present purposes, such analyses of singular or small groups of texts (as opposed to large-scale typological studies undertaken in formalist literary theory from a range of post-war resources) are justified on these methodological grounds, where neither universal laws nor intractably situated ethnographies constitute the main aim, strictly speaking. What is being sought is more of a mid-range theoretical and methodological approach to the auto/biographical text. This approach does not denigrate the individual life narrative, nor does it pre-clude our capacity to make at least limited conclusions or generalizations, which makes recognizing genealogical interrelations and similarities among texts possible in the manner of what Wittgenstein referred to collectively as 'family resemblances'. Here the utilization of (some) locally applied literary concepts, taxonomies and terminologies (e.g. genre, canon, corpus, diegesis, metaphor, synecdoche, etc.), as well as intertextual and narratological con-cepts, are not out of place as analytic touchstones. A combination of close textual reading of a relatively small number of auto/biographical texts in regard to certain rhetorical strategies therefore forms the basis of the meth-odology adopted in the following chapters.

Writing and not talking

It is also worth pointing out that this study concentrates on life writing, as opposed to other life history forms (the most ubiquitous of which by far in sociology and criminology is the biographical interview, as mentioned pre-viously). The reasons for this have to do not only with the comparatively rich development of auto/biographical methodologies that emanate from the humanities disciplines outlined thus far, and the need to incorporate these into the social scientific analysis of auto/biography, though this in itself would be a valid reason. In addition, there is the important issue of this particular sample group, which for obvious reasons is nearly impossible to access while in prison, and often even after release. For serving and former prisoners who are mem-bers of organizations (such as the Provisional IRA), there are formidable issues to do with negotiating access to potential participants via an apparently grow-ing and sophisticated group of 'gatekeepers'. Similarly, there are significant ethical and data protection issues to take into consideration, as well as the right to privacy. In addition, for those who put themselves forward to participate in academic research, many are experienced in using the research interview to 'grandstand' or otherwise try to appropriate the research process for their own purposes. The auto/biographical text offers the advantage of bypassing or overcoming some or all of these obstacles. What is more, because the published autobiographical text by radicalized prison writers by its nature has the group orientation in mind as an implied audience, they arguably afford a more authentic and representative insight into the radicalized or 'terrorist' world-view, and thereby a unique glimpse of the underlying processes and/or causes of radicalization from the 'inside', as it were.

What types of things do we find that are of significance to radicalization in these texts – in terms of what it is, how it happens and who it happens to or is directed at? As mentioned previously in this chapter, and as constantly reiterated in the research literature on radicalization, culture is key. In this respect, common features include the life course (especially young adult-hood), emotional and group bonds, the family, friendship, the 'Other' or the enemy, belief and gender. While many of these also figure in the existing research literature on radicalization, most have yet to be sufficiently or comprehensively explored, or exploited for their cultural meaning or relevance to the broader understanding of radicalization. What also emerges is the reliance upon a body of *language, symbolism* and *myth* that these prison writers are able to draw upon, often in creative and innovative ways, in developing a range of shared tropes and cultural narratives relating to subjects such as evil, chaos, loyalty, honour, war and the self. In many cases, these innovations not only facilitate the development and transmission of resistance cultures historically and internationally, and they also provide a fertile resource for creative innovations to broader cultural forms of narrative storytelling in society at large (e.g. Franklin, 1978). There is also the immense importance of the (imprisoned) *body* as a seminal if somewhat neglected primary source for recovering experiential knowledge, and facilitating communication by and among radicalized actors, forming a foundational basis of many resistance cultures, regardless of more abstract ideological principles. The same can be said for the similarly neglected yet key areas of *sexuality, childhood, memory, consumption, time, risk* and *doubt*. While admittedly this comprises a rather long and daunting list of cultural factors, it is certainly not comprehensive. There is plenty of scope to delve into any number of other cultural influences and forms in terms of their impact upon radicalization as something that happens to a distinctive group of individuals, and its impact on society in general. For the purposes of this study, I will try to show by reference to the interesting (if also often challenging and often disturbing) corpus of political prisoner life writing how the interpretations of these various and universally shared tropes help us to better understand radicalization, if only by stressing their familiar and universal commonality as fundamental to the cultural life of modernity.

What is a political prisoner?

As with other types of inmate groups, it is important to recognize that the category of 'political prisoner' is discrete and overlapping, as well as extremely diverse. As in the case of terms like 'radicalization' (and indeed 'terrorism' and 'autobiography'), the term 'political prisoner' has remained stubbornly resistant to definition. The Red Cross defines a political prisoner broadly as 'a person who has committed offenses for political motives', while Amnesty International simply resorts to the tautological: 'a political prisoner is a political prisoner' (in Dwyer, 2008: 204). For many political prisoners, their autobiographical writings show them to be much less amenable to simply 'writing off' their time in prison, instead they use writing itself as a way to recover a sense of collective purpose with those who do or might share their political views, as well as a sense of personal autonomy and resistance in the prison environment. This group is probably the most attuned to what Goffman recognized as the need to retain as much as possible a strong identification with their pre-carceral identities, not least because many (though by no means all) of these prison writers come from the middle or upper classes and feel the acute need to resist the stigma of incarceration as much as possible. This type of political prisoner group is often made up of those who are incarcerated for political offences that are (or are perceived to be) in opposition to the interests of the current state power regime. Their 'crimes' are often associated with their writings or other expressive endeavours, as well as their refusal to participate in or endorse what are deemed to be significant aspects of public life, or alternatively their active participation in unsanctioned versions. These are the so-called 'prisoners of conscience', exemplified by figures such as Nawal El Saadawi, Wole Soyinka, Rosa Luxemburg, Victor Serge and Aung San Suu Kyi. For other political prisoners, particularly those involved in paramilitary, revolutionary or other types of politically inspired, symbolic or criminal violence, incarceration – like death – is regarded as just another occupational hazard of being a revolutionary, a soldier, or otherwise 'on active service' (often referring to themselves as 'prisoners of war' or POWs). This group is represented in the canon of political prisoner auto/biography by figures such as Bobby Sands, Countess Constance Markievicz, Jeremiah O'Donovan Rossa, Emma Goldman, Alexander Berkman, Nelson Mandela, Emmeline and Sylvia Pankhurst and Jack Henry Abbott. For other political activists who have unintentionally ended up in prison – or in detention, in forced exile or on the run – after deciding on a whim to take up arms as part of resistance groups, the 'pains' of usually long-term incarceration is something that comes as nasty shock for which they were signally unprepared. This group is well represented by the unnamed Guantánamo Bay detainees interviewed by Sharon Curcio (2005). Still others find themselves imprisoned for political offences because of their protests for ideological reasons on behalf of others with whom they sympathize or identify, often in the company of 'fellow travellers' or friends; many (though by no means all) of these individuals view their 'processing' through the criminal justice system as an integral part of their protest action, inspiring their subsequent writings about life in prison as a way of articulating and further advancing the cause for which they act. Such political prisoners are represented in the canon of prison autobiography by the likes of Margaretta D'Arcy, Jean

Middleton, Angela Davis and Ruth First, among others (note the prominence of women in this rather altruistic category). Then there are those political prisoners who are incarcerated because of their identity, sexuality, religion or ethnicity, such as those held in concentration camps, internment or labour camps. This group is represented by what have in many instances become the culturally seminal life writings of figures like Anne Frank, Primo Levi, Alexander Solzhenitsyn, Violet Kazue de Cristoforo, and Jeanne Wakatsuki Houston, Mine Okubo (again, it is worth noting the distinctive presence of children, families and immigrants and/or diaspora populations in this particular category). Finally, there are those who are incarcerated for political reasons to do with religiously oriented practices such as scapegoating (e.g. Judith Ward, Gerry Conlon and Hugh Callaghan), martyrdom (Saint Perpetua and Saint Paul) or prophesy (Jeremiah);[11] these writings often chronicle miscarriages of justice by means of personal testimonies of witness or 'confession'.[12]

Some, notably penal abolitionists, argue that the designation 'political prisoner' can ultimately be applied to *all* prisoners, since their incarceration is traceable to political causes such as poverty, racism, social exclusion, unemployment and marginalization. In addition, there is an interesting and substantial contribution to the genre of political prisoner life writing by those who, strictly speaking, never actually served any time in a penal institution, but rather use this designation metaphorically to explore their own identities in relation to existing political structures and the possibilities for widespread social change. This group is represented by writers such as Betty Friedan, Maria McGuire and George Orwell. Some political prisoners only adopt this identity after the event, as it were, either during or after their period of incarceration for ordinary criminal offenses (Dwyer, 2008), e.g. Jack Henry Abbott; others become more *fully* radicalized during their incarceration for relatively minor political offences (e.g. Bobby Sands). For the purposes of this present study, I am minded to adopt something akin to Amnesty International's definition 'a political prisoner is a political prisoner', in conjunction with an auto/biographical methodological approach, in which case I treat any example of life writing by a writer who *is* or *represents him or herself to be* a political prisoner. This means that any or all of the varieties of political prisoner cited above can and often do appear in the following chapters.

While this is not an exhaustive typology, it is also not mutually exclusive; writers in one category can also (and usually do) come under one or more other categories, as illustrated for example by Ruth First, who as an academic and political journalist was also an idealist who endured detention and other forms of harassment by the apartheid South African government, on behalf of and – as she recounts in her autobiography *117 Days* – in solidarity with her friends. It is this fluidity that militates against the prima facie case to deal only with the life writings of violent, extremist or militant prisoners in this project devoted to the study of radicalization. This is not only because the boundaries between the categories are very loosely drawn and permeable, but also because many of these prisoners actually *become* radicalized, or become more *fully* radicalized, during or after the period of their incarceration, as we will see in their life writings.

The sociological and criminological literature on prisoner autobiography has tended to concentrate on the writings of 'criminals' rather than those produced by political prisoners. This is most likely because prisoner writings have generally been the subject of criminological research, the main purpose of which, as previously stated, is to advance the critical understanding of offender identities as opposed to the struggle over political power between individual prisoners and the state. In addition, although there has been some attention devoted to the influence of class on prisoner auto/biography, factors such as 'race', age, religion, gender and disability have received much less consideration, except to make general but nonetheless important observations such as that women prisoners are much less likely to write autobiographies (e.g. Nellis, 2002). The following chapters, while by no means being able to adequately consider all of these influences on political prisoner autobiography, therefore attempts to focus more closely on the impact of variables such as religion, 'race' and gender on these writings, in addition to the undeniably important issues of conjugal, identity and friendship and kinship networks, the life course (particularly childhood) and the presumed 'silence' of women political prisoners.

Understanding resistance cultures: why are these texts so important, and what can they tell us about the modern state?

Twenty years since its first publication, Barbara Harlow's book *Resistance Literature* (1987) remains a landmark in the scholarly study of what she designates generically as 'writing within a specific historical context, a context which may be most immediately situated within the contemporary national liberation struggles and resistance movements against Western imperialist domination of Africa, Central and South America, and the Middle and Far East' (Harlow, 1987: 4). A professor of English literature, Harlow's analysis is framed within the conventional genre distinctions of literary analysis, designated by different sections into the separate genres of poetry, narrative (primarily the novel) and memoir. In her reflections on literary theory and history, she argues for the convergence of meaning in literature as the site of human imagination, philosophical aesthetics, and perhaps most importantly, personal and political *struggle*, as generating a cultural discourse against oppression in the quest for liberation. While the individual works of resistance literature she cites are grounded within the political and historical specificity of the particular power struggles within which they are produced, at the same time, Harlow insists, there is nevertheless a generic quality pervading these texts vis-à-vis 'the role of culture and cultural resistance as part of the larger struggle for liberation' (Harlow, 1987: 10). As such, the proximity of these texts to their immediate physical and geopolitical contexts is at the same time determined by their belonging to a 'larger collective struggle throughout the world' (Harlow, 1987: 11), locating them at the cleavage between the particular conflict from which they emanate and more generally linked to the very idea of the struggle for liberty as a common human desire in (modern) cultures. The dialogical nature of this micro–macro relationship represented by the resistance literature text is echoed by the dialogical character of its influence on the culture of armed liberation struggle as a generic phenomenon, making it 'not only a product of culture but a *determinant* of culture' (Cabral in Harlow, 1987: 12, original emphasis). In other words, literature is (from the perception of the state, at least) dangerous, or in Georges Bataille's (2006) word, even 'evil'.

This complex and tense dialogic incorporating the personal suffering of the radicalized individual insurgent as the result of penal incarceration on one hand, and the claim to legitimacy of the global political nation state as the defender of the individual citizen's rights on the other, makes international comparisons between texts and the cultural products of resistance around the world possible, to some extent. Harlow argues that the importance of these texts to the development of cultural ideologies of resistance within and among insurgent actors and groups internationally is not to be underestimated, and that moreover that the extreme importance of the cultural form of resistance is 'no less valuable than radicalization, armed resistance itself' (Kanafani cited in Harlow, 1987: 11). We can therefore claim that it is as important to attend to these texts as cultural forms of resistance in the effort to understand and respond effectively to the *culture* of armed struggle or political violence as it is to concentrate on the physical or political manifestation of the phenomenon itself.

What are we to make of the somewhat awkward association between political prisoner life writing as a literature of resistance and struggle against the state, and the prominence of its production in the auto/biographical format – probably the most paradigmatic conventional genres of the colonial and sovereign white male (Danahay, 1993)? Harlow exonerates this link through what she calls post-colonial irony, whereby the conventional auto-biographical form affords an occasion for the transgression of the colonizer's language by the oppressed, and hence the creation of a new voice:

> Irony might not only have been a kind of displaced revenge on the part of the oppressed colonized seduced by the west, but would have also allowed the francophone North African writer to take his own distance on the language by inverting it, destroying it and presenting new structures to the point where the French reader would feel a stranger in his own language.
> (Khatibi in Harlow, 1987: 23)

In other words, genres of resistance literature are derivative of the colonial cultural forms against which they 'struggle' for liberation, if in an ironic way:

The word for resistance used here, *mu'āradah*, translates the term *muqāwamah* conventionally used in Arabic to suggest popular, organized resistance to colonial occupation or imperialist oppression and gives a literary-critical implication to the idea of resistance. *Mu'āradah*, while it does have the literal meaning of confrontation, opposition, or resistance, is also the designation given to a classical Arabic literary form, according to which one person will write a poem and another will retaliate by writing along the same lines, but reversing the meaning. This translation into Arabic of the Arabic word for resistance also suggests a larger and collective political agenda to the linguistic task of the literary translator.

(Harlow: 1987: 24–5)

Drawing on the work of Edward Said, Harlow claims that the derivative or allegorical character of resistance literature points to the importance of filiation and allegory as a key factor in political struggle:

Al-Jahiz's fable, in its retelling by Abdelfattah Kilito, raises allegorically a number of questions relevant to resistance literature: access to history for those peoples who have been historically denied an active role in the arena of world politics; the problem of contested terrain, whether cultural, geographical, or political; and the social and political transformation from a genealogy of 'filiation' based on ties of kinship, ethnicity, race or religion to an 'affiliative' secular social order.

(Harlow, 1987: 22)

Achieving this
in what could not have been more pointed terms: '*All third-world texts* are *necessarily*, I want to argue, allegorical, and in a very specific way: they are to be read as what I will call national allegories, even when, or perhaps I should say, particularly when their forms develop out of predominantly western machineries of representation, such as the novel.'

A little farther down on the same page, Jameson lays out his thesis even more exactly: 'Third-World texts, even those which are seemingly private and invested with a properly libidinal dynamic – necessarily project a political dimension in the form of national allegory: the story of the private individual destiny is *always* an allegory of the embattled situation of the public third-world culture and society'.

(Jameson in Bensmaïa, 1999: 151, emphasis added by Bensmaïa)

Bensmaïa, an Algerian himself, reacts against this tendency among 'first world' critics, represented here by Jameson, to identify 'post-colonial' texts first as a sort of homologous genre, and second to interpret them as intrinsically 'allegorical' in terms of their compulsion always to tell the story of the nation state as a priority, even as they narrate their most private, intimate and even sexual personal experiences. While recognizing Jameson's good intentions with respect to his advocacy of 'third world' literature, its inclusion into the literary canon and its worthiness in terms of critical interpretation, Bensmaïa nonetheless objects to the implication that the nation state (with or without the 'post' designation as always somehow proximate to its status as being residually 'colonial') is in some sense always at the forefront of the writer's mind, a determinate factor in the exercise of individual authorial imagination manifested in 'third world' writing. Why the compulsion to read constantly this 'allegorical' and indeed 'political' dimensions into such texts of the 'third world', 'Chinese', 'Middle Eastern', etc. when the same is not done (or at least not so insistently) with 'western' literary texts is the question:

> To answer this question [of interpretation] even tentatively, it seems crucial to effect a displacement, or more precisely a recentering, of the question and to inscribe it in a critical and theoretical context where the notion of 'allegory' would no longer introduce the same characteristics of interpretive stability and transparency we have granted it until now with Jameson. In this case, the people, as well as the men, women, and events evoked in the novel, 'are not simply historical events or parts of a patriotic body politic' but rather 'a complex rhetorical strategy of social reference where the claim to be representative provokes a crisis within the process of signification and discursive address' (Bhabha, 1990: 267). And in fact, as soon as the reference to the 'allegorical' dimension of a text is no longer susceptible to a purely historical or even political explanation, as soon as the ideological or political analysis of a text is no longer grounded in a confusion of 'reference with phenomenality,' of the linguistic with natural or historical reality, 'it follows that, more than any other mode of inquiry, including economics, the linguistics of literariness [becomes] a powerful and indispensable tool in the unmasking of ideological aberrations, as well as a determining factor in accounting for their occurrence' (de Man, *Resistance* 11).
>
> (Bensmaïa, 1999:154–5)

De Man's approach to the text differs from Jameson's in that it does not display the same propensity to reduce the act of critical interpretation to the search for allegories of nationalism, but rather opens up the interpretation of the text to the wider possibilities afforded by the diverse 'allegories of reading' in de Man's phrase. However, this is not to say that de Man relinquishes the task of interrogating texts from a political standpoint; rather, 'the unmasking of ideological aberrations' within and across all texts through, for example, the exploration of the use of rhetoric and metaphor, can expose the political and nationalist ideological dimensions (such as they are) within, between and across texts, irrespective of their designation as part of a 'third world', 'post-colonial' or 'western' literary canon. This is what I have strived to do in my interpretations, to subject to the same critical scrutiny such allegorical texts of nation/self in the mode of post-colonial subject (e.g. the prison autobiography of Bobby Sands) and colonizer (the autobiographical poetry of William Wordsworth) (Dearey, 2007) while retaining from de Man the insistence that the analogous use of allegorical rhetoric in these texts – while observably similar – at the same time evokes the ostensible resistance to assimilation by the author(s) as it does the incompatibility of meaning that lies at the heart of such (post)colonial representations of nation/self. It is as essential for the critic/analyst to resist conflating these distinctive yet allegorical spheres of meaning as it is to resist relinquishing the *real* pain and suffering of those prisoners involved in resistance struggles to the merely linguistic referents of genre or narratological categories such as irony or figuration or indeed the vortex of language or the text:

> [T]he logical and grammatical model of the narrative also has become 'rhetorical' not because we have, on the one hand, a literal meaning and on the other hand a figural meaning, but because it has become impossible to decide by grammatical or other linguistic devices which of the two meanings (that can be entirely incompatible) prevails.
>
> (de Man quoted in Bensmaïa, 1999: 155)

Far from simplifying the study of radicalization by viewing it through the telescopic lens of life writing, such are the difficulties of interpretation and the complexities involved in entering the 'world of the text':

> Above all, it is surely a question of being aware of the tenuousness of landmarks and of giving ourselves the means to 'survey' a world that the Text—'which muzzles the world with its intransigence' and 'tolerates only acquiescence' (Djaout, 115)—did not manage to yoke. From this, the tragedy crossing this text, which manages to find neither its subject, its object, its direction, nor its 'place' of inscription, reveals its link to the insurmountable conflict existing between the 'pedagogical' enterprise of 'telling' the story of the nation as if it were given to narration—by thus recounting itself, identifying itself or giving itself an identity through the story told!—and the 'performative' endeavor, which is that of 'writing' (the nation) and which turns out to be, above all, the bearer of a compulsion to repeat (history) that at every moment risks losing the whole project in cacophony or perhaps even madness.
>
> (ibid.:156)

Hence it is necessary to remember that the act of storytelling is in many ways just that – an act, a performance – and moreover one which is prone to comic, tragic or other forms of self-parody or pathos. Notwithstanding the implicit pedagogical or didactic purposes of such 'acts of literature' (to use Derrida's phrase) as a method of imparting representations or images of the nation, or indeed competing nationalisms or identities, these texts are not, Bensmaïa is reminding us, simply 'revealed' truths of the way things are, recorded via the unbiased narrative conventions of objective history or self-representation. Instead, they are to be seen as the wildly 'cacophonous' performances that they are, i.e. acts of writing, which even so are to continually bound to the national histories from which they struggle to become free. In many ways, radical or revolutionary writers write not to rationalize, identify or allegorize with history as it has been presented to them, but rather write 'instinctively' to differ (ibid.: 159). As is the case with many feminist theorists, the compulsion to auto/biography represents an urge to reformulate extant notion(s) of subjectivity with a view to (re)articulating alternative emancipatory theories of agency capable of eliding the very same ideological structures of power and domination historically linked to certain normative ideals of the self. That this form of writing is so closely linked to the cultural ideal of the masculine, colonial, nationalist, individual and sovereign self that is pivotal to the political hegemony that is being struggled against is in many ways ironic, to say the least (Battersby, 1998; McNay, 2000). The problem of central concern for feminism, post-colonialism and other dissenting ideologies is their ambivalent faith in the possibility of expressing alternative forms of subjectivity and processes of subjectification/ subjection in the pre-existing medium of autobiography, without reproducing its negative historical and ideological connotations.

Life writing, power and resistance: gender and disclosure

The emergence of auto/biography as a definitive cultural object (Dilthey, 1976; Daniel, 1994) marks the prioritization of certain 'natural' processes of subjectivity enshrined in the commonsense praxis governing agency and identity formation. These social practices are concerned, for instance, with notions of the ostensible narrative unity of the life and the individual subject, the specular accessibility or transparency of the subject to itself, culturally specific religious/ confessional practices of self-examination, the relative social status of the author, the parameters of authorial creativity, access to writing materials, time to write, and so forth. Recognition of the potential malleability of these social norms in recent times has led to a distinct shift in focus from critiques that claim to substitute or replace auto/biography with new and improved versions derived from less objectified, referential or socially sanctioned principles of subjectivity and/or representation to those that are reciprocally informed by the hitherto suppressed presence of a diversity of autobiographical voices and texts (Smith and Watson, 1998: 5). This is due largely to the influence of feminist, post-colonial and postmodern theoretical critiques on literary and social theory. In other words, what we could call the theodicy of individual being, which forms the societal basis of subjectivity – that is, the vindication of the epistemological subject in a world dominated by the moral evil and suffering it has largely brought about – is ultimately resolved in the feminist/post-colonial apologetics of diversity, transgression and inclusion. Written from prison, these same auto/biographical texts are further imbued with, and embedded within, the history and shifting power structures of the modern state and the ongoing contests for its appropriation by other political actors.

In view of this, it is not surprising that auto/biography is of special and intensive interest to feminist theory on account of the deeply challenging and often problematic nature of subjectivity and representation at its foundation. In fact, nowhere in autobiography studies have models of identity and issues of identity politics achieved the conceptual prominence as they have in the study of women's life writing, especially in relation to developments in feminist epistemologies linking subjectivity to agency, power, patriarchy, ethics and aesthetics (cf. Stanley, 1992; Gilmore, 1994; McNay 2000; Battersby, 1998; Elam, 1994). From one perspective, this is due to the possibilities that auto/biography presents as a potential source of critique, capable of destabilizing the unified patriarchal social models of subjectivity, as well as its capacity to reconstitute the fractured and absent (female, disenfranchised male, child, aged, disabled, ethnic, etc.) models of self, establishing and disseminating alternative modes and technologies of subjectivity as the basis of consciousness-raising and/or political resistance.

However, as we have seen in post-colonial, poststructuralist and cultural studies theory, this enterprise is intrinsically problematic. The principle objection has been that, in the past, autobiography has tended towards androcentrism and the (re)generation of androcentric interpretive strategies, at the expense of gynocentric models (Schweickart in Kadar, 1992: 4). In its ideological function, autobiography privileges forms of life writing that prioritize and reproduce dominant versions of objective and truthful narrative structures, marginalizing those narratives that display a lesser objectivity, coherence or regularity. It has also tended to valorize certain notions about what constitutes the personal or the unitary subject (P. Smith in Kadar, 1992: 5) in cultural archetypes of identity. Despite trenchant criticisms of Cartesian and Enlightenment influences on subjectivity and representation in discourses such as autobiography (see Judovitz, 1988), there is nonetheless a strong tendency in some strands of modern thought to interpret autobiography in a quasi-Cartesian manner, insofar as it remains a discrete 'literature of possibility' as well as a 'literature of resistance', which emphasizes the possibilities for self-determination and emancipation in processes of identity construction. This accounts for much of the attraction towards autobiography from a range of theoretical perspectives, even in the shadow of autobiography's dubious ideological past (cf. Danahay, 1993). This means that, paradoxically, the major objection to autobiography stems from the same cultural impulse as the main valorization for the form, in the sense that both are essentially political though diametrically opposed in terms of the ideologies of individualism they seek to promote – universal, monolithic and univocal versus specific, multivocal, inclusive and diverse.

For feminism and beyond, the full ramifications of autobiographical discourse analysed according to the principles of social constructivism have not yet been sufficiently mapped or articulated. Nevertheless, the critical force of women's autobiography on the phallocentric canon, which is predicated upon the rejection of masculinist rhetoric and its related ideologies of power, have been generally welcomed as representing a genuine opportunity for effecting possible social change. While many (mostly male) political prison writers will not be fully or consciously aware of this dimension of the auto/biographical text, there is an implied understanding of its potency as a form of self-expression, and a mechanism for continuing the collective struggle in an unequal, punitive, occupied and/or conflict situation. At the same it, the optimism surrounding the emergence of women's auto/biographical writing and feminist auto/biography theory introduces the problem of developing new rhetorics of subjectivity that are adequate to serve as templates for (women's) writing and identity formation beyond the simplistic opposition of male/female dualisms (Brée, 1988; Bell, 1985). This accentuates the vexed problem of feminist rhetoric versus the rhetorics of femininity in relation to the homologous social categories of 'woman' or 'women' under the generic rubric of 'women's writing' (Elam, 1994). Examples of how these aspects of auto/biographical writing are negotiated in practice, in such localized and diverse contexts in which the projection of unity to outsiders is paramount, while the internal reality is closer to ongoing argumentation and jockeying for power, is as important in the development of feminist/women's life writing as it is in other radicalized contexts. Hence the problem of disclosure in competing life/collective histories and their reception are key themes, and will be investigated in the examples that follow by women as compared to men.

Chapter 3

'There are so many roots ... '

Sex, sexuality, gender and the body in political prisoner radicalization narratives

'There are so many roots to the tree of anger that sometimes the branches shatter before they bear.' This is the opening line of Audre Lorde's auto-biographical poem 'Who Said it Was Simple' (1982), describing the brief moments of communal relaxation among a group of women activists in a coffee shop prior to a protest march. After reflecting on the complexities of gender, sexuality, sisterhood and race among these women involved in the 'struggle' alongside the male waiters who serve them and the 'girls' they hire to do their housework to free them up for protest marches, Lorde ponders the worrying aporia of emotions (mainly anger), desire and the servicing of bodily pleasures and appetites that make their resistance possible. She concludes the poem with the words, 'Which me will survive all these liberations?'. A perusal of the autobiographical writings of other radical women suggests that Lorde is not alone in her struggle to make sense of these complex and contradictory influences on her political activism. Given that the root of radicalization, 'radic-', itself means 'root', the implication of her observation of the multiplicity and contradictory nature of the various 'roots' of radicalization, as it is actually experienced and happens to real people, casts substantial doubt on the 'scientific' efforts to reduce it to a neat series of developmental stages, let alone produce a formula that has predictive and hence preventative capacity. Rather, the stories recounted in this chapter would appear to expose a messier and more complicated diversity of 'processes' of agency and self-determination, but at the same time these stories also reveal patterns that are more or less distinctive to this sample group. Among these patterns is the gendered nature of radicalization, and how gender, sexuality and the body shape and influence the radicalization narrative vis-à-vis these individuals' 'journeys' or pathways into – and also out of – extremist groups. This chapter is devoted to exploring and explicating how the modern phenomenon of radicalization is shaped and framed by gender, sexuality and the body. Though these kinds of stories are present in virtually all life writings by or about political prisoners, for the purposes of brevity and comprehensiveness, I will concentrate on a group of inter-related texts generated from the conflict known as 'The Troubles' in the

north of Ireland[1] in the 1970s and 1980s. This concentration on one particular conflict and the texts produced within this specific socio-cultural context is intended to demonstrate the analytic potential of the intertextual
interpretation of these types of texts, and is intended to sit alongside the
other more comparative analyses produced in the other chapters.

First, a bit of background. When I first started this research, I set out to
examine the less analysed role of gender in radicalization as represented in
political prisoner life writing. After all, as the research literature summarized
in Chapter 1 continually reiterates, we know that gender – mainly in the
form of 'masculinities' (read here young Muslim men) – is a key factor in
radicalization and extremist/terrorist subcultures. At the same time, the role
of women (or to a very much lesser extent 'femininities') represents the 'dark
figure', and hence the worrying trend in radicalization and terrorism
whereby (radical) women and feminine subcultural practices and ways of
knowing remain either absent from or enigmatic within counter-terrorism
policy frameworks. The initial plan was thus to examine the issue of gender
in political prisoner life writing, focusing on the radicalization narratives
contained therein, and the preconceived questions more or less present
themselves: why there is such a strong 'gender differential' in this area, i.e.
why are men so overrepresented in these types of offences, and why the
(apparent) dearth of political prisoner writing by women? In what ways is
radicalization gendered, if at all? And what do the influence and representations of gender narratives in political prisoner life writing tell us about radicalization and the terrorist threat more generally? These initial research
questions were founded with and continue the work of Barbara Harlow by
insisting on the inclusion of women's life writings in the form of resistance
literature as a sub-genre of political prisoner life writing, and its impact on
social movements, oppositional consciousness (Mansbridge and Morris,
2001), cultures of extremism or resistance, and social change. They were also
informed by the theoretical work in criminology with respect to the influence
of masculinities on criminality and crime, posing the further question: if it is
the case that the increased radicalization of women and their participation in
terrorist crime is due to their greater assimilation of masculine (criminal)
behaviours and identities, or if radicalization narratives or resistance cultures
are becoming more 'equal', i.e. more inclusive of gender difference, and if so
how gender politics thus function within these groups. Consideration was also
directed towards a more detailed analysis of the especially disruptive and
terrifying enigma of radicalized or terrorist women: what women's status as
the 'ultimate deviants' in a criminological sense (Young, 1996) reveals about
the implications and function of gender in political prisoner life writing.

Upon undertaking the work of reading many examples of the life writings of
these politically radicalized prisoners, it became clear quite early on that the
common perception of an apparent dearth of such texts by women is unjustified, though the production of these texts is patchy and uneven – among some

radical groups, such as the Weathermen/Weather Underground and the various Black Power movements, there are a (growing) number of autobiographies and memoirs relating to the radicalization of (former) members written by both women and men. In the context of 'the Troubles' in Northern Ireland, bio-graphical representations of radical women appear to far outnumber the pub-lication of autobiographical accounts by women members of paramilitary organizations, while the production of such autobiographical texts by the male membership constitutes something of a publishing industry in its own right; biographies, compared to the women, constitute a much lesser proportion of these life writings, though they are still in evidence. The reasons for these and other disparities with respect to gender and the articulation of radicalization narratives within their subcultural and in wider cultural contexts will be examined in the first section of this chapter, taking as an example the auto/ biographical representations of some of the radical women variously involved in 'The Troubles' of the conflict in the north of Ireland, converging around the figure of Mairéad Farrell. The second key aspect that presented itself during the period of my initial research was the unexpected – a better term would probably be previously overlooked – prominence of stories about sex, sexuality and the primary influence of sexual relationships and the body within these radical sub-groups and the pivotal role they were accorded in the life stories of these radicalized actors. According to these stories, for many radicalized actors, sex, sexuality and the formation and breakdown of sexual relationships constitute both the way into (radicalization) and also the way out of (de-radicalization) extremist groups and terrorism. What is more (as the case of Farrell also attests) the sexualization of radical women contained mainly in popular or biographical accounts affords a way for the broader socio-cultural efforts to deal with the anxieties that arise when a nice, pretty, middle-class young woman of good upbringing becomes a terrorist: as in the case of Patty Hearst (Graebner, 2008), this raises urgent questions about the potential for *all* young women to become radicalized – a possibility that immediately calls for mechanisms for neutralizing the political agency of (all) women.

   Quite apart from the ubiquity of these types of stories, why should they be considered significant or important in explaining radicalization, when evi-dently (referring again to the literature review) current thinking on radicali-zation would indicate that they are not? The exploration and development of sexual codes and practices, and gender difference, provides the framework through which dynamic radical cultures of resistance are articulated and played out. This accords with Jeffrey Weeks' declaration: 'To an unexpected and unusual degree, sexuality has become a battleground for contending political forces, a front-line of contemporary politics' (Weeks, 2003: 92). To this end, as Weeks explains, the obsessional interest in sex and sexuality that characterizes contemporary modernity is a product of the historical 'priva-tization of morality' resulting from the influence of secularism and individu-alism that have disembedded sex from its moorings in religious cultural traditions. Consequently, especially during periods of rapid social change, sexuality becomes increasingly important as an arena where the macro and micro struggles for power and emancipation take place, incorporating a broad diversity of issues regarding the articulation and representation of the self and (sexual) desire as the source of 'intimate citizenship' and global politics.

In his book *Telling Sexual Stories: Power, Change and Social Worlds* (1995), sociologist Ken Plummer notes the extraordinary proliferation of sexual storytelling throughout the modern period, and its increasing ubiquity in 'late modern' societies – an indication of the rise in stature of a new form of civic life that he calls 'intimate citizenship'. This new form of political being reflects the cultural prominence of narrative storytelling in the emergent and complex polis of modernity, as much as the act of telling stories about previously hidden or secreted intimate and/or sexual experiences in a public forum represents a particularly modern form of emancipation and empowerment (especially for gays, lesbians and women). Plummer rightly asks: why do we want to tell and (perhaps even more importantly) hear or read these sexual stories? Far from being voyeuristic or perverse, these stories reveal fundamental and systemic aspects of modern (sub)cultures, including the functional and cultural contribution of 'radical' groups to the manifestation of protest, consciousness raising and social change.

> This book has argued that stories and narratives depend upon communities that will create and hear those stories: social worlds, interpretive communities, communities of memory. The telling of sexual stories that can reach public communities of discourse has been a central theme. Without lesbian and gay stories the lesbian and gay movement may not have flourished. Without the stories told by abuse survivors, the whole rape movement would probably have floundered. And recovery tales identified in their narratives a whole scenario of hitherto undetected concerns that have entered a public arena of debate. And these stories work their way in to changing lives, communities and cultures. Through and through, sexual story telling is a political process.
>
> Hence the analysis of sexual stories is not just a quirky interest, or even a titillating, voyeuristic one. It is central to an understanding of the workings of sexual politics in the late modern world.
>
> (Plummer, 1995: 145)

Sexual storytelling is thus a radical act, a way of recovering a sense of empowerment and emancipation, as well as contributing to widespread social change. It is not only political through and through, it is elemental to the operation of contemporary politics and foundational to our ability to shape and make sense of the rapidly developing global political world.

The review of the research literature in Chapter 1 strongly indicates that sex, sexuality and the body does not, as yet, constitute a recognized cultural determinant or causal factor in the phenomenon of radicalization, and so neither does sexual storytelling form a promising site for analysis. On the surface, this may be slightly puzzling, as there is a school of thought that takes seriously the sensual, emotional and intimate bonds of cultural aspects as diverse as family life, friendship bonds, enjoying hip-hop music, illicit drug taking, being part of a street gang, following fashion, etc. as crucial to the construction and maintenance of terrorist or extremist identities. It is almost as if sex is too embarrassing, or maybe too obvious, to form a 'discrete' area of research into radicalization by the police or security services. The much-repeated promise of the granting of 72 virgins in paradise to the successful *shaheed* (martyr) in Islamist subcultural narratives is probably the most obvious, if overlooked, example of what I am referring to here. However, the neglect of this area of modern political life is, I will suggest, imprudent, especially where the topic of social change initiated by radical sub-groups or individuals is concerned.

Hence the questions that emerge are *who* can tell these sexual stories; *what* they tell (and just as importantly, do not tell); how these stories are articulated in terms of their cultural and mythic references, and the development and impact of subcultural strategies of disclosure on official and expert knowledge of radicalization and terrorism; and *why* we (in resistance and broader culture at large) want to hear these stories, as the commodification and market consumption of the 'radical' and/or 'terrorist' subject – particular women – becomes ever more common in popular cultural production. Finally, how are such stories about sex, sexuality and the body to be interpreted and incorporated into official discourse by policy-makers and others who make important decisions or have a specific interest in radicalization?

Who are these radicalized women: sisters in the struggle, sexual bait, or pawns in a game of political brinkmanship?

When we read the life writings of women political prisoners in Northern Ireland, what do they tell us about the politics of gender and radicalization: is gender a unifying, neutral or divisive force among radicalized individuals and/or groups? Irrespective of the nature of radicalization (whether 'process' oriented or otherwise, a question that I will return to again over the course of this study), the question of gender and its function as a formative trope in the burgeoning identity politics and radical subcultures, especially during the 1960s and 1970s, immediately asserts itself. Do women become radicalized in the same way as men? Do the same issues and factors contribute to the continuation or development of their radicalization to violent or terrorist action? Do they experience and make sense of their radicalism in the same or different ways?

What seems to emerge from the research literature is the view that, while the male influence dominates in radical subcultural groups (with the exception of exclusively female groups, such as the women suffragists or the women's movement), the experience of being a member of these groups is far from equal or 'gender-neutral'. In her analysis of Islamic fundamentalism, Milton-Edwards (2005: 2) focuses on the gendered nature of extremism, claiming that the ideology of Islamic fundamentalism in particular 'is not gender-neutral but is represented as a specifically male business' (ibid.: 2). This characterization of the 'business' of fundamentalist political extremism as essentially 'male' (as opposed to being described as shaped by the more socially or culturally constructed ideologies of 'masculinity') is instructive, if perhaps raising more questions than it answers. In any case, what Milton-Edwards, along with other commentators, seems to be suggesting by this remark is that the manifestation of extremism intrinsically extends to the exploitation and oppression of women who are, as a result of patriarchal hierarchies in which these groups typically operate, especially vulnerable to manipulation by the men who would seek to capitalize on their comparative weakness as agents in society at large, thereby enhancing a sense of empowerment and potency (over women) within these cultural sub-groups as an elemental part of their radicalization.

This sense of empowerment and agency mined from the inequalities of patriarchy is not limited to men, however – some women can benefit from these normative gender dichotomies too, and this realization has been used to great effect to facilitate the exploitation and manipulation of women by male leaderships. This is observable across extremist groups internationally. In Pakistan, for example, by reproducing, reinforcing or even exaggerating cultural practices that are oppressive or exclusionary to women in wider society, radical groups are able to control vulnerable women and girls by making them feel powerful and precious as the objects of 'protection', and control other women and subsequently entire families and communities through them:

> Young girls are particularly vulnerable to recruitment to extremist ideology because few other paths are offered them. In countries like Pakistan, fundamentalist religious schools are already carefully inducting young women, realizing that by indoctrinating them, they are able to control an entire family. A woman goes home from the mosque, educates her children, and talks to her neighbors, and thus the ideology flourishes and grows. This is the first step toward militarizing women.
>
> We are already seeing the next step. Recently in Islamabad, a group of women, wielding sticks, demanded that video shops be closed and music stores banned. They attacked a house where they felt immoral behavior was taking place and kidnapped the women living in the house. Some of these female militants sitting in judgment of others were barely 15 years old. That is the effectiveness of the proponents of fundamentalist ideology. Today, they are raiding a house against 'immoral' fellow Muslims

and tomorrow they may very well choose to strap on bombs and become suicide bombers against 'infidels.'

(Obaid-Chinoy, 2007: 6)

Such attacks by women upon other women in the name of political extremism by radicalized women is not limited to the young or to Islamic or Middle Eastern groups. In her memoir *To Take Arms: A Year in the Provisional IRA* (1973), Maria McGuire tells how radicalized Irish Republican women were encouraged by the male leadership to disparage and even physically disrupt peaceful protest by other women's groups, putting paid to any latent sense of alliance with non-violent groups or 'sisterhood' with other women active in the struggle for liberation. The male leadership was able to sever or prevent the ties of sisterly solidarity by focusing the Provisional IRA (PIRA) women's attention not on gender similarity, but on class difference, a seemingly counter-intuitive strategy given McGuire's own privileged middle-class background, but one that seems to have resonated even with her, if only temporarily:

Several 'peace' campaigns began, organized by women in Derry and Belfast. They were seized upon eagerly by the press as representing the wishes of ordinary people in defiance of the tyrannical IRA; we considered them middle-class and called them the 'peace at any cost brigade'.

(McGuire, 1973: 105)

Establishing common cause between men and women PIRA volunteers was accomplished by reference to the deaths of past martyrs for 'freedom', and the necessity not to 'betray' them, as a priority over gender identification between women activists who advocated violence or non-violence as a means for pursuing their political objectives:

But [PIRA Army Chief of Staff Sean] Mac Stiofain's oration assumed the most importance, in view of the Derry women's movement; and he said that to accept the Whitelaw proposals would be a compromise that betrayed the men and women who died for freedom in 1916. Direct action against the Belfast women's campaign was taken the following day, when the formidable Maire Drumm [grandmother and much revered Irish Republican who served as Sinn Féin Vice President and Commander of the women's republican league *Cumann na mBan*, who was later assassinated in her hospital bed by Loyalist paramilitaries in 1976] led a detachment of Provisional women into their meeting and wrecked it.

(ibid.: 106)

In a similar vein, Susan Stern (2007) tells how, despite their vociferous promotion of gender equality, the 'Weatherwomen' were not only encouraged to denigrate the non-violent activism of their liberal feminist contemporaries in the women's movement, but were regularly encouraged to personally and sometimes viciously attack other women members in the frequent 'criticism-self-criticism' sessions that were a central part of the group's practice.[2] As in the case of other extremist groups, even well-educated and otherwise well-mannered middle-class women, such as typified the members of the Weather Underground, were encouraged to indulge in such openly conflictual and often deeply personal and aggressive diatribes against others, including other politically active women even in their own group, and more often close friends or intimates in their own small cell or collective. This reproduces in the context of radical politics the propensity for women to be the victims of violence as well as verbal and psychological abuse within intimate domestic relationships, whether between women and men (Edwards, 2002; Browne and Williams, 1993) or among intimate same-sex interpersonal relationships (Burke and Follingstad, 1999). Such divisive and belligerent practices, and the difficulties for the victimized partners to resist or escape them, are not merely dependent upon the socialization norms of heterosexism (Brown, 2008); in extremist subcultures, they serve to polarize and exacerbate gender difference both within and between other radical groups; and they more deeply entrench traditional ideologies of gender-specific roles and identity politics as a way of exerting control over women, despite the constant invocation of rhetoric about gender equality, revolution or freedom as prophylactic or counter-narratives. This would seem to be commonplace among radical groups internationally and across religious, educational, political and class divides. It is a formative element of extremism that emerges from and reinforces the ideological and embodied reciprocity of dependency and violence among and between individuals and groups. Women are thus discouraged from availing of civic remedies of escape in favour of other modes of 'empowerment' that can form a potent means of recruitment while patently contradicting their own self-interests:

> Indeed, many well-educated, Western-born Muslim women are susceptible to recruitment. I wrote an article that looked at Muslim religious schools in Mississauga, Canada. There, young Canadian-Muslim women are being told to shun the Western world they live in. These women, brainwashed into covering their faces and adhering to sexual segregation, are continually told that their Muslim brothers are dying in battles to defend their honor so that Western men are not able to 'defile' them. Ironically, they reject the very political system that gives them the choices they currently enjoy. This is a difficult problem because in societies like Canada and the United States, where multiculturalism and freedom of religion are not only encouraged but a bedrock of societal belief, many people do not question the teachings being put forth in religious schools. It is a fundamental tenet that females have the right to an education and the right to practice the tenets of their faith. Unfortunately, these empowered women are learning a very extreme interpretation of Islam, one in direct conflict

with the society they grew up in and against which they, and their children, are bound to clash in the future.

(Obaid-Chinoy, 2007: 6–7)

What we observe here is the general lack of neutrality concerning gender in politically radical groups internationally. These groups tend to be dominated by males, consequently the incorporation of masculinist patriarchal structures is used not only to manipulate and control radicalized women, but ironically also to attract them, by offering women the prospect of having power over other women both within and outside of these sub-groups, and hence encouraging a sense of divisiveness and separatism among politically activist women. As Cockburn (2000) points out, it would be a mistake to suggest that no women derive any benefit from this situation, but at the same time, by discouraging or disrupting a sense of political solidarity among women, or indeed appropriating the definitional and functional role of political identity *as* women, these same women are made more (not less) vulnerable to violence, oppression and exploitation within these extremely patriarchal groups. For women who have become sufficiently radicalized to join extremist groups or take part in politically motivated violence, the option of identification or alliance with other radical women outside the group is almost always immediately foreclosed (except of course where women as well as men are encouraged to appropriate the suffering of the usually amorphous and 'helpless' colonial 'Other' as their own (Trnka, 2003)). Violation of this interdiction can lead to exclusion or punishment (possibly even by death) as dictated by the male leadership, as in the case of Maria McGuire.

In her analysis of the competing national loyalties, activisms and conflicts negotiated by Protestant women in Northern Ireland, Myrtle Hill (2003) points out the very important and often overlooked dimensions of fragmentation, conflict and disagreement that were as characteristically a part of social and resistance movements during the late 1960s and 1970s, as were the equally emotionally charged bonds of filiality, solidarity and altruism. The depth, commonality and probable ubiquity of internal dissent is an essential dynamic of these groups that tends to be overlooked, downplayed or even hidden in 'official' historiographies or, in the case of auto/biographical representations, what turns out to be hagiography or, in the terminology of Audre Lorde, 'biomythography', meaning an ' ... integration of mythic and quotidian, the non-linear chronology, and the blurred line separating fact and fiction that these two texts exemplify' (Weekes, 2006 [online]). In many ways, this compulsion to construct the past via 'biogmythography' constitutes a reaction to the perceived need in the present moment to portray to the world an image of consensual mutual solidarity as the realities of internecine conflict, internal power struggles and interpersonal strife – while true – could be seen to serve the interests of oppositional groups. While some of the trouble can be attributed to personality clashes within resistance groups, many 'real life' stories of time spent as a member of these groups indicates that tensions are more often the result of external factors, particularly where women or 'others' (e.g. those with alternative identities in terms of 'race', sexuality, disability, etc.) who identify with other or competing narratives of emancipation and resistance are involved. Alternatively, feelings of personal obligation or group loyalty can act as powerful deterrents for sharing these types of stories, at least publically, thereby obscuring the internal tensions, contradictions and dissents through what can amount to a group or self-imposed conspiracy of silence, mainly (though not only) on the part of women.

In practical terms, the diverse pressures of identity politics virtually guarantees the incursion of issues such as gender, sexuality or race equality into the power dynamics of these militant groups, even if these individuals openly eschew membership or even publicly deride the aims, theories or membership of other identity groups as a way of displaying loyalty and solidarity to 'the cause'. The need to perform (sometimes continually) such 'acts' of loyalty on the part of individuals can be suffused with a sense of urgency, and fraught with emotion, as the intergroup dynamics within communities can strongly impact the development of competing ideologies and group subcultures as unique entities separate and distinct from any potential 'fellow travelers'. According to Hill (2003), this was particularly evident in the burgeoning civil rights and women's movements and paramilitarism in Northern Ireland during the 1960s and 1970s:

> The emergence of the women's movement in Ireland as elsewhere was associated with second wave feminism and the wider civil rights movement of the late 1960s. However, in Northern Ireland it was affected by, and itself impacted on, broader movements for social justice in the region. While disagreement about methods and principles was not uncommon amongst women activists, the ongoing political and military struggle heightened existing differences and injected a sense of urgency and emotion into all proceedings.
>
> (Hill, 2003: 75)

As the Women Against Imperialism (WAI) member and prison protestor Margaretta D'Arcy relates in her autobiography *Tell Them Everything* (1981), the tensions between women's groups primarily devoted to non-violent means of protest and the political aspirations of militant women involved in 'armed struggle' alongside men in paramilitary structures (such as the IRA) were not limited simply to the realm of ideological politics. Sexuality, intellectual conventions around language use and debate and other concerns were also brought to bear as means of maintaining silences, blindnesses and other modes of self-protection for radicalized women among and between the various activist groups. In D'Arcy's case, this was not exclusive to women in the IRA. There was pressure on her and the other

WAI women members to pay the fines imposed by the court rather than go to jail, as this gave rise to difficult questions about the relationships between socialist women's groups like the WAI, People's Democracy (PD) and the Provisional IRA, with their unspoken tensions and assumed solidarities. Even at a WAI conference, these issues were apparently never openly discussed, leaving D'Arcy with a sense of disempowerment, subjugation and fear, despite being herself at the centre of the protest that led to her imprisonment with Irish Republican women:

> These issues were never discussed [at an academic women's conference held at Trinity College, Dublin]. No one ever tried to explain why pressure was put on us to break our word and pay the fines. There was one other possible motive—ordinary human fear. To go into jail as an advocate of international socialist feminism without being a member—or wholehearted supporter—of the IRA, meant that we would be in a minority among the other prisoners. How would they treat us? And what about women personally liberated through lesbianism, how would they retain their independence in such a Catholic-conservative environment? Was it fear primarily of the other prisoners; or simply that the women were unable to face the atrocity of the no-wash protest? I shall never know: it was never discussed.
>
> (D'Arcy, 1981: 36)

D'Arcy's reference here to lesbianism and Catholicism in relation to the other women inmates, whose ranks she would soon be joining, is revealing. Her anxiety is about how the PIRA inmates will respond to lesbian women in the WAI, not fear of being subjected to the sexual abuse of predatory lesbians already inside the prison (IRA or otherwise), as is the common theme regarding women prisoners' sexuality as represented in popular culture and mainstream media. Neither does her account of her time in Armagh Women's Prison relate any instances of sexual intimidation or abuse, whether directed towards other women or herself (something which the stridently honest and forthright tone of her book would indicate she would not have hesitated to reveal. Rather, D'Arcy's narrative relates a generally strong and supportive environment among the women inmates on the wing, who despite their dire conditions and diverse political affiliations, generally speaking shared a vigorous sense of solidarity and overall a high morale.

This strongly contradicts the representation of radical women's sexuality, political affiliations and the power dynamics among women inmates in Armagh Prison as represented in the ghost-written account, attributed to the SAS member Scott Graham, and what could be considered the biomythographical representation of PIRA member and one of the Gibraltar Three, Mairéad Farrell in the book *Shoot to Kill* (2002)[3] (hereafter *STK*), which would appear to be closer to the populist view of radical women's sexuality and power hierarchies in prison. After renewing the sexual relationship with Mairéad that constitutes the first part of the book following her release from Armagh Women's Prison for terrorist offenses, Scott the narrator presents a portrait of Mairéad-the-prisoner as a young, pretty, innocent and naïve ingénue who was the object of desire of every 'butch' inmate on the wing. At one point he relates that she learns that these women are playing cards 'for the right to have sex' (*STK*: 219) with her. He contrasts this with his own 'loving, gentle' sexual relationship with her, as he describes it from her point of view:

> Remember, Scott, I was a wee innocent girl of 18 when I went inside. We had made love lots of times but always in a loving, gentle way although it was passionate between us. But some of those women in there had been inside without a man for years and whenever someone like me, young and innocent, came inside, we were like lambs to the slaughter.
>
> (*STK*, 218)

According to Scott, Mairéad told him that on more than one occasion she was advised by a fellow inmate to accept one of these women as her 'lover' in order that she might also act as her 'protector'. Though she would 'do whatever she liked with her', she would also jealously guard her against the constant predations not simply of the threat of sexual violence, but also of repeated instances of 'gang rape' that would leave her 'a wreck' as a result of the constant fear of attack by these brutally violent and sexually insatiable women, inmates as well as 'screws' (*STK*, 218–22). Mairéad duly accepts the sexual advances and protection of Marie-Therese, an older IRA prisoner, whose 'girlfriend' Mairéad becomes and who was 'larger than me and more powerfully built' (223), 'hard' looking but with a 'gentle' side (not unlike how Scott represents her describing himself). Eventually, Mairéad reveals how she begins to take a more 'active' role in her sexual encounters with other women inmates, and even develops a taste for violence and aggression in her sexuality, transferring this prediction to her later 'screwing' with Scott, whom she asks to 'do whatever you want. Use me ... use my body ... abuse me in any way you want ... fuck me and screw me everywhere and take no notice when I plead with you to stop' (*STK*, 217). Scott recalls how different this was from their previous sexual encounters prior to Mairéad's incarceration, and how she would thereafter ask him to bite her during their 'lovemaking' sessions, as this was the type of sado-masochistic violence she was subjected to and had internalized in her sexual practices within the prison.

This representation of women sexuality in prison, and indeed Scott's huge curiosity about it given the time and space he devotes to it in the text, is typical of a hegemonically masculinist view of female desire both in general and in all women only environments, particularly the women's prison. This reflects a wider philosophical and social hierarchy of the modern subject, with the male at its pinnacle, epitomized by Hegel's interpretation of Aristotle in his seminal (the word is used here intentionally) *The Phenomenology of Spirit*, in which the *telos* of history and consciousness is driven by desire for the (lesser) 'other' subject with a view to break 'from nature, then eventually [take] nature back into itself and [transcend] it' (Ferguson, 1993: 47); this is often by implicitly or explicitly violent means of 'overcoming' through the dynamic transcendence (*Aufhebung*) as represented in Hegel's syllogistic view of the progression of history. The model of the desiring subject is fundamentally based on the obsessive need for conflict and ultimately 'transcendence' through an act of triumphant overpowering followed by a final assimilation by capitulation. When this resisting 'other' is represented by a woman, with her close association to nature, the syllogistic process is facilitated by numerous and multiple (re)encounters with her whereby she is ' ... continually reencountered and transcended: "nature is the object of a perpetual reconquest" (Wyschogrod in Ferguson, 1993). The passions must be subordinated to reason, to lift *man* above the level of animal' (Ferguson, 1993: 47, original emphasis). In other words, man's desire for this 'other' feral woman is at once driven by the non-rational, repetitious passion of nature, which, when finally exhausted, will eventually result in the return of phallocentric rationality and the decisive act of subordination, represented by the re-inauguration of the institutional apparatus of state control, achieved through an act of violence and ultimately death.

In his psychoanalytical deconstruction of the revolutionary violence that characterizes the modern age, Žižek (2008a, 2008b) offers the following resolution of this sort of phenomenon as representative of the problem introduced by Kant and observable in the current cultural products of radicalization: i.e. the desire to subvert (often by means of extreme if not also righteous violence) the material–historical connection to temporal tradition by restoring the 'rootedness' of the present to a previous 'golden' age. This can be understood as a type of Sadeian sexual fantasy, to subvert nature's cycle of generation/corruption by first total clearance of the ground, total violation of (natural) law – creation *ex nihilo*, an 'absolute crime'. This is an outcome of the influence of sublimation, defined as

> a process that diverts the flow of instinctual energy from its immediate sexual aim and subordinates it to cultural endeavor ... Sublimation, which is often mentioned in the literature, by emphasizing the desexualization of goals and the social valorization of the object, remains both an essential concept and an unresolved question for psychoanalysis.
>
> (De Mijolla-Mellor, 2006)

Combined with *thanatos*, the death drive:

> The death instinct or death drive is the force that makes living creatures strive for an inorganic state. It does not appear in isolation; its effect becomes apparent, in particular through the repetition compulsions,

when a part of it is connected with Eros. Its tendency to return living creatures to the earlier inorganic state is a component of all the drives. In this combined form, its main impetus is toward dissolution, unbinding, and dissociation. In its pure form, silent within the psychic apparatus, it is subjugated by the libido to some extent and thus deflected to the outside world through the musculature in the drive for destruction and mastery or the will to power: this is sadism proper; the part that remains 'inside' is primary erogenous masochism.

(Delion, 2006 [online])

As Žižek (2008a) explains, it is the combination of these two primal psychic forces – sublimation and death – that accounts for the violent conflict that characterizes the fantastical revolutionary political narrative characteristic of the modern age:

It is therein that Lacan locates the link between sublimation and the death-drive: sublimation equates to creation *ex nihilo*, on the basis of annihilation of the preceding Tradition. It is not difficult to see how all radical revolutionary projects, Khmer Rouge included, rely on this same fantasy of a radical annihilation of Tradition and of the creation *ex nihilo* of a new (sublime) Man, delivered from the corruption of previous history. The same fantasy also inspired the Jacobinical revolutionary Terror: Revolution must erase the body of the people corrupted by the long reign of tyranny and extract from it a new, sublime body.

(Žižek, 2008a: 261)

On this reading, the (male–civic) 'body politic' has the qualities of the sublime, while the implied presence of (female–corporeal) sexualized body marks the boundaries dividing the bodies that matter: 'Ultimately, in this society of men, it is Man himself who is an insurmountable obstacle to men – and not Woman, who plays no decisive role' (Abbott, 1982: 119). Even when expressed metaphorically, the misogyny underpinning the ideology of such extreme and violent revolutionary ideology is evident, as for example in this description of the enemy: 'For Americans to be shocked and disgusted at senseless murders and at crimes of extreme violence against the innocent is exactly identical to an old, worn-out prostitute expressing moral indignation at the thought of premarital sexual relations. Tell America that' (Abbott, 1982: 127). This tendency to attack the enemy represented by the western nation state indirectly by reference to the 'other' sex is also observable in the intragroup conflict that pervades much of the revolutionary rhetoric of the Black Power movement as represented in the contemporaneous life writings of women members (e.g. Davis, 1990; Perkins, 2000). In this regard, both women and men members expose the faults and prejudices of their comrades of the opposite sex in the movement to critically identify them with the oppressive and exploitative tactics of the US government (Dearey, 2006).

This combined ethos of Hegelian with Freudian sublimation and death is in many ways consistent with the basic narrative arc of *STK*, reflecting a distinctively conventional masculine ethos of the desiring subject and his relationship to the feared yet desired Other, a narrative of psychic desire that is either an analogy or part and parcel of the philosophical narrative of modernity and the state. However, these stories about sex and the telling of sexual stories by former radicalized individuals do not simply reveal a latent culture of conflict and dissent within these extremist groups; they also reflect the narrative qualities shaping the subcultures of political violence – including the attractions of joining such groups as well as the shortcomings that form at least part of eventual reasons for leaving – as described in the life writings of many erstwhile members, especially women. The substantial attention devoted to the topic of sex and sexuality in the life writings of radical women group members in the post-war period suggests that this is a significant if hitherto overlooked variable in the phenomenon of radicalization.

These stories representing the ganglions of desire in terms of the gendered and sexual subjectivities and geographies of extremist subcultures are multiple, contradictory, ironic, ambivalent and confused. In many ways, this reflects what Durkheim in his social theory considered as the role of sexuality in modern society as ' ... essentially a site of moral ambiguity' (Gane, 1993: 52). On the one hand, sex represents the arena for the most grossly immoral acts, while on the other, it ensures the continuation of the species and of the social organism itself. It is the basis of that most effective form of social regulation and integration, conjugal obligation, and at the same time the origin of the most dreaded temptation, infidelity and betrayal. According to the memoir of the former Weather Underground member Jan Alpert *Growing Up Underground* (1981), her one-time best friend, occasional lover and erstwhile colleague in the underground, Pat, seemed to enjoy the perks of 'free love' and was unaffected by feminism. For Durkheim, however, the arguments typically put forward by Communists and other radicals as to the emancipatory power of 'free love' are counter-intuitive, given free love's reliance on the pleasure principle and its antithetical relation to the very idea of 'the social' (which often means self-denial in favour of collective harmony or the greater good). While the promise of 'free love' interpreted as unlimited sex and/or unfettered sexuality can provide a powerful attraction to potential recruits to radical groups, the patriarchal social hierarchies commonly found in radical or extremist subcultures can give rise to many ambivalences, contradictions and discontinuities; this does not preclude radical women or feminist groups, as in the cases of Alpert, where radical women can potentially be the objects of unfounded claims to sexual conquest by their so-called 'sisters' in the struggle.[4] Combined with the emotional intensity of competing sexual relationships such as described by McGuire, Alpert and Stern (in addition to

Graham), this potent mix of passions can lead to violence inflicted on group members considered to be inferior by their superiors, usually upon women by men (Gane, 1993: 53), as in the case of Mairéad Farrell. Durkheim recognized the violent impact of this sort of intense way of living on individual consciousness and on the ability of the group to function: 'a very intense social life always does a sort of violence to the organism, as well as to the individual consciousness, which interferes with its normal functioning' (Durkheim in Schinkel, 2009: 81). This forms an important and commonplace repressive strategy for counteracting or neutralizing the political agency of radical women, and it is often carried out within intragroup interactions as well as characterizing the historiographical representations of these movements.

Sexual places and spaces, and radicalization in contemporary geopolitics

Having considered the women characters in these stories, we may wonder who are these violent men, what is their role in these sexual stories, and what about the places or scenes of these dramas – specifically in relation to women's confinement? As a (radicalized) woman, Mairéad is on the 'outside' (or at best at the margins) of the process of historical progression; in the immediate situation, however, it is Scott who is the real 'outsider', at least from the perspective of Mairéad's community. Though *STK* admits little or no tension in the narrative with respect to who will eventually emerge victorious, the multifarious 'inside–outside' dichotomies in the narrative suggest that there are various and unstable formations with respect to who or what is the authentically 'rebellious' or 'complicit' subject or cause in the unfolding of the project of modernity. This is probably most evident in the spatial organization of the text, mainly with respect to the places and spaces on the borders or in the anonymous pubs and city streets where Scott and Mairéad meet, and in the hidden spaces of the prison and the military barracks. Spaces and places have particular resonance in terms of shared social understandings of sexuality and the body, especially where 'other' or 'queer' spaces like the prison and deviant, stigmatized 'criminalized' subjects like radicalized women or women prisoners are concerned (e.g. Brown, 2000). Mallan and Stephens (2002) explain how different spaces are linked to normative notions of sexuality and the appropriateness (or otherwise) of the 'objects' of love or desire who typically inhabit these spaces. Consequently, appropriately 'bounded' private spaces like 'the nation, regions, cities, and the home' (Mallan and Stephens, 2002: 1) are mapped as the normal domain of women, and are underpinned by assumed ideals of heteronormativity, denoting within these spaces the delimited maternal arenas of organization, collective relationships and care. Similarly, the public, undomesticated, unbounded or wild spaces like the countryside, city streets and solitary travel are the appropriate domain of men, suggestive of progressive temporal purpose as opposed to repetitive and non-productive occupation of space, and the more risky, exciting and bodily pleasurable space for the seeking and playing out of sexual desire (Mallan and Stephens, 2002). By being at once the more or less exclusive domain of women, and modelled on the domestic space of the family home, the (women's) prison complicates this dichotomy by simultaneously reinforcing the polar restrictions of gender and heteronormativity while at the same time consistently undermining them (particularly the latter). Such closed spaces of the prison, boarding school, barracks, retirement homes, etc. can evoke the claustrophobic feelings of dread and fear; the quasi-public and risk-laden environment of the women's prison, at least from the outside, provides a forbidden and thus attractive site of fantasy and fascination, a secret and hidden place for the imagination of the acting out of (forbidden) sexual desires by those for whom the ever-present threat of danger and violence evokes the spatial qualities of wild or untamed spaces, such as linked to the normative sexuality of men. Indeed, the closer and more proximate they are, as Brown (2000) argues about the closet, the more flooded with desire they become (as in the case of the public toilet as potentially transgressive and unbridled sexual space). 'Space is a shifting signifier which points to but does not anchor meaning across social, cultural, and territorial dimensions' (Mallan and Stephens, 2002: online). But of course, a major part of the attraction to proximate spaces is the promise of their being occupied by the equally proximate Other(s) and the possibilities afforded for the performance of desire between desiring subjects (e.g. Butler, 1999), which means that they are therefore never (completely) closed off or destroyed. This accords with Ferguson's (1993) remarks that, though oppressive and exclusionary, patriarchal societies do not destroy feminine or 'other' subjects, and neither are they always and everywhere 'rebellious', nor are their male counterparts always 'complicit' with the power structures of modernity. Therefore 'gynocentric' feminist solutions, whereby women's norms of subjectivity supplant those of men, are not the answer. Rather, a clearer recognition of the constructivist and interpretive dimensions of subjectivity and gender relations, and how they frame cultural discourses of liberation and resistance in the places and spaces where these dramas are played out, is the way forward.

Ferguson recommends that deconstructing the various cultural texts reflecting this phenomenon is at least part of the necessary work involved in arriving at any potential understanding of (and hence any possible solution to) socio-political 'problems' such as radicalization. The reality is that it is not always easy to tell who or what is the source of the threat (if any), how lasting it is or from whence it originates. Instead, Hegel's narrative posits that the dominating presence of the underlying desire for these other subjects is a testament not merely to their triumphant exclusion or manifest control, but also to the relentlessness of their demand for (and the need for) their inclusion as an ongoing concern in the quest for liberation (Ferguson, 1993). In this sense, the history of modernity is not so much a story about the final enunciation of *freedom* by the nation state as it is about the continual negotiation of *struggle* (*jihad*) between political actors (individual and collective), and that the actors and identities in this narrative of struggle and conquest are fluid, messy and ambiguous.

By way of an interpretation of such a radical text, it is arguable that the narrative arc traced in *STK* reiterates the geopolitically oriented 'intertwining discursive formations of racial and gender dominance, parallel discursive strategies [that] produce and maintain the privileges of men/whites/the west by constituting women/people of color/the east as other and lesser' (Ferguson, 1993: 39). This complex narrative strategy has its origins in the masculinist/phallocentric foundationalism of modern philosophy: 'In the articulation of western discourses of subjectivity that privilege masculinity, Hegel is a pivotal figure. Like Hobbes, Descartes, and Machiavelli, Hegel's fingerprints are all over contemporary notions of selfhood and desire' (Ferguson, 1993: 39). In other words, the appropriation of women's desire and female sexuality within a violent, often sadomasochistic, (political) narrative constitutes a vanquishing, fetishizing and/or commodification of women's subjectivity at the same time that it reinforces the potency of hierarchical male power structures:

> While very different from Hobbes in his teleology of development toward greater community, from Descartes in his approach to reflection, and from Machiavelli in his expectations of the state, Hegel shares with these and other figures in western thought an insistence on the primacy of separation and conflict over interconnection and affirmation and on the constitution of desire via domination.
>
> (ibid.: 40)

In a Foucauldian sense, space is intrinsically linked to concepts of power (Mallan and Stéphens, 2002: 2); the same can be said with regard to subjects as well as spaces. For Scott, his association with Mairéad means that the usually distant and closed sexual domain of the woman's prison and the subjectivity of a terrorist woman are now excitingly proximate and eminently penetrable. In *STK*, the fascination with Mairéad as terrorist woman/feral lover is reflected in the continual curiosity, risk-taking, anticipation and exhilaration, related in detail by Scott as soldier/narrator in his sustained efforts to continue his secret sexual liaison with Mairéad and, through her, to penetrate the secret sexual space of the women's prison as well as the secret domain of the terrorist cell and the colonized Irish 'Other'. For the typical soldier, this represents a significant extension and intensification of the normal field of struggle, and a potentially rich site for the satisfaction of previously denied desire – but this time transferred from the chaotic space of the battlefield to the potentially equally violent and aggressive domain of a penal institution, where combatants who have been apprehended instead of killed are housed. For a member of the elite SAS, it has a further dimension of the individual heroism of covert action: Scott is not only penetrating enemy lines but also the body of an even more rare elite female combatant and, what is more, a woman who Scott claims has been promised as marriage partner to a member of a highly placed Republican family. This alone constitutes a powerful, almost mythological tale about the conquering of a nation through the sexual violation of 'its' women (Aretxaga, 1997), eliding the alternative narrative, whereby Scott would allow himself to be used as bait in a 'honey trap' with which to capture Mairéad and process her and her comrades through the less passionate and private (and potentially more revealing) arena of the criminal justice system (or vice versa).

The influence of gender on the (post)colonial political struggles such as in the north of Ireland have their roots in emergent mythologies of gender as much as in modern political ideologies of the state. As Valente argues, after the nineteenth century, the cultural mythologies of Irish nationalism and sovereignty incorporate an imperialist ideology of colonialism which is itself founded upon an extreme idealization of 'gender disjunction, exclusion and stratification' (1994: 189) as the model for civil society, social order and social control:

> In figuring the conquerors as the exponents of a principle coded and celebrated as masculine (encompassing an aggressive will to historical progress, technical mastery and rational transcendence, et cetera) and the conquered as the embodiment of a principle stereotyped and dis-counted as female (encompassing a passive repose in organic cyclicality, affective immanence and domestic concerns, et cetera), imperialist dis-course has inscribed a vicious symbolic circle in which sexual and socio-economic dominance reflect and authorize one another. Colonial rule and expropriation were naturalized as the latest historical signifiers of an inherently gendered cosmos; gender hierarchy and male control were naturalized as the ultimate referents of the colonial mission.
>
> (ibid.)

This applies not just to Ireland, but to all post-colonial societies. Valente finds that it has resulted in the development of an Irish nationalism enshrined in its literary culture what displays a rhetoric of 'colonial hypermasculinity' (Nandy in Valente, 1994: 193) building on the virility of the warrior tradition in Irish mythology, and latterly expressed in the language of patriarchy and militancy observable in the writings of Pearse, Moran, Griffiths, Gonne, Robinson and Yeats (Valente, 1994). It is this deeply mythological story of victory in war via the violation of the 'Other' in the form of women – and of the 'Other's' women – that underpins the 'shoot to kill' stratagem, more appropriate to a war paradigm of terrorism, which has been continually denied by the British government in favour of a more criminological para-digm. The perception of women as part of the traditional 'spoils of war' has persisted for centuries; despite efforts in modern times to countermand the practice of rape and the sexual enslavement of women and girls by comba- tant forces through dictates of human rights governing warfare and the behaviour of soldiers, it would seem that this practice is at least as common a feature of conflict as it ever was – probably more so. According to the philosopher Claudia Card (2002), this is in part due to the convergence of sexism and racism in this type of war crime or crime against humanity, whereby the conqueror's power over their enemy is physically inflicted on the bodies of women and girls as living symbols not just of their national, but also of the racial superiority of their conquerors. While Scott's revelations of his highly sexualized relationship with Mairéad suggests her willingness as a participant, and therefore the consensual nature of their relationship, in a fabular sense, this is nevertheless evocative of what the Weathermen termed 'wargasm' (Morgan, 1989: 154–79), whereby the culture of military–terrorist conflict is underpinned by the sexualization of violence against women. Morgan cites a US Army chant to illustrate her meaning with respect to the close proximity – even conflation – of sex and violence in the hypermasculine culture of militancy:

This is my rifle,
This is my gun.
One is for killing,
One is for fun.

(in Morgan, 1989: 154)

In the case of *STK*, the ideological connotations of the purported victory and clandestinity of Scott's sexual prowess in relation to his affair with Mairéad represents a powerful analogy of the colonial history between Ireland and Britain that constitutes the story's primary meaning. The character of Scott is able to penetrate the Irish Republican movement on its own home territory to its most intimate and treasured core, i.e. the body of a revered and later mar- tyred heroine and warrior queen (a sort of modern Queen Meadhbh, as central protagonist in the foundational myth of Irish nationalism epitomized by the myth of dying young rebel warrior, Cúchulainn). Scott's relationship with Mairéad, though apparently known – but not acted upon – by the British security forces, remains a secret to his less knowledgeable enemy (the PIRA), who incidentally relies on secrecy as a primary weapon in the struggle. What is more, in the end, following her release from prison and continuing campaign of 'active service' in Gibraltar, Scott is able to reveal that Mairéad not only enjoys but actively invites the violence, aggression and (virtual performance of) rape that characterizes their sexual relationship, to the extent that both their sexual and political 'struggle' culminate in her eventual, violent and unlawful killing by the British State (according to the eventual European Court of Human Rights judgment of 1995). As in the infamous *Story of O* (Reage, 1976),[5] the strong implication is that the dénouement of a woman's 'willing' participation in sadomasochistic sex is ultimately her own death, which is what she has really desired all along (Sontag, 1983). According to Scott, Mairéad constantly refers to how she loves his 'muscles' and his power over her. More than anything, this biographical narrative of Mairéad Farrell utilizes the fetishization of radical women's sexuality (see Craig, 2002) to tell the story of how a weaker, sub-jugated, 'feminized' nation not only *desires* its own domination and destruction at the hands of its superior colonial masters, but indeed this is its deepest and most secret fantasy. In this sense, *STK* comprises a potent narrative mytholo-gizing the legitimacy of colonialism in the post-colonial age, expressed through the cultural medium of a story of terrorism sutured to a tale of 'true romance'. Tension and fear in the narrative are resolved not by simply killing the other, but through a process marking the close interweaving of the modernist philo-sophical ideologies of sexuality and desire culminating in domination by violent force ('desire' and 'force' are the concepts favoured by Hegel). This provides the focal point in the mind of the soldier/thinker, in philosophy as in combat:

> The one who wins the struggle does so not actually by killing the other (for that would leave no one to give recognition) but by being prepared to kill the other and to die in the fight ... The first becomes the master/lord, the second the slave/bondsman.
>
> (Ferguson, 1993: 42)

The irony is that, even in the Hegelian philosophical narrative of spirit, it is the slave/bondsman who is the most knowing and ultimately triumphant.

For the most part, *STK* reads, as Eager (2008) has commented, more like a fictionalized than an authentically realist narrative of the life of a radicalized militant woman; this is particularly true of the ending, in which Graham claims not only to have been present at the shooting of Farrell and her two male IRA colleagues on Gibraltar, but to have been the one to have positively identified her at the scene, and even looked her in the eye moments before her death (Graham, 2002: 324–5). The narrative is almost exclusively devoted to a description of the prolonged sexual liaison that Graham claims to have had with Mairéad, spanning her early career as a new PIRA recruit through to her life following release in 1986 after a sentence of more than 10 years, and then up to the time of her unlawful killing by British SAS officers in 1988.

Recovering other stories and the politics of disclosure in political prisoner life writing

How does *STK* compare to other contemporaneous texts describing the radicalization and life stories of Mairéad Farrell and the other radical women with whom she associated? Relatively little has been written about these women compared to their male counterparts in the Irish Republican movement; however, it is worth noting that Graham's account of Farrell's life in Armagh Women's Prison differs substantially from that of her one-time fellow inmate Margaretta D'Arcy (1981) or the accounts of prison life recorded in interviews with a number of Irish Republican women prisoners who served with Farrell in Mary Corcoran's *Out of Order: The Political Imprisonment of Women in Northern Ireland, 1972–1998* (2006). In the latter work, sexual violence as experienced by the women inmates is mentioned, but only in relation to the highly emotive and politically contested practice of strip-searching the women inmates by prison staff. The signal presence or fear of rape attributed to Farrell by Graham in *STK* is never mentioned by the former inmate women interviewees. Can we thus conclude from this that such sexual violence among the women prisoners, or indeed the presumed 'affair' between Scott and Mairéad, never happened? Not quite. As noted in the previous chapter, the analysis and interpretation of these life stories are fraught, and rely upon a deeper knowledge of the tropes and narrative devices used by such actors to reveal, as well as conceal, themselves and their social worlds is necessary. In this vein, as Corcoran (2006) notes:

> homosexuality [in prisons] is either not mentioned or disguised under terms such as 'relationships' ... [Nevertheless] 'butch' and 'femme' lesbian roles, or other quasi-marital relationships, were central to women's identification and structure.
>
> (Ward and Kassebaum cited in Corcoran, 2006: 73)

Similarly, though the pairing of a British SAS soldier on active duty in Northern Ireland with an active service PIRA operative would normally be considered highly unlikely, such overtly sexual liaisons are not unheard of. Morgan (1989) cites Patty Hearst's eventual marriage to one of her former bodyguards (echoing the romantic narrative trope 'Reader, I married him'), in addition to the confessed attraction by one of Morgan's former unnamed women radical feminist colleagues (and herself a one time object of her own sexual infatuation while Morgan herself was married) to a male FBI agent/interrogator while she was in prison. It is probably best to admit that we are in very tricky sexual–political territory here. On the one hand, to admit the possibility that these types of stories are true, especially those such as represented in the *STK* narrative is to allow or even encourage the fetishization and appropriation of radical women on the grounds of their presumed violent sexuality; this would thereby facilitate the normative phallocentric stratagem of neutralizing their political agency by negating (and commodifying) them as mere sexual objects. On the other hand, to suggest that such liaisons must by their nature be fictional or logically impossible, based only on the ideological foundations reliant on the preservation of such oppositional dichotomies (e.g. heterosexual/homosexual, masculine/feminine, violent/passive, radical/conservative, etc.) is to deny the permeability of these boundaries, and the propensity for radical women (and men) to transgress them as an elemental part of their political radicalization as well as of their general human being.

As Winders (1999: 121) notes, drawing on the feminist theories of Irigaray, Cixous, Judovitz and Keller, either reading reiterates the 'sexual asymmetry' that has formed a critical foundation for modern western phallocentric societies that deny the polymorphousness of women's desires. This 'sexual asymmetry' has functioned to negate the political agency of radical women and transform their radicalization and radical identities into the fodder for masculinist desire, and their own social stigmatization and alienation as (doubly) deviant women. It is thus not surprising that women political prisoners such as those interviewed by Corcoran have adapted and internalized self–representative strategies that maintain silence or ways of avoiding disclosure concerning their sexuality and practices within and without prison.[6] However, these issues go much further than the practical and normative implications concerning the social demands for women to actively monitor and protect their public reputations as sexual beings in light of society's insistence on mapping women's bodies according to the 'geography of pleasure'. Scott's claims that his pleasure in Mairéad's body was reciprocated in her pleasure in his 'muscles' is thus somewhat undermined by the resolution of the narrative in which she (and her comrades) are identified and violently and unlawfully killed – the very same event and strategy of dealing with radicalized terrorists that has continually been denied at the official level, but which nevertheless with a kind of crude irony provides the title of the book. These same asymmetrically sexist and exclusionary practices, based on the hypocritical denial or paradoxical reaffirmation of such dichotomies, underpin the praxes of alienation and radicalization by misinterpreting the ease with which the living, desiring and sexual body exceeds these political ideological rules and rationalized frameworks:

> Irigaray, radically questioning the primacy of the autonomous (masculine) subject and employing the female body with its diverse 'geography of pleasure' as metaphor, strikes at unitary, phallic modes of knowing as domination (or, as Judovitz argues, at a subjective politics of representation inaugurated in modern epistemology by Descartes) accompanied by the denial of the polymorphous character of female desire and (as with Cixous) the multiplicity of feminine modes of knowledge. Keller, as a leading example of an American feminist who draws upon recent French feminist thought as well as object-relations theory to formulate a powerful critique of 'normal science' as 'male'—a conclusion she qualifies somewhat—historicizes the constructed, masculinist gesture of radical division; of knowing as distancing, alienation, and objectification.
>
> (Winders, 1999: 121–2)

The central organizational structures of family 'relationships', and the contingent heteronormative gender roles in society as a whole (as well as in radical groups), are not just imported into the prison environment, nor do they simply greatly reinforce and facilitate the institutional surveillance and control of incarcerated women; they also (as with remarks on the family in Chapter 4) enable practices regarding the hiding or non-disclosure of what actually happens in these places, and among the embodied, desiring subjects who occupy them, not least in relation to what might be regarded as deviant or perverse practices among the new and ideologically opposed collection of in(ti)mates. This extends significantly to all communications with the outside world, if not with respect to the message, then in terms of the secrecy of the chosen media of communication:

> Admonishing my mother to caution would be dismissed with impatience. The only way to persuade her to act to safeguard her own freedom, I decided, was to insist, for my sake and theirs, that she take the children away. With infinite trouble I wrote thirty urgent words to send a signal by a laborious procedure that had been devised for a time of extreme need. (I had previously alerted my mother that I would use this way to reach her.)
>
> (First, 1965: 55–6)

Unlike many male prison writers, Ruth First does not divulge what this 'laborious procedure' was – although then again the woman political prisoner Nawal El Saadawi (1983), in a similar situation, does. It is very difficult to imagine what these communication mechanisms might have been in First's extreme circumstances, but these are a secret she maintains to the end. Similarly, Morgan's (1989) divulgence of the sexual attraction between her former colleague and an FBI agent suggests that such feelings might be more common than is at least openly acknowledged; the same may be said for the sorts of implied yet strongly denied disclosures about intimate relationships such as that involving Morgan and Alpert, or indeed what constituted the bonds of intimacy from the not always consistent perspectives of the desiring subjects in question.

The felt necessity by women to hide or distort these experiences under the guise of 'friendship', or to subvert them into the organizational structure of 'the family' as promoted by penal policy in women's prisons, makes it difficult if not impossible to completely reject the veracity of these often competing or conflicting stories. While women members of the IRA may or may not have chosen to remain silent on the issue of intragroup sexual violence inside or outside of prison (again, Maria McGuire (1973) represents a rare example of a former PIRA member who provides public revelations of the sexual advances and/or infidelities of the married PIRA male leaders with whom she was associated, at the same time that they trumpeted their commitment to traditional Catholic family values), radical women prisoners like Susan Stern are much more forthcoming in their autobiographical accounts of life both inside and outside of a woman's prison. Stern maintains adamantly throughout her memoir that she remained (often regrettably) unable to indulge in the sexual practices with other women group members as dictated – at times virtually required – by the organization's leadership as part of the 'smash monogamy' campaign; she was only ever able to overcome this impediment of desire towards another woman while she was beyond the control of the Weather Underground leadership, while in prison.

Stern (2007) tells of an instance when it was mandatory for a woman who entered a collective household of Weathermen to have sex with every male resident in the house, a practice represented as a 'bonding' exercise to function in the interests of providing better 'security' in within terrorist cells – notwithstanding the fact that the same commitment to engage in such 'security' or 'bonding' exercises did not apply to new male residents/recruits. She also recounts – and has received harsh criticism and claims of denial for – what she describes in detail as her presence at the rape of a fellow Weather-woman by a visiting member of the male national leadership (ibid.). What these stories and many others indicate clearly is the strong cultural presumption of the sexual availability of women, and the dominating influence of practices such as the 'smash monogamy' culture of radical groups during the sexual revolution of the 1960s. They also show how these enhanced the capacity for radical groups to attract and recruit disaffected (and sexually frustrated) men by the instrumental use of women, and to subsequently control the sexuality of the women they managed to recruit. This dynamic of exploitation and control is as true in the broader narratives about radical women in popular cultural forms as it is in the subcultural storytelling of these extremist groups – maybe even more so. Consider the example of the feral and ultimately self-annihilating sexuality of Mairéad Farrell as represented in *STK*, or the beautiful but ruthless young IRA assassin Annette in the film *Patriot Games*: such blatant fetishization of radical women as physically exotic, sexually promiscuous, dangerous, prone to sadomasochistic violence and in need of taming (or, even better, killing) are paraded in contemporary culture as representations of them as political agents. With respect to the irresistible beauty and sexiness of terrorist women as represented in popular culture, many young women want to be like them; with respect to the acceptability to fuck them and then dispose of them (including through murder), many men want to gain access to them. Irrespective of the acceptability or otherwise of the political ideologies they adhere to, this is a crude example of false consciousness by which women's capacity as political agents to contribute to or shape socio-cultural change are continually fore-closed and reformulated in ways to continue the oppression and exploitation against which most if not all of these women struggle to be free.

To return to D'Arcy's portrayal of Farrell in her prison memoir – though admittedly her account spans a relatively short period of time in the prison, arriving for a 91-day sentence which would have been approximately three years into Farrell's 14-year sentence for her part in a hotel bombing – there are serious points of discrepancy between the two biographical narratives of Farrell. Compared to the common practice by prisoners to write about their time inside long after their release (Morgan, 1999), D'Arcy's account, published in 1981, is somewhat unusual in that it was written relatively contemporaneously to her period of incarceration in 1979. Nor is Farrell the main subject of the memoir, but rather one of the figures she encounters in her time on the 'dirty protest'[7] with the Republican women prisoners. D'Arcy recalls Farrell's authoritative role in the prison as the Officer Commanding on the wing, in charge of the other IRA prisoners, negotiator between the protesting women and the prison governor, staff and the hierarchy of the Catholic church, and main liaison with the organization on the outside. This was a very responsible and demanding role, which according to D'Arcy, Farrell carried out with a great deal of authority and ability under extremely difficult circumstances where she had little advanced notice of whom or what she would be required to deal with on any given day:

> Mairead's task was infinitely more intricate—to ride the ever-changing currents and winds affecting life in jail from society outside. Disturbances deriving from the relationships of the Northern Ireland Office with Westminster; pressures via the Catholic Church; via the Unionists; back again to pressures brought against the Catholic Church; from the Vatican via Britain, from America and the elections via Britain; against America via NATO via Britain; against the Northern Ireland Office via the screws; against the Provos via the public and so upon us, inside. The repercussions flowed through the jail from the constant visitors, the press, the British Information Service, the Prison visitors, security. And how did we know the importance of each new official visitor? By the artistry of Griff, the cook, as revealed in how he prepared and served up our dinner each day.
>
> (D'Arcy, 1981:68)

This description of Farrell does not match the more fetishized heterogeneous male fantasy type, nor the story of life in Armagh Women's Prison as heavily reliant on the exploitation of the women prisoners by each other, and the manipulation for them to join groups. Nowhere in her book does D'Arcy indicate that either of these was the case; she does not appear to have been coerced or cajoled to engage in any unwanted activity of any kind – sexual or otherwise – nor to join gangs or groups for her protection (PIRA or other). If anything, she bemoans the lack of any organized position on her own (WAI) group's chosen form of protest, apart from abstract political rhetoric:

> Instead, high-falutin marxist jargon was bandied back and forward: 'idealism', 'petit bourgeois', 'individualism', 'martyrdom', etc. No-one in that hall knew exactly who the Armagh Eleven were [herself and the

other WAI women arrested for protesting on International Women's Day]. The women who had decided to pay the fines were identified to the conference. I was going to jail, and yet I couldn't tell anyone. The talk was that the Armagh Eleven have decided to become as distanced, as abstract as any other cause set up by the male left-wing groups. A more personal approach, a sisterly identification, were badly needed, and were lacking. I was alone and must take the consequences.

(ibid.: 36)

The diversity and complexity of women's political opinions, alliances and forms of activism make it extremely difficult to come to any reliable and decisive conclusions concerning their real nature in terms of individual motivations, collective meaning or causal processes. One radicalized woman's story can be totally different from another's, and even the act of telling these stories can silence, appropriate or occlude those of others involved in such struggles. Hill (2003) explores the relationships between a range of women activists and organizations operating in Northern Ireland during the 1970s, claiming that to a significant extent both the contemporary and historical focus on 'the Troubles' has effectively undermined the actions and achievements of women engaged in more specifically 'feminist' actions, as well as masking the contributions, activism and indeed radicalism of women from the Protestant and Unionist community. 'While all left-wing groups are vulnerable to fragmentation, the experiences of women in Northern Ireland during this period is a particularly difficult and emotive reminder of the multiple identities and conflicting loyalties held by women everywhere' (Hill, 2003: online), not just politically active or indeed radicalized women. As echoed in Chapter 5 these kinds of tensions, conflicts and shifting patterns of emotional connection and political alliances characterize all human relationships, not just among women or radicals. While this may make the picture more complex, there is still reason not to give up the study and analysis of such aspects of these groups in despair, but rather to probe further into how and why such patterns of interaction function regarding a specific dependent variable – in this instance, radicalization.

Even given these real and complicated tensions, at least in terms of intragroup relations, the life writings of women political prisoners such as the South African anti-apartheid activist Jean Middleton (1998) and Student Nonviolent Coordination Committee (SNCC) and Che-Lumumba member Angela Davis (1990) among others demonstrate how the radical quality of their activism is often narrated as characterized by a sense of reciprocity and solidarity, even if this is not (or not always) actually the case. For women political prisoner life writers, their stories about how and why they came to be radicalized as individuals are often told according to their involvement *with* others with whom they empathize or wish to identify (e.g. workers, other women, the oppressed, ethnic minorities, etc.); by contrast, the life narratives of radicalized male political prisoners often stress the altruistic qualities of their actions *for* others, undertaken on their behalf. Possibly in contrast to Hill (2003), Hargie and Dickson (2003) argue that there is a tendency toward collective or 'community development' work by women in Northern Ireland, which is particularly evident among Catholic women, with evidence that ' ... estimates that some 6,000 women are actively involved, while identifying a less fully evolved tradition of engagement within Protestant areas' (ibid.: 296). This could be down to the less individualistic culture of Roman Catholicism in comparison to its Scottish-Irish-influenced Protestant counterpart, which is culturally more disposed toward an ethos of self-sufficiency, or alternatively to the even more deep-seated 'herd instinct' of people to stick with their own – not just in response to the ideology of religious obligation, but also with respect to class, age, racial and/or gender norms:

> Thus, people have a range of in-groups as well as the politico-religious one. We identify more with those of the same age, gender or race, as well as with those who have similar interests and hobbies. These identities interact with, and in certain contexts will take precedence over, the politico-religious one.
>
> (ibid.: 303)

In this regard, the male prisoners typically view themselves and their suffering as a symbolic or even iconic representation of the communities with which they identify themselves; by contrast, it is typical of the women not only to fail to claim this status, but actively to eschew any particular iconic or representative role as an individual, instead focusing on their ordinariness or typicality, and actively identifying with other women as 'just one of the girls', while at the same time recovering a particularly powerful sense of agency as one of a collective group. Notwithstanding efforts by male leaders to disrupt a sense of 'sisterhood', feelings of friendship and/or solidarity between women can be a powerful force, propelling individual like-minded women into radical activism and possible recruitment, as in the examples of Middleton (1998), Saadawi (1983) and D'Arcy (1981). However, the realities of the pressures of clandestinity and particularly group incarceration of women political prisoners, due in part to their usually small numbers in comparison to the men and the lack of adequate accommodation within the prison system, can mean that the realities and distinctive 'pains of imprisonment' (Sykes, 1958) suffered by these women can have a lasting and devastating impact on their sense of self and bonding as a collective in comparison to the men. The close proximity in which many women political prisoners are forced to live while detained or sentenced prisoners can be the cause of considerable stress and be the cause of factionalism (as in the example of Jean Middleton (1998)), as well as strengthen solidarity ((as represented in the prison autobiography of Margaretta D'Arcy (1981)).

The centrality and fluidity of the gendered body in political prisoner life writing by men and women

These reflections help us understand why these types of writings are often so innovative, imaginative, disruptive, disturbing and creative in relation to other more established genres, which can become extremely formulaic, unchallenging and predictable in terms of their characterizations, scenes, language and plots (Franklin, 1978, 1998). It also helps explain what is frequently observable in political prisoner life writing, as adeptly argued by Maud Ellmann (1993), i.e. the exaggerated fluidity and instability of gender norms in these narratives, undercut by a dual reliance upon extreme and biologically essentialist notions of gender difference, and how this dialogic results in the 'doubly deviant' effect of feminization of male prisoners in their writings, if not in their subcultures and in wider culture more generally. For the male Irish Republican prisoners in the H-Blocks, it is the physical capacity of the male body – its folds, hollows and cavities – as opposed to (penile) extension and muscular bulk – that become the hallmarks not just of the masculine potency of the male prisoner (the pinnacle of the revolutionary soldier), but also of male utility and instrumentality (the aim of classic industrial capitalism). Male IRA prisoners who could hide a range of contraband materials in their bodies without being detected by the authorities were lauded by the sub-group as they played an important role in continuing the resistance campaign on the 'inside', making collective elision of the prison regime possible by facilitating direct and uncensored communication between the prisoners and the outside world. In Feldman's (1991) view, this instrumental use of the (again, male) prisoner body marks its political conversion into a 'weapon' of war to be used by skilled insurgent soldiers who see themselves (despite their incarceration) as still engaged in battle against the state. In O'Hearn's (2006) biography of Bobby Sands, the collective nature of these prison protests forms a major strand of the narrative of Sands's meteoric rise to the status of martyr-hero-artist-chronicler. This is a complex auto/biographical construction, in part forged from the largely unsung or subjugated 'feminine' work of his cellmates who 'service' his needs as author by secreting writing materials and his proliferating output within their own bodily cavities, functioning as surrogates to the eventual birth of the revolutionary artist. In this way, the dichotomous character of gender norms is retained within prison, for example in the presumed role for his cellmates in latter years to function in a subordinate role, whereby their duty was to provide not just 'storage' but 'transport' for his writings by secreting them in their own bodies, or storing 'comms' or materials like pens, paper and radios, thereby feminizing their bodies and subjectivities in contrast to his masculinized identity as master and commander. This became an assumed duty of sharing a cell with Sands (Ellmann, 1993), as the other prisoners took to calling Sands's cellmates Bobby's 'mules' (O'Hearn, 2006: 243). This form of resistance and solidarity was not just

limited to communications, but also extended to the transport of other contraband materials, such as tobacco and other 'entertainment' materials, the
source of an alternative leisure and consumption culture within the prison
(ibid.: 217), whereby the bodies of less privileged male prisoners were used to
recreate the political and fraternal geography of the domestic space.

Additionally, the ability of the male body to endure and adjust to pervasive
danger of violent physical assault (something more normatively related to
violence against women in the domestic realm – see also Crawley and Crawley's (2007) analogy between the quasi-privacy of prison and the domestic
sphere and the cathartic bonding power of prison violence for male prisoners
and staff) that form the new basis of power and masculinity in Ellmann's
view. As in the citation below, the 'political football' metaphor could apply as
much to the bodies (specifically the genitalia) of men as it could to the
abstraction of politics as a (typically man's) game in Northern Ireland in
general, simultaneously affording an opportunity for intertextual identification with the life writings of heroic Irish Republican prisoners of the past.
Coogan tells this story about his interview with an IRA member who had
undergone police interrogation:

> Hanaway underwent the 'five techniques'. When it was all over, he told
> me, lowering his voice because his wife was in the room, 'My privates
> were the size of a football from the kicking.'
>
> 'How did you manage to get through it all, I asked him? 'I kept
> thinking of *The Last Words*, and I thought of what those me went
> through and I said to myself, sure what am I getting—nothing! So I
> stuck it out.'
>
> (*The Last Words* is a book about the last words and writings of the
> executed 1916 leaders. It is doubtful if any political science course
> includes it on its reading list but such works have more relevance to the
> making of a revolutionary than the learned tomes that are written about
> them afterwards.)
>
> (Coogan, 1971: 439–40)

Something as basic as bladder control indicates how the body can be used not
so much as a weapon against the state (as it is often attributed in the prison
resistance of men (Feldman, 1991)) but, as in the case of Ruth First, as a
symbol or site in the prisoner's determination to at least try to withstand the
mortification of the self via the disintegration of the basic norms of civilized
behaviour. This indicates that there is more than one 'narrative' of the body
and political protest inside or outside of prison, generated by the enforced need
to 're-articulate' (in both senses of the word) the body in prison:

> I remained locked in for a stretch of seventeen hours, still without
> using the po [First refused to use this instead of the toilet]. My bladder

passed the jail endurance test as well if not better than any other part of me.

(First, 1965: 66)

It is worth remarking that women also played a vital, though perhaps less celebrated, role in this subversive communication network, and how this worked. In his biography of Bobby Sands, O'Hearn (2006) records the substantial contribution to the protest effort made by the women of Sinn Féin's POW department, coordinated by the redoubtable figures of Marie Moore and Mary Hughes. Both women visited the 'blanket men' in prison often, and Moore was responsible for recruiting a 'network' of young women to pose as 'girlfriends' for the prisoners in order to be able to kiss and embrace them during prison visits without arousing suspicion (in actuality, these physical contacts were enacted between strangers and designed for the exchange of messages between the prisoners and organizers on the outside). This was a difficult, dangerous and disgusting task, as the protesting prisoners had not washed or cleaned their teeth or hair for months or years, and reeked from the stench of the faeces that covered them and their cells. Often materials were exchanged by means of oral and anal transmission:

> It was hard for the young women to go into jail day after day and kiss somebody who was completely dirty to get communications coming from all parts of his body. 'Sometimes you felt like being violently sick before you got out with the communications,' says Moore, and sometimes they had to swallow them and wait until it came back out again.
>
> The women swallowed their pride as well as the comms. They were doing things that went against much that they had been taught. Not only had they to receive items that the men had been holding internally, they also had to secrete comms, supplies, and even miniature radios and cameras on their bodies.
>
> The job got harder as the prisoners' demands increased. As the women became known, the prison authorities held them back for special searches. After the searches, packages had to be passed to the prisoner ... But the ordeal was still not over. The women still had to get their comms back out. They stank because the smell of the communications was unbelievable. Even the Sinn Fein office back in Belfast stank from the comms that were opened and transcribed there. A local businessman gave Moore a bottle of expensive perfume to spray the comms before she opened them.
>
> Despite the ordeal, day after day, month after month, the women kept up their visits. None of them ever stopped working for Marie Moore.
>
> 'They all just carried on.'

(O'Hearn, 2006: 242–3)

Getting caught exchanging contraband with the prisoners could land the 'girls' in serious trouble with the authorities. These young women remain nameless, but are described as being of 'dating age' similar to those of the young male prisoners, in their teens or early twenties. O'Hearn relates how their performance of the 'girlfriend' experience was not simply restricted to the role of communications (which at times could mean visiting twice a day, every day), but also to ' ... look their best in an effort to keep up the prisoners' morale while they did their job of communications' (ibid.: 242). The duration of this prison protest campaign meant that these women 'were in jail nearly as long as the prisoners' (ibid.: 242). In other words, the demands placed upon them were quite considerable, reflecting a newly emergent idealization of femininity within the culture of Irish Republicanism, which comprised an exaggerated version of the unstinting and selfless servicing of the men's needs, based on the exploitation of social norms surrounding intimate relationships, albeit a contribution by these young women that has remained largely invisible and unremarked.

From my readings of a considerable amount of prisoner life writings, critical commentaries upon these, and qualitative interviews with Irish Republicans, I have yet to come across any reference to the performance of the same types of 'boyfriend' experience for incarcerated Irish republican women (or for that matter women providing the same service for the women prisoners) as 'Marie's girls' did for the men. The handling of 'comms' from and into the women' prisons has not been subjected to the degree of detailed attention it receives in O'Hearn's and Ellmann's books with respect to resistance practices among the male prisoners, or indeed the function of these recovered founts of power within prison as mechanisms for completing what O'Hearn refers to as the 'fuller' radicalization of republican prisoners like Sands. This could be seen as part of a broader cultural trend in which the protest actions of women political prisoners, especially in Northern Ireland, generally receive considerably less attention than those of the male prisoners, due at least in part to the depth of public distaste for the violation of norms of decency and femininity in relation to the women prisoners on the blanket or 'dirty' protest (or on hunger strike, for that matter). As previously mentioned, in the case of the women PIRA prisoners who took part in the blanket/dirty protest, menstrual blood was added to other faecal material smeared on the walls and ceilings of their cells, even framing pictures of holy figures such as the Virgin Mary; this occasioned extreme disgust and was subsequently suppressed by the powerful men within the broader community who witnessed these sights first hand, notably the then Cardinal of All Ireland, Tomás Ó Fiaich and the journalist Tim Pat Coogan (Coogan, 1980). In recent years, however, there has been a growing consciousness and determination among feminist commentators to recover and expose the gendered dimensions of political prisoner protest, and to reiterate the symbolic significance of menstrual blood and menstruation as a 'weapon of resistance' against the state by radicalized women (O'Keefe, 2006: 535; Aretxaga, 1997).

O'Keefe (2006) argues that it is the genuinely subversive qualities of menstruation and menstrual blood, and their relation to the generative power of the female body, that represents such a threat to the rational hegemony of the nation state. As D'Arcy (1981) chronicles in her prison autobiography, the young women on the dirty protest are well aware that they are risking not just their own physical and psychological health, but also their very fertility and the immanence of future generations by their actions as a consequence of their vulnerability to infection. The anxiety that their bodies 'would not let them down' as a result of their chosen form of protest had the potential to place in doubt the very survival of their ethnic groups, and even provided an occasion for some empathy and consciousness-raising from the male prison protestors:

> I was most scared about possible vaginal infections, which quite a few suffered from. We never changed our knickers or jeans, but one had to have some protection there. Most of the women wore sanitary towels but there were no sanitary belts, so much of the time in the exercise yard was spent in furtively hitching the towels into place out of view of the TV monitors. The problem of not washing during menstruation was solved by changing the tampax much more frequently than one would outside. Also I had a period only once while inside, which relieved my problem. In the beginning you could get as many sanitary towels and tampax as you wanted. But then surgery came round and informed us that we were going to get them only on the first day of the month, and you had to choose between tampax or towels. The whole problem of menstruation had been a taboo area, never discussed in the Republican News. Eilis once talked in the yard about how the men in the Blocks were becoming educated. 'Some of those wee lads know nothing about periods. One of them was asking, does it come out from a hole, just pouring down? It had to be explained to them. They are beginning to understand what we are going through. The shortage of sanitary towels. They don't know how we stick it.' And so on and on. While they thought the authorities were indifferent to their appeals for help when their periods were too heavy or too frequent, a new area of sympathy and understanding had been discovered, from the men in the Blocks. Some of the girls said that they preferred too many periods than none at all: 'It is healthier,'—anything to indicate that their bodies would not let them down over the no-wash protest.
>
> (D'Arcy, 1981: 80)

But at the same time, D'Arcy's experience of the dirty protest led to some very unexpected 'alliances' with respect to the trialling of a new negotiating strategies, and the emergence of a bizarre composite sense of political agency, conflict, identity and the materiality of history embedded in the physical prison space:

Every morning there are hundreds of flies on the walls, on the floors. We swat them. I feel like the proverbial white hunter. I try to have a truce with them, 'You can have the walls but leave my body alone.' No way, they crawl up my legs, land on my face, I hide under the filthy grey blanket, they sneak in, no mercy. No surrender. I am Paisley, I lash out, jumping on my springs and on my bars. Don't slip, they will get their revenge if I end up with a broken back. I can't go to surgery. Carefully get them: some of them are stunned, I think they are dead, no, they recover. They are like the Provos, unconquerable, they are everywhere, and then the little ones that live in the skirting boards (even though the cells are supposed to be cleaned each time we are moved), hundreds of years of filth are ingrained in the floorboards, thousands of flies live there. And in some of the cells there are fleas. One morning we were changing cells and the screws got into a panic when they were moving the mattresses, hundreds of fleas flew up, the screws ran shrieking out into the wing. The male screws in their weird outfits came along with disinfectant putting it everywhere. The female screws are frightened of the fleas because they will be infected by them and who wants a flea-ridden screw to screw?

(D'Arcy, 1981: 78–9)

The male prisoners also wrote about the flies, using them as a trope to describe their political (as opposed to biological/familial) situation. A significant example is contained in Bobby Sands' prison autobiography, *One Day in My Life* (1983). Sands' use of the snow imagery to combine the multiple meanings of erasure/silence/invisibility/purity with the ethereal and cyclical image of nature is explored in the following excerpt, this time in the summer, when he recounts the frightening and repulsive experience of waking up with thousands of maggots crawling all over his naked body, on his face and in his beard:

I'll never forget that, I said to myself, reflecting on the morning I woke up and my blankets and mattress were a living mass of white maggots. They were in my hair and beard and crawling upon my naked body. They were repulsive, and dare I say it, frightening at first.

(Sands, 1983: 52)

But again, though this is a shocking and revolting experience, Sands is able to immediately reassert his control of the situation through his autobiographical writing, even turning the narrative of the situation to their mutual advantage:

But like everything else I had come to terms with them sharing my cell with me. At night I could hear them actually moving about the floor,

> disturbing little bits of paper, now and again causing a rustling noise as
> they headed in the direction of my mattress, where they would finally
> embed themselves and in the warmth harden into an egg-like cocoon
> before hatching into flies.
>
> (ibid.: 52)

In other words, his body provided the heat for incubating the larvae, while in
their own way they provided him with the inspiration to write, in the first
instance by 'disturbing bits of paper' (a play on both meanings of the word
'disturbing'). Bearing in mind the prohibition on writing under the Prison
Rules at that time, and the extreme punishment regime he was under while
on the blanket protest, it is perhaps a little surprising that among the excre-
ment and rotten food on the floor, there were actually bits of paper suitable
for writing upon, even in the tiny mode of writing that he was reportedly
forced to adopt. This in itself makes the mention of the rustling paper that
much more significant as a possible instance of writerly invention.

Over the years of his incarceration, Sands' eventual desensitization to the
maggots and his much remarked interest in ornithology (an obsession with
birds that also forms a common trope in prisoner writing) led him to
identify an alternative purpose for the maggots. As an expression of his
agency in an extreme situation, this represents a rather conspicuous example, as the presence of the maggots as a particular nuisance is in itself
intended by his captors to be as part of his 'special' punishment. Once
again, this shows his determination to construct an alternate narrative
direction and framework for the events comprising his specially tailored
punishment regime (comprised by himself, the other paramilitary prisoner,
the prison staff and management, the Northern Ireland Office and the
British Government). In the following excerpt, he uses a kind of transli-
teration – i.e. the systematic representation or spelling of the text written of
one alphabet using the corresponding letters of another (as coincidentally
he does in the example of transliterating Russian text into English, evoking
again the intertextual reference to Solzhenitsyn suggested in the title of
his prison autobiography) – to translate the wriggling white maggots
from their natural and punitive discursive contexts into one that focuses
primarily on the exploration of his political and artistic agency as a writer
and his construction of a particular altruistic type of autobiographical
voice:

> But the maggots had another use, as I quickly discovered. I soon
> became so used to them that I would gather them up in my hands off
> the floor and from the rubbish piles in the corners. There would be
> thousands of them wriggling and sliding about. Having gathered them
> together between my palms, I would throw the white wriggling mass
> out of the window, scattering them over the jet-black tarmacadam

yard and against the black background their white wriggling little forms were easily spotted. The wagtails came fluttering about in a frenzy, their quick little legs darting them from one maggot to the next, feasting upon what to them must have been a delicacy. Within two or three minutes the yard would have been cleared of every single maggot.

(ibid.: 52–3)

As in the prison life writings of Rosa Luxemburg (1946), nature features prominently – if not in the recovery, then in the urge to preserve a viable sense of subjectivity and humanity from beyond the 'territorial' realm of the conventionally political – as does the need to be creative in finding 'another use' for its manifest realities as the source for political inspiration and physical endurance. For Luxemburg, nature, and her intuitively perceived role in it, provide a paradigm model and logic for her political activism as the source of personal experience (as an embodied being and a woman), a source of knowledge and experience that makes life worth living even in the most dire physical and material circumstances:

On the background of the monotonously grey sky, there towered in the east a huge cloud of an amazingly beautiful rose colour; it was so detached from its surroundings that it looked like a smile, like a greeting from afar. I breathed with a sense of renewed freedom, and involuntarily stretched out both hands towards the enchanting vision. Surely when there are such colours and such forms, life is lovely, life is worth living?

(Luxemburg, 1946: 29)

It is no use for me to tell myself not to be silly, seeing that I am not responsible for all the hungry little larks in the world, and that I cannot shed tears over all the thrashed buffaloes in the world (they still come here day after day drawing the lorries laden with bags). Logic does not help in the matter, and it makes me ill to see suffering.

(ibid.: 47)

In his study of the oral life histories of former (male) PIRA prisoners, Feldman (1991) finds this 'entanglement' of the 'political' (violent) with the 'apolitical' (natural, animal)

renders these figures evocative allegories of arbitrary victimage. The entanglement of nature with the violent political life of men is a profound confirmation of boundary collapse and deterritorialization. In turn, domination of the animal body is a metonym for the politicization of the human body and its unfixing from all customary social references by political violence.

(ibid.: 82)

But is nature, as perhaps is being implied, really 'apolitical' or 'non-violent'? From the point of view of most people, this would be an absurd question, but the prison life writings by the likes of Luxemburg and Sands would suggest that this is not how they saw – or more to the point – experienced it. In Sands's story about the maggots, the arbitrariness of political or apolitical violence, whether in the human or natural world, isn't just about the designation of 'victimage', but simultaneously about benefit, even beneficence of the consequent suffering of victims (including, in this case, himself). While Sands finds himself in a truly horrendous situation – cold, alone, starving, in pain, covered in filth and infested with maggots – he is still able to see the possibilities of advantage for others (in the immediate situation, the birds, but potentially extending beyond the realm of nature) afforded by his own personal suffering. In other words, he is still able to exercise his agency, as martyr but also as caretaker and life-giver. While this could be seen as an effort to politicize nature, it also suggests the usefulness of nature as a way of simultaneously depoliticizing or apoliticizing the politically induced punishment and suffering of prisoners like Sands and Luxemburg, providing them with a sanctuary from their otherwise extreme political existences – or simply from extremism full stop.

In this same episode, Sands describes how the white maggots which he doesn't throw out of the window eventually turn into an inescapable nuisance in the form of a mass of black flies that line the walls and ceiling and cling to his face and naked body day and night, describing them matter-of-factly as a 'black cloud ascending in panic as I stirred ... a pest and very annoying' (1983: 52). This other discovery about the maggots is revealing in terms of the plurality of possible meanings with which he perceives his current situation. Most strikingly, the black-on-white symbolism of the flies on the white walls and ceiling of his cell and on his pallid skin at once replaces the white-on-white metaphor of effacement, voicelessness and erasure represented elsewhere in the book by reference to the snow (see Dearey, 2005) with the allegorical presence of the written word as visual record. Prisoners have for centuries if not millennia used the walls of their cells and any other materials to hand for the purposes of self-expression through writing. The construction of this alternative narrative – recouping from the institutional punishment regime the means for his own individual agency – hinges on the black-and-white metaphor for writing; while it is insufficient to completely alleviate his suffering as a result of this annoying and disgusting pestilence, the metaphor is nonetheless significant if only because it interrupts the course of the official narrative with respect to the intended objective of his incarceration – i.e. silence, retribution and incapacitation. Here again, he is taking the initiative for determining the discourse of his 'special category' punishment status into his own hands, and away from those who have been responsible for his internment. What is more, by leaking from the beyond the prison walls, these stories of suffering and life-giving agency provide a new and potent site for the storytelling and invention of political agency as a source of radicalization by others outside the prison and long after the events being narrated.

However, while his recovery of a mode of agency through writing and the re-establishment of authorial control may to some degree disrupt the development of the official or contiguous historical narrative of these events, at the same time it intensifies the underlying tension in this new narrative development. This can be seen in his reversal in the previous passage of the black-on-white image of writing to the white-on-black metaphor depicting the white maggots on the black tarmac in Sands' prison autobiography, which overturns the normative image of writing as stable and unambiguous, as in the image of black ink on a white page. The implied ambiguity of this symbolism can itself be read as a constitutive element of his alternative view of writing and of the world it portrays as seen in 'black and white' (in both the literal and Manichean sense) terms – a seminal trope, as we have seen, in the cultural discourses of radicalization and terrorism. In this context, the protean meanings of black-and-white images are not only multiple and diverse, but also intrinsically unstable and uncontrollable; this includes, of course, the problems of recording events by putting them in writing, and also the complications involved in perceiving the world in extreme and unyielding moral terms (again as in the cosmic Manichean struggle between good and evil troped as black and white), and by extension the polarizing ideologies of racism or sectarianism. The reversal of the black-on-white image to the white-on-black of the maggots on the tarmac also evokes challenges to the discourses of social realism, for instance in the form of the photographic image, the 'negative' from which reproductions of the original images of reality are produced on paper.

With regard to the white-on-black metaphor as a representation of writing, it is also notable that Sands' description of the maggots on the tarmac refers to their constant 'wriggling', their inability to stay still, in contrast to the normal permanent image of written script. This conveys the strong impression that, despite his cast-iron will and manly resolve to 'win' in this present battle with the state authorities, not even he is sure how these events will be recorded or interpreted historically for future generations, nor even what their true meaning in the current social context really is. Despite his apparent success in recovering a sense of agency from the power of writing, and the normative permanence of the written word, unlike Solzhenitsyn's (1963) anti-hero Shukov, Sands nonetheless remains anxious and uncertain as to how the events in which he finds himself at the centre will, in the end, be written in historical memory; neither is he entirely confident of the 'writtenness' of life itself, either as an individual life story or as an extension of Irish nationalism in the long history of Northern Ireland (Coogan, 1980). Like Shukov, however, Sands hides a deep if latent uncertainty about his capacity to personally survive the political events in which he is embroiled long enough to find out. Shukov severs ties to his family by refusing to request or receive parcels from them, Sands severed ties with his former wife and young son, and refused to even mention them in his (published) life writings. The limitations of his agency as an individual, embodied human being and also as an individual writer are all too evident in the face of an institutional regime resolved to enforce its authority to the limit, even to the point of death, as are the emotional burdens of maintaining marital and fatherly bonds in a situation in which this death will not be avoided. In contrast to O'Hearn's rather hagiographical representation of Sands as a strong and resolute, fully radicalized warrior against his British oppressors, his own sense of personal failure, impotency and loss, and the potential silence threatening his own suffering and that of his 'people' leave him open to a palpable if latent sense of doubt.

At the same time, however, there is also the possibility that his own personal resolve to resist this regime, and to write about it and its potential to disrupt the contiguous narrative history of these events in Northern Ireland, also affords an alternative view on the ambivalent nature of freedom and constraint in a supposedly civilized modern and global society. If this is the true nature of the 'struggle for freedom' in developed modern societies, the brutality and chaotic nature of its diverse and competing narrative realities poses a strong challenge to the ideological rhetoric of freedom and liberty as the unified and rational domain of patriotism and national pride. Bobby Sands' prison autobiography represents an alternative narrative construction of the life–national history, in its challenges to, and reconfiguration of, the conventional contiguous historical narrative on synchronic lines. These innovations by prison writers are notable as signal influences on modern contiguous narrative and its normative hold on the history of civilization and the nation state, as evidenced by the influence of prisoner writing on the development of canonical literature (Franklin, 1978; Carnochan, 1995; Morgan, 1999). At the same time, Sands' innovation and originality as a prison life writer has been attenuated by the reproduction of a distinctively phallocentric auto/biographical voice; this is evidenced by his reliance on some of the canonical auto/biographical devices (such as the rhetoric of substitution, and the language of sensory deprivation and death) to convey a potent self-image as essentially masculine, and how this echoes the egocentric and anti-altruistic social ethos of conventional autobiography (Dearey, 2007).

A consideration of some of the intertextual dimensions of this text, in terms of its use of metaphor and its specific relationship to other prison writings, suggests that *One Day in My Life* marks a significant political moment in historical narrative and life writing. By examining in detail Sands' treatment of metaphors like letters, writing, maggots and snow, an image emerges of a man who is in many ways exploring the limits of his agency and identity, not so much through political argumentation but through *writing about writing*. This concentration on writing itself is consistent with the theorizing of Julia Kristeva (1982; 1984), specifically her insistence on the function of writing within resistance cultures as an activity that is at once a means of survival – in a sense, writing (for) one's life – and a way of putting one's own life experiences on record in contestation of official versions. In his prison writings, Sands conveys his determination but also a strong sense of his deep, underlying anxiety concerning the meaning and substance of the whole enterprise at which he finds himself at the centre. As a committed but also in many respects reluctant participant in this extraordinary and violent political struggle, Sands's autobiography shows how much he relies on his agency as a writer – as much as a soldier – to maintain his sense of commitment to 'the cause' while in prison. His concentration on the metaphor of the *pen* reinforces this distinctively masculine autobiographical voice, as well as to its putative cultural resonances as described in Chapter 2. This is evidenced by, among other things, the fragility of his grasp upon narrative in this text, an underlying anxiety over internalizing a 'native' post-colonial subjectivity, the potency of the cultural mythic symbolism accorded to the figure of the dying young warrior in both English and Irish mythology, and his compulsion to (re)produce the exemplary and autonomous individual self perhaps in a manner perhaps most recognizable in canonical masculine autobiography of the English Romantic period (Dearey, 2005).

The impact of these life writings by political prisoners is in many ways contingent on the capacity of these texts to flow out of the pen and leak beyond the prison walls. However, these are words that suggest other modes of gender and sexuality than merely the pen as penis or the ultimate penile extension for the radicalized extremist in prison. Even within the PIRA movement during the period of the 1970s and 1980s, the visibility of and levels of public interest in political prisoners as shaped by gender is ambiguous, shifting, contradictory and complex. While the menstrual blood of the women protesters in Armagh Women's Prison was considered generally too much of an offence to norms of feminine decency for public consumption, the physical condition of the male prisoners was especially amenable to public visual display (e.g. through images painted on gable wall murals, photographs or drawings in the press or printed on leaflets, or in the dramatic tableau performed in public sometimes by (women) sympathizers or relatives). This is arguably due to the visual similarities between the 'Blanket men' and the images of the scourged Christ in the visual iconography of traditional Catholicism practiced in Northern Ireland. The Irish Republican women prisoners, by contrast, who were attired in filthy but ordinary modern clothes, presented less of an alluring and mythically evocative image (had they been confined together naked, the ensuing situation with respect to the public appetite for representations of their prison sufferings might have been different). We are accustomed to seeing the iconic Christ-like image of the Blanket men and hunger-strikers, but it is unlikely that the cultural link was anticipated by the Irish Republican leadership; more likely it was a matter of serendipity, and could have been easily foreclosed if the prison or state authorities had given sufficient thought to the consequences of denying the male prisoners the relatively simple request of being able to wear their own clothes (something all prisoners in UK prisons are now able to do by right). Such were the unreflective vagaries of the Northern Ireland Office under the leadership of the Thatcher Government.

This is not to say that Irish Republican women have never featured in the public eye, nor that they have never written about their experiences of political resistance and protest in prison. The focus of public attention in a successful hunger strike by Irish Republicans in British prisons who sought to be returned to serve their sentences in Ireland following a car-bombing campaign in London in March 1973 was overwhelmingly on the women, sisters Dolores and Marian Price. According to Coogan, this was in large part down to the power of the women's writings about their experiences in prison:

> Two of the men arrested with them, Hugh Feeney and Gerard Kelly [later members of the Stormont goverment], also went on hunger strike with the same demand and were also force fed for a period which lasted over 200 days, and were also ultimately successful. But somehow the men's struggle never captured the public's imagination in the same way that the girls did. Apart from the fact of being women, Dolores wrote poetry and Marian had a descriptive touch about her writings which made her letters on forced feeding particularly arresting.
>
> (Coogan, 1971: 410)

Notwithstanding the power of the Price sisters' prison life writings, it is also possible that part of their cultural potency as a source of public interest (in comparison to the men) was their implicit connection to the forced-feeding of the suffragettes in British prisons,[8] suggesting that the cultural memories of such events in prison are especially durable, even possibly beyond their delineated ideological boundaries. Despite the duration, endurance and suffering of the various forms of prisoner protests undertaken by Irish Republican prisoners throughout the twentieth century, however, it was the hunger strike that would epitomize the unique spirit of Irish nationalist resistance more than any other. As Coogan astutely observes, this is at least partially due to the 'strength of weakness' at the heart of this experience, what Vaclav Havel has called 'the power of the powerless' (1978):

> Of all the facets of the decade-long campaign, the most typically Irish was hunger-striking, that powerfully weak form of protest in which, as we have seen in other eras, the case of the participation seems to the public to get morally stronger as the victim gets physically weaker.
>
> (Coogan, 1971: 410)

In political terms, 'weakness' is a characteristic most conventionally associated with femininity, although, as political prisoner life writing and resistance cultures demonstrate, it is not the exclusive biological preserve of women, and neither is radicalization solely a dimension of essentialized masculinities. The slipperiness and instability of (often polarized and exaggerated) gender dualisms are particularly observable in the life writings and resistance cultures of political prisoners, both male and female. For many Irish Republican women prisoners, these experiences have proved to be enduringly difficult to discuss, let alone write down, due to the deeply entrenched cultural idealizations of women and the importance of cleanliness and purity in the public maintenance of their identities (Aretxaga, 1997). Along with the public distaste for realistic accounts of the Irish Republican women prisoners as departing too radically from idealized cultural norms of Irish femininity, this could at least partially explain the comparative (or perhaps apparent) dearth of autobiographical prison life writings by women prisoners in comparison to the large and ever-growing corpus of writing by the men. At the same time, as Mary Douglas argued, the linkage in the public imagination of female sexuality with dirt and the commodification of the female nude (e.g. as bather or odalisque) represents an established cultural mechanism for encountering and negotiating the body and its boundaries (Nead, 1992). The iconic figure of the female nude raises the transgressive and threatening spectre of female sexuality, disease and dirt (especially where working-class or other deviant women are concerned), at the same time as it resolves this threat through the aesthetic and ritual ordering of cleanliness and purification in a cathartic and beautiful image of the female nude. This lays the cultural foundations for the easy representation of radical working-class women such as Farrell in the biographical format, translating their life stories into commodified and fetishized ciphers of feral sexuality, and thereby sublimating any authentic political agency in the interests of appealing to a hegemonically male erotic fantasy.

The auto/biographical representation of male Irish Republican prisoners is somewhat different; a dichotomous gender difference persists, but even in moments of extreme or relative weakness, a distinctively male potency is regained. In the development of his iconic identity and subjectivity as a non-conforming political prisoner, Bobby Sands represents a unique compilation of distinctly feminine and masculine elements, generating his growing commitment to himself no longer as a revolutionary soldier, but as a resistance *writer*. In many ways, this contrasts to the compelling and enigmatic qualities of Sands's identity as an enduring symbol of 'the Troubles', which (as the recent critically acclaimed film of Sand's prison life by artist Steve McQueen indicates) has made him an enduring source of fear, dread and loathing, as well as nobility, sacrifice and fascination. Alongside the popular cultural depiction of the Islamist terrorist on the rampage, Sands has provided the paradigm image of the captive terrorist/political prisoner. It is notable that Sands is never depicted as engaged in the act of reading or writing in prison (Whalen, 2007), let alone singing, studying, partying or teaching (all of which he did a lot of in prison), and neither are the many terrorist prisoners depicted in popular cultural forms like television and films who often bear a striking resemblance to him. Instead he is almost always shown as the target (if not victim) of sadistic violence by those acting on behalf of the state, or alternatively the subject of his own masochistic self-immolation, occupying the prison cell space for the purpose of enduring extreme physical and emotional suffering in the quest for a united Ireland. According to O'Hearn (2006: 209), Sands' nascent identity as fully radicalized political agent finally begins to emerge when he rejects his role as participant in an ongoing series of prison protests designed to (re)gain various privileges within the prison and devotes himself primarily to the task of writing. Having already adopted the pen name Marcella, the name of his youngest sister, he reprises the appropriation of the female voice that has been elemental to masculine autobiographical and resistance cultures since the nineteenth century (Dearey, 2007), helping to attenuate any collateral loss of self endured as a result of his incarceration. These radical transformations constitute a pivotal stage on the path to his death on hunger strike and his subsequent emergence as an iconic figure of modern resistance movements.

With respect to the intertextual influences on a prisoner like Sands, we may well ask: what was he reading during his period of incarceration? Though there is evidence in his prison diaries that he had consumed the usual diet of Irish Republican resistance literature, his reflections on these texts are few and far between, in favour of a rather unexpected literary corpus. In his prison notebook, Sands records that he was particularly partial to, and influenced by, that most colonial of British writers, Rudyard Kipling. Sands can be associated with his determination to exploit the 'strength of weakness' by embracing both his compulsory and selective feminization as a starving political prisoner; Kipling's example must have shown him how he was nonetheless able to retain and build upon his personal and collective desire for revenge and the vanquishing of his enemy through warfare, if not through actual combat, then by means of the fundraising and propaganda linked to the written word. As Michael Holroyd points out, this is particularly notable in Kipling's life writings and his success in transforming the book into a battlefield, a site for engaging heroically with the enemy, and ripe for revenge in a kind of 'boys' own' world of fantasy and daring-do, albeit one charged by a spirit of vengeance and military aggression:

[T]he inspiration for much of Kipling's work was revenge, and the creation of a cleansing boys' world in which he imagined himself performing all the military and athletic deeds that poor eyesight and health had denied him ... His books turned the world inside out, making it a battlefield where the nameless enemy within is exposed and vanquished.

(Holroyd, 2002: 71)

Other commentators on Kipling's work similarly recognize the ambivalences and ambiguities inherent in it, and in relation to his influence on culture in general in terms of his endorsement of vulgarity, encouragement of hooligans and fundraising for soldiers' families in the nineteenth-century British empire:

> While Attridge covers a range of sources from canonical literature to more ephemeral material, he devotes a considerable amount of his study to the cultural influence of one man, Rudyard Kipling. Thus three of his seven chapters trace the impact of Kipling's *Barrack Room Ballads* (1892) from its ambivalent reception, through the contemporary anxiety that his 'vulgarity' gave a voice to the hooligan, to the popular poetry of the war that mimicked Kipling's balladry or reacted against it. Kipling's role in the war as fund-raiser (the sale of 'The Absent-Minded Beggar' [1899] raised huge sums for soldiers' families) and as propagandist with *The Friend in South Africa* is well known, but Attridge is good on the way in which the war polarized other contemporary writers. As he shows, those who wrote pro-war poetry included not only such obvious contenders as W. E. Henley, Alfred Austin, and Henry Newbolt, but even the elderly Algernon Charles Swinburne, whose 'The Transvaal' (1899) appeared in *The Times*. Opposed to the war stood Thomas Hardy, who preferred to portray the individual in conflict with the nation rather than as a synecdoche of it.
>
> (Daly, 2005: 306)

The 'anxiety of influence' (to adapt Harold Bloom's memorable phrase) in relation to the intertextual linking of Sands with Kipling is palpable, not least in the limitations this influence imposes upon the creative process (whether literary or political) as a result of the necessarily ambiguous and contaminating influence of one's role models. This formative influence is exacerbated by the similarities of the nineteenth-century world inhabited by Kipling that were in many ways analogous to Sands' twentieth-century world; both (albeit for different reasons – i.e. incarceration versus physical disability) found themselves physically unable to participate fully as conventional warriors in fighting what was not just a crisis of imperial hegemony, but moreover a crisis in masculinity, who nevertheless still hungered for engagement with the enemy and the opportunity for the heady experiences of victory and revenge. For many middle-class British men during the Victorian era, this crisis presented itself in their doubts about the certainty of belief in their own opinions and conscience, and consequently their moral authority to rule themselves, their families, or anyone else for that matter. As Tosh (1997) explains, this overwhelming sense of crisis converged on the rising levels of anxiety manifest in middle-class men's apparent inability to control 'their' women, children, or settle once and for all the 'Irish question' (coincidentally, this convergence of socio-political forces also fuelled the emergence of the feminist 'first wave' and the corpus of women political prisoner auto/biography that emanated from this period as a sub-genre of resistance literature in its own right (Joannou, 1995)). What is more, the growth of new philanthropic social legislation throughout the late nineteenth century felt to many men like a humiliating exercise in public emasculation, as did the surfacing in the public domain of male homosexuality – as epitomized by the infamous trial of Oscar Wilde, which again coincidentally resulted in the production of two of the most canonical of prisoner life-writing texts in *The Ballad of Reading Gaol* [1895] and *De Profundis* [1911], both in Wilde (1999). This challenge to the anti-altruistic[9] ethos that characterized the emergence of the distinctively modern culture of individualism in the early modern period (Gaukroger, 1995) was, to many privileged, middle-class British men of the colonial era, an invitation to view women, children, the poor and ethnic minorities as adversaries in a zero-sum game of political power, in which their gains were the men's losses.

> As Elaine Showalter [in her book *Sexual Anarchy*] has pointed out, the novels of masculine quest in the 1880s and 1890s, like those of Rudyard Kipling, Rider Haggard and Joseph Conrad, expressed acute fears of 'manly decline in the face of female power'.
>
> (Tosh, 1997: 54–5)

It would seem that Kipling's work provided a similar soothing effect for the incarcerated, weakened and effeminized Bobby Sands during a crisis in masculinity in Northern Ireland, though one that would simultaneously fuel ' ... a growth of irrational and paranoid responses in both society and culture' (ibid.: 55) well beyond the prison and the IRA.

Sands' mention of his fondness for the writings of Kipling in his prison journal (Sands, 1998: 223–4) is suggestive not only of the postmodern irony of simultaneously undermining and endorsing the values of the colonial power with respect to the crisis of masculinity shared by colonizers and revolutionaries, but also in the importation of preferred narrative forms of storytelling – notably the fairytale. Kipling's use of the fairytale form as a way of narrating the colonial crises of nationalism and gender is discernible in the use of this genre by Irish nationalists during the 1970s and 1980s; this is evidenced in what has become the popular commonplace of the 'a year and a day' fairytale temporality employed by men and some women Republican writers for their autobiographical accounts of their radicalization 'journey': e.g. Bobby Sands' *One Day in My Life* (1983) and Maria McGuire's *To Take Arms: A Year in the Provisional IRA* (1973). Coogan singles out this type of 'confessional' literature generated by now-dissident IRA members Maria McGuire and Peter McMullen, both of whom reported their disillusionment with the IRA as a result of callous disregard for the lives of innocent victims (1971: 433). This seems to be a sub-genre of resistance literature of the de-radicalization variety, troped along the lines of 'I was a radical [fill in the blank]' exposé (e.g. Morgan, 1989; Gartenstein-Ross, 2007; Husain, 2007; Begg, 2007; McGuire, 1971), in which the often young, idealistic ingénue is (temporarily) seduced into extreme or fanatical interpretations of their true beliefs by charismatic leaders, the promise of belonging and friends, the lure of power and/or money, the promise of sex, the ability to change society for the better, or all of the above, before eventually seeing through the façade of unjustified or self-serving violence, and reconnecting to the original values of the core authentic self.

This essentialist and recursive tropology of the life classically symbolized in a one-day narrative has been expertly deconstructed by Paul de Man in his essay 'Autobiography as De-facement' (de Man, 1984). This trope has become thoroughly integrated within the canon of prisoner writing, most notably in Solzhenitsyn's classic *One Day in the Life of Ivan Denisovich* (1963), and applied in an analogously canonical way, in the manner of Wordsworthian life writing, in Sands' prison life writing. This tropology offers the classical masculine autobiographical subject an established and conventional way of restoring a sense of agency to the sovereign self, through for instance the incorporation of diegetic narratives recounting the suffering (mainly) of others, and using this as a method of accumulating political capital enacting moral entrepreneurship and reinforcing individual legitimacy at a time of crisis (Dearey, 2007).

What is important for women political prison life writers is not so much the restoration of the sovereign self through the auto/biographical act, but rather the breaking of silence, whereby the mimetic function of autobiographical writing in the act of *telling* as a decidedly rebellious act especially for a woman, as exemplified by Margaretta D'Arcy's determination to *Tell Them Everything* and Maria McGuire's refusal to be silenced even under threat of death:

> For these reasons, I decided to come to Britain to tell what I knew about the way the Provisionals have been conducting their campaign. I know that many members of the Provisional movement consider me a traitor. But for me the ultimate betrayal would be to remain silent.
>
> (McGuire, 1973: 10)

This represents an interesting reversal of the more masculine dictate issued in the IRA recruit's manual *The Green Book*, which is adamant about the value to the cause of not being seen or heard, and certainly not 'telling':

> The most important thing is security, that means you:
> DON'T TALK IN PUBLIC PLACES:
> YOU DON'T TELL YOUR FAMILY, FRIENDS, GIRL-FRIENDS OR WORKMATES THAT YOU ARE A MEMBER OF THE I.R.A. DON'T EXPRESS VIEWS ABOUT MILITARY MATTERS, IN

OTHER WORDS YOU SAY NOTHING to any person. Don't be seen in public marches, demonstrations or protests. Don't be seen in the company of known Republicans, don't frequent known Republican houses. Your prime duty is to remain unknown to the enemy forces and the public at large.

(in Coogan, 1971: 545)

This idealization of radical subjectivity as unyieldingly covert and invisible (exemplified in the IRA by the silence of Bobby Sands while under interrogation at the Castlereagh Detention Centre, as told by O'Hearn, 2006) to D'Arcy's and McGuire's radical acts of disclosure – and other women prisoners' refusal to (fully) disclose – are instructive. As the women's writings urgently insist, they are not and do not experience their incarceration like the fairytale princesses held in the highest tower, waiting for their handsome princes to come to their rescue. Rather, they see themselves as women and as political agents, with their own set of distinctive motives and objectives, which may or may not always be in harmony with those of the male political prisoners or leadership of resistance organizations. Nevertheless, as Angela Davis (1990) acknowledges, the compulsion to write an autobiography about one's time in prison is not undertaken lightly; neither is it an especially welcome prospect but more akin to a stoic duty. That these women often obliquely reference the 'year and a day' temporality of the fairy tale is suggestive of the feminist concentration on the fairy-tale narrative as a focus of public debates about gender during the 1970s (Haase, 2004). Notwithstanding this compulsion to 'tell', the cultural machinery of the modern capitalist state still retains powerful mechanisms for silencing, and/or perverting and commodifying, the radicalization rationales and imagery of radical women.

Conclusion

Radicalization is a gendered phenomenon. Men and women tend to become and experience their radicalization against and according to dominant and dichotomous gender norms in a diverse yet patterned variety of ways. These dualistic and essentialist norms are often exaggerated within extremist subcultures, and also form the cultural basis within which the radicalization of men and women is either romanticized or sexualized (respectively) in popular cultural forms, such as film, music and television. This typically results in the neutralization of (radical) women's political agency, and their further exploitation and manipulation within a succession of linked patriarchal social orders, that reinforces colonial and conflict-oriented political philosophies of modernity based on progress, oppression, exploitation and assimilation; it also glosses radical subcultures as potent imaginary sites for the compulsive playing-out of often violent and sadomasochistic sexual fantasies of power and the source of commodification, leisure and consumption. On a more micro level, the life writings of political prisoners indicate that sex and sexuality are also key aspects of their own stories about how they became (and in some cases ceased to be) radicalized. Many men and women alike would seem to have been attracted or recruited because of existing sexual or intimate relationships, or the promise of emancipation from restrictive sexual mores and/or the increased availability and variety of sex. They subsequently often become disillusioned with or leave these groups because of the breakdown of these relationships, or dissatisfaction with the manner of social interaction and intimate bonding with respect to sexual expectations (often dictated by the male-dominated leadership).

In addition, the body – notably the suffering body of the political prisoner – represents a potent symbolic weapon in the resistance 'struggle' by the individual and his/her collective against society and/or the state. In this context, as these stories show, the general trends are again highly gendered. For male political prisoners, the fluidity and malleability of gender as a social construction (as opposed to biologically or essentialist determination of physical anatomy) functions as a powerful source of creativity, innovation and recovery of power among the most fully radicalized of political actors, especially in prison. Though the men import into the prison environment dichotomous and exaggerated versions of gender identity, they are able to interpret these in fluid and unusual ways as a site for eliding the power and surveillance regimes of the penal system. This enables them to 'read' their protest actions into a variety of possible mythical–religious narratives and thereby to gain a public platform for their 'hidden' sacrifice and suffering. For women political prisoners (especially in Northern Ireland, but also elsewhere), anatomy is definitely destiny: essentialist and narrowly construed norms of femininity tend to limit or occlude their protest actions, divesting them of symbolic meaning in the public sphere due to implicit violations to social norms of taste and decency. These reflections on gender, sexuality and the body suggest that, at the level of public policy-making, there is currently too little awareness of the role of these variables on the emergence of radicalization *and* (as opposed to 'in') prison, and hence not enough is being made in counterterrorism strategy of links to governmental departments with responsibility for equality in the areas of sexuality, gender and race/ethnicity.

It is through the production and dissemination of these life writings within groups and internationally that resistance cultures develop and flourish, using these iconic life stories to provide a sense of immediacy and to 'humanize history' in a way that dry doctrinal or philosophical tracts never can. These texts serve a strong functional and ideological role in their ability to converge shifting, complex and contradictory socio-cultural aspects relating to a great diversity of identity and social change, and to sometimes even reverse hegemonic social discourses of terror and punishment in order to communicate a group's message in a powerful way that is relatively simple and easy to understand in a culture well acquainted with the auto/biographical text and gender norms. By including in these texts the telling of sexual stories, radicalized political prisoners enhance the readability and increase the public demand for these sorts of stories, and their influence is felt well beyond extremist politics, as they tap into and advance ways of articulating and discussing 'intimate citizenship'. As will be investigated in the next chapters, many of these stories and experiences generated from prison actually originate in childhood and family life, or conform to the cultural construction and epistemologies of the child and the family as an analogous site for resistance and social control. In this respect, there is an urgent need to recognize and incorporate policy-making in the areas of schools, families and children as well as race, sexual and gender equality into counter-terrorism and national security strategies.

Chapter 4

'I felt myself turning cold like the bottle of Coke'

Children, childhood and 'the child' in political prisoner life writings

A friend of an enemy is an enemy. Childish but true.

(Abbott, 1982: 193)

The pivotal role of emotional ties and the collective bonds of identity among friends (i.e. young Muslim men in Sageman, 2004) and sexual intimates (in the case of women, e.g. Morgan, 1989; Dworkin, 2000) have featured in the research literature on radicalization and have further developed through the lens of political prisoner life writing in the previous chapter. What emerged from the micro-analysis of these life stories was the prominence of sex, sexuality, the body and gender difference in radical subcultures, and their attendant auto/biographical representative forms, as well as in the broader cultural narratives in general about the nature of the terrorist threat, and how these enable us to trace the ways into – and reasons for wanting to get out of – such radical groups. A key factor in the analysis of the life stories written by and about radical women was – in contrast to the mysterious and enigmatic figure of the female terrorist – the all too familiar image of the woman trapped in an institutional hierarchy of exploitative and often violent relationships in which her desire to actively contribute to socio-political change is readily sublimated to the needs of male-dominated subgroups and thus neutralized, ultimately becoming the object of commodity exchange in capitalist popular culture (in the form of films, novels, television drama, etc. in which the narrative denouement is more often than not the violent killing of these women). Telling stories about sex and sexuality is a crucial part of the auto/biographical representations of what life in a radical group is like for both women and men, and why they were attracted to join these groups and make these sorts of life choices in the first place, and subsequently to devise their modes of action in order to achieve their political aims. But, even in an age obsessed with sex and the production and consumption of sexual stories (Weeks, [1986] 2003; Plummer, 1995), is sex really that important as a variable in the radicalization process, or do these auto/biographies – as perhaps unwittingly implies in Jane Alpert's (1981) introductory remarks – simply focus on this area of radical subcultures as a way of deflecting individual culpability for their violent actions or simply making their stories more entertaining and enticing for the reading public, enabling them to raise their public profiles and sell more books?

One way to address this question is to examine another key element closely related to the influence of intimacy via gender, sexuality and the body on radicalization and radical subcultures: the role of children, childhood and family relationships in the radicalization narratives of political actors in their prison life writings. Each is closely related to the study of intimacy and the private sphere, and as such it is justified to investigate whether or not they both feature as elemental influences on radicalization in these life writings. If they do, does this influence manifest itself in different or similar ways? The political relevance of children, childhood and family relationships have until recently remained severely underestimated, or at least woefully under-researched, not least due to substantial difficulties arising from concerns over access and research ethics, in addition to the general theoretical and methodological estrangement of terrorism and security studies from these areas classically identified with the private sphere linked to femininity (which, as noted previously, tend to lie outside the parameters of the rationalized nation state). However, this does not mean that the family and the private sphere have not featured as the object of concern about national security. It has been argued that, for example, the intergenerational transmission of political militancy via the family (typically through the dynastic practices of intermarriage between members of Irish Republican families) was key to the development of radicalization and the entrenchment nationalist mythologies and subcultures among Republicans in the interwar years (White, 1993). While such dynastic practices relating to the transmission of radicalization subcultures and attendant values through marriage are still in evidence among terrorist groups to this day (e.g. Jamaah Islamiyah (Ismail, 2008)), even where radicalization in Northern Ireland diverges from this practice after the Second World War, the influence of the family is still in evidence. The more specific emotional qualities of obligation and identity bonds that shape filial relationships mainly between young men have been noted in the recent research literature, and highlight the role of affective experience modelled on the sibling relationships of 'brotherhood' (and, where appropriate, 'sisterhood'), as well as the metaphorical representation in nationalist cultural discourses of the state in the form of 'mother' or 'fatherland' (Valente, 1994).

Notwithstanding their concentration on interpersonal violence carried out by men upon women and children in the private sphere, as noted in the previous chapter, feminists have for some considerable time been cognizant of the political ramifications of violence which are fundamentally linked to the political hierarchy and power regimes of the domestic space. The contemporary rhetoric of political violence among 'jihadists' to pursue a campaign of violence 'at home' is in itself highly suggestive, reiterating the signal importance of the domestic geopolitical space as the preferred arena for the power struggle, not least as evidenced by the available data on the 'top-down' recruitment strategies of Islamist groups in constructing 'shadowy' networks (Bush, 2002) founded on a core base of family members (Ismail, 2008).

While 'the family' is a consistently prominent feature of any politically conservative agenda, at the same time families are foundational to what Marty and Appleby (1993: 3) term the 'defiant society'. Ironically, both conservative and revolutionary interpretations of the family share identical roots in the common conviction, prominent in the twentieth century, ' ... that control of the moral and spiritual formation of children and young adults is the certain path to the eventual transformation of society as a whole, including the state' (ibid.: 3). Nevertheless, the general tendency is to overlook or derogate the family to at best a kind of secondary status in the study of discrete social phenomena presented as 'social facts' and (largely) subjected to empirical analysis has been a feature of social scientific research virtually since its inception:

> No doubt one of the reasons why little of the exegetical and critical literature concerns itself with [Durkheim's] conception of the relations between the sexes is a consequence of the fact that these three basic subjects, 'men', 'women' and 'children', are not constituted as objects in their own right but appear as one of a series of primary divisions against which are projected the more obviously constructed foreground topics. It is 'law', 'suicide', 'religion' etc., which organize commentaries in relation to problems of moral integration and social density. It may be seen that the general avoidance of his ideas on this subject— so complete incidentally that neither of two recent presentations, Giddens (1978) and Thompson (1982) pays any attention to them at all ...
>
> (Gane, 1993: 24)

Gane levels the same charges of neglect of the family and childhood in the study of sexuality and conjugal relationships as key factors shaping the social and material formation of moral integration, social density and culturally specific forms of anomie (citing Tiryakian's analysis of late modern culture, 'sexual anomie' is seen as being especially pertinent as a key motivating factor determining all three (Gane, 1993: 24–5)).[1] There are a number of important points being made here. First, it is important to reiterate that families, children and childhood are closely proximate, but yet utterly distinct in conceptual terms, making the analysis of radicalization viewed through this prism less than a simple matter. Second, and of equal import, is the issue of social integration, a concept that Durkheim considered especially important as a way of gauging the normality or pathology of the state of social cohesion and/or functionality. Indeed, we observe that the European Parliament has been *inter alia* drawn to the issue of integration with respect to the radicalization of foreign nationals in member states: 'In the majority of cases, third-country nationals have inte-grated well within the Member States of the EU. However, if integration fails it can provide fertile ground for violent radicalization to develop' (Communica-tion from the Commission to the European Parliament and the Council, 2005: section 2.4). While it is unclear if such references to 'third-country nationals' refers to them as individuals, groups, or both, the EU focus on interfaith and cultural dialogue in the integration of new immigrants/immigrant populations strongly suggests that the family and family practices are under scrutiny.[2]

There is growing evidence that experts and practitioners in terrorism and security studies are increasingly acknowledging the relevance of the family in terms of its emotional and relational bonds in the construction of terror net-works and membership recruitment; yet they lack the theoretical and metho-dological framework through which to conceptualize 'the family' or indeed childhood and/or 'the child' as the potential source of political violence or other forms of seditious action or demands for social change as resistance to governmental hegemony. It is beyond the parameters of this study to provide anything like a comprehensive review of such theoretical and methodological approaches to childhood and family studies, though some of this research literature informs the theory, and analyses are included in this chapter. What I would say from the outset is that the incorporation of children, childhood and the family into the study of radicalization is unlikely to simplify, at least in the short term, what is already an extremely complex topic. This is due in no small part to the hugely diverse and adaptable nature of what we think of as 'the child' and 'the family', and how historically diverse these notions have been and are becoming, even if we limit ourselves to the modern era. At the same time, there is little realistic prospect of increasing the knowledge base and thus enhancing counter-terrorism policy with respect to the acknowl-edged areas of community cohesion and social integration in terms of young people and families, without substantial efforts to incorporate these meth-odologies and epistemologies into existing frameworks. Thus in this chapter, I will delve into a wide range of political prisoner life writings to explore the extremely diverse and innovative resistance strategies developed by children or remembered childhoods, and how these stories have given rise to alternative discourses or radicalization as the basis of identity politics and social change.

Children and childhood in politics and the law

In her autobiography *Growing Up Underground* (1981), political radical and former terrorist bomber Jane Alpert begins the book with the following statement:

> The commitment I made that night led me eventually, through a cir-cuitous route, to forms of protest more dramatic than picket lines. In November 1969, after I had helped to set off bombs at eight

government and corporate buildings in New York, I was arrested, pleaded guilty, and went underground, where I spent more than four years. I still don't understand all the forces that drew me into the conspiracy or the underground—any more than I understand exactly why I raised my hand at that CAC meeting. But I am certain that politics was only one part of what inspired me. While I am proud to have moved decisively against the Vietnam War, I also know that my motivations stemmed as much from a longing for acceptance as from a passion to rebel, as much from the kinds of relationships I formed in childhood as from my outrage at the United States government. How I came to believe and act as I did—and later, in a spirit of renunciation, to surrender and go to prison—is the core of this autobiography.

(Alpert, 1981: 17–18)

She ends her memoir with this overall assessment of her life experiences in terms of what led her to engage in the violent protests and what eventually led her to renunciate these activities:

Certainly personal rage and pain, more than politics, had led me to break violently with my parents in adolescence, to bomb buildings, and later to reject the left with all the hostility I could muster. In the past few years I had gained some inner peace and self-control. My surrender [to the FBI] had helped. So had writing the book and professional counseling, my family's steadfastness and Ed's [her new partner] undemanding love.

(ibid.: 372)

In between, Alpert provides sometimes a great deal of detail with respect to the specific qualities and consequential influences of the emotions passions and intimate friendship, family and sexual relationships that she later considered to have been key factors leading her to act as she did. For now the focus of attention is on the quality and influence of the relationships and indeed emotions and other ways of knowing and sources of meaning formed in childhood singled out by Alpert that I would like to discuss. As we will see, life writers like Alpert, Thai Jones (2004) and Ed Husain (2007) tend to assign much of the 'causal' influence of childhood on the adolescent urge to rebel against parental and other institutional forms of authority; however, other examples of life writing display some of the more nuanced and ambivalent qualities of childhood and children's agency on contemporary politics more generally.

Children's roles in politics and international relations has historically been a much neglected topic, but the 'politics of childhood' increasingly is being recognized as an important and complex aspect of global politics, extending to all areas of conflict and peacemaking. Recently, scholarly research on the cultural articulation of contemporary problems concerning the new threats to global security shows promising signs that political scientists are taking the experiences and lifeworlds of the child and/or the culture of childhood seriously as significant sites for exploring how political conflicts and crises are understood, narrated and interpreted (in Paul Ricœur's phrase, 'brought to language'). This trend is exemplified by the political scientist Stuart Croft's deconstruction of children's films like *The Incredibles* in his book *Culture, Crisis and America's War on Terror* (2006). In the context of more conventional political science theory, Professor of International Relations Alison Watson (2006) has noted that children play an active and directly relevant part in the modern geopolitical landscape, the available evidence demonstrating that millions of children worldwide are deeply involved in a range of diverse, and sometimes dangerous or extreme, political activity: children labour, they fight, they seek refuge, they participate in political debate, they consume, and above all they *resist*. What we see from the stories recorded in political prisoner life writings about conflict and politics is that children retain and take the memories and experiences of childhood, if not the actual resistance strategies, with them into adulthood, often drawing strength from them in their later resistance efforts or identifying them as seminal moments in their personal radicalization narratives constructed retrospectively in adulthood. This covers a range of theoretical–psychological mappings of childhood experience, from the sort of quasi-psychoanalytic uncovering of the distinctive quality of parent–child relationships as the source of personal desire and later resistance and self-emergence identified by radicals like Jane Alpert (1981), to more quotidian descriptions of the discrete events of everyday interaction with strangers cited by the black revolutionary James Forman (1985). These stories are evidenced by a number of examples of political prisoner life writings, a selection of which will be further examined over the course of this chapter.

Increasingly, international relations experts who study the dynamics of conflict and peacemaking are becoming aware of the important role of children's storytelling about their experiences of conflict (whether acquired first, second or third-hand, or as remembered stories from childhoods long past) and how these shared narratives can facilitate possible futures of continued violence or transformative peace (McEvoy-Levy, 2006). The undeniable reality is that many children throughout the world endure horrendous and systemic exploitation, oppression and abuse. As Watson (2006) argues, this reality itself constitutes a driving force behind much of the foundational discourse of universal human rights as a way of tackling this huge injustice. Yet despite what some may regard as international paternalistic concern for children and their welfare, and the failures to adequately protect children and other vulnerable people from the hazards of modern conflict, the view is emerging that children are also active agents within the global political environment, and are adept in developing strategies of dealing with and reacting to these often pressing and sometimes extreme situations in which they find themselves.

Nevertheless, idealizations of the presumed innocence and purity of child-hood and the need for (adult-run) governments to control and protect the public imaginary space of childhood as a prophylactic for ensuring nationalist visions of the future are fundamental to the modern ideologies of the nation state (Corsaro, 2005; Brocklehurst, 2006) – and indeed its enemies[3] – endure. Brocklehurst (2006) argues that cultural conceptions of childhood ' … vary with the priorities of society and providers of security' (2006: 171), covering a wide spectrum from passive innocent to ruthless killer, rendering children as potent symbols in discourses of nationalism and the security of the nation state. These increasingly extremist and/or violent nationalist discourses often turn on rhetorical arguments for children to cease from or engage in violent military action,[4] or indeed to be (or not, as the case may be) the legitimate targets of terrorist violence (bin Laden, 2005). This general trend can be con-strued as an instance of what McNamee *et al.*, (2005) term the 'double status' of childhood, whereby children are seen as both 'subject' (*vis-à-vis* the notion of agent, i.e. the actively feeling, knowing, desiring category of personhood) and 'object' (more often the object of parental and/or state manipulation, fear, protection and control, but otherwise an empty designator of civil status or a cipher of the emergent political rhetoric of conflict). 'By fulfilling the roles both of the unquestioning combatant and of the innocent, children serve as tools of violence and a means of testing the waters of reconciliation' (Durana, 2008: 116). In practice, this fundamental dualism serves to occlude both the recognition of the agency and meeting of the needs of children by its tendency to deny the child as needing and acting 'subject' in favour of children as incomplete, unstable 'object' of parental and/or state institutional control. It is this tendency that forms the basis of the politics of nationhood, whereby childhood, its objectification and its control is ideologically manifest in the *law* as a way of nominally dealing with each side of the dialogic of childhood, while only really dealing with the object status of children at the expense of their subjective agency and development (McNamee *et al.*, 2005). What is more, this legalistic ideology also creates a cleavage between children and adults – and we may add a cleavage between adults from their own child-hoods – which encourages the proliferation of discourses of conflict and crisis converging around the child:

> By the same token, and using exactly the same mechanisms [e.g. the enshrined 'incompetence' of children according to their 'minor' status in relation to adults, state institutions and the law], the law also therefore acts to reinforce the boundaries between adulthood and childhood.
>
> (ibid.: 234)

The conceptualization of 'the child' in the eyes of the state serves as an instrument of reification for childhood and children, enshrining the power-lessness and insubstantiality of the child in the law; unwittingly this makes children and childhood the source of considerable resistance and a potential site of contestation of power and control by virtue of its ephemeral qualities, mystery and invisibility to the state. In many respects, the empty and enigmatic qualities conventionally designating the child in politics and the law reflects the dualistic conceptualization of the public/private sphere which has tended to treat women in a similar manner. As with women (and other 'deviants'), this extends to the places and spaces children typically inhabit, particularly the family and school.

Should the problem of violent radicalization be tackled in school?

It is not just through the objectivizing political ideology of the law that the nation state filters and represents images of the child. As I write, children and families are also finding themselves at the forefront of UK Government policy-making as the dual locus for fighting its enemies by tackling violent extremism (particularly that of an 'Islamist' stripe) via their families, communities and schools:

> Our goal must be to empower young people to come together, with their families and the wider community, to expose violent extremists and reject cruelty and violence in whatever form it takes. Schools can make an important contribution, being a focal point for local communities and helping to build mutual respect and understanding.
> (Department for Children, Schools and Families [UK], 2008a: 3)

The targeting of children and families as sites for dealing with the potential hazards they represent in their daily practices and cultural forms – whether as a conduit for the intergenerational (or intragenerational) transmission of radicalization or resistance, or as a domain for disseminating preventative programmes or facilitating 'intelligence gathering', or 'exposure' exercises via the family (along with school) – means that they have come very much onto the radar in the 'war on terror'. Is this focus on children and families justified by the evidence, and will the policy strategies on which they are based, such as the one developed by the Department of Children, Schools and Families and other governmental bodies actually work as preventative interventions by the state, or are they more likely to make the problem of radicalization worse?

In recent years, a number of elements of youth culture, such as gangs, popular music, games, videos, kinship and filial relationships, religious practices, masculinities, violence, etc. have been highlighted as points of concern in the research literature on violent extremism (e.g. RAND, 2007). While governmental agencies have honed in on 'youth' as a particular object of concern with respect to the causes of violent radicalization, there is also evidence that it is seen as part of a potential long-term solution:

Programmes targeted at youngsters in their most formative years and at an age in which they are most vulnerable to fall prey to violently radical ideas, can have very fruitful outcomes. The promotion of cultural diversity and tolerance can help to stem the development of violently radical mind-sets ... The 'Youth' programme therefore contributes towards preventing violent behaviour from taking root in young people.

(Communication from the Commission to the European Parliament and the Council, 2005, Section 2.3)

But, while the European Commission seems to favour the 'carrot' approach to preventing the inculcation of violent extremism and radical ideas in young people by actively encouraging the values of diversity and tolerance, the 'stick' is never far away. These programmes are not only limited to ordinary participation in civic life, but can also extend into the areas of policing and law enforcement: 'Schemes should be considered which involve the police and law enforcement authorities engaging more at the local level with youth' (ibid., Section 2.5).

How effective such policy initiatives are in preventing violent extremism or countering terrorism, or how unifying or empowering they are from the point of view of children and families in the everyday practices of their public and private lives, is an important question, and one that will be borne in mind throughout this chapter. While there is a certain logic to targeting such cultural *loci* in the fight against radicalization and terrorism, and while peaceful prevention is infinitely preferably to bellicose cure, at the same time, there is something discomforting in the notion of subjecting children and families to yet more surveillance and control in the interests of (at best) forestalling public anxiety over terrorist violence, or in the worst-case scenario actually fuelling radicalization by making young people feel even more under suspicion, and hence even more susceptible to alienation. The increased 'responsibilisation'[5] (Garland, 2001) of children and families in largely Muslim and/ or immigrant communities for the task of dealing with the problem of radicalization and extremism is of questionable value, not least because of its tendency to leave unaddressed (or under-addressed): the socio-economic inequalities that tend to strongly affect these communities, and which foster anger and discontent; the vulnerability of family members to violence and abuse in the private and/or domestic sphere (Heidensohn, 2002); the claimed propensity of British children to already suffer from demonization or criminalization (UNCRC, 2008), and to already suffer comparatively low levels of happiness and well-being in comparison to other children internationally (Unicef, 2007). In light of these findings about the state of childhood and family life in (immigrant) communities in Britain, there is as yet insufficient evidence to support the claim that making these families, children and their communities who are already living under such strains responsible in this way will alleviate the pressures towards radicalization or empower them to feel resilient to withstand them. If anything, the prima facie argument to the contrary would seem to be founded on firmer ground.

Childhood, radicalization and schooling in political prisoner life writing

Education, especially higher education, has featured in recent research on radicalization as a particular source of concern (e.g. Abuza, 2006; Sageman, 2004; RAND, 2007). Certainly with respect to the external social shaping of childhood in modern 'developed' societies, school – along with the family – is a major influence on the social construction of childhood and the real-life experiences of being a child. Though it not the case for all radicalization narratives contained in political prisoner life writings, there are a great many examples in the genre in which childhood experiences of school life and family relationships are either indicators of or influences upon the radicalized future to come. For instance, whereas Ed Husain (2007) and Malcolm X (1965) credit their experiences of racism from their teachers as the initial source of their latent radicalization and eventual resistance, for others writers like Patty Hearst (1988), childhood stories about rebelling against teachers (by in her case telling a nun teacher at her Catholic convent school to 'Go to Hell') function more as a trope foreshadowing as opposed to causing their adult experiences of radicalization.

As Sue Middleton (1987) points out, biographical research on the political impact of schooling indicates that schools are not just the places where the abstract liberal ideologies of emancipation, or (alternatively) the Marxist reproduction of class difference are played out by (active) staff upon their (passive) pupils; for women in particular, being involved in education can have a reciprocal and politically radicalizing effect on educators as well as students. This raises doubts about the implied presumption of school as a place where power or agency flows from the top down, i.e. from staff to the students, in the form of ideological moulding or social control. Certainly the Department for Children, Schools and Families (CSF) report (2008) does not countenance the possibility identified by Middleton that teachers may in actuality be radicalized by the real-life experiences of learning as a result of the reciprocal process of dialogue or exchange of ideas with pupils and their parents in an open-ended and non-hierarchical educational forum. The alternative realities of an institutional educational environment built on surveillance and hierarchical control represented by the CSF model will not be lost on the types of families or their children who are seen to adhere to the sorts of 'extremist' or 'radical' views in question. An elemental part of this worldview by those families who are extremist is commonly to claim a sense of victimization by, and adversarial stance against, the institutions of western(ized) governments from the outset, including state institutions such as schools. Such a preventive strategy delivered through schools-based initiatives could thus potentially make an already fraught situation even worse for some British children and their families, and thereby possibly make young people even more vulnerable or susceptible to radicalization. For some families, such a strategy will not so much represent a remedy to a potential and generic threat, but may instead be perceived as an extension of a pernicious policy-making logic on the part of the state which views them and their children as passively vulnerable to anyone pedalling extremism, or alternatively portrays them as unwilling to live up to their duties as responsible citizens by actively contesting or reporting such encounters at every turn, thereby offering them the unattractive choice of being seen either as deviants or collaborators.

In light of recent scholarship on the decline of the 'traditional' family, it is arguable that the influence of factors like childhood and schooling are becoming increasingly significant in the construction of social discourses about security and risk. According to Goddard (2005), the political importance and expediency of children and childhood in a globalized world have risen in inverse relation to the decline of traditional adult social ties such as marriage and the extended family, and the sense of 'security' they offer, making children into both the rationale behind and the curative for increasingly urgent experiences of adult 'insecurity':

> Children have become more important, some argue, because adult ties have become more fragile (Jenks, 1996). For example, Hutchinson and Charlesworth (2000: 577) have noted, with respect to the United States, that 'there has been a recent sharp rise in the sentimental and emotional value of children, as marital ties have weakened and become less significant in the lives of many adults'. As Block reminded us ... *it is insecurity in a context of uncertainty that often drives an increased interest in children.* If we look at the UK case, we can see that the post-1997 Labour Governments have been much more interventionist on child welfare policy than their predecessors (Little, Axford and Morpeth, 2003; Fawcett, Featherstone and Goddard, 2004).
>
> (Goddard, 2005: 269, emphasis added)

In short, with respect to international politics and intranational conflict, families, children and childhood 'matter' a great deal – or at least are seen to do so by the state – especially during times of political insecurity, and in light of the decline of traditional societal structures such as marriage, the extended family and religion. However, while ' ... a variety of global pressures have led to increased interest in children in recent years ... this has not necessarily led to an increased interest in their own voices and priorities' (ibid.: 270). Perhaps it is time for policy-makers to develop a more reflexively aware attitude towards past tendencies to target children in this way, and develop more authentically participative and empowering models for the integration of children as valued members of the civil society, not least by listening to them and taking their concerns seriously, rather than regarding them as the objects of moral panics or institutions of social control, such as schools.

Voicing childhood: sociological views of 'the child'

The concept of 'voice' is a frequently articulated challenge to research on or about children. Some experts in the area of government policy-making stress the difference between the experiences of children and the experiences of childhood *as remembered or reconstituted by adults* (whether by other adults or later by the grown-up child him/herself), and the consequences of these different perspectives on the authenticity of the 'voices' of children in policy-making – an important consideration in the present study where what are usually presented in auto/biographical form are recollections as opposed to contemporaneous representations of childhood:

> There is a clear logic, in a context in which the experience childhood is changing rapidly, in basing policy responses at least partly on the views of children rather than on the potentially misleading perspectives and out-of-date memories and experiences of adults. Some of the language of the Agenda for Children suggests that the concerns of the sociology of childhood with the subjectivity of children is moving beyond academia and into the decision-making realm of policy-makers. Indeed, the influence of such perspectives is explicitly acknowledged by the authors. It is fortunate that in this context the authors have both academic and policy interests; in most such studies, the links between ideas and policy are insufficiently acknowledged and analyzed.
>
> (ibid.: 266)

But is this view of the presumed qualitatively significant differences between past and present childhood conceptually consistent with the constructivist stance in the sociology of childhood, which seeks in every instance to distance itself from any essentialized notion of childhood, children or 'the child'? Does the insistence on representations of childhood experienced by the individual and contemporaneous child reify the present and deny the manifold experiences of childhood, notably as manifest but also continually emanating from both individual and collective memory over time?

In his landmark book *The Sociology of Childhood* (2005), the renowned sociologist of childhood William A. Corsaro recounts the demise of theoretical approaches that rely on the division between the child and adult in favour, in the first instance, of constructivist and interpretive perspectives that ' ... argue that children and adults alike are active participants in the social construction of childhood and in the interpretive reproduction of their shared culture. In contrast, traditional theories view children as "consumers" of the culture established by adults' (Corsaro, 2005: 7). These theoretical approaches contrast with the traditional 'deterministic' theories of child socialization, whereby society appropriates and actively shapes (or more actively seeks to disempower or control) the passive and docile object known as 'the child'. The constructivist models of childhood view the child as an active agent in the dialogical process of their own (re)construction of the world, in which both they themselves and their cultures are continually re-formed and reconstituted in an ongoing process that resists finality or overdetermination. The various aspects of childhood or 'the child' are thus fundamentally undetermined, open and available to interpretation, or are otherwise continually under negotiation or in process (Corsaro, 2005: 7). Even so, Corsaro cautions, constructivist accounts have their limitations. One is the virtually myopic focus on individual (normally psychological) development of 'the child' or childhood as a developmental life stage 'passed through' on the way to adulthood: 'Constructivism offers an active but somewhat lonely view of children ... Another limitation of constructivist developmental psychology is the overwhelming concern with the endpoint of development, or the child's movement from immaturity to adult competence' (Corsaro, 2005: 16)

As a more viable alternative, Corsaro suggests the 'childhood as a structural form', a view associated with the work of Jens Qvortrup, who

> further develops the notion of viewing childhood as a structural form by contrasting it with perspectives that focus on childhood only as a period of life. He places these perspectives in three general categories. The first is the typical psychological view, which is individual and personality oriented. In this view, childhood is forward looking or anticipatory, and is determined by an adult perspective. The second is the psychoanalytic view, which is also individual and personality oriented, but here the interest individual adulthood requires the retrospective examination of the individual's childhood experiences. A third view is the life course perspective. This perspective is a mix of individual and nonindividual approaches, in that it follows single individuals from childhood to adulthood or vice versa while at the same time stressing the impact of historical and societal events. All of these views are similar to the traditional theories of socialization ... in that (1) they focus on the anticipatory outcomes of childhood (that is, children becoming adults), and (2) they consider childhood and adulthood as necessarily belonging to different historical periods. Qvortrup argues that, by conceptualizing childhood as a structural form, we can move beyond these individualistic, adult-oriented, and time-bound perspectives to pose and answer a wide range of sociological questions.
>
> (ibid.: 30)

Corsaro further describes how the historical study of childhood has been developed using a range of cultural and latterly auto/biographical data sources, extending from Philippe Ariès's groundbreaking *Centuries of Child-hood* (1962), a study of the child in medieval European society from artistic representations of children as like small adults, to later sixteenth-century notions of children as sweet innocents, subjects of 'coddling' mainly by women. In the eighteenth century, this view of the child as docile adult-in-the-making, pure, innocent and unformed, was augmented by a social dimension that also required him or her to be subject to moralizing and dis-cipline by institutions organized and managed by adults. In many respects, this was in response to what were increasingly becoming images of the child as the object of moral panic, suspicion and fear, as a result of their perceived lack of general controllability and self-control.

Corsaro details how the traditional 'grand theories' of childhood as pro-pounded by Ariès and Lloyd de Mause (*The History of Childhood* (1974)) have given way to less abstract and universalist approaches. Among the most significant of these are a number that make extensive use of the historical materials of childhood, mainly in the form of children's autobiographies, let-ters, diaries and notebooks, and the various official reports of children's experience (e.g. as used in the courts or reported in the press). An example of this approach includes Linda Pollock's landmark *Forgotten Children* (1983), in which she uses just these sorts of auto/biographical records to seriously question many of the assumptions contained and continually reproduced in the grand historical theories of childhood by experts like Ariès and de Mause. Another example of such a groundbreaking study of childhood is Barbara Hanawalt's *Growing Up in Medieval London* (1993), in which she 'captures the lives of London children and youth in the fourteenth and fifteenth cen-turies' (Corsaro, 2005: 68) using court records, coroners' rolls, literary sources and contemporaneous advice books to recover a sense of children's everyday lives. Similarly, the authors Lester Alston (1992) and David Wiggins (1985) also make substantial use of resources comprising autobiographies, life nar-ratives, personal testimonies, diaries, games and nursery rhymes to recreate the richly evocative sense-making practices and active (and often resisting) role of slave children in their own daily lives. Other examples cited by Corsaro that refer mainly to diaries to reconstruct the lives of American pioneer chil-dren at the turn of the twentieth century is Elliott West's 'Children on the Plains Frontier' (1992) and David Nasaw's (1985) use of court records, bio-graphies and autobiographies to study children's experience of American urbanization from the late 1890s to the early 1920s, as part of his research on the 'newsies' or youngsters who sold newspapers on the street. These seminal studies, all of which use a rich and diverse range of auto/biographical data, represent innovative and creative examples of how to use these types of bio-graphical data or life writings effectively to both challenge previous assump-tions encased in 'grand' theories or metanarratives of childhood, and also to introduce new insights into the study of children, childhood and the family. This adaptation of such microanalysis of children's life writings (and the life writings of childhood) in the study of radicalization and other political phenomena can help to address the situation whereby

> The relative silence of scholars in international relations has been regrettable: holding back the development of a much needed conceptual bridge between the micro-level study of children's everyday lives and theorisation about the actions of states in respect of warfare, security and defence.
>
> (Jason, 2007: 323)

Symbols, myths and knowledge: representations of childhood in political prisoner life writing

The available evidence suggests that even very young children are aware at least to some extent of the political circumstances in which they live, and are active in acquiring and shaping the language and symbols of conflict. In their research into young children's attitudes towards the conflict in Northern Ireland, Connolly and Healy (2003) find that even children as young as 3-to-4-years old ' … are actively engaging with the social and cultural events that surround them and are attempting to make sense of them' (ibid.: 45). Their interviews with 3-to-4-year olds indicate that this process starts at an even younger age: 'The general repertoire of cultural markers and symbols that the children had learnt and assimilated at a much earlier age was now providing the basic language and knowledge to try to describe and make sense of what was going on' (ibid.: 50). Where or how these discourses and cultural symbols were learned are not explicitly stated, though the strong implication is that this is at least exacerbated through pre-schooling and later in primary and secondary education (via segregation of the religious groups) while being primarily passed on within families in a variety of ways. This was evidenced by the stories the children told about articles given to them by family members, and their awareness of their significance as symbolic markers of identity, such as an Irish tricolour flag given to one girl by her grandmother, and another boy who recognized a Rangers football shirt and was able to discuss its relevance to his community/identity because he had been given one at home. This suggests that the way children make sense of politics and conflict is not simply about learning a vocabulary of language and symbolism and then gradually constructing from this developing a body of knowledge as they mature; the sense-making process is much messier and more complex, embedded as it is in the everyday practices and narratives of ordinary family life, which includes in this instance ritual occasions such as birthdays and gift-giving, and their casual but effective utility for the inculcation of certain 'tribal' political views, such as are attached to the implicit meanings symbolized in a football shirt, which can be in some way understood by a very young child. While this systemic embedding of such sectarian cultural identities, knowledges and practices in the everyday lives of families is key, other researchers interpret these same findings in a way that insists on the foundational influence of such symbols in early childhood as the basis for later and incremental sense making praxes throughout childhood and later life:

> This research [Connolly and Healy 2003] clearly demonstrates the importance of cultural images for young children living in Belfast as signifiers of the segregated communities they live in. For the youngest children such images represented the notion of belonging to one group and not the other. As the children aged, the symbols could be used as a means to explain the apparent differences between communities. For all the age groups the ability to recognise 'the other' could mean safety or affirmation of their own culture. These findings have been supported by other research, for example McGrellis (2004). The importance of cultural images is subsumed in the oldest group of children by the importance of history. The historical context of 'the troubles' informs the language used by the oldest children, that is, they become aware of the meaning behind the cultural images. This knowledge of history, or rather the importance attached to it, has been highlighted since as an instigator for involvement in paramilitary activity (McGrellis, 2004).
>
> (McKie and Lombard, 2005: 179–80)

While such research findings suggest that families are at least complicit in the preservation and transmission of the symbolism, language and mythologies of the politics of difference and conflict, there is also evidence that external influences on children and families can strongly influence – if not overwhelm, in the most extreme instances – this process embedded in the day-to-day (re)production of family life. Schools or the organization of schooling are often also complicit in this process.

Understandably, and rightly, the vast majority written on the subject of terrorism and childhood focuses on the damage and suffering children are forced to endure as a direct and indirect result of conflict and violence, or how to deal with children's fear of terrorism, and the trauma they suffer as a result of it. The journalist Obaid-Chinoy (2007: 4) describes this as the 'stealing from children of their childhood', the 'robbing of families of their innocence', which in turn has a lasting effect on children and their families, making them the perfect recruits for future terrorist action. Their immaturity, naïveté, material and emotional neediness, lack of judgement, knowledge and sophistication, inability to comprehend the consequences of their actions, propensity to risky behaviours and susceptibility to the functional faux-parental structures of protection and socialization make children particularly vulnerable to violence, exploitation, manipulation and intimidation.

It is this inherent vulnerability attached to children and childhood, coupled with the increasing awareness of the intrinsically anarchical and potentially dangerous virtual world of the World Wide Web that constitutes a binocular focal point of concern for government policy-makers and law enforcement, especially in more 'developed' societies. Claims about a purported link between child pornography, the sexual abuse of children and terrorism have recently appeared in the western media, drawing attention to the utility of highly sophisticated paedophile communication networks (especially those online) for the purposes of covert communication between terrorists, and also the discovery of images of child pornography in the possession of terrorist suspects on their arrest (Kelly, 2008; Kerbaj and Kennedy, 2008; Kerbaj *et al.*, 2008; Council of the European Union, 2007), leading to calls for more interagency cooperation between those working in child protection and counter-terrorism. The government's concerted efforts to construct an effective prevention strategy is in many ways built upon the notion of the vulnerability of children and their families to such pernicious and predatory external influences, which are seen as requiring addressing by the state in order 'protect' (as well as to 'target') them:

> As a country, we are rightly concerned to protect children from exploitation in other areas. We need to do the same in relation to violent extremism. As I speak, terrorists are methodically and intentionally targeting young people and children in this country. They are radicalizing, indoctrinating and grooming young, vulnerable people to carry out acts of terrorism. This year, we have seen individuals as young as 15 and 16 implicated in terrorist-related activity.
> (Director General of the Security Service, speech to the Society of Editors' Annual Conference, 5 November 2007, quoted in Department for Children, Schools and Families, 2008: 12)

Hence the primacy of the child *protection* model used in policy-making on children is linked into the *prevention* strategy that is a main strand of current counter-terrorism policy. This is not without its ironies, not least of which is the responsibilization thesis that is foundational to the (crime) prevention strategy mentioned previously, which seeks to divest responsibility for crime prevention onto the affected communities themselves. Given the recent catastrophic failures in the child protection systems in the UK, is this amalgamation of the crime prevention model with the child protection model the most appropriate or potentially effective way of dealing with the issue of radicalization, particularly in the UK? Or could the surveillance and stress often experienced by families who become the object of the child welfare system (as separate but additional to the police) possibly make the situation even more acute, with respect to the inculcation of feelings of stigma and victimization, or further complicate the relationships between children and the various adults charged with their 'care'?

Interventions by external actors or outside institutional agencies in these 'traditional' relationships and areas of family life can be extremely fraught.

In her research carried out in Pakistan, Obaid-Chinoy (2007) observes how the material vulnerability of children and families can create a rift between children and their traditional or normative culture, a gap in which extremist ideologies can take place (through coercion, cajoling or other incentives), providing in many circumstances a virtually irresistible alternative for many children who are forced to fend for themselves and their families in desperate circumstances. In such extreme socio-economic contexts, the bonds of parental care toward the child can be utterly destroyed by the crushing brutality of poverty exacerbated by the destructive impact of war; indeed, the financial inducements offered by terrorist groups (and also other predatory groups who would exploit children for their own ends, such as paedophiles and people traffickers) that are provided to families in exchange for their children can be as tempting as means of physical survival, even at the expense of social bonding and community cohesion (Singer, 2005; Obaid-Chinoy, 2007). Poverty and violent conflict similarly affect children and families by their negative impact on social infrastructure and the lack of provision of education and healthcare, further aggravating children's situation by making them more prone to being victims and/or participants in violent conflict. While it is clear that these factors have a material impact on boys and young men recruited as soldiers in terms of the construction of alternative masculinities and a resulting sense of empowerment, there is also a profoundly damaging impact on women and girls, with respect to the inculcation of a deep sense of damage, resentment and intolerance which, can eventually be passed down to future generations.

The severing of bonds to traditional culture – particularly with respect to learning religious tradition and transmitting the meaning of religious symbols and texts – can have devastating consequences in terms of uprooting such symbolic modes of meaning from their normative socio-cultural context. This cultural disruption can have a particularly destructive effect on those who are already vulnerable due to other inequalities such as poverty or gender, and pervert the meaning of religious ideas such as 'martyrdom' and 'sacrifice':

> [P]oor parents collect economic rewards for the sacrifice of their sons and daughters to suicide terrorism and receive selected passages from the Quran—without any proper context—which show that their children died following the instructions of the Prophet. Solitary women, especially, sometimes gain a distinctive social status in the community, aside from monetary support, for being the mother of martyrs.
>
> (Obaid-Chinoy, 2007: 6)

While poverty and lack of education can be exploited by religious fundamentalists within patriarchal societies resulting in a vicious cycle of deprivation, intolerance and violence, it is crucial to recognize that this phenomenon is not exclusive to Muslim countries, nor to the 'developing' world. As

Githens-Mazer (2008) points out, both history and symbolism matter a great deal, as the

> legacy of a painful and unresolved colonial past and process of partition. Regardless of other cases, this ... cast[s] light on mechanisms and content which help to explain how myths, memories and symbols of the colonial and recent past inform contemporary resonant repertoires of myths, memories and symbols, which in turn serve as bases for radicalization among some Islamists from North Africa. This radicalization is further underpinned by concern over, apathy towards and outright hatred of what is perceived as western anti-Islamic behaviour, and particular concerns over what are viewed as the injustices of Palestine, the Balkans, post-9/11 Afghanistan and Lebanon in 2006.
>
> (Githens-Mazer, 2008: 565)

This disruption of tradition with respect to the interpretation of sacred texts observed by Obaid-Chinoy among Afghan refugees in her home country of Pakistan is very interesting and instructive, as it is observable in other contexts with a number of variants and differing outcomes. We may ask in the context of western societies, however, which are comparatively much more secularized, if such incursions into traditional familial relationships and cultural texts, rituals, symbols, etc. are similarly so direct or simple as factors in the radicalization of children and young people. Most American or British children – even those raised within religious or 'fundamentalist' families – grow up in the knowledge that their so called 'traditional' values are not universally shared by those around them, and are frequently openly challenged, misrepresented or even pilloried and ridiculed within the dominant culture and in the media. These children and their families are, in response, often quite sophisticated in their ability to absorb and subvert the influence of secularism and its attendant cultural hegemony on their local subcultures, including sometimes direct attacks on and public ridicule of their own religious practices and beliefs (see Marty and Appleby, 2003). Similarly, we may wonder if the extreme manifestation of poverty, illiteracy, patriarchy and deprivation as described by Obaid-Chinoy (2007) in Pakistan, and their influence upon children and families, is analogous to the situation in the west. While there are obvious observable differences between 'east' and 'west', it is important to note – as Rebecca de Schweinitz (2005) insists – that such 'extremes' of poverty, ignorance, violence, exploitation, poor housing, neglect and manipulation are by no means limited to the conflict-addled regions of the 'third world':

> some observers suggested that the 'conditions in the poor south [of the United States of America]—or in places such as Harlem' were more 'tragic' than those which surrounded refugee children in World War II Europe (Universal Declaration of Human Rights, 1949: 141 in de

Schweinitz, 2005: 57) ... [T]he lives of many children in both the rural South and America's cities still bear no resemblance to the childhood we idealise.

(de Schweinitz, 2005: 65).

So, while clearly there are children in the richest countries of the world who live in what are describable (at least relatively) as extreme levels of poverty and deprivation, it is less clear whether or not there is any congruence between the propensity and extent of radicalization of children found in, say, rural Pakistan, and those in urban Harlem, Birmingham or Bradford. Open-source data on the backgrounds of terrorist suspects in western societies would suggest that individuals from backgrounds of extreme poverty and deprivation in the west do not (as yet) constitute a particularly high-risk group for radicalization or terrorism; if anything, the available data indicates just the opposite, and that it is the affluence of middle-class family life that affords distinctively propitious opportunities and motivations for later radicalization among white western extremists. The link between family, education, childhood and middle-class culture in real-life radicalization narratives will thus feature prominently in this chapter.

In the following sections, I will explore the construction and influence of children, childhood and families in the life writings of a selection of individuals from the 'west', as well as one from the 'east', who were incarcerated at some point in their lives for political reasons, and how and in what sense these experiences form part of the narrative of (eventual) radicalization. In these texts, the link between children, childhood and family life and later radicalization is indeed very nuanced and complex, but what we do not see is any simple correlation between the extremes of poverty and other forms of deprivation and later terrorist action. In fact, many (though not all) of these political prisoner life writers come from privileged, middle class backgrounds. While the basic literacy required to write their life stories would tend to foreground individuals from relatively more privileged backgrounds over the lower-class inmate population, this is not always the case; some prisoners (including many poor women and girls, see Voglis, 2002) actually learn to read and write in prison in order to write their life stories, or alternatively find an amanuensis. Neither do we encounter children and their families as passive or docile victims who are in need of government surveillance, control or 'protection' from the machinations of terrorist recruiters to whom they are generally easy prey. Instead, what emerges from these texts are a number of discernible patterns concerning the considerable *agency* of children and families, even in the most dire circumstances, and their ability to elide these protection regimes in order to make their own choices about how to best deal with what are often the extremely unsettling or traumatic experiences of systemic prejudice, injustice and discrimination at the hands of the state or its representatives in the course of their ordinary public and private lives. These responses by families in the form of radicalization life histories – as we will see in the case of the Weathermen (or later Weather Underground Organization)[6] – can be violent, non-violent, a mixture of the two, or an alternating cycle at different stages of the organizational/life course. School, *consumption* and other leisure or extracurricular activities tend to figure prominently here,[7] as does the blindness of society at large and the state to recognize the impact of the sometimes astonishingly unjust situations to which these children and families are subjected, often at the hands of the state as well as extremist groups. Here it is *racism* that emerges as an especially key variable, the source of daily and ongoing humiliation, strengthening the barriers to life chances, and encouraging and legitimating resistance among the young as above all a logical and considered strategic response. As scholars increasingly point out, for example, children in the U.S. asked to recite the pledge of allegiance and salute the flag in racially segregated schools, whether black or white, settled or immigrant, have every reason to distrust authority and rebel against society and its hypocritical morals (e.g. Pei, 2003) when they can observe for themselves the flimsiness and hypocrisy of such performances of national unity, liberty, justice and belonging. Any pre-vention strategy on the part of government policy-makers should therefore concentrate not just on the construction and publicizing of 'counter-narratives' designed to halt or reverse radicalization from external sources, but must also be more attentive to the internal dynamics of life as a child or family in con-temporary society as the basis for widespread and enduring anger and resis-tance. Racism and other forms of inequality, deprivation and discrimination continually and negatively impact the integrity and integration of millions of individuals, through no particular fault of their own and without the predations of evil recruiters spreading messages of hate. Additionally, radicalization is shaped by the internal dynamics of adolescent rebellion against parental authority has also been credited by radicalized political prisoners as a primary source of their radicalization (e.g. Alpert, 1981; Husain, 2007).

Let us now turn our attention to these life stories in order to explore these aspects in greater context and detail.

'I felt myself turning cold like the bottle of Coke': the reconstruction of childhood tradition and youthful rebellion in radicalization narratives

In his bestselling autobiography *The Islamist: Why I Joined Radical Islam in Britain, What I Saw Inside and Why I Left* (2007), Ed Husain accords a great deal of significance to his childhood experiences – including memories of school, family life, religious tradition and observance and peer networks. For Husain, it is the severing of the Muslim holy texts from their traditional familial context that forms the basis of his narrative of radicalization and eventual de-radicalization. *The Islamist* can be divided into three main parts: childhood spirituality formed by family and traditional practice, youthful rebellion marked by the departure from 'authentic' spirituality and the politicization of Islam, and the final conversion to true spiritual Islam, returning to the family fold and starting his own family. The first part of the book comprises a brief history of a happy childhood, brought up in a vibrant, multicultural London. Husain describes growing up in a loving extended family that was guided by the influence of a deep and moderate observance of Islam (his paternal grandfather was a teacher of Islamic tradition and worship, much in the traditional peripatetic mould). He describes how his childhood was shaped by love and the authentic spirituality of traditional Islam. Racial/ethnic strife were not a part of his childhood experience of growing up as a Muslim in multicultural Britain (not unlike the childhood recollections of Gerry Adams in his description of a 1950s Belfast, which he characterizes by the peaceful and tolerant intermingling of the Catholic and Protestant population in his autobiography *Before the Dawn: An Autobiography* (2001)). However, notwithstanding the sort of idyllic recollection of childhood that appears throughout Adams's corpus of autobiographical writings (see also *Falls Memories: A Belfast Life* (1994)), there is in Husain's autobiography an indication in the narrative that things are not quite as tolerant and harmonious as they might have seemed; this is epitomized in the story of an encounter the young Ed has with one of his teachers. In this story, the 9-year-old Ed is scolded by his teacher, Mr. Coppin, for forgetting to help set the tables for the communal school lunch:

> 'You're in trouble, young man! Do you understand?'
> 'Yes, Mr. Coppin,' I said. Then he said something that I have never forgotten. Of me, a nine-year-old, he asked, 'Where is your Allah now then, eh? Where is he? Can't he help you?'
>
> (Husain, 2007: 4)

This callously disrespectful invocation of his religious tradition comes as a shock to the boy, and is regarded by the adult Husain as a pivotal moment in his childhood. The story is evocative of a previous narrative device used in another important text of a life of political radicalization that ends with a spectacular de-radicalization and spiritual conversion to authentic Islam – that of Malcolm X. In his famous autobiography, Malcolm similarly recalls what he considers to be an equally revealing and even more devastating throwaway remark by one of his teachers, to the effect that he should be more realistic in his stated ambition to become a lawyer, that such a profession was not 'realistic' for one such as him:

> Mr. Ostrowski looked surprised, I remember, and leaned back in his chair and clasped his hands behind his head. He kind of half-smiled and said, 'Malcolm, one of life's first needs is for us to be realistic. Don't misunderstand me, now. We all here like you, you know that. But you've

got to be realistic about being a nigger. A lawyer—that's no realistic goal for a nigger. You need to think about something you *can* be.

(X and Haley, 1964: 118)

For Malcolm, according to Dyson (1995), this 'devastating rebuff' (5) from his white teacher at the middle-class Mason Junior High School completes Malcolm's negative assessment of white middle-class culture that was already in process, an event that concludes the narrative of the racist murder of his father by white vigilantes, and the traumatic and destructive intervention of middle-class social workers in his family, which included the committal of his mother to a mental institution and the dispersion of the children into the care of extended family or foster care. This dismissal of 'well-meaning' but essentially racist middle-class liberalism is reinforced in Malcolm's immediate introduction into the society of the black bourgeoisie in Boston where he then lived with his older half-sister, a culture with '… its social pretensions and exaggerated rituals of cultural self-affirmation, leading him to conclude later that the black middle class was largely ineffective in achieving authentic Black liberation' (ibid: 5). This attitude towards the ineffectiveness and lack of authenticity of the black and white middle classes, and the subsequent introduction into the 'street culture' of Harlem, initiates his radicalization, and unites the narratives of Husain with Malcolm X, as does his eventual conversion to 'real' Islam and his subsequent de-radicalization. (We will return to the topic of street culture in radicalization narratives later in the chapter.)

As previously mentioned, the Sinn Féin activist, one-time political detainee and later Member of Parliament in the devolved regional government in Northern Ireland, Gerry Adams has devoted a significant amount of his considerable corpus of autobiographical writings to the seminal influence of his childhood growing up in the working-class areas of Belfast. Yet unlike Husain (2007) and Malcolm X (1965), Adams's recollections of his childhood are characterized by a sense of nostalgia (which at times verges on the saccharine) in his representations of his hometown and his family traditions and upbringing. Notably, there is not the same presence of a symbolic story recounting the shock of being confronted with the secondary status he was accorded as a member of the Catholic working-class in Belfast. In *Before the Dawn: An Autobiography* (2001), Adams implies that this is owing to the fact that, due to the segregation and ghettoization of Belfast in the 1950s, virtually all of the people he came into contact with as a child were more or less just like him, i.e. poor, working class, and above all Catholic. Similarly, schools were (and to a large extent still are) segregated along sectarian lines, and so he – like most children – did not have the same sorts of disrespectful and racist encounters with his teachers as Husain and Malcolm. Yet his stories about his childhood nevertheless present revealing insights into the development of his political character and his later radicalization. Two of these stories are recounted early in his autobiography: one relating to his experiences of responding to exhortations by his peers to commit an act of violence on an 'innocent' creature, and the other recalling what can be interpreted as a symbolically important consumer exchange experience. In the first story, the young Gerry is out and about with a number of other boys in the neighbourhood when they come upon a frog:

> 'What's that?' he shouted. We all turned to where he stood in slightly longer grass.
> 'Look,' he pointed again.
> It was a frog. A large green frog. I caught hold of it, feeling it cold and clammy between my palms, its heartbeat against my fingers. It's legs squirmed as it struggled to be free.
> 'Give it to me,' said Frank Curran.
> 'What for?' I asked.
> 'You can blow them up.'
> 'What do you mean blow them up?' I asked.
> 'You can put a straw up its arse and blow it up,' Frank said.
> 'You're not doing that,' I said. 'It's not your frog, it's mine!' ...
> 'I want to blow it up,' said Frank ...
> 'I wouldn't mind see it getting blown up,' said our Paddy.
> 'You can make it so big it's like the bladder of a football sometimes. You blow and blow and blow. And then the frog goes pop!'
> They all looked at me and at the frog. The spear carriers were especially interested.
> 'Look!' I shouted. 'There's a rat!' For a second they turned around and away I ran from my erstwhile comrades.
>
> (Adams, 2001: 11–12)

The repeated exhortations and pressure by his peers to 'blow up' the frog, and his stratagem for distracting the other boys (who included his own brothers, who were also keen to blow the creature up) and resisting this course of violent action can be read as a metaphor for his later activism in the political wing of the Irish Republican movement (Sinn Féin) as opposed to the IRA, and his eventual involvement in the secret talks with John Hume which led to the 1998 Good Friday Agreement and the peace process. In other words, Adams is portraying himself as very much an individual, albeit one who was and remains a member of a powerful and strong collective social group, yet who was (and is) not inclined towards violence or to follow the crowd, and that this characterizes the boy as well as the man. In many ways, the stories Adams tells in his autobiography about his childhood are arguably meant to give an indication of his political make-up as a grown man, one who (as it turns out) is not averse to using distraction or subterfuge to subvert the mindlessly violent designs of his peers against defenceless 'innocents'.

A second story records Adams's attitude toward (parental) authority, and how a well-judged act of defiance could in the end lead to a positive and mutually rewarding outcome. On asking his father and mother if he could ' ... go down to Kennedy's Bakery in the morning and get a pillow-slip of mixed-ups [assorted bread, cakes and rolls]' (ibid.: 14) his father tells him to ask his mother, and she tells him in no uncertain terms that he certainly is not to, as she does not want 'the whole street talking about us' (15). In any event, he sneaks out of bed early in the morning to meet up with his friend, who has also been denied permission to go to the bakery. The boys have worked for weeks selling kindling wood door-to-door around side streets where they are not known so that their mothers won't find out, and have the money to buy two full pillowcases full of fresh baked goods each.

> Back across the river, he sneaked into his house, I sneaked into ours. I put two or three buns to one side in a hidden place for our Paddy, Liam and Sean. The rest I arranged neatly on our dining-room table. A ticket of bread, five farls, six baps, some nice crusty rolls. And then, the pile of pastry. I shook the crumbs, coconut flake and crusts out of the pillow-slip for our Rory, patted him on the head and then padded my way upstairs into bed.
>
> Everybody was delighted when they got up later, though my ma gave off a wee bit.
>
> 'I told you not to go down there,' she scolded. But that was all.
>
> When he came back that night my da said everybody on the building site was jealous of him. He was the only one who had buns. Even our Margaret was impressed. She said nothing, but I knew. After that, Joe and I went down to Kennedy's every so often. But now my ma always gave me the money.
>
> (Adams, 2001: 16)

What is interesting and suggestive about these three very well-known life narratives describing famous lives of radicalized and subsequently de-radicalized actors is their foundation in the experience of childhood and family life. Malcolm, Adams and Hussain each recount incidents in their childhoods that they later deem to be of substantial importance upon their later radicalization as adults; in two of these, the boys are forced to endure very negative racist encounters with adults entrusted with their education, which will later prove pivotal in their reaction against the racism they thus learn about in society as a whole. While Adams does not suffer such a racist indignity (mainly due to the external organization of his community along sectarian lines),[8] his resistance to peer pressure to conduct an act of violence and his defiance of his mother's injunction, the later rewards and approval he receives for these acts and the justification of his actions at the time, represents a foreshadowing of the narrative arc that his political life narrative will take. It is not inconsequential that these stories usually take place either in school or in the context of leisure or consumption activities, as they figure as prominent sites of power and conflict, as well as pleasure and enjoyment, in everyday family life. Certainly, leisure and consumption feature prominently the life writings of other radical figures (in addition to the following, see also Becker, 1978).

In his autobiography *The Making of Black Revolutionaries* (1985), the founder member of the Student Non-violent Coordination Committee (SNCC) James Forman records the following incident from his childhood in the chapter entitled 'Childhood and Coca-Cola', in which he is refused service by a white woman working at a drugstore fountain during a family vacation to visit his aunt in Memphis, Tennessee, on the way back home to Chicago. Instead of being allowed to sit at the counter on the high gleaming stool and drink his fountain Coke from an ice-cold and shapely glass as he wanted, the woman makes him go into the back to be served his Coke there straight from the bottle by a black man, with whom he has the following conversation:

> 'But … but … I don't want a Coke from the bottle. I want to sit up there and drink my Coke from a glass. Why do I have to drink it here?'
>
> The man looked at me. Something was wrong. I didn't know what, but something. A fear swelled up within me, the fear of the unknown.
>
> 'Where are you from?' he asked in a sympathetic voice, although there was annoyance in it too.
>
> 'I don't understand.'
>
> 'You have to drink your Coke back here. You can't sit on those stools.'
>
> 'But … why?' By this time I had the cold Coca-Cola in my hands. It was very wet and very cold, and I felt myself turning cold like the bottle of Coke. Something dreadful was wrong and I could not understand why I was crying, what was the matter, who this man was, what right he had to tell me where I had to drink my Coke, why I couldn't sit on the stool.
>
> 'Where are you from?'
>
> 'Chicago.'
>
> 'Well, don't you know?'
>
> 'Know what?'
>
> 'Boy, you're a nigger,' he said in a flat voice.
>
> 'A what?' I asked. I heard him and I didn't hear him because I didn't really understand the word.
>
> 'A nigger, and Negroes don't sit on the stools here.'
>
> (Forman, 1985: 19)

Forman concludes the chapter with these reflections on what the later fully developed 'Black Revolutionary' would retrospectively cite as the 'first step' of his radicalization 'journey', this devastating sense of humiliation and loss of innocence he experienced on this occasion as a child:

> My experience that day was not unusual—hardly. You could almost call it a cliché of the black experience, so often has it happened to our children in one form or another. But I buried it deep, and 'forgot' about that bottle of Coca-Cola for many years. Later, in graduate school, I would write down all the racist confrontations of my life—and only when they were all on paper, and I was racking my memory to make sure none had been forgotten, did this one come to the surface.
>
> It must have been a horrendous day for me, more than I realized at the time. It was, in fact, the first step on the long journey of a black man in a strange land.
>
> (ibid.: 20)

This account is significant in terms of the contrast upon which the narrative pivots, that is not the disruption of a sacred text from its traditional or normative cultural context (as in the case of Husain), or an occasion on which to stand up to peer pressure (e.g. Adams), but rather an analogous disruption of an icon of American consumer culture – an icy glass of fountain Coca-Cola – from what was the previously experienced innocence of racism in the context of an otherwise loving and supportive childhood in the freedom of a beautiful hot sunny day. This experience was clearly upsetting for the young Forman as it was later to be considered by the grown man – nevertheless, so utterly common as to be 'cliché'. It is instructive that the experience was at least temporarily forgotten but later recalled during an exercise in what can be called 'memory mining' by a more mature and also more politically engaged young adult who is better able to interpret his memories through and into an existing political ideological narrative.[9]

As with Malcolm and Husain, the utterance of racist epithets by 'well-meaning' adults to children who are in a position of authority, or whose actions are otherwise intended to 'educate', and their role in carrying out the social labour of labelling, as well as deriding and disempowering the child, is extremely pertinent to the reconstructed narratives of radicalization in political prisoner life writing. On this point, it is important to note that these incidents all occur in what for the most part constitutes the child's experience of their own designated public spaces – in the cases of Malcolm and Husain, the formative arena of school; for Adams and Forman, that of the familiar marketplace of their (or their extended family's) home town. The black feminist activist and fellow SNCC member (and also Che-Lumumba member and erstwhile Black Panther) Angela Davis records an incident similar to Forman's in her autobiography, drawing attention to the importance of the 'trivial' desires of children and the impact of their systematic frustration by ideological forces like racism on their burgeoning sense of identity:

My childhood friends and I were bound to develop ambivalent attitudes toward the white world. One the one hand there was our instinctive aversion toward those who prevented us from realizing our grandest as well as our most trivial wishes. On the other, there was the equally instinctive jealousy which came from knowing that they had access to all the pleasurable things we wanted. Growing up, I could not help feeling a certain envy. And yet I have a very vivid recollection of deciding, very early, that I would never—and I was categorical about this—never harbor or express the desire to be white. This promise that I made to myself did nothing, however, to drive away the wishdreams that filled my head whenever my desires collided with a taboo. So, in order that my daydreams not contradict my principles, I constructed a fantasy in which I would slip on a white face and go unceremoniously into the theater or amusement park or wherever I wanted to go. After thoroughly enjoying the activity, I would make a dramatic, grandstand appearance before the white racists and with a sweeping gesture, rip off the white face, laugh wildly and call them all fools.

(Davis, 1990: 85)

In this passage, Davis provides an insight into the types of coping and resistance strategies that children are compelled to develop in racist societies, if only, in the first instance, as a way of being able to satisfy their own 'wishdreams' in a dominant cultural that regards the desires of these children as subject to the powerful cultural barrier of taboo (in this case, dominated by race). The use of dramaturgy and the performance of race using an imaginary white 'mask' in order to be able to do what she wanted and to 'pass' is evocative of Fanon's influential *Black Skin, White Masks* (1968), a common trope for making sense of and dealing with the subjugation of colonialism, even for children, especially those like Davis who grew up in the Jim Crow south. By invoking the dramaturgical play of 'dressing up', masking provides the young Angela with a way of fulfilling her forbidden or 'taboo' desires and at the same time undercutting what the adult would later encounter as the vileness of racism with the playfulness and amusement of childhood *jouissance*. Leisure time and particularly consumption form key nodal points for the development of such resistance strategies for these radicalizing children. Davis follows this story by recalling an incident while out shopping with her sister Fania, a story with a twist in the tale in terms of the humiliating narratives of racism and the influence of the 'exotic' by acting out in reality a 'childish daydream':

Years later, when I was in my teens, I recalled this childish daydream and decided, in a way, to act it out. My sister Fania and I were walking downtown in Birmingham when I spontaneously proposed a plan to her: We would pretend to be foreigners and, speaking French to each other, we would walk into the shoe store on 19th Street and ask, with a thick accent, to see a pair of shoes. At the sight of two young Black women speaking a foreign language, the clerks in the store raced to help us. Their delight with the exotic was enough to completely, if temporarily, dispel their normal disdain for Black people.

(Davis, 1990: 86)

After being fawned over by a succession of compliant and willing white assistants (including the shop manager) and served at the front 'whites only' section of this Jim Crow shop, the girls eventually bring the 'game' to its triumphant crescendo:

Eventually I signaled to Fania that it was time to wind up the game. We looked at him [the white shop manager]: his foolish face and obsequious grin one eye-blink away from the scorn he would have registered as automatically as a trained hamster had he known we were local residents. We burst out laughing. He started to laugh with us, hesitantly, the way people laugh when they suspect themselves to be the butt of the joke.

'Is something funny?' he whispered.

Suddenly I knew English, and told him that he was what was so funny. 'All Black people have to do is pretend they come from another country, and you treat us like dignitaries.'

I had followed almost to the t the scenario of my childhood daydream.

(ibid.: 87)

Though Davis's narrative is similar to that of James Forman in terms of the childhood scene that takes place in a local shop, the closure of the narrative pivoting on the twist in the plot is very different, as is the sense of agency and empowerment on the part of the storyteller and her sister. The normal racist contempt that is otherwise effortlessly conveyed by the characters of the white shop assistants in her hometown of Birmingham, Alabama, is in Davis's narrative disrupted by the playing out of her 'childish fantasy' in the company of her sister. In this episode, as in so many recounted in her autobiography, Davis presents herself as a powerful character even while she is forced to live in a social environment that is institutionally engineered to deprive her and others like her of power, and how she uses her knowledge and intelligence as a formidable resource not simply in living out or 'masking' her fantasies, but moreover in reversing the humiliating dynamics of the racism she is forced to endure by manipulating these 'masks'. Childhood – in terms of its dramaturgical proximity to role-playing and play-acting, and as a prime originary point for consumer-led fantasy and desire – provides a key resource for the radicalized imagination. In Davis's autobiography, this is developed from her earliest childhood memories of resistance consisting of sitting in her front yard with other black children shouting 'cracker' and 'redneck' at passing white motorists, to something much more sophisticated and direct in terms of the impact of her 'play-acting' on the ability of white people to maintain their dominant social roles. In contrast to Forman, the advantages afforded to Davis by her middle-class upbringing by educated and politically aware parents, and her experiences of cosmopolitan life in New York – and indeed the girls' knowledge of French – are key factors in her ability to transform this fantasy scenario into a reality, or at least to tell the story in this way. Notwithstanding the fact that her auto-biography was primarily written in response to charges of murder, kidnapping and criminal conspiracy (in which she was not directly involved, and for which she would eventually be found not guilty), Davis's non-violent radicalization and her attendant sense of agency has been deeply entrenched throughout her life. It is arguable that this is because she has taken or adapted opportunities for other more intellectual or 'consciousness-raising' forms of resistance, largely due to her access to the best education, international travel, career advancement and other opportunities. Without these, her radicalization could possibly have taken a very different and perhaps more violent form.

From an analytic perspective, what are we to make thus far of these examples in terms of what they can tell us about radicalization as represented in the life writings of political prisoners, and how they relate to the existing research literature on the radicalization 'process' undergone by such politically 'radical' individuals? First, despite the admittedly anecdotal nature of these various stories, there are striking differences in these narratives, as well as perhaps some surprising similarities. Certainly, the link between the extreme circumstances recorded by Obaid-Chinoy of the appalling poverty and deprivation endured by the Afghan refugee children she observed in Pakistan and their resulting vulnerability to radicalization (among any number of social evils) by extremist groups seems well established as a prima facie case: both logically (i.e. from a common-sense point of view) and methodologically in the research literature – reinforcing the finding that poverty, deprivation and violent conflict *causes* radicalization. We may ask, however, how many or what proportion of radicalized individuals who are currently the target of attention by the security and intelligence services of any number of what Bobbitt (2008) calls 'market states' fall into such relatively obvious and 'extreme' circumstances? Few if any of the radicalized 'enemy within' figures in capitalist nation states would fall under this category of poverty and deprivation. While the definitive answer to this question is strictly speaking only available to those who have access to what is often highly confidential evidence about these suspects, open-source data available from media reports on terrorism trials would suggest that the proportion of radicalized individuals from this type of extremely deprived background is indeed very low. What is more, it would seem that, due to their lack of education and other personal and material resources, many of these individuals with little or no education or other cultural or political resources to draw upon normally make up the 'not very valuable foot soldiers' who in the words of one Guantánamo Bay detainee 'are recruited to carry out the violent attacks and to become suicide bombers, [and that the] entire operation of recruitment, training, and implementation ... may take no more than 24 hours ... ' (Curcio, 2005: 56). This suggests that despite their acute dangerousness, individuals from this group are unlikely to be 'high-value' operatives.

This leads us to consider then the more intricately contextualized life narratives constructed by radicalized actors such as Husain, Forman, Malcolm X, Adams and Davis cited above. Let us first further consider Ed Husain's autobiographical account of his 'journey' into and then out of radical Islam, specifically his childhood and later adult relationship with his Islamic faith as the pivotal point upon which his radicalization–de-radicalization narrative turns. Books and private reading figure prominently here, as does the influence of one particular school teacher, Mrs Rainey: 'I now wanted everything to do with Islam. There was one problem: Grandpa and my parents taught me by setting an example, by *living* faith. Mrs. Rainey [Husain's RE teacher] taught us with books' (Husain, 2007: 20, original emphasis). As in the case of Malcolm X's autobiography, books, school and an influential teacher become increasingly significant at this stage in these young lives, symbolically marking in the narrative the interruption, in Husain's case, between his connection to the authentically 'spiritual' Islam of his family and the 'extremist' interpretation of the religion by a succession of politically oriented groups with which he later becomes involved. The break from family, tradition and scholarly interpretation is continually foretold in the narrative by the incursion of a small number of extremist texts, most notably the writings of imprisoned radicals such as Mawdudi, Qutb and Nabhani, each of whom drew on the writings of previous radicalized prison writers. Notwithstanding Ed Husain's use of the autobiographical format, he singles out the practice of directly referencing the life of the Prophet (*sira*) as the basis of 'theological' knowledge, which, according to Husain (2007), enables the extremists (particularly literalist and fundamentalists such as the Wahhabis) to effectively bypass centuries of religious tradition, mystical experience and theological commentary, in order to put forward reductive, partial and simplistic arguments based on such biographical 'evidence'. Husain suggests that this constitutes a perversion of the *sira* tradition, and hence a distortion of Islam, by linking the life of the Prophet with the spiritual development of the self in a decidedly political context amenable to 'galvanized action' on the part of the individual:

> The Qur'an has depicted a path, the Straight Path (*Siral al-Muslaq'lin*), which when followed revolutionizes the whole of life. It brings about a transformation in character and galvanizes us into action. This action takes the form of purification of the self, and then unceasing effort to establish the laws of God on earth, resulting in a new order based on truth, justice, virtue and goodness.
>
> (Towards Understanding Islam website: www.al-islamforall.org/litre/englitre/Undislam.htm)

Husain describes the highly potent and motivational ethos pervading radical Islam, which was very attractive to young Muslim men in Britain, offering as it did a potent cultural resource for recovering a sense of masculine identity and building upon this as the basis of revolutionary and world-changing activism (e.g. Husain, 2007: 75). At the foundation of these observations rooted in childhood and family experience is a composite of a cultural traditions of life narrative (*sira*), prisoner life writing and the possibilities for the (re)construction of a new masculine self, one that is active and powerful, different from the subservient and passive subjectivity of the child or indeed the subordinate 'minority' male. As an institution that continues to dominate the lives of children to this day, schools and teachers, as the authority figures who oversee the lives of their students for much of their day-to-day lives, are hugely important. Perhaps one of the edifying lessons of the stories about Mr Coppin and Mr Ostrowski is that more attention should be devoted to the disciplining and surveillance of *teachers* (as opposed to children and their families) with respect to the quality and content of their communications with their students as a simple, low-level, low-cost but still potentially effective preventative to future discontent and later radicalization (cf. Department for Children, Schools and Families, 2008).

One of Husain's main theses is the supposed dichotomy between 'radical' (read 'political') Islam versus 'spiritual' (read 'real') Islam, the former being comparatively unconcerned with things like prayer, tolerance, family, tradition, the spiritual life, the influence of holy people and religious observance in the single-minded pursuit of the global Islamic state. The resolution of this dichotomy in Husain's personal narrative of spiritual epiphany, however, remains quite dualistic in its perspectives on these supposedly contrasting and mutually exclusive realms of religious experience. But is it true to say that any of the 'great' religious traditions is fundamentally apolitical? Among Husain's conclusions is his insistence on the need for 'moderate' 'spiritual' Muslims to take more of an active role in monitoring and regulating the perception and reality of Muslim religious practices in the media, and in social, political and cultural life, fighting back against the incursion of the radicals; indeed, this has formed a major objective of the Quilliam Foundation, of which he is a founder member. However, questions arise concerning the effectiveness of such a strategy or expectation in the Muslim community as a whole, and whether or not it is entirely realistic or even desirable as an outcome of a de-radicalized life story in terms of influencing public policy on counter-terrorism. Why should Muslims who are uninvolved in such criminal activity, and whose religious traditions are distorted by unorthodox, extremist interlopers, be assumed to have to answer for their antisocial and destructive actions? Is it not possible that such demands on the part of moderate, law-abiding citizens function to continue the pathologizing of the Islamic faith, and further increase the very alienation that it is meant to counteract? The lessons of Northern Ireland in this regard should be learned, whereby the often media-driven public demand for distancing and repeated denunciation itself becomes the negative and damaging phenomenon of the 'politics of condemnation', which feeds into the hands of the extremists. If terrorism should be treated as a criminal offense and not a political or much less religious activity, as the current director of RUSI Professor Michael Clarke has recently suggested in his commentary on the UK trial of the airline bomb plot, then shouldn't these narratives be restricted as much as possible to the legal–judicial domain and the individual offenders involved, rather than implicating their communities in any formal or informal ways with respect to the deliberate pursuit of criminals?

For Husain, the radicalization process is rather abruptly brought to a halt when the promises of his group leader and 'friend' Waj to be like a 'father' to him in preference to his real father is not realized when his fatherly attentions are needed. The failed promises of the extremists, combined with the more inclusive and less paranoid Islam that he observes first-hand as practised in places like Syria, start to take their toll on his radicalized certainties. While leaving such groups is not straightforward, as even Husain's life writing suggests, the interruption of the radicalization 'process' is often due to the failures or contradictions of internal or intragroup relationships, or indeed other disappointments, rather than the condemnation of external or non-member political elites or ordinary citizens. Hence the value of counter-radicalization strategies based on the condemnatory performances of extremists by communities – or indeed the incursion of 'counter-narratives' at school – is at best questionable, or at least remains to be proved.

What are we to make of the meaning of consumption in these stories? The lives of children, like women, have for centuries been effectively silenced through their consignment by patriarchal social structures to the private sphere. As Watson (2006) has noted, however, children play a variety of roles, and childhood represents a significant 'site of knowledge' in the public world of global politics, not least in the international marketplace. In addition to their active roles in the shaping and transmission of ideologies of education and belief, children are also vital forces in the globalized consumer economy as both subjects and objects of considerable amounts of consumption activity: ' ... in rich countries in particular, the child has become an important customer in the effort to sell more goods' (Watson, 2006: 238). This shifting dynamic to the concentration on – and perhaps in many respects dependence on – children as primary consumers and objects of consumption (and international sources of cheap labour to produce many of these same goods) in capitalist market economies is significant in terms of raising the profile of children and childhood as important sites of economic, social, cultural and political activity in late modern global capitalism. This observation becomes even more significant in terms of radical politics in light of Baudrillard's thesis on the consumer society.

A major theme throughout Baudrillard's work, he argues that the emergence of the consumer society in late modernity marks the demise of Marxist structuralism in a number of its key aspects, including recognition that (1) late modern capitalism is no longer founded on the overly deterministic economic structuralism model based on the activity of material production; (2) revolutionary change through class struggle by the proletariat and the associated ideology of the dialectic of historical progress founded on revolutionary conflict are an impossibility in the new consumer society (not least given the seduction of consumerism for what were the working classes in the wake of the total consolidation of market capitalism and the state); and (3) the classic icon of the alienated revolutionary subject as the source of political agency engaged in resistance of the social forces of the state is culturally and politically obsolete (Gane, 2003: 152–6). In its place, Baudrillard posits the inauguration of a 'radical' social landscape of 'hyperreality', one in which the material and structural aspects of reality are overwhelmed by their symbolic, semiotic and simulacral meanings, where the death of the real results in the ' ... world apprehended as fable and narrative' (ibid.: 158), a world in which the *agency* of the revolutionary subject passes to the *object* of consumer desire. In this postmodern world dominated by consumerism, time, space and subjectivity become transgressive, excessive, and unbounded by traditional normative structures, reflecting the non-linear, non-progressive, non-cumulative, intensive, chaotic, ecstatic and contradictory logic of hyperreality: ' ... [T]he symbolic order is articulated on metamorphosis in ritual time and space. What is new in Baudrillard's version of the symbolic order is that it is active, dynamic, strategic and based on challenge of radical illusion' (ibid.).

Baudrillard's thesis on consumer society elicits a number of possible insights with respect to these narratives or fables about the significance of childhood experiences of consumption, and their presumed narrative outcomes for these radicalized actors. An implicit sense of this that is power available to children *as consumers* is contained in the narratives of Forman, Adams and Davis. Forman's recollection of his childhood experience of being out and about on his own and purchasing a Coke with his own money draws attention to the richly imaginative and intensely felt emotional lifeworld of the child – reiterated in Davis's story that relates a complex and vivid vocabulary and sense of drama, to include not simply desire and its collision with taboo but also 'wishdreams' – and the child's awareness of and deep sense of attachment to their socio-economic cultures. Forman's wondrous and extended anticipation of consuming that fountain Coca-Cola at the drugstore counter-relays an intensive involvement in the burgeoning consumer culture of post-war America, of which he was at an ideological level completely conscious and personally invested, even as a youngster who otherwise knew little of the ways of a racist world inhabited by his extended family and other member of his 'race'. It is the thwarting and exclusion from not just this encounter but the contamination of all future consumer exchanges that makes the loss so devastating, and hence makes his alienation from hegemonic American culture so complete. Seiter (1995) acknowledges the tendency in what she identifies as being mainly male-dominated scholarship on consumer culture and culture in general that on the one hand blames women and children vis-à-vis the family for their overwhelming interest in shopping and consumer goods while, on the other hand, chides them for their weakness to hedonistic consumption, identifying these activities and interests as something that need to be censored, overcome or controlled, presumably by a cabal of elite white men (not unlike dominant public attitudes toward radicals or revolutionaries). At the same time, Seiter emphasizes the innate scope for creativity and palpable sense of agency that is offered by consumption activities, and their attraction for those for whom fulfilment of their desires is often otherwise foreclosed in social terms. She subsequently focuses on the two perspectives of the consumer culture of the child that depend on their position in the hierarchy of (consumer) society:

> that of privileged children like my own, with money to spend and confidence that they really count and deserve gratification; and that of children ... whose circumstances do not resemble those of the media world, who participate much more marginally in the consumer economy of childhood, and who have faced at a very young age the frequent and abrupt denial of their desires.
>
> (Seiter, 1995: 3)

As Forman's narrative in particular strongly suggests, however, these stories of childhood consumption are saturated with symbolic meaning, and indeed take on quasi-ritual significance as inaugural points into the transitive ways of passing on knowledge of 'race' that form the basis of (later) radicalization. This accords with Baudrillard's thesis on the symbolic transference of revolutionary agency from the radical subject to the consumer object (or prehaps its reversal), and his view of the significance of ritual experience of space and time; that the best way of studying contemporary society and manifold manifestations of 'radical' hyperrreality is not through macro structuralist ideological analysis, but rather through the anthropological study of micro social behaviours and their reliance on simulacral symbols, rituals and narratives relating to such object-based experience. This view accords with new experiences of childhood in a global consumer economy; these include those such as Rauch's (2007) ethnographic study of adolescent girls in Bolivia and the function of the ritual aspects of consumption in their everyday negotiations and performances of belonging and difference to the various and complex identities and community groups to which they are linked, including national, racial, regional and familial. According to Rauch, it is through the performative and ritual qualities of consumption that children (like adults)

> may negotiate their connection to others at the same time that they may be identified by particular categories. As Brubaker and Cooper

(2000: 6–7) point out, the notion 'that "nations," "races," and "identities," "exist" and that people "have" a "nationality," a "race," an "identity"' obscures the material and symbolic processes through which those relationships and collectivities emerge and evolve.

(Rauch, 2007: 356–7)

It is the deconstruction of these 'obscuring' material and symbolic processes that opens up new horizons in understanding radicalization. These observations provide important insights into the significance that is evidently accorded to consumption rituals, objects and symbolic encounters by writers like Davis, Adams and Forman, and how readily the childhood experience of thwarted (or, in Adams's case, occasionally fulfilled) desire and marginality can be translated into radicalization narratives that assume fabular qualities as the basis for the historical or mythical modelling of the entire political collective, which are in turn based heavily on what are identified by members as symbolically rich ritual experience.

As Gane (1993) reminds us, the Durkheimian conception of ritual hinges on its capacity for the 'formulation of social reproduction' (27) and is (alongside education) a concept that informs the ongoing interpolation of ideology between the living individual and the apparatus of the state (*qua* Althusser). For Durkheim, ritual and education are the two main poles upon which the indoctrination of moral ideology in modern societies is communicated (usually) to children, as well as being the primary mechanisms through which the child first comes to form attachments 'outside himself, and is "above all the means by which society perpetually recreates the conditions of its very existence" (Durkheim, 1956: 123, cf. Althusser, 1971: 123–29)' (Gane, 1993: 27–8). In terms of the representation of such experiences in life narrative forms, ritual also demonstrates the utility of a consumer culture that 'provides children with a shared repository of images, characters, plots and themes [providing] the basis for small talk and play, and it does this on a national and global scale' (Seiter, 1995: 7), functioning as a model for recovering, developing and communicating resistance cultural forms among individuals and in later life. The adult revolutionary might develop a more nuanced or worked-through understanding of the ideological foundations of American consumer economics that are rooted, for example, in racism, but the child has already grasped this at the core of her very being, internalizing the inherent strategies of creativity, language, symbolism, narratives, images, etc. as the basis of an alternative agency that is suitable for the pursuit of forbidden desires on both a local and global scale. What is more, the childhood experience and stories of total immersion in the pleasures and pains of consumer desire can also be found in the often emotive and sometimes profoundly hedonistic or frustrated descriptions of what it's like to be a radical or part of a radical collective (e.g. Stern, [1975] 2007; Becker, 1978). This is not to infantilize radical actors, but rather to stress first the nature of radical subculture, and in particular its incorporation of symbols, narratives, imaginative strategies and emotional and relationship practices that originate or are normatively situated in the cultural arenas of global consumerism and childhood; second it reiterates the centrality and ambiguity of the civil space as a place where children and families are only relatively 'free' to exercise their agency through individual choice and opportunity (e.g. through shopping). As Shapiro (2001) argues, both the family and the global civic domain are deeply ambiguous 'stages' on which ' ... a dramatizing of the dilemma of justice ... torn between familial obligation and civic attachment' (22) are played out. In this context, it is worth noting the language use of experts in radicalization and terrorism, as exemplified by Brian Michael Jenkins's expert testimony to the US Committee on Homeland Security, in which he refers more than once to terrorist recruitment venues as 'retail outlets' (Jenkins, 2007: 5, 8), or the more generic references to the proliferation of global terrorist organizations such as those linked to al-Qaeda as 'franchises' or al-Qaeda as a 'brand'. These same civic dramaturgies are also enacted, for many children, in the proliferating malls and shopping centres that form a part of their main designated public spaces, within which they are at once the objects of welcome and desire, and of deviance, criminality and fear. As Shapiro notes, these fundamental tensions, ambiguities and dilemmas existing between familial obligation and civic attachment (2001: 22) are continually staged, and must be negotiated by children in both their public and private lives and dealt with by the adult adjudicators of the state in an appropriate manner (or at least one that doesn't aggravate what can be an already tense situation).

Though this can be difficult for children, the task and its rewards are not simply negative from the child's point of view. For many social actors, the powerful attraction of consumption forms a focal point for individual expressions of agency, creativity and bonding between like-minded peers, as well as comprising an occasion for the satisfaction of individual material, emotional and identity needs. Yet research into the impact of consumer culture on children has found more pernicious links between television violence and childhood aggression, and the blurring of boundaries between childhood and adulthood (Schor, 2004: 14–16); these are issues that strongly influence what are regarded as positive (i.e. socially productive) versus negative (socially destructive) radicalization, which hinges on the acceptance of (non) violence as a legitimate way of pursuing political aims and the view of children as potential contributors to the carrying out of radical or terrorist action. As Schinkel (2009) points out, however, it is important to bear in mind the distinction between violent and non-violent resistance, and its productive and/or destructive consequences is itself far from clear.

The question now is: how do these experiences, memories and stories translate from narratives of childhood to those that somehow explain or tell the stories of how or why individual actors became radicalized? Forman's richly evocative and detailed narrative contrasts with his simultaneous reference to this same experience as so common as to be virtually a 'cliché' for most black Americans. His additional reference to 'forgetting' this 'deeply buried' memory of what he later deems to be a decisive experience of his childhood is instructive. This can be identified as part of the 'politics of forgetting' whereby '[t]oday, the memory has become [sic] to be seen ... as cure to the pathologies of life' (Huyssen, 1995: 6), while at the same time forgetting has established itself as the best strategy for navigation through the social world' (Misztal, 2003a: 2). In other words, in a political forum, the act of forgetting comprises a pivotal if (sometimes) temporary strategy that is adopted by children to negotiate the conflicts and dilemmas of their social worlds in the here and now; remembering these past stories constitutes a way in which memory can later become a way of dealing with or even a curative to social evils, such as racism or abuse. Misztal (2003b) explores the ostensible yet dialogical contrast between *social remembering* – which enables a sense of meaning linking personal experience to collective culture (via myth, ritual, history, and so forth) – and *social forgetting* – which encourages the (at least) temporary deletion of memories in a way that is consistent with the insistent demands of identity and civil society in the present moment. Misztal argues that social forgetting is essential for the maintenance of certain functional levels of social solidarity in the face of painful or potentially disruptive personal experience. Her reflections are applicable to the solidarity-inducing yet potentially nation-disrupting memories of the collective and individual memories of many black Americans. It could also, as Feldman (2003) contends, be regarded as an instance of the commodification of memory in 'a highly disposable marketplace of insistent history' where divided communities in conflict are virtually 'choking on historical memory' (60). In this context, the highly synchronic and consciously (s)elective nature of remembering and forgetting in such stories as observed by Feldman adds significantly to the emotionally charged and volatile political atmosphere that in turn lends itself to the rationalization of often extreme acts of interpersonal violence; responsibility for this violence is excused or diffused by the individual's assumed position as both victim and perpetrator (a paradigm instance is provided in Alastair Little in his autobiography *Give a Boy a Gun* (2009)). This ambiguity relating to the double-edged power of remembered personal narratives, and its commodification as cultural and political capital in a volatile and fast-changing global marketplace is detectable in a great deal of black American writing, as illustrated by the closing lines of Toni Morrison's novel *Beloved*: 'This is not a story to pass on' – a distinctly antithetical impulse to the inherently social act and epistemologies of storytelling in which such stories are meant to be told and retold, as well as sold and resold. Forman's selective forgetting and later elective remembering enable him to live though the trauma of the original event in a way that is sufficient to be able to reclaim a sense of identity and solidarity (with others and with his own childhood self), and at a temporal remove that does not so urgently threaten his burgeoning sense of identity as a child, at which time memory is allowed to return and to do its (personal and political) work. The manifestation of this phenomenon is particularly evident during times of rapid social change and/or other 'tensions' involving families, communities and states:

> In times of rapid social change or interstate tensions, nation state, ethnic groups and families may draw on versions of history to create or fuel differences. Mead (1932) asserts that pasts are remembered and reworked in ways that meet the needs of groups; these may include the state, families and other forms of collective identities such as religious or political parties.
>
> (McKie and Lombard, 2005: 174)

At this point it is important to reiterate the methodological and epistemological difficulties of dealing with such recovered memory as research data. As Farrall (2009: 175) states, these stories are not 'factual' representations of the past – and so must not be treated by the researcher as such – but rather are presented and must be analysed as 'subjective' truths. At the same time, from the perspective of cultural criminology, it is just as crucial to acknowledge that this does not render such auto/biographical memories useless or meaningless for social scientific research. On the contrary, as Farrall (2009) illustrates in his case study of wrongful conviction based on Angela Cannings' autobiography, and as argued in Chapter 2 of this book, the existence of a sizable corpus of life writings – such as that represented by vast and growing number of political prisoner auto/biography – makes the establishment of patterns and comparisons possible, and so can be a rich and promising site for understanding radicalization. Still, as any scholar and indeed 'ordinary' reader of auto/biography will attest, it is a vital and established convention of reading these texts not to take these outward declarations at face value, not least when it comes to the (recovered) domain of (contested) memory. The authors of auto/biographical texts often (un)consciously incorporate into their writings the basis on which these contestations and suspicions are rightly or wrongly founded. On the part of the reader, this can be identified by the declarations of acquired memory, forbidden or taboo stories (often the most delectable, repeated and thus marketable kind), or the inclusion of large amounts of direct quotations, often by others or long after the events in question. A similar claim could be made about the 'true crime' genre, though it enjoys huge cultural priority over 'expert' discourse.

Such common elements of life writing often elicit both the interest and suspicion of readers, as do other considerations, such as creating an enticing and readable narrative, which large numbers of people might wish to buy. In the 'Acknowledgement' of her autobiography *Growing Up Underground* (1981), Jane Alpert makes a number of significant admissions in this regard. We learn that this particular autobiographical project took some four years to finish, during which time a fully completed version was 'abandoned' on the advice of her editor (8), who urged her to start the project again, thereby adding two-and-a-half years, more than double the time taken to complete the original book. In addition, Alpert consulted several commentators on the period in question and experts in biography and publishing with a view to 'improving' the final version of her memoir:

> Nancy Milford read an early draft of the prologue and gave me the counsel of a skilled biographer in character portrayal. Susan Brownmiller, over innumerable lunches and dinners and sometimes in saunas, listened with critical attention to the story of my life, telling me what was interesting to readers and what was not ... Finally I thank Ed Cripps: for never losing interest in tales he had heard a hundred times, for bearing with my refusal to show him some chapters, for unsparing commentary on those he saw, for an occasional 'Good enough' and a rare (but thrilling) 'It's terrific,' for countless handkerchiefs, and at the end for typing until dawn, for cutting up and gluing together what I was too bone-weary to edit one more time, and even for learning my voice so well that he could write a few of my sentences (which I promptly revised).
>
> (Alpert, 1981: 8)

The final text generated by these and other influences is significant with respect to the authenticity and strategic reading of the final work. Compared to other 'classic' prison life writings, such as Oscar Wilde's *De Profundis* and *The Ballad of Reading Gaol* (1999), the editorial and other revisionist presences are much less in evidence, not least given the circumstances under which they were written – alone in his cell, with access to only one page at a time (Wilde had to relinquish the piece of paper he had written in order to be issued with another page, and thus had no opportunity for revising the final text, though some minor revisions were made to the final edited copy by his friend and literary executor). From a formalist literary standpoint, the sometimes rambling and fragmented quality of the overall narrative detracts from its aesthetic beauty, but also suffuses it with a sometimes almost visceral authenticity, given the palpable sense of the writer's pain and passion at the moment of putting pen to paper. In contrast, in Alpert's memoir, the dominance of the themes of sexuality, and the detailed renderings of sexual practices (including her early stories of sexual awakening as an adolescent) and encounters between the members of her own and other radical groups suggests a knowing presence of the publishing marketeer, and the presumed demand among the reading public to read such intimate and at times salacious stories. As in the case of the British Conservative MP and former cabinet minister Edwina Currie (2002), the timely production of sexual stories among political intimates can function as an injunction to the public to remember them, as well as an occasion for making money out of their pasts. Though perhaps not quite as blatant, in Alpert's case there is also a strongly implied sense of answering or settling scores with others (often former colleagues or associates underground) who have also written or spoken publicly about their relationship with Alpert; this enhances the heightened sense of intertextuality among the great and still increasing number of radical autobiographies to emerge from this heady time in US political history. Given the still unsettled and undecided meaning of these events on current political narratives (e.g. Bill Ayers' influence on president elect Barack Obama), the revisionist impulse of unfolding contemporary forces upon the autobiographical memories of these writers is not to be too readily dismissed.

This dynamic quality of memory and writing emphasizes not just the dialogical role of memory and forgetting in politics and political autobiography, but also the dialogical nature of childhood and the life course as the (recoverable) site for later adult political knowledge, consciousness and resistance.

Childhood memories and ways of knowing in radicalization life stories

The extant literature on terrorism acknowledges the role of remembered 'past harms' as a spur to later radicalization and terrorist action (e.g. Chakrabarti, 2005; Biggar, 2003; Gibney *et al.*, 2008). It is not sufficient, however, to simply recognize that radicalized or terrorist subjects reference these sorts of memories in their explanatory discourses. It is important also to appreciate the significance and role that this type of remembering has for the individual concerned and for his or her collectives and resistance cultures in general. The significance of childhood as a 'site of knowledge' (Watson, 2006) is reiterated elsewhere in Angela Davis's *An Autobiography* (1990), where she records her reaction to the Marin County Court House, part of the Civic Center complex designed by the famous architect Frank Lloyd Wright, where she was tried for murder, kidnapping and criminal conspiracy charges:

> For the courtrooms, he [Wright] had used a motif of circles. In the one where my first court appearance took place, the ceiling had a large round panel with lights encircling it. The fixtures of the room were arranged to correspond with the circle above —the judge's bench, the jury box, and the tables for the prosecution and defense—all were strategically placed to form a circle.
>
> Later I discovered that in designing the courtrooms, Wright had had something very definite in mind. He wanted to depict the nature of justice in the United States. The participants in a trial, he believed, should not be seen as struggling against one another. On the contrary, judge, jury, prosecutor and defendant are holding hands around a circle in the common pursuit of justice.

When I learned about Wright's hand-holding message, I thought about the game we used to play as children— 'Ring around the rosie, Pocket full of posies ... Ashes, Ashes ... ' —and the way the game itself picked certain children to be 'out.' There was absolutely nothing I had in common with the men sitting around the courtroom circle. My comrades, my friends and I—we all saw these men as the manipulators of a judicial game that was rigged against me. We therefore had to continually strengthen the people's movement that was our only hope of beating the odds.

(Davis, 1990: 287)

This story powerfully evokes how – even for a highly educated 'intellectual' revolutionary – the knowledge of childhood is powerfully enduring as a resource for the current task of sense-making of politics in the present adult moment, even trumping the ideological Marxism that she espoused with, in this instance, the symbolism of elite social engineering expressed through architecture. It also reveals not just how the memories from childhood of individual experience are significant sites of knowledge for the grown adult, but also how *text* (in this instance, the text of a nursery rhyme) is used by children as a way of understanding events that present themselves as the chaotic and upsetting experiences that are regularly encountered in their world (as noted previously in the lives of black children in America). Analysis of 'traditional' forms of storytelling like nursery rhymes by experts in child cognitive development has established the relationship between this type of storytelling and the autobiographical experience of ' ... thinking and feeling, and the contribution of storytelling to the inner world of affect' (Collins, 1999: 77). This cognitive connectivity strengthens the child's ties to other language and expressive arts, including writing, talking, reading, drawing and acting, and formatively shapes their access to auto/biography and to narrative, ' ... two areas of human experience in which the human need to story as a way of making sense of that experience is a crucial factor' (ibid.: 77). Furthermore, as Collins argues, these essentially subjective and personal aspects of storytelling shape the broader arena of culture that is affected by the processes of narrative. Davis's citation of this particular nursery rhyme is also interesting, in that it has been commonly associated in the popular imagination with the mediaeval plagues in Europe, and even linked with the demand to show obeisance to a monarch through politically symbolic and collective acts of physical prostration such as kneeling or curtsying to the King or Queen ('we all fall down!') (Opie and Opie, 1997). However, in their research into the origins of this particular nursery rhyme, Opie and Opie found that the rhyme, as it is now generally known, dates back only to the late nineteenth century, and that the 'a-tishoo' references suggest not so much a reference to the mode of communication of plague, but rather a more whimsical and empowering symbolism adopted to describe the imaginative capacity of clever children: 'It would be more delightful to recall the old belief that gifted children had the power to laugh roses' (ibid.: 365). At some level, it would seem that the political connotations of this text as a way of helping the child to make sense of what are otherwise chaotic or unsettling events, or indeed the playful power of the 'knowing' child, made a durable impression on the young Angela. It also demonstrates how important texts such as these are to children (as well as adults) in interpreting their lifeworlds and negotiating power struggles throughout the life course, and that the relationship with some texts established in childhood (like the Bible or Qu'ran, in Ed Husain's experience previously discussed) have enduring influence for both the individual and collective, not least in the reproduction of civic and resistance knowledge and cultures, and the sense of individual empowerment.

The verdict of Davis's famous trial, as previously mentioned, cleared her of all charges, and she has not been involved in any violent or terrorist activity throughout her long career as a radical militant activist. As the story about her and her sister's 'game' with the shop assistants demonstrates, education (even higher education) need not be perceived as a threat to national security as a radicalizing influence. Neither are the symbolic meanings of, say, civic architecture as shared and uncontested as they are generally purported to be. Davis's life writings represent an important case in point: irrespective of government conspiracies to criminalize her for her political beliefs and aspirations, her education and intellectual endeavours have throughout her longlife history as a self-confessed revolutionary consistently allowed her to live out her activism in a fundamentally non-violent way (though nevertheless one that has been disruptive, radical and even militant). Higher education has been noted in the research literature on radicalization as a possible 'cause' of terrorism, or at least substantial contributing factor (e.g. RAND, 2007: 39). What Davis's and First's life writings suggest, however, is that the opposite might actually be the case – a university education may actually *prevent* terrorist violence by enabling radicalized militants to devise more personally rewarding, imaginative and non-violent modes of resistance and protest. Perhaps it is the case that the often localized, non-violent and (sometimes) non-criminal character of these protests by the majority of university-educated activists (Ida B. Wells represents another notable example) indicates the true influence of higher education as a contributing factor in what is the falsely assumed escalating 'process' of radicalization initiated at university which results in terrorist action. It could be that the relationship between higher education and radicalization is strictly speaking more (weakly) correlative than causal, and there are other more salient contributing factors that link higher education with terrorism – notably underemployment and lack of opportunities for new graduates due to social marginalization (Atran, 2003). Another possibility, which the life writings of radicals like Davis (among many others) suggest, is that higher education as an isolated dependent variable actually *inhibits* or *prevents* politically motivated violence and terrorism by providing radicalized actors with a broader conceptual canvas and more sophisticated and reflective resources for pursuing social change in a less violent or destructive way, as the extant research on social movements (e.g. Mansbridge, 2001a, 2001b; Mansbridge and Morris, 2001; McAdam *et al.*, 1996) would indicate. Given the sheer numbers of people who participate, or have participated, in higher education, if this were to be a causal or strongly correlative variable in radicalization, then it would be reasonable to expect that the numbers of radicalized terrorists would be much higher than it actually is. While some life writings, such as *The Islamist* (Husain, 2007), indicate that individuals can become radicalized while at university, this seems to be more commonly a result of being separated from friends and family at a young and impressionable age, or simply falling in with the wrong crowd rather than a pedagogical outcome, and so must be treated with caution.

As a distinctive 'site of knowledge' for political radicalization and its consequences (particularly imprisonment), childhood experiences and childhood consciousness represent major touchstones in the prison life writing of the Egyptian author, physician and activist Nawal El Saadawi in her book *Memoirs from the Women's Prison* (1983).

For Saadawi, childhood marks the cleavage between the two worlds of freedom and imprisonment, myth and reality, the material world and the transcendent: it is a shibboleth with which to make sense of the previously unknown. Again, the memories and rationality of childhood provide links between two very different subjectivities and lifeworlds, enabling her to comprehend, or at least deal in the moment with, the chaos and trauma of her detention.

Real children, as well as childhood, feature in Saadawi's prison life narrative. She details the brutality of imprisoning 'ordinary' women prisoners and their children together, writing: 'If there exists a hell on earth it must be the mothers' cell at the Barrages Women's Prison' (Saadawi, 1983: 43). She voices the great injustice here, mostly because the reasons behind the incarceration are often not the fault of the women or the children, but rather of the men in their families, and the social influence of Egyptian patriarchy in general:

> Behind every one of these women prisoners is a man: a father branding his daughter for a life of thievery, a husband beating his wife into practicing prostitution, a brother threatening his sister so she will smuggle hashish and hard drugs for him, the head of a gang stealing a young female child and training her to beg in the streets ... the pits of society, the very lowest of the low. The tortured on earth. The other face of the system.
>
> (ibid.: 44)

The phrase 'since I was a child' or 'since childhood' appears repeatedly throughout Saadawi's memoir, to the extent that it provides a framework for the narrative:

Since childhood a dream has inhabited my imagination: I write my words and people read them—today, tomorrow, the day after. When does not matter, for people will read them. Those are the people who make a homeland, and my homeland has become those people.

(ibid.: 204)

Writing: such as been my crime ever since I was a small child. Ever since I was a child I have hear my country grandmother say, 'How much the government has lied to us, daughter of my son!'

(ibid.: 202–3)

Since childhood, I've had a passion for solitude. I've not had a room in which I could shut myself off, for the number of individuals in every stage of my life has been greater than the number of rooms in the house. But I have always wrested for myself a place in which I could be alone to write. My ability to write has been linked to the possibility of complete seclusion, of being alone with myself, for I am incapable of writing when I am unable to give myself completely to solitude.

(ibid.: 129)

But since childhood I have abhorred rulers and authority—ever since I saw my mother rebel against my father when he raised his voice against her, and every since I heard my father cursing the king, the government, and the British.

(ibid.: 117)

Saadawi thus uses childhood as a reference point for how childhood experiences and parenting, and even her own parents' childhood experiences, can affect later political activism, and form the original life experience from which to learn to resist and rebel:

She [Sadaawi's mother] gave me life, and she has given me the revolution ever since I was a child.

(ibid.: 119)

My father and mother used to encourage me to participate in the nationalist demonstrations against the King and the British. During the 1919 Revolution, my father had been a student of Dar al-Ulum in Cairo, Egypt's major teacher training institute. In the company of some of his classmates, he participated in beating up a party of English soldiers. A bullet splinter wounded him in the leg, and he returned to his village, Kafr Tahla, carried on a donkey cart.

My mother had been a young pupil in elementary school in Cairo at that time. She went out into the street with some of the other girls from her school to call out slogans against the British. The police arrested her and kept her in the police station for a full day before she returned home.

(ibid.: 153)

As with other political prisoners like Ruth First, Saadawi's recursion to childhood marks a huge disruption in what is the norm progression of chronological time:

> I drew my fingers from the soil and looked up: a head resembling my grandmother's, wound in a black kerchief. The features, though are different, and so is the voice. So is the time.
>
> Time becomes confused for me here. I don't know if I am the child playing in the dirt or the woman caged inside the prison. My childhood and adolescence, and all the stages of my life, seem to be intermeshed into one period of time, or it is as if there is no such thing as chronological time.
>
> (ibid.: 110)

This is a very interesting and revealing passage, as it shows how the prison experience works to dissemble cultural structures that normally comprise the progressive, chronological life course as narratively organized through a series of relatively distinct developmental stages. Childhood thus becomes a way of understanding life in prison, not necessarily because prisoners are infantilized (as indeed they often are), but because the separation of the stages of life and its progression disintegrates, making what were the formerly obsolete or distant life stages (past childhood, future death) suddenly seem not just relevant and available, but concurrent, collapsing into a consuming and amorphous *present*. The over-riding presence of death in political prisoner writing, exacerbated by these experiences of time, can be a liberating and empowering but also very volatile and dangerous phenomenon (as also represented in the prison life writings of the IRA hunger striker Bobby Sands (Dearey, 2005)):

> From the inner selves of human beings threatened with death emerged the tyrannical demon—the latent strength long imprisoned, the stored-up energy suppressed since the remote past, since childhood, since birth, or rather from before birth, ever since those human beings were foetuses in their mothers' wombs.
>
> The prison administrative staff hastened to us. What had happened? What had lifted the lid and revealed the rebellious demon caged inside the seashell?
>
> (ibid.: 184)

In her prison memoir, Saadawi makes a great many of links between her experience of prison and her experience of childhood. These also include her experience of pain and pleasure, and learning about love as in adolescence (30); the childlike joy to be found in daily rituals such as making tea (39); and the recovery of communal experience of living as one of a group of women and girls as in another type of 'total institution', the boarding school, and the joys of collectivity and problems of aggression this entails (40).

As is repeatedly demonstrated in prisoner life writing, the boundaries between bodies and minds are blurred, as are virtually all the other boundaries that we rely upon to create the images we create to represent and reproduce it in cultural forms and everyday social interaction, especially the boundaries delineating gender, power and desire, the public and private world, childhood and adulthood, individuals and collective groups (including families) and time and space. These significantly affect normative narratives and experiences of belief, liberation, identity and embodiment, enabled by deviant social labels (such as prisoner, rebel, artist, 'black sheep', etc.) not just to stigmatize and punish, but also to explore alternative narratives of imagination and experience. In this section, I have quoted from a range of political prisoner life writings, and argued that children and childhood are significant factors in the phenomenon of radicalization. These stories reveal a great deal about *who* is likely to be vulnerable to radicalization as a result of being influenced by external forces such as extremist groups or state security forces, not just in places where children live in environments of extreme poverty and conflict. Such 'extremes' of poverty, deprivation and violent conflict can lead to an endemic culture of fatalism among individuals and communities, which can exacerbate the recruitment vulnerable children and young people to violent extremist or terrorist groups; however, these are neither necessary nor sufficient as causes of radicalization, as the relative advantages of those who become radicalized in 'western' societies indicate. Instead, the life writings of political prisoners supports the view that childhood represents an important 'site of knowledge', which is implicitly or explicitly acknowledged as a seminal factor in the radicalization narratives of political actors. Throughout their lives, children develop what, in many instances, turn out to be richly evocative and intensely imaginative worlds and motivational memories of feelings, narratives, texts and rationales, and the sorts of everyday coping skills that can later be of use to the adult radicals and political activists, particularly those who are sent to prison (perhaps also for those who end up dying as a result of their terrorist action, but this link is of course extremely difficult, if not impossible, to prove). Despite the complexities of specific environments, and the chaos and trauma brought on by poverty, adult unemployment, the ongoing threat of immanent violence, and fear, this knowledge begins to accumulate at a very early age, as children ' … are actively engaging with the social and cultural events that surround them and are attempting to make sense of them' (Connolly and Healy, 2003: 45).

However, while children may acquire knowledge of the language and symbolism of conflict and the realities of violence from an early age, their powers to develop a sophisticated understanding and mechanisms of interpretation remain underdeveloped, at least for some time. While this pool of knowledge may manifest itself in their adult lives as 'radicals' or 'soldiers', this is of course not an inevitable outcome. It is therefore important not to stigmatize these children or their families or communities unduly as producing a unique or abnormal 'substrate' of memory for the purposes of radicalization – such knowledge, memories, practices and strategies function as the resource for all adults in negotiating their daily lives, for better or worse. Youthful rebellion – such as described by Husain (2007) – against parents, the family and the local community can also undoubtedly play a part in radicalization, and it does in many if not most families in other social-psychological contexts. While some writers, like Saadawi, indicate that they learned their radicalism from their parents, other radicals like the Russian Bolshevik Victor Serge in his *Memoirs of a Revolutionary* (2002) insist that they initially eschewed the life of a revolutionary simply because it is what their parents did, and they wanted to be different (at least at the start of their lives as independent of their parents), although in the end this is precisely the kind of lives they pursued. Still other writers, as will be shown in the next section (e.g. Jones, 2004), tell stories about family political histories that significantly complicate these delicate emotional, development and familial links.

Is the intergenerational transmission of radicalization down to middle-class parenting practices?

In her landmark research on child-rearing practices in middle-class and working-class families, the sociologist Annette Lareau (2003) found that childhood is, in her view, 'unequal' with respect to the level and quality of active involvement of adults in the lives of the children in their care. Among other things, she argues that the 'concerted cultivation' of middle-class children's in comparison to the 'accomplishment of natural growth' model of child-rearing in lower-class families results in the greater sense of middle-class children's own agency and ability as individuals to act on behalf of others. But of course this does not mean – nor does Lareau suggest – that children's from lower-class or poorer backgrounds are unwilling or unable to engage in acts of resistance or contribute to resistance cultures, nor that individuals from more privileged socio-economic backgrounds are destined to take active and challenging stances on issues of social change based on their personal experience or preferences. Nevertheless, as Trnka (2003) has suggested in her analysis of the Red Army Faction or Baader-Meinhof group, there is a notable tendency among contemporary extremist groups to include among their membership many middle-class individuals who have a highly developed (and sometimes over-inflated) sense of their own agency and propensity to appropriate the suffering of others in their 'struggle' for liberation as an expression of their cultural heritage.

The family biography of the son of Weathermen and later Weather Underground activists Thai Jones (2004) writes about how just such a situation emerged to facilitate the development of the then Weathermen under the leadership of his father Jeff (himself the product of a middle-class family headed by a father who was once incarcerated as a conscientious objector) into a violent terrorist organization:

> *Was this all?* Wondered Jeff, as he arrived around 10:00 P.M. and saw a few hundred people beside the bonfire. If there had been a thousand of them, it might have seemed an army. This was a sacrifice, a play-acting troupe of soldiers armed with cardboard swords and shields. Then he made the mental adjustment that Weatherman had trained him for. There weren't many, he figured, but they were the right ones, the vanguard. He had known most of them for years. They had marched together, been arrested together, had their heads beaten in together. They had the same jokes, like the one about Marion Delgado, the five-year-old kid who, just for kicks, placed a twenty-five-pound slab of concrete across a railroad track to derail a passenger train. *New Left Notes* had printed his grinning picture, kneeling over the rails in overalls as he reenacted his heroic deed. For Weatherman, he had become a half-serious symbol of the damage that the small were capable of wreaking on the powerful.
>
> Jeff took the bullhorn and faced the crowd. 'I am Marion Delgado,' he said, and cheers rose from those who knew the joke.
>
> (Jones, 2004: 178)

In this story, we see the middle-class adult and Weathermen leader Jeff identify himself politically with the violent action, read as resistance, of a Chicano boy living in poverty.

These stories demonstrate what we might call the fluidity of children's and families' actions on unrelated others who choose to interpret these as political within their own symbolic realms of meaning. What the Weatherman example particularly shows is the desire of middle-class and generally well-educated young radicals to ally themselves with, and build their political allegiances upon, the experiences and actions of the poor and dispossessed, or alternatively with the anarchy of extreme violence that is inflicted on 'innocent' victims sutured to the institution of childhood or to real children. To what are we to attribute such political idealizations of children, the family and violence within radical or resistance cultures, not least in the case of the Weathermen, a group with a distinctively homogenous membership, overwhelmingly white, privileged, educated people in their late teens or twenties, many of whom had severed ties with their own families, and vehemently sought to 'smash' the monogamous marital relationship that forms the normative basis of the family?

Here we witness once again the relationship between the family via the child and childhood and the state, characterized as it is by mutual dependency and ongoing tensions, fear and conflict, through which they exist in shifting patterns of cooperation, competition and 'care'. This binding up of children and the family with the disciplining exercise of 'legitimate' violence by and against the state foregrounds the shifting patterns of politically symbolic violence in late modernity. Whereas Foucault (1977) identified the idealized object of 'legitimate' (i.e. state) violence in pre-modern times to be directed against those who threatened the sovereign (whether in the form of regicide (Foucault, 1977) or parricide (Spierenburg, 2008)), in contemporary modernity this position has been usurped by those who threaten violence against 'innocent victims':

> Moreover, the subject of what used to be regicide is no longer a king that apparently fell out of grace with God or the gods; it is the 'innocent victim' of the political individual, and his or her death is first of all punished because it is unlawful, because it offends the state, like any murder.
>
> (Schinkel, 2009: 87)

Drawing on existentialist theory, Schinkel (2009) argues that this tension in the legitimating infliction of violence on innocent victims in the public versus private spheres results in a paradox in which the achievement of its aim – the monopolizing of violence – by the state would thus eradicate all private violence, and thereby make itself obsolete by eliminating its core function, i.e. to legislate and punish illegitimate interpersonal violence (mainly among intimates). Such a totalizing monopoly on violence within the private sphere would arguably have a similar effect on the family (and by extension other quasi-familial sub-groups), rendering it a crude instrument of the law, and therefore also obsolete. Schinkel concludes that this paradox reveals the legitimating violence carried out by the state is reliant upon the existence of 'non-legitimate private violence' (ibid.: 87) directed primarily at 'innocents' and intimates by which it is sustained. The same could be said of the reliance of familial or radical sub-groups upon the illegitimate (or disproportionate) infliction of violence by the state as a legitimating impulse for their continued existence.

How are such paradoxes, based on a deep and underlying sense of mutual dependency and consent underscored by violence and the desire for legitimation, resolved? For Schinkel, the resolution comes in a political logic of this interdependency of the state in relation to the violent/criminal expressed in the political rhetoric of evil, rendered in the form of a tautology:

> The discursive exorcism of the criminal from society cleanses society itself from illegitimate elements—a secularized form of 'deliverance from evil'—and of blame for the illegitimacy of the criminal, thus ensuring that a society of properly subjectified subjects remains a *communitas perfecta*. As soon as subversive elements appear, these are excommunicated as existing 'outside society'. This leads to a tautological self-definition of the

social system by means of a state–society differentiation: it is what it is, because it is not what it is not.

(ibid.: 89)

The predominance of mutual dependency is, according to Shamgar-Handelman (1994), disrupted by the disintegration of a sense of agreed social consensus and the distancing of the social–normative 'centre' of society from a proliferation of non-conforming 'peripheries' (253).

> The wider the distance between the centre and the periphery is (whether this distance results from legitimate social pluralism, or from social changes that reduce public support for the central values of society), the more will conflict of interests and competition between the family and state come to the fore.
>
> (ibid.: 253).

So, while the interpersonal violence against innocents (e.g. children) that characterizes the family's hegemony over the private sphere and intimate relationships is constitutive of the 'evil' against which the state depends for its legitimacy, the family's normative role in bearing and rearing children nevertheless places them in a position as 'society's creditor' (ibid.: 254), whereby the state is morally, culturally and materially (in the sense of maintaining a durable population) indebted to and dependant upon the family. The basis of this contractual relationship is usually on the unspoken knowledge of common-sense, negotiated at the verges of the state–family spheres of public–private life, mainly carried out through incremental agreements on the details of minimum standards for caring for children. 'However, events that change the moral order of society (such as revolution, extreme change of regime, the overthrow of colonial rule, etc.) are the events that tend to carry in their wake a comparatively clear statement of family–state relations' (ibid.: 254). Shamgar-Handelman observes that this cooptation of children, childhood and practices such as child-rearing within the family by 'extreme' political forces, such as in the Communist ideologies of the former USSR and the Nazi regime in Germany, substantially affected their capacity to contest and eventually win control of the state.

Viewed through a criminal as opposed to political lens, the tension between children and the state symbolized in the political rhetoric of the ability (or not) of parents to control their children is equally substantive and consequential in terms of perceived threats to national security and the possibility of regime change. RAND (2007) and Sageman (2004) note the rise in levels of juvenile crime levels during and after episodes of war, and consider it a key independent variable in the radicalization process. Olujic (1998) makes the same empirical link:

During the war [in Croatia] there was an increase in the rate of juvenile crime. Serious crimes committed by minors increased by 53 percent between 1991 and 1992 (Ministry of Labor and Social Welfare 1995). In the unsettled atmosphere after the official end of hostilities, the rate of juvenile crime continued to rise—up an additional 48 percent between 1992 and 1993—returning to its prewar level only in 1994.

(Olujic, 1998: 326)

Here the idealization of 'the good child' (in preference to its deviant or criminal other) is one who is wholly subjugated to the moral and cultural values of the dominant political order; this is a social construct that is essential to the (re) generation of civic ideology and an insurance policy for its future reproduction via the family in cooperation with and support of the state. The story told by Thai Jones about his father's appropriation of the short life and violent death of Marion Delgado represents the other side of the coin, as it were; it encapsulates the rhetorical cooptation of children's lives by radical sub-groups as models for resisting or frustrating the relentless growth of state power through the suffering of its weakest and most vulnerable members. As Trnka (2003) contends, however, such acts of political appropriation are not merely opportunistic: they represent extensions to colonial oppression by actively subverting or inhibiting the development of resistance cultures among those 'others' who are actually suffering poverty and injustice (disproportionately women and children). Instructively, as Shamgar-Handelman (1994: 264) points out, none of these political strategies that are centred on the child/innocent seek the empowerment of children in terms of enhancing their active contributions to political life or improving their life chances or levels of protection (including, importantly, those who are troublesome, criminalized or otherwise labelled as deviant). Ironically, she argues, this is one of the few political strategies that is yet to be genuinely implemented by any political group in the current political crisis. Instead, the political roles accorded to children are to function as the object for political demands for more intensive measures of social and/or familial control, or alternatively as a site for contesting existing social norms, and encouraging resistance and dissent, in order to facilitate the emergence of already privileged (white, middle-class, young) adult groups into positions of power. Seen from these perspectives, the 'good child' is not one who lives a good, healthy or happy life, but rather one who can engage in activities that are preservative/destructive to life or property as long as their activities are readable through the (conservative/revolutionary) violence of the adults who are themselves vying for state power.

Conclusion

In this chapter, the notional implications of children, childhood and 'the child' have been considered as contributive or constitutive aspects of the phenomenon of radicalization as represented in the autobiographical writings of those who have been at some point imprisoned for what they perceive as their political offences against the state, and their role – if any – in their retrospective narratives of radicalization. References to the scholarly and public policy literature on children and childhood, as well as radicalization and terrorism, have informed the analysis of these life narratives focusing on the child and/or childhood in opposition to the state. A number of patterns are observable in these narratives, and are subsequently relevant with respect to current analysis and policy-making in this complex and contested area of political and cultural life.

What we find in these stories is a great diversity of richly detailed and emotionally evocative and imaginative landscapes upon which later radicalization can be written and indeed read – by the writer him/herself and/or by others. In contradiction to the conceptual image of the child in legal and policy-making discourses as weak, vulnerable or passive (McNamee *et al.*, 2005), what emerges from these stories are representations of children and childhood that are saturated with intensive meaning for their narrators, often hinging on a sense of childhood agency (as in the case of Angela Davis's recollections) or the injustice of racism (as in the cases of James Forman, Malcolm X, and Ed Husain). This is not to deny that some children are forced to live in appalling situations of extreme poverty, violence and deprivation, in which the urgency of the struggle for survival by the family or community collective can result in a hugely destructive sense of fatalism, which drives children into the arms of terrorist recruiters (e.g. Obaid-Chinoy, 2007). But even in situations where children are identifiable by their weakness or vulnerability to such exploitative or criminal influences, many of them are nevertheless able to display an immensely creative and imaginative capacity to act strategically and effectively in resisting these external forces, whether they emanate from extremist sub-groups or the state, and that these childhood experiences would appear to be available for these radicalizing purposes throughout their lives. To put it another way, childhood provides *the* template for knowledge about power and resistance for many radicalized actors, at least as much and in some cases more so than political or religious ideologies.

While children and childhood are culturally identifiable with the private and domestic sphere, it is instructive that many of these stories take place in what can generally be identified as the public world of the child – in families, certainly, and among friends, but also predominantly in school and also in the outside world and in the marketplace. The often detailed micro orientation of these stories centring on consumption and education provide valuable insights into the manner of agency or injustice and its linked outcomes for the radicalized individual(s) concerned. With respect to the school environment, the issue of racism is particularly notable, specifically the racist remarks of 'well-meaning' teachers to their pupils. While currently the UK Government is directing attention to the issue of radicalization of children in schools, it is far from clear that the sorts of incidents recorded in the life writings considered here would come under scrutiny, let alone be adequately addressed according to guidelines provided in the government's 'toolkit' for countering radicalization among children and families in schools. The focus is too much on the role of school authorities to reinforce surveillance and 'counter-narratives' in response to any signs of extremist views, with too little emphasis on the potential (if unconscious or unintended) stigmatizing behaviours of even a minority of teachers and other school staff in relation to the children and their families. As Corsaro (2005) and Lareau (2003) indicate in their studies of class-based practices of child-rearing and the evolutionary political agency of children, the effectiveness of strengthening the already considerably enhanced practices of social control in relation to middle-class children by their parents and teachers would suggest that this represents a counter-indicative or perhaps even counter-productive strategy for preventing later radicalization. Rather than encouraging 'net widening' (Cohen, 1985) in schools with respect to their function as a state institution of social control, perhaps a better approach would be to find more authentic and less deterministic ways of empowering children and their families (particularly those from less advantaged backgrounds) to encourage their sense of agency and participation in civic life through a more inclusive and empowering process. This would, for instance, enable them to point out and demand redress for what they consider unacceptable behaviour on the part of school staff or others in positions of authority over them who (at present) stand to benefit from current initiatives designed to increase their powers of surveillance and control. This could have the long-term advantage of building a sense of civic participation and responsibility among those children and families who often, as the research shows, feel intimidated and powerless in the face of educational and child welfare authorities who do or could accuse them of deviance from 'moderate' norms.

Another factor identified in this sample group of life writings is the importance of consumerism and consumption as scene-setting and plot devices for the originating point of radicalization narratives. As in the case of children, and their capacity to participate and contribute to the commandeering of the world of politics by adults, consumption as an activity and area of cultural life tends to be denigrated as at best frivolous, at worst the arena for the indulgence of envy, pride, hedonism and greed (Campbell, 1998). The view is encouraged that children are particularly susceptible to temptation, manipulation and self-destructive choices as consumers, forming the target of corporate advertising and inflicting 'pester power' on their poor, put-upon parents, who are frequently reminded in the media about the cost of raising a child. However, as researchers in the area of consumption studies note, the culture of consumerism is a vital part of the political ideology of late modernity, especially in the west. In the wake of the erosion of class, employment and other rigidly hierarchical economic structures, it provides a rich and fertile ground for the ongoing free play of identity construction, leisure, imagination and emotional life. Consumer objects are elemental in the making of the modern child,[10] and the objects that children make are among the most treasured in the world.[11] The point is that while children are sometimes shamelessly targeted by corporate advertisers or others who would exploit or manipulate them for their own selfish ends, at the same time children quickly develop a sophisticated sense of (shopping) nous, and can actively engage in the production, marketing and sale (e.g. the classic lemonade stand or the paper-round) of consumer goods, thereby becoming full participants in the global economic community. As with adults, consumption provides a canvas on which the desires and aspirations of individuals can be projected and represented; the frustration or denial of these desires or their humiliating denigration in the public world of the child, as these stories show, can be hugely upsetting and alienating experiences for those who are on the receiving end of this type of marginalization; they can form the foundation upon which later and cumulative experiences of alienation and anger (and potentially later radicalization) are projected and (re)constructed. Perhaps it is time to take children more seriously as global consumers and producers, as well as manufacturers and contributors to the modern world and global politics.

Apropos Jack Henry Abbott's (1982) statement, quoted at the beginning of this chapter and further supported by the many and multifarious citations of childhood as a prime resource for the tactical knowledge and survival strategies necessary to cope with the demands of political radicalization and/or imprisonment, in many ways it is no exaggeration to say that childhood provides the *logos*[12] of radicalization, if not also of terrorism. Any parent or teacher will quickly recognize the logic employed by ideologues such as Osama bin Laden (2005), whose rationale is basically founded on a principle that justifies the use of violence against civilian populations because – and I paraphrase here – 'they (or their friends or governments) started it' and 'we will stop hurting you when you stop hurting us first'. Such logic also underpins a traditional model of child-rearing, in which pain (often in the form of corporal punishment) is inflicted on the defenceless (if no longer deemed to be 'innocent') child in the name of 'love' and 'care'; as a mechanism of discipline and control, this is reminiscent of the altruistic sentiments frequently alluded to in radical/terrorist justifications and ideologies, and indeed the policy responses by western governments. This alignment of childhood with radicalization is not meant to infantilize or demean, but rather to explore the deep and complex cultural sources of knowledge, reason and emotion by which these social phenomena emerge and are dealt with. This is consistent with the meaning of *logos* as a concept that guides the search for structure and order in the form of rational knowledge with respect to what is otherwise chaotic and frightening experience. This link is further supported by the cognate need to 'tell' that is also cited in this definition, which we see reproduced in the proliferation of auto/biographical texts by imprisoned and other radicalized actors, as well as the profoundly generative capacity (*logos spermatikos*) regarding the 'intelligence' that these texts contain, how these are used by other radicals or extremist groups to construct similar ideological subcultures and organizational structures based on this knowledge, and their as yet underutilization as a source of knowledge and information on the part of agencies who seek to 'counter', frustrate or alternatively predict and prevent this generation of values, philosophies and ideas.

While it is a fallacy to conclude that children or the experiences of childhood 'cause' radicalization, or that children are passive or naïve recruits to extremist groups, the texts of political prisoners recording their life stories strongly suggest that they are important factors in the manifestation of radicalization, whether in real, symbolic, epistemological or rhetorical terms. What is more, the salience of childhood as an independent variable gives rise to some discrepancies with respect to viewing radicalization as a 'process', or at least a realist/materialist process that is rooted in a discrete progression of linear chronological time. If radicalization is to be regarded as a process rooted in childhood, then the length and breadth of this process is significantly broadened, probably to the point of making any short (e.g. four-step process) model meaningless; this is not least because in the interim, prior to the onset of adulthood, children are reliant on the filtering of peer networks and family life, class and ethnic identities, and associated life chances, myths and memories of past harms as hermeneutic devices for interpreting and making sense of their emergent body of knowledge. As the sociological literature on childhood demonstrates, childhood as a notional life stage is to some extent (depending upon your viewpoint) socially or culturally constructed, i.e. it is a product of a constellation of social, economic, political and cultural factors that affect the representation practices in question. It is along these lines that consideration has focused on the impact of childhood mainly as a site of knowledge recollected from the social conditions of prison, the disintegrating influence of which upon time and space calls to question the priority of 'process' modelling of radicalization.

To return to intrafamily relationships and childhood experiences, the studies cited by Corsaro (2005) among others raise interesting and challenging questions as to the agency of children and the daily milieu within which they experience and internalize cultural values within the family, and how these affect their perceived self-image, life chances and interactions with the 'outside' world. While middle-class children are generally susceptible to greater, more intrusive and microscopic levels of control by their parents at home, at school and in their leisure time, the relative paucity of 'home-grown' terrorists who originate from the lower classes in western societies would suggest that these more intensively controlled childhood environments are not effective in preventing or forestalling later radicalization (thus bringing into question current government policy that advances the development of such middle-class practices of the micro-management and social control of children and their daily lives). On the contrary, the inculcation of a highly developed sense of identity, power and commitment, fuelled by the choice-driven political agenda of western consumer culture, means that the children of the western middle classes are especially prone to the very cultural aspects of radicalization cited in Chapter 1, such as a heightened sense of agency, individuality and superiority, and the desire to instigate and achieve social change, not least on behalf of others. While the lives of deprived, demonized, marginalized or criminal children might leave them with a sense of political apathy or passivity relative to their middle- or upper-class counterparts, they are still susceptible to feelings of discontent and anger against society, which can fuel later radicalization; a global social context in which the divisions between rich and poor are becoming increasingly pronounced and entrenched, means that even if a relatively small proportion of these children become radicalized, it is still a potentially serious threat. Viewed through the lens of class conflict, the lives and actions of these lower-class children can (as shown by the Marion Delgado story, and the many stories about poor or disadvantaged children told by Zawahiri, bin Laden, etc.) provide powerful iconic images and tropes useful for extremist sub-groups as a way of codifying the social injustices and inequalities overseen by the state, irrespective of class identities.

From these observations, a number of questions arise. How does the ostensibly significant levels of participation within radical movements of middle-class individuals affect their interpretation of designated symbolic acts of resistance linked to childhood or the family as a spur to radicalization (whether in relation to themselves or to others)? What influence does the relative autonomy and independence from adult/parental control that is experienced by working-class and poorer children have on their political futures as adults, or on those of other adults who would make political capital out of these experiences? Do the resistance strategies of children (of whatever class) inculcate a sense of fatalism or activism, or does it make any discernible difference at all to how they perceive their sense of agency in their worlds? Though these would provide the basis of a fascinating long-term ethnographic study of radical families and children, the recruitment of such families, given their fears about disclosure, makes it unlikely that such research is currently feasible, or indeed ever would be. In the meantime, there are some auto/biographical texts relating to the lives of families, often written by the grown-up children, and we will now turn to these in order to try to find some answers to these questions in the next chapter.

Chapter 5

Is radicalization a family affair?

A tale of two families

'The family' is an exceedingly important yet equally contested notion in contemporary society and in scholarly debate. The sheer diversity of this fundamental social institution has led many to refer to it instead under the guise of 'famil*ies*' or the more generic designation 'kinship relations'. Yet it is this very diversity that demonstrates the great capacity of the family as social institution to absorb significant levels of social, political, cultural and economic change, and still endure as one of the most foundational and influential entities shaping a fast-changing and globalized modern world. For millennia, kinship and marriage relations in whatever form have proved to be fundamental to most if not all societies because they have provided important models for the construction and indeed study of the social, whether modelled on the theories of evolutionary Darwinism (e.g. in the work of the nineteenth-century Swiss anthropologist J. J. Bachofen), diffusionism (Robert Lowe), functionalism (Malinowski and Radcliffe-Brown) or structuralism (Lewis Henry Morgan, Marx and Engels). These theories have posited different ideological narratives of the social from the perspective of the family throughout the nineteenth and twentieth centuries, focusing on key aspects, such as the progressive development of societies through a series of historical stages, the non-linear reproduction of cultural practices and behaviours, the emotional bonds of sentiment and blood ties, or contract-based exchange relationships between opposing factions or groups, respectively (Macfarlane, 1986). Like society, the family (and indeed childhood) as an institution has persisted over long periods of time and across different cultures, although its individual members have changed; unlike societies and the state, families have the biological capacity for physical (re)production, thus ensuring their continuation and endurance (Shamgar-Handelman, 1994).

The relentless temporal, biological and generational qualities of the family are reflected in its ideological and daily practices, to the extent that '[w]e can see families as reproducing themselves both literally and ideologically' (Dallos, 1997: 174) in reaction to diverse and ongoing dialogical influences. Above all, this temporal and biological regeneration, and ideological and cultural reproduction, take place under the further influence of the *agency* of individual

family members and their shifting alliances. This situation is significantly complicated by its contextualization within the highly individualistic culture of
globalized modernity that exacerbates the fluid – or 'liquid', to use Bauman's
(2003) famous expression – or Giddens' (1992) 'pure relationship' based on
emotional intimacy, which are increasingly credited as being formative characteristics of contemporary family life. Dallos (1997) reiterates the agency of
families within the ideological culture of the nation state when he writes, 'Above
all, these decisions suggest the possibility that families do not simply absorb
ideologies and discourses wholesale, but that they translate them within their
own "family culture", that is, the traditions and current dynamics within their
own family' (174). Nevertheless, in his Reith lecture 'Family', Anthony Giddens
(1999) suggests that the experience 'on the ground' is not simply one of confidence or empowerment pertaining to the agency of the family or their individual members when it comes to making decisions about (let alone living out)
their sexuality, identity and lifestyle choices, child-rearing practices, relationships or emotional ties; in a globalized world, these decisions may be characterized, shaped or influenced by a comparatively wide variety of choice, but
can also be reacted to with resistance, anxiety, uncertainty, dissimilitude and
dissent, both within and without the family, thereby attenuating any burgeoning
sense of agency or emancipation from the traditions or conventions of the past:

> Among all the changes going on today, none are more important than
> those happening in our personal lives – in sexuality, emotional life,
> marriage and the family. There is a global revolution going on in how
> we think of ourselves and how we form ties and connections with others.
> It is a revolution advancing unevenly in different regions and cultures,
> with many resistances.
>
> (Giddens, 1999)

What Giddens calls the 'catch all' category of the 'traditional family', and
the periodic calls for its reinstatement by politicians and/or the institutions of
the state when faced with seemingly insurmountable social and political
crises, serves as a tried and tested way of trying to reassert state power
through the institution of the family by shoring up its traditional powers to
control deviant youth, women, homosexuals, etc. as part of the unwritten
'contract' between the family and the state. Yet current attempts to construct
explanations of radicalization in the form of political 'narratives' based on
'tribal' or 'traditional' cultural practices that are consolidated and symbolized in practices like marriage, religion and the education and socialization
of children have instigated a proliferation – if not an explosion – of different
and even contradictory or counter-productive responses. Some of these have
pointed the finger at the functional qualities of tribal or traditional marriage
practices to consolidate quasi-dynastic bonds of solidarity among radical
actors (e.g. White, 1993; Ismail, 2008); others have suggested that changes to

traditional practices around marriage in response to 'western' cultural influence are responsible for the emerging 'homegrown' security threat. A notable example is provided by Malik's argument that

> ultimately ascribes Siddique Khan's [the 7/7 bomber] radicalization to his choice to marry for love, instead of an arranged in traditional 'village' fashion, the alienation which ensued between him and his family and the way in which Wahhabi-ite groups preyed upon this alienation in order to recruit him and indoctrinate him into an al Qa'eda outlook.
>
> (in Githens-Mazer, 2008: 555)

An exhaustive review of the expansive literature on the family is well beyond the constraints of this study. However, from this substantial corpus of literature, we can gain a number of general insights about the family that are useful for analysing its particular role (if any) in the phenomenon of radicalization. Dallos (1997) sets out the following general criteria for studying the family:

> It can be argued that choices and the beliefs underlying them, operate at three distinct by interconnected levels:
>
> 1 *The socialcultural* – what is perceived as acceptable and desirable in any given society.
> 2 *The familial* – how people in families jointly negotiate decisions, based partly on the internalizations of cultural discourses and partly on their joint evolution of a set of shared beliefs.
> 3 *The personal* – each family member has a more or less unique set of personal beliefs: for the parents this may emanate from their accumulated experience prior to forming a family; for all members personal beliefs also develop from contacts outside the family, and so on.
>
> These three levels need to be considered simultaneously to provide a comprehensive picture of 'the family'.
>
> (176)

This chapter will thus consider the socio-cultural, familial and personal aspects of family life as described within political prisoner life writing.

Families serve important ideological functions within society, whether traditional and modern, 'western' or 'other'. In particular, they are core concerns of government with respect to reinforcing – and challenging – the institutions of the state. From a policy perspective, families are about reproducing and transmitting the normative cultural values of a society through mechanisms like the production and socialization of children, and other patterns of daily interaction. As Dallos (1997) has noted, families reproduce themselves both literally and ideologically in a continual but also active sort of way in which family members don't simply 'play out' predetermined roles, but are agents in their ongoing reproduction, alteration and transmission vis-à-vis their own distinctive 'family culture'.

Families are thus pivotal in the ongoing development, manifestation and immanence of the past, present and future of societies. How this happens, and in response to what particular internal and external forces, are salient to the present study.

> Each family or grouping can be seen as to some extent creating a unique interpersonal system of meanings and actions, a version of family life which develops from the amalgamation of its members' negotiations and choices based upon their personal and shared beliefs and histories.
>
> (Dallos, 1997: 176)

The signal importance of this role, coupled with the implicit agency of the family in adapting their own discrete cultures, can cause a deep sense of unease from the perspective of the institutional powers of the state, which (as Enlightenment principles would have it) favour the principles of objectivity, uniformity, conformity and rationalization above the more discrete, subjective, anecdotal, localized character of family life (Inwood, 2005). Families can thus be viewed as either the idealized structural form for ensuring the future of the state, or alternately an instrument for resistance and change, and therefore as the object of suspicion due to its individualistic and localized interpretations of cultural life such as religion, ethnicity, sexuality and identity, or other nationalist, political, economic or working practices that are elemental to everyday life. This suspicion on the part of the state can lend itself to attacks upon the family and its discrete cultural forms when they are viewed as not being in alignment with or support of institutional government, especially during times of political upheaval when the state is already under pressure, in conflict or otherwise in crisis:

> Attacks on the family are typical of revolutionary periods. Christ told his disciples to leave their parents and families and so to follow him. The French, Russian, and Chinese revolutions all undermined the traditional family structure in those countries in an attempt to speed the progress toward a new social order. The Israeli kibbutz is another example of the same social process.
>
> (Dallos, 1997: 183)

What is more, such attacks on and panics about the family often emanate from public performances by politicians, and other moral and political entrepreneurs, as a result of their anxieties about the status of the family itself and its perceived instability with respect to its internal capacity to adequately and predictably perform the social–moral roles ascribed to it. As Dallos again succinctly points out, this critical view of the family has an impact not only on the idea of 'the family' and family units, but also on the individuals who comprise them. In response, families devise ways and means of dealing with the public anxieties surrounding what might be presented as unusual or undesirable belief systems, patterns of behaviour or socialization practices. Such adaptations are made more compulsory and urgent when linked particularly to a broad variety of 'othered' families, including those affected by disability, addiction, unemployment, alternative parenting structures (e.g. 'lone' parents, same-sex, interracial or intercultural, extra-marital, etc.), 'fundamentalist' moral–religious orientation (e.g. the Purity Movement) or indeed any 'extreme' political views. These families are often compelled to adopt a range of coping strategies to limit the leaking of what might be regarded as deviant family norms or practices into the public domain, and thus pre-empt possible outside interference or state sanctions. For many families, this equates to a strong need to reinforce and defend the public private divide that both advantages and disadvantages families and/or family members, and to disseminate among and within families the work of creating boundaries regarding *disclosure* as a way of protecting (or alternatively displaying) their own preferred 'internal worlds':

> More broadly, families are also expected to undertake certain duties, such as the 'appropriate' socialization of children. Similarly, the recurring public 'panics' about the family 'being in crisis' and in moral decline, falling apart, not shouldering its responsibilities and so on, are likely to be absorbed by family members and further regulate a family's internal activities and external relations. Each family will develop a set of beliefs governing the boundary between its private, internal world and that of a public external outside. Some families, for example, appear to hold to the belief that whatever happens 'under their roof' is essentially private and should be free from outside interference, whilst others expect, and even invite, outsiders to help manage their affairs or are keen to interact with other families and the local community.
>
> (ibid.: 177)

These largely defensive practices around disclosure by families would seem to be an important correlative to what Lynn Jamieson (2002) terms 'disclosing intimacy', which is characteristic of the private and intimate relationships typically found within modern families. 'Disclosing intimacy' is the phrase Jamieson uses to distinguish the special type of intimacy shared by two or more persons in a relationship based on the mutual shared communication of personal emotions. In this sense, it is about the dissemination of a certain type of 'internal' knowledge in the knowledge-based political economy of intimate, often familial, relationships in contemporary western societies, mainly to do with the disclosure of the *self* to *another* (Ricœur, 1994). In the context of 'western' modern societies, it is argued that disclosing intimacy is becoming more and more privileged as a mechanism for negotiating the increasingly manifold and intrusive forms of surveillance and institutional mechanisms of social control – many of which are targeted at the family – through the power of individuals to exercise their discretion over both the quality and quantity of non-externalized 'information' or 'intelligence' (the nomenclature depends on the interest attracted by the government agency in question). In the context of this study, the strategies for delimiting and negotiating disclosure extends to a range of 'intimacies' determining not just feelings, but also the sharing (and contesting) of a wide range of family ideologies, myths, practices and beliefs that impinge upon politics within and without the family, and indeed the state's reaction to these knowledges and practices to which they can only ever partially comprehend or gain access, but nevertheless according to which they are compelled to make decisions or take action.

Do families 'cause' radicalization?

This is a rather crude but nonetheless immediate phrasing for asking what, if anything, families have to do with fostering or transmitting radicalization across or among the generations. The available research literature in this area is disproportionately sparse in comparison to the attention devoted by academics and policy-makers to other 'causal' factors, such as class, ethnic, political, historical or theological ideologies, or even the emotional bonds of friendship. This dearth of research on radicalization and the family is perhaps somewhat puzzling given the available evidence that radical politics (often though not always associated with violence) tends to 'run in families' (e.g. Ismail, 2008), though precisely how this happens is subject to change even within a discrete radical group. For example, in his interviews with Provisional Irish Republicans, White (1993) identified the shift from the more or less stable, predictable dynastic transmission of republican nationalism maintained via the family in the 'Official' IRA from the generations spanning the 1920s to 1969, and the change to a more fluid system that predominated in the 1970s and 1980s of (inter)personal and self-recruitment based on individual experiences (often in response to internment) and other filial or conjugal bonds – although again, the precise nature of the correlation between radicalization and close interpersonal relationships is important to note, particularly in relation to women (who may or may not be the wives and girlfriends (WAGs) of violent extremists) and young men (who may or may not rely on tightly knit cell-like groups for a sense of belonging). While the family clearly presents an interesting if as yet opaque or at least insufficiently understood influence on radicalization, it is probable that the lack of research in this important area is down to three main factors, which have featured already in this study: (1) the lack of familiarity with, or in-depth and theoretical knowledge about, the family among counter-terrorism and security studies scholars and policy-makers (especially in comparison to policy-makers in other areas of government); along with (2) the deeply entrenched theoretical, analytical and practical frameworks that preserve an overly abstract, macro view of the 'traditional' (criminal) family, which is overly determined by their deprived economic circumstances and geographically situated in localized working-class areas; and (3) the secrecy and strategic frustration of disclosure by families, most of whom jealously guard their right to privacy, and resist what is often regarded as the incursion of outside agencies into 'their business'. Each of these factors represents a significant barrier to understanding how and in what ways the family is implicated in radicalization; taken together, they exert a significant negative impact on professional knowledge and the integrity of research outcomes.

However, there is evidence, from a criminological perspective, on the economic and class determinism of the 'deviant' family, that at least the first two aspects are changing, taking more account of the influence of the life-worlds of different families at different times and in different places, in response to shifting patterns and understandings of families' work patterns, economic and leisure behaviours, identities and needs. In their ethnographic case study of 'glocal' organized crime in 'Downton', Hobbs and Dunnighan find that:

> Downton has witnessed the transformation of the local criminal neighbourhood firm during the second half of this century from traditional family-based associations, deeply entrenched in the traditional overtones of working-class parochialism, to a networked system displaced from the resonance of nostalgic criminal locales. The firm becomes re-invented in the form of temporary collaborations, momentarily suspended within the traditional networks of a market environment drained of any capacity to translate territorial control into market sovereignty. Contextualised within Downton as a locality, the transformation of the traditional family firm into either individualistic mutations or actively disorganised deviant scavengers, is reflective of dramatic economic changes that the region has sustained since the turn of the 1960s. Stripped of the traditional industrial contours that once shaped and structured community life (local labour market, neighbourhood ecology, extended family networks and leisure time), Downton's working-class population began to fragment against the backdrop of a redundant industrial landscape, fracturing the community's material base and creating new crucially blurred socio-economic coalitions.
>
> (Hobbs and Dunnighan, 1998: 291)

While it is an oversimplification to mark the dividing line between the so-called traditional transmission of radical or criminal cultures or identities through dynastic family lines to a more individualistic choice-based economy in the wake of the social movements and economic changes of the 1960s and 1970s, there is perhaps a nugget of truth to it. However, though as will be shown in the remainder of this chapter, the realities on the ground, as it were, within particular families shows quite a lot of diversity and complexity where these two models are concerned. Family histories such as that of the Argentine freedom fighter Tamara Bunke, aka 'Tania the Guerrilla', the self-professed Cuban revolutionary who died with Che Guevara while fighting government militia in the Bolivian jungle, provides a paradigm case of the 'traditional' family model of radicalization (Rojas and Rodríguez Calderón, 1971), but at the same time illustrates just how distinctive and probably unusual such cases, and their legacies and influences, actually are in the contemporary cultural context.

In situations where not just individuals but whole families are incarcerated, the entire family and its individual members are under considerable stress, and this can and usually does affect every area of family life in a range of ways. Though there are a small number of studies devoted specifically to the impact of imprisonment for political offences upon individuals and their families in the academic literature, they mainly relate to the narrowly psychological impact of particular traumatic events rather than broader sociological meanings of conflict or trauma generally (Koopman, 1997). Even where wider cultural context is taken into account, the focus of attention is still chiefly on the development of therapeutic interventions for the treatment of individuals affected (e.g. Kinzie, 1989) as a more urgently pressing concern. As Koopman (1997) has rightly observed, there are significant methodological issues that need resolving with respect to delivering reliable and confirmable findings on the impact of political trauma on families and communities in the social sciences disciplines; sociology, anthropology, politics and criminology, for instance, take a broader view of the meaning and consequences of such 'events', and the way in which they impinge upon collective areas of family and community life including practices of child-rearing, affective bonding, identity formation, idealization of citizenship and security, and family rituals such as the production and consumption of food. Ethnographic and other 'reflexive' forms of research such as auto/biographical methods (Davies, 1999) – especially where auto/biographical records of these events are publicly available – are thus justified as a way of gaining important insights into this important area of life. In the following sections, I will concentrate on two examples of autobiographies based on the incarceration of radical or politically imprisoned families: Jeanne Wakatsuki Houston and James D. Houston's *Farewell to Manzanar* (1973) and Thai Jones's *A Radical Line* (2004).

Farewell to Manzanar

Farewell to Manzanar (1973) is regarded as a classic American text of the Second World War era. Authored by Jeanne Wakatsuki Houston with her writer husband James D. Houston, it is the story of the Wakatsuki family's experience of incarceration in a Japanese internment camp during the Second World War. As an autobiographical 'project', *Farewell to Manzanar* is an intensely familial as opposed to individual story, as it was 'told' by Jeanne Wakatsuki Houston to her author husband James, who then wrote the book (Rayson, 1999). Through the dual perspective of the narrator as girl and (later) woman, the narrative recounts the attack and subsequent disintegration of the Wakasuki family in the wake of the Japanese army attack on Pearl Harbor, which initiated the US involvement in the war and the resulting policy of interning Japanese-Americans in secure camps. The central narrative focus for this autobiography is on the humiliation and eventual physical and psychological collapse of Jeanne's father in the wake of government and public responses to Japanese Americans by the authorities, and how her mother and older siblings were forced to assume the shared roles of providers, carers and leaders of the newly structured family, and consequently deal with the aftermath in their reintegration into 'free' American society and the radicalizing repercussions on their own self-images and family life in the present and through future generations.

In this book, we see graphically how the experience of family imprisonment can reverse or reorder the dynamics of the parental and marital relationships. In this uncompromisingly revealing and forthright work, the authors disclose how Jeanne's father, a proud and dominant Japanese man, is reduced to an abusive and dependent alcoholic as a way of dealing with the trauma of humiliation and imprisonment, and how the older children of the family and the mother must step in to care for him and take up the leadership roles of carers and providers, promoting at least the image of a functional family in a situation of extreme hardship and duress. As Olujic (1998) notes, this is an experience that is common to families during wartime, and shows the strength and agency of children in dire situations engineered by the state:

> Parents, of course, experience great difficulty and hardship in adjusting to displacement and their new circumstances. Some become extremely depressed or abusive. In some families, when one or both parents are too overwhelmed, a teenage child may assume responsibility for the entire family.
>
> (Olujic, 1998: 323)

In her essay on Japanese women's autobiography, Rayson (1999) discusses the detrimental effects of internment on Japanese-American families, and argues that these negative consequences impinging on Japanese-American cultural identity account for the comparatively rare autobiographical accounts of life in internment camps written by men, for whom the experiences emanating from the humiliation of incarceration are things they wish not to remember and recount but to suppress and forget. She argues that for the women, the task of life writing has ironically been less fraught because they are more accustomed to oppression within the family, lack of self-esteem and discrimination from society at large. The comparatively larger numbers of 'ethnic autobiographies' (Rayson, 1999: 132) by women in the post-war period can also be explained by the greater inclusion of (Japanese) women into public sphere, in the form of their increasing participation in the workforce and education and growth in immigration.

Jeanne describes how, following the disappearance of her father for more than a year after he was first taken into custody by the FBI, her mother was obliged to take on the role of main provider and deal with the immediate difficulties of their forced evacuation from their family home. Although her mother had always worked in the factories and canneries surrounding their home in a small fishing town of southern California, this had always been in the context of a secondary economic role to her husband's primary role of provider, even though it seems her financial contribution to the household was essential due to the risky ventures her father was prone to embark upon as breadwinner (trying a number of 'schemes' to enable him to provide a living for his large family, while at the same time avoiding the humiliation of having to work for someone else). Notwithstanding this, her secondary status meant that her mother's financial contribution to the family was fundamentally overlooked.

Even as a working-class Japanese-American woman, however, Jeanne's mother was hardly a docile or passive subject in her new role as head of family. The story is recounted of her efforts to sell valuable family items when the family was forced out of their home for the second time, when they both badly needed the revenue and were also unable to bring all of their belongings with them from their resettlement house to the internment camp:

> The secondhand dealers had been prowling around for weeks, like wolves, offering humiliating prices for goods and furniture they knew many of us would have to sell sooner or later. Mama had left all but her most valuable possessions in Ocean Park, simply because she had nowhere to put them. She had brought along her pottery, her silver, heirlooms like the kimonos Granny had brought from Japan, lacquered tables, and one fine old set of china, blue and white porcelain, almost translucent. On the day we were leaving, Woody's car was so crammed with boxes and luggage and kids we had just run out of room. Mama had to sell the china.
>
> One of the dealers offered her fifteen dollars for it. She said it was a full setting for twelve and worth at least two hundred. He said fifteen was his top price. Mama started to quiver. Her eyes blazed up at him. She had been packing all night and trying to calm down Granny, who didn't understand why we were moving again and what all the rush was about. Mama's nerves were shot, and now navy jeeps were patrolling the streets. She didn't say another word. She just glared at this man, all the rage and frustration channeled at him through her eyes.

He watched her for a moment and said he was sure he couldn't pay more than seventeen fifty for that china. She reached into the red velvet case, took out a dinner plate and hurled it at the floor right in front of his feet.

The man leapted [sic] back shouting, 'Hey! Hey, don't do that! Those are valuable dishes!'

Mama took out another dinner plate and hurled it at the floor, then another and another, never moving, never opening her mouth, just quivering and glaring at the retreating dealer, with tears streaming down her cheeks. He finally turned and scuttled out the door, heading for the next house. When he was going she stood there smashing cups and bowls and platters until the whole set lay in scattered blue and white fragments across the wooden floor.

(Houston and Houston, 1973: 13–15)

This story evokes the potent pain and irrepressible spirit of this woman who is put in an impossible situation by an illegal response of the US Government to its own citizens in wartime.

This story about the self-destruction of valuable family china represents a major act of resistance for this Japanese matriarch. In traditional Japanese culture, articles such as fine pottery, porcelain and china are considered to be highly valuable as family heirlooms handed down through the generations. As such, these articles and their bestowal to subsequent generations comprises a potent cultural symbol that represents the continuation and maintenance of ancestral family ties, the transmission of Japanese ideals of beauty and craftsmanship through the ages, and the sharing of prosperity from past to future generations across time and space. The development of techniques and artistic conventions in pottery and porcelain-making has particular symbolic resonance with respect to the cultural development of a distinctive sense of Japanese identity, particularly as these aesthetic codes have evolved and changed in relation to centuries if not millennia of bellicose and peaceful interaction and engagement with other cultures, historically mainly in relation to Korean and Chinese practices. Mama's act of defiance in the face of pressing material need for her own family in the present moment, and its broader symbolic meaning as a forced act of desecration of her cultural identity and values as a Japanese woman and head of family, powerfully and symbolically evokes the duress inflicted upon thousands of Japanese-American families during this shameful episode of US history, and the impact upon their sense of national and ethnic identity that endures over the generations. It also shows how even lower-class, dutiful and law-abiding working-class immigrant women had it in them to carry out painfully self-destructive acts of defiance in the cause of resistance given the situational circumstances, a very volatile and undesirable outcome, not least one orchestrated and carried out by a self-professed enlightened democracy.

The visual imagery of this story is also striking in its evocation of another strong image associated with traditional Japanese culture – at least from the perspective of popular American knowledge of it – namely Hokusai's famous wood print *The Great Wave off Kanagawa*. The image of Mama standing at the centre of a sea of broken shards of translucent blue and white china seems to metaphorically locate her within the turbulent, if also beautifully powerful, waves of Hokusai's celebrated work. This imagery adds an extra dimension to the cultural meaning and interpretation of the story. As Finley (1998) notes, Hokusai's print depicts the great power of nature compared to the relative weakness of human beings. The giant waves are poised to descend on two boats, which are difficult to discern among the dramatic, gigantic and tumultuous waves; even the majestic Mount Fuji in the background is dwarfed by the centrality and power of the sea storm (Finley, 1998). The contrast between the natural and human realms in terms of their disparate power is inverted in Jeanne's story about her mother, since in this version it is Mama who represents an unstoppable force of nature and the salesman the futility if presumptuousness of humans and the comparative insignificance of the US state.

This vision of her mother as a powerful, irresistible force, and a woman acting in defence of her family in opposition to the capitalist or market state accords with certain feminist interpretations of Hegelian philosophy in relation to women and the family. In her exploration of the section in Hegel's *The Phenomenology of Spirit* (*PS*) entitled 'The Ethical World. Human and Divine Law: Man and Woman' (Hegel, 1977: 267–78), Starrett (1996) expands upon Hegel's notion of the role of women and the family in relation to the state, and their 'critical' potential for resisting state powers, in order to affect real and lasting social change. In the research literature and in conversation with practitioners and policy-makers, there is ample evidence that many in the security services have a basic familiarity with the conflict-based phenomenology of knowledge and the 'politics of right' devised by Hegel, and that it exerts a seminal influence on the contemporary understanding of the nature of political conflict – epitomized in the syllogism 'thesis–antithesis–synthesis', which is explicated most definitively in *The Phenomenology of Spirit*. Yet there may perhaps be less familiarity with this particular section of the text devoted specifically to women and the family. Here, as Starrett points out, Hegel reflects upon the pivotal idea of 'crisis' and the 'critical' as the driving forces of politics, history and knowledge, and the contribution of individuals to the relentless development of consciousness as represented in the first instance by their coming into conflict with the legal–rational codes of the state. According to Hegel, this fundamental yet rather static and abstract 'phase' or 'stage' of development represented by the law is effectively interrupted in the first instance by the 'ethical' stage, in which women, men and the family feature prominently. At this initial phase of crisis, Hegel sees the family emerge as a distinctively *radical* force for opposing the totalizing hegemony of the (state) law, by virtue of the family's immediate participation and rootedness in the 'essential' and 'natural' order of ethical life. This connection epitomized by the family specifically in relation to

women, pivots not just on the usual link to cyclicality, fertility and reproduction represented by birth as an implicit challenge to the law and the state,
but also on women's relationship to the 'dead' in the form of traditional,
spiritual and ancestral ties to the past, and subsequently to the present realm
of 'experience' and 'sensibilities', thereby effectively undercutting the comparatively attenuated temporality and legitimacy of the rationalized state:

> Hegel then develops the radical, cross-temporal character of the family,
> embeds it in an experiential context, and clarifies its deep cross-temporal
> source of legitimation: 'The family ... weds the blood-relation to the
> bosom of the earth ... The family makes [the dead individual] a member
> of the community [*PS*, para. 452] ... [and] the divine right and law has
> for its content and power the individual who is beyond the real world'
> (*PS*, para. 452).
>
> (Starrett, 1996: 258)

This oppositional movement, in which women and the family feature prominently alongside men (understood here as real-life individuals constrained
more by family than legal–rational ties), brings into 'critical' confrontation the
seminal 'being-toward-death', or 'risking death in order to achieve independence' (ibid.: 259), which is characteristic of the radicalized or (more often)
terrorist ethos. Hegel is here on the side of the radicalizing influence of the
family and its transformative impact on society represented by the law, and the
consequential influence of women's activism and their willingness to risk
engagement with death and destruction in order to accomplish its 'ethical'
directives. The reason behind Hegel's defence of this type of 'being-toward-
death' on the part of individuals within families is that it preserves the 'spiritual' or 'divine' aspects of the *ethical* law by circumventing the totalization of
the family by the legal-rational ambitions of the state. Though Hegel's
uncompromisingly essentialist view of women is not without its own critical
problems, his implicit recognition of women and families as occupants of what
we would call the private sphere is instructive: it exposes their oppositional
power and determination to resist state domination in order to protect their
interests and autonomy against the overzealous incursion of the state when it
mistakenly insists that there is only one law (*PS*, para. 466). Read against this
background, Mama's act of defiance and destruction is one that has the real
power to terrify or bring into crisis the crude rationality of the legal–juridical
nation state, as it simultaneously preserves the ethical 'spirit' of family life
expressed through intergenerational ties to the dead (and get to be born).

At this point, it is worth pausing to consider other possible or competing
interpretations of this story and the affective–political–economic dimensions
that underpin it and endow it with meaning. From a Durkheimian perspective,
another interpretation of this narrative is possible, this time without reference
to (or possibly with a different view of) the death-driven force of *thanatos* as

devised by thinkers like Hegel or Freud. Though there are overt references throughout Durkheim's work that he took a similarly essentialist view of women as Hegel (as typical of men of their times), there are also suggestions that his view of the sexes relied on the formative effects of social organization of power, domination and institutional authority – encapsulated in the moral–sacred domain of the family. According to the thesis developed in *The Division of Labour in Society*, the formation of normative gender roles in modern societies is a consequence of the increased specialization of labour that characterizes complex 'organic' societies; hence the presumed 'weakness' and lack of intellectual and political agency of women is a consequence – not a cause – of their progressive social segregation to the private domestic sphere (notwithstanding the close link with the biological work of care and reproduction, which in the work of Durkheim and others have tended to reflect the essentialist view of women). With respect to managing relations between the family and the state, for Durkheim, reciprocity and equilibrium are key as underpinning the unwritten social 'contract' between the two. When the powers of the state (usually expressed through the inauguration of newly repressive or intrusive forms of regulation or social control, which is itself a sign of social abnormality or pathology) become or are experienced as excessive, or result in new pressures upon the family, what were previously the domain of the private sphere have a tendency to transform into urgently public concerns, or even what have come to be known under the banner 'moral panics', which frequently place the moral functionality of the family in question (as for example in the rise of knife crime among youngsters, and the consequent social critique directed at black, urban, working-class or one-parent families). Such moral panics highlight fissures and divisions in the 'conscience collective', and the subsequent unequal application of repressive pressures on some families can be so intensely damaging as to threaten the whole of the social fabric. Hence Durkheim argued that the consequences of the incursion of 'absolute' power of the state into the sphere of family life, as these stories evidence, can be devastating not just for individual families but for the whole of society:

> This aspect of the argument is clear: out of the initially strong and repressive *conscience collective* there develops a society with extensive administrative responsibilities over the family but with a 'regression of collective sentiments concerning the family' (Durkheim, *The Rules of Sociological Method*, 1964: 157). But in opposition to the formation of conjugal society as a moral sphere based on the contract of two free parties, the role of the state begins to insist upon obligations which are not in any way contractual, in fact they appear to become more absolute: 'as domestic obligations become more numerous, they take on ... a public character. Not only in early times do they not have a contractual origin, but the role which contract plays in them becomes smaller'. The social tendency seems to consist in an increasing state involvement: 'social

control over the manner in which they form, break down, and are modified, becomes greater' (ibid: 210).

(Gane, 1993: 35)

The manifestation of this type of repressive absolutism with respect to the exercise and scope of state power (often encouraged by populist attitudes of deviance and stigma, fuelled by latent sentiments of difference) over individual families is epitomized by the internment of Japanese-American families during and even some time after the war. From what was the previously 'hidden' or publicly silent domain of the private family emerge stories that endure as indictments of state power and exemplars of women's empowerment and ethical and political agency at such vital political junctures as represented by violent conflict and/or war. In an increasingly globalized society in which national populations are significantly determined by patterns of international migration and multiculturalism, these life stories reveal latent or repressed contradictions in the conscious collective of society as experienced by individual citizens with ever more increasingly complex identities in relation to the family and the nation state. This is reflected in the alternative representation and meaning of the 'death drive' (*thanatos*) in *Farewell to Manzanar*. While the Wakatsukis are a proud and loyal American family, they retain a strong and – it turns out – necessary connection to their traditional Japanese roots (the 'roots' of which form the basis of their radicalization (*radic-* or 'root' stories)). Mama's 'drive' toward 'death' represented by the her attachment to previous generations is not so much a Freudian 'death wish' or Hegelian invitation to confrontation with the state as it is an illustration of her continued belonging to her ancestral Japanese culture and the moral values passed down through the generations of her family, including her American family. These are ties that bind and, in response to illegal state repression, radicalize and endure.

In contrast to the familiar Hegelian narrative, which represents the rather abstract historical progression of collective and individual consciousness mainly through conflict and (ruthless) assimilation of the other, a Durkheimian interpretation of this story suggests that the production of a more urgently demanding moral tale in which individuals and families such as Jeanne and her family are compelled to negotiate very damaging and repressive state regimes in their ongoing efforts to maintain a sense of collectivity and identity (at both familial and national levels). Such heart-rending stories reveal the resilience and resourcefulness of families under duress, as well as the potentially damaging impact on the whole of the social collective in the presumptive efforts by the state to purge or protect itself from the 'enemy within'. While such stories are painful to tell, their significance for the authors, their families and communities in texts like *Farewell to Manzanar* are crucial as a way of establishing a unique historical record of their experiences of what really happened during (and after) the war, and thereby facilitating the arduous process of recovering a sense of dignity and justice based on the public dissemination of these truths that don't tend to feature in the official records. Like other examples of family political prisoner auto/biography (e.g. *The Diary of Anne Frank* and many life writings produced by survivors of the Holocaust), it is no coincidence that such texts often become cultural classic texts. This is not least because they form a vital source of cultural capital in helping to ensure that these stories are preserved and (re)told throughout the generations, so that there is some hope that lessons will be learned and such events will never happen again.[1] As Durkheim and indeed Hegel (in his writing on women, men and the family) suggest, these texts are important because they express deeply felt experiences about the moral crisis affecting the social collective of American society that would otherwise be repressed, ignored or silenced by the institutional mechanisms of the state.

In its implicit references to potent cultural language and symbols that are known to both sides of a community in conflict, the stories in *Farewell to Manzanar* express how the storyteller can convey experiences saturated with meaning in a relatively brief narrative through the imaginative and innovative use of shared cultural symbols in the narrative. Among other things, this demonstrates how powerful storytelling is as a way of articulating and communicating the sense of frustration, injustice, chaos and isolation that is experienced by these writers and their families at the time, and how significant such experiences and their own ethnic cultures are in their subsequent attempts to make sense of the macro political events in which their and their family's lives have become 'dictated' (in both senses of the word). It is common in political prisoner life writing for these kinds of stories about the real-life experiences of exploited, oppressed or marginalized individuals – rather than intellectual ideological manifestos or religious sermons – to feature as the primary influences upon later radicalization (of the people involved and others who identify with them). The act of writing itself is therefore to be regarded as a highly political act of resistance, a way of reacting and responding to the injustices and inequalities of a 'civil' state with the creativity of human imagination augmented by the richness of cultural symbolism and ethnicity expressed in popular forms of storytelling (e.g. auto/biography). What is more, the act of writing these stories and disseminating them to a wider public in addition to a private family audience forms the basis of constructing a mythical family past for future generations by reading/translating the family's present experiences and situations into the symbolic language and narrative forms of their traditional past, providing families – even those who are living through political crises – with a sense of continuity and resilience. While religious symbolism often facilitates this functional role (e.g. Marty and Appleby, 1993), this does not always have to be overtly the case, and neither do such traditional metanarratives have to be referenced or imported in their entirety, but can be drawn upon anecdotally or 'sampled' – in contemporary cultural parlance – as in this story about the family china. In her analysis of such life experiences and their encapsulation using traditional symbolism as the basis for organized collective political resistance, Rugh (1993) puts it thus:

Resurgence movements grow out of such a social and economic context—one that for various reasons has become intolerable to many people. By drawing on familiar symbols and values, such movements are capable of mobilizing a consensus among their followers to move in what appear to be new and promising directions, offering potential solutions to the ills that affect individual lives. The process is made easier by an encapsulating ideology which clarifies and identifies approved directions for the changes.

(Rugh, 1993: 155)

Though few would consider *Farewell to Manzanar* to be a radical or revolutionary text, it is clearly intended to affect a deep-seated *change* in American society that is sufficient to prevent such an outrage happening ever again. In this sense, we may detect in many of its anecdotal stories the kernel of what Rugh (1993) and others identify as more overtly and fully formed examples of resistance narratives and their power to influence, especially when sutured onto or 'read into' other fundamentalist metanarratives such as those of religious persecution (which, by referring to the continuing victimization from the past, predict that such outrages will be forthcoming in the future, hence the need for militant action in the present) or analogous familial or cultural myths or ideologies. This analysis highlights the importance of considering not just the narrative representation of radicalization or the radicalizing influence of auto/biographical texts by professed 'extremists', but also those unallied to ostensibly fundamentalist or extremist ideologies. This is consistent with the definitional issues considered in Chapter 2 concerning the designation of who is a political prisoner, and the shifting and permeable boundaries within this extremely diverse and unstable group. This problematic is exemplified by the radicalization stories of the Wakatsuki family designed to facilitate social change and the radicalization stories told by others framed by those with a seditious or violent political agenda: while there are clearly differences between these generic types of radicalization narratives, they both share at least one overriding and common aim – to transliterate what is often encountered as the chaotic and traumatic experience of ordinary personal life into auto/biographical form, and to use this as the basis for the recovery of a sense of agency on behalf of the individual, in order to facilitate social change. Importantly, this resurgent agency on the part of the individual is linked to a source of language about the self (e.g. auto/biography) that is both ubiquitous and commonsensical, which greatly assists in the facilitation of this complex cultural process. Though these stories may or may not be embedded in extremist ideological narratives of history, they are linked to enduring and potent cultural symbols that have the capacity to suffuse these stories with resonant meaning that can profoundly influence others – if not convincing them to join the 'struggle' themselves, then persuading them of the rightness of 'the cause'. As the philosopher Paul

Ricœur (1994) explains, this phenomenon reveals a number of revealing insights into the nature of the self and how it shapes political realities in modernity: first, that the self is essentially embodied, not an abstract product of the Cartesian cogito, but rather enabled by and constitutive of its cultural and material surroundings and relationships with others; second, the dual nature of the self – what Ricœur calls the *ipse* and *idem* aspects of identity – is essentially temporal, ensuring the durability or sameness of the self over time, while at the same time opening the possibility for radical innovation and change to the self and society initiated on the part of the individual embedded within his or her physical and cultural situation.

The story of Mama's resistance, which is recorded early in the text, sets the tone for Wakatsuki's autobiographical account of life as a Japanese internee, not least by enabling her to portray her mother as a powerful woman even given her desperate circumstances, and thereby enabling her own use (by proxy) of the autobiographical voice for what she eventually reveals at the end of the story to be her own act of defiance. This is a testament to Hegel's and Durkheim's theses that women and families can emerge into the public/political domain as powerful forces for change when placed under the duress of the abuse of power by the state; equally, it is a warning for states not to incur too lightly or obtrusively into the 'private' lives of real families. This is in light of the fact that the use of the autobiographical 'I' and the public dissemination of these stories is typically not easy for women, and even less so for Japanese women. As Rayson (1999) indicates, for many Japanese women, the usual difficulties of women writing autobiographically are compounded by the culture of silence surrounding Japanese norms of femininity. As with the fraught issue of disclosure in Black autobiography,[2] the breaking of this silence by speaking out in the form of life writing does not simply annul the culture of silence, but brings with it the task of adapting innovative ways of creating new cultural reservoirs of silence – what Rayson terms the creation of new 'masks' – as a form of protection against possible attack or denigration by the dominant culture. These women differ from radical women like Susan Stern or Maria McGuire in that they are less comfortable with 'brazening out' the accusation of betrayal of their femininity and the codes of normal conduct that they are bound to by their radical sub-groups and by society at large. As has been noted, writing autobiography implies a certain amount of vanity on the part of the individual writer; Japanese as well as women and men from other ethnic backgrounds often adopt an ostensive display of modesty as a way to countenance what for many women writers itself constitutes a radical if not openly rebellious act (Rayson, 1999: 133). At the same time, there seems to be an abiding awareness of the productivity of women's life writing during important events in American history (e.g. the emergence of American nationalism from the captivity narratives of frontier women in the eighteenth and early nineteenth centuries (Namias, 1993); suffragette autobiography during the late nineteenth and early twentieth centuries (Joannou, 1995; John, 2003) and the preponderance of women's life writing during the sexual revolution of the 1960s and 1970s (e.g. Jellinek in Rayson, 1999). Through the use of elliptical, ironic, oblique, humorous and anecdotal styles of writing, these women are able to reconstruct a sense of self that is durable, yet malleable enough to sustain the narrative impulse to reveal enough (though just as significantly not too much) while retaining and enhancing a sense of integrity and self-belief (Jellinek in Rayson, 1999; see also D'Arcy, 1981).

There certainly is a lot of this type of writing in *Farewell to Manzanar*, which is what makes it so powerfully evocative of one family's experience of a time of conflict and chaos in American history, and it has the ring of truth about it, as well as probably being quite representative of the experiences of hundreds of thousands of Japanese-Americans. As in Shoah literature, the use of obliqueness, anecdote and (most controversially) humour in popular cultural forms make these stories compelling and bearable to tell and to read, while at the same time generating their own problems in the telling of stories about war crimes and other atrocities. While commentators like Zandberg (2006) acknowledge the innovative capacity of these popular and often satirical stories to critique conventional forms of collective memory, ultimately he castigates them for their inability to offer anything by way of viable alternative. As Gilman (2000)[3] contends, however, while in no sense was the Holocaust 'funny' (not least in the remembering in family histories of the loss of beloved parents and children), the use of humour and laughter in storytelling about this seminal event in twentieth-century history nevertheless highlights the timeless juxtaposition of comedy and tragedy that is characteristic of humanist – as opposed to distinctively religious, ethnic or nationalist – discourse. While this represents a disturbing decoupling of Shoah narratives from their roots in Jewish cultural history, at the same time, ' … it offers rereading of the Shoah as the place of heroic action' (Gilman, 2000: 308). As has been argued throughout this book, the recovery of 'heroic action' via individual agency is a key element of radicalization and a major factor attenuating the difficulties of telling and hearing these painful stories. Alternatively, as Rasmussen (2009) argues in her analysis of women's life writings about their experiences of breast cancer, recourse to the new conventions of feminine humour represented by the genre of 'chick lit' enable these women to tell their experiences while at the same time being able to elide the 'rhetorics of triumph and horror' or the reductive status of victim.

Despite the damaging experience and lingering sense of guilt and shame that result from their time at the internment camp, there is quite a lot of humour and laughter in *Farewell to Manzanar*. Following the family's first night in the makeshift cabins of the camp, they awoke to find themselves covered in a fine white dust as a result of the sand blowing into the drafty hut.

A skin of sand covered the floor. I looked over Mama's shoulder at Kiyo, on top of his fat mattress, buried under jeans and overcoats and sweaters. His eyebrows were gray, and he was starting to giggle. He was looking at me, at my gray eyebrows and coated hair, and pretty soon we were both giggling. I looked at Mama's face to see if she thought Kiyo was funny. She lay very still next to me on our mattress, her eyes scanning everything—bare rafters, walls, dusty kids—scanning slowly, and I think the mask of her face would have cracked had not Woody's voice just then come at us through the wall. He was rapping on the planks as if testing to see if they were hollow.

> 'Hey!' he yelled. 'You guys fall into the same flour barrel as us?'
> 'No,' Kiyo yelled back. 'Ours is full of Japs.'
> All of us laughed at this.
>
> (*Manzanar*: 23–4)

The children's joking about their situation made it possible for the adults, in this case the mother, to resist succumbing to complete despair. This demonstrates how important children are – not just as dependants to be cared for and protected from the desperation of their conditions, but as agents who contribute to and enable adult resistance to their incarceration, by for example making fun of the absurdity of it. At the same time, the children's fun was not always to the benefit of the survival of the family unit or the adults, to say nothing of the experts in the camp assigned to ensure the children's well-being. As in stories recounted in other such texts, the consumption of food and mealtimes together prove to be a key indicator of family life (particularly as viewed from an outsider or expert perspective):

> Kiyo and I were too young to run around, but often we would eat in gangs with other kids, while the grownups sat at another table. I confess I enjoyed this part of it at the time. We all did. A couple of years after the camps opened, sociologists studying the life noticed what had happened to the families. They made some recommendations, and edicts went out that families *must* start eating together again. Most people resented this; they griped and grumbled. They were in the habit of eating with their friends. And until the mess hall system itself could be changed, not much really could be done. It was too late.
>   My own family, after three years of mess hall living, collapsed as an integrated unit.
>
> (ibid.: 37, original emphasis)

While the families were able to adapt survival strategies in the camp from the *Issei* (first generation of Japanese) memories of life in a ' … small, crowded country like Japan' (ibid.: 33), they were nevertheless unable to withstand the relentless, compounded and extended 'pains of imprisonment' that were visited upon them in the camp. The impact of internment would continue have a lasting effect on American culture for generations to come.

Jeanne Wakatsuki Houston ends her narrative with expressions of how radicalizing her family's experiences have been on her and will be for the rest of her life, forming part of her personal 'inheritance' from her parents and to future generations of her family:

> They were sitting on the steps like that—Mama hunched, Papa tending the blackening rings—one morning a few days before we left camp. Now that smell and those voices in the wind from the orchard brought with them the sign I was waiting for: the image of a rekindled wildness in Papa's eyes. Twenty-seven years earlier I had carried it with me out of camp only half understanding what it meant. Remembering now, I realized I had never forgotten his final outburst of defiance. But for the first time I saw it clearly, as clearly as the gathered desert stones, and when I left today for good I would carry that image with me again, as the rest of my inheritance.
>
> (ibid.: 198)

Despite the Wakatsukis family's multiple efforts to prove themselves worthy (and even patriotic) Americans after being released from the camp (like the great majority of other Japanese-American families) is described in the book, Jeanne's story is essentially one that exploits the ubiquitous popularity and audacity typical of the auto/biographical genre to conduct an act of retrospective resistance against the indignities inflicted upon her family. The need to expose the dysfunctional and disintegrating inner workings of her family during this period and afterwards, though undesirable, was in the end a price worth paying in order to get her meaning and the stories of their experiences across to the wider reading audience, to make them public and visible. The impression is given that this is not just an act of defiance on behalf of her own family, or generally of Japanese-American families who suffered the humiliation and pain of internment. She also reads the suffering they endured to the suffering of another group of American outcasts, the Okies, who were forced to evacuate their land on the Great Plains and relocate to the west coast as a result of natural (drought) and man-made (depression) disasters (ibid.: 150). In short, it wasn't them, Japanese-Americans, it was the government – and part of the proof lay in the fact that their experiences were by no means an isolated case.

Here the power of storytelling is once again revealed as a way of making sense of marginalization and oppression on innocent citizens by the state, through in this instance, the narrative device of diegesis referenced in the previous chapters. Hearing stories about the lives of others who have also suffered at the hands of their communities had a special attraction for the young Jeanne. She recalls how she nearly (much against the wishes of her parents) converted to Catholicism, such was her fascination with the stories of the martyrs told by the nuns and priests who visited the camps as missionaries:

They passed out candy. But what kept me coming back, once I started, were the tales of the unfortunate women like Saint Agatha, whose breasts were cut off when she refused to renounce her faith ... [The mother superior loved to] tell us about Saint Agatha, or Saint Juliana, who was boiled alive, or Saint Marcella, who was whipped to death by the Goths. I was fascinated with the miseries of women who had suffered and borne such afflictions.

(ibid.: 44)

This suggests how important narrative and storytelling are to the children as ways of making sense of and enduring their incarceration, a childhood strategy that for the authors was also embraced as an adult way of making some sort of sense out of these painful and chaotic events. To this end, while the writer's own individual cultural or ethnic tradition can provide the inspiration or form for these stories (as in the one about the broken china), Jeanne's story about her attraction to Catholicism (a tradition to which her family was previously unaffiliated) illustrates that these stories don't have to be from the child's own ethnic or religious tradition to be meaningful for them but can be borrowed or adapted from those of other ethnic or social groups. This casts new light on the influence of religion on radicalization as distinctively fluid.

Part of the pathos of Jeanne's story is the feeling that this has actually happened and probably will happen again in the 'land of the free'. What *Farewell to Manzanar* communicates is the revelatory power of storytelling as an act of resistance and a way of coping with the vagaries of political upheaval and its aftermath in the everyday lives of ordinary families, and the repercussions for future generations. The stories Jeanne tells are dialogically shaped by the stories the internees tell and hear:

The stories, the murmurs, the headlines of the last few months had imprinted in my mind the word HATE. I had heard my sisters say, 'Why do they hate us?' I had heard Mama say with lonesome resignation, 'I don't understand all this hate in the world'.

(ibid.:151)

This is evocative of the 'who are they and why do they hate us?' political rhetoric about terrorism referred to in Chapter 1, which is based on a highly dualistic and mutually exclusive worldview in which the 'Other' constitutes an implicitly evil and wantonly violent presence, with no sense of proportionality or possible reasons for their actions. However, for the Watkatsuki family, this hate is all too familiar, manifest as it is in the polymorphous forms of racism that are endemic in American society in the daily course of social interaction in the life of the young Jeanne (such as at school, with 'friends', at majorette practice and performances, dances, etc.).

As with Ed Husain and Malcolm X, Jeanne's first awareness of herself as the object of racism originates once again from a white teacher who taught her and her brother and sister following the family's first expulsion from their home in southern California to a Los Angeles ghetto prior to their final relocation to the internment camp:

> Kiyo and my sister May and I enrolled in the local school, and what sticks in my memory from those few weeks is the teacher—not her looks, her remoteness. In Ocean Park my teacher had been a kind, grandmotherly woman who used to sail with us in Papa's boat from time to time and who wept the day we had to leave. In Boyle Heights the teacher felt cold and distant. I was confused by all the moving and was having trouble with the classwork, but she would never help me out. She would have nothing to do with me.
> This was the first time I had felt outright hostility from a Caucasian.
>
> (ibid.:16)

Jeanne admits that prior to this she was no stranger to racism, revealing that while living in the predominantly white middle-class town of Ocean Park she was unused to the company of other Japanese people and feared them as *yo-go-re*, or 'uncouth' (ibid.: 12). In other words, she and her family were not just the victims but also the purveyors of racist views against fellow 'Orientals', a revelation that is typical of the unflinching honesty of this book. It is also indicative of the influential power of the auto/biographical text as the author is able to turn her challenging reflexive gaze upon the nature of American society by decentring the characters and interrupting the rhetorical contiguity of the narrative, thereby constantly disrupting and forestalling the simplistic assignment of the good–evil or racist–non-racist dichotomy. There is good *and* evil everywhere and in everyone – and even the victims of racism can sometimes unwittingly be racist themselves; what is more, this is a much more worryingly complex state of affairs than the theodicy-oriented 'war on terror' discourse of global conflict would imply. This capacity to acknowledge the contagion and trauma of racism both suffered and inflicted by the autobiographical subject represented in *Farewell to Manzanar* helps the reader and writer to 'swerve' (to use Gilmore's (2001) word) many of the jurisprudential anxieties over the truthfulness and actual harm suffered by this family as represented in the autobiographical form of subjective, non-legal testimony. By revealing what must be many uncomfortable truths about both extra- and intrafamily trauma, the authors endow the narrative with credibility and Jeanne's own autobiographical voice with a strong sense of honesty, dignity and integrity.

Though the Japanese-American families caught up in the trauma of mass internment during the war would eventually receive redress through the courts and an apology from the US Government, the exposure in this memoir of the various liminal traumas suffered by this family render it meaningful not in the objective form of a legal test case, but as an alternative 'limit case' of confession and testimony in the autobiographical form. Such alternative narratives are necessary because within the legal–rational culture of modern nation states, such stories could not otherwise be told (Gilmore, 2001: 146). For many who experience trauma in and through the family, the ability to tell their story is often the only meaningful sort of 'justice' they will ever have, often forming the basis for transforming oneself and one's way of living as well as the identities and lives of those in a similar situation (ibid.). Such testimonials are important for disseminating to the public at large the kind of trauma suffered in everyday life by ordinary families like the Wakatsukis, and these stories can inspire a determination for cultural change in an immediate and personal way that is lacking in the cold objectivity of the legal–judicial process.

As in the case of Ed Husain (2007), the situation with respect to the young Jeanne's experience of her white teachers and school was similarly mixed. Her experience of a teacher in the internment camp had a positive lasting influence on her:

> What I see clearly is the face of my fourth-grade teacher—a pleasant face, but completely invulnerable, it seemed to me at the time, with sharp, commanding eyes. She came from Kentucky. She wore wedgies, loose slacks, and sweaters that were too short in the sleeves. A tall, heavyset spinster, about forty years old, she always wore a scarf on her head, tied beneath the chin, even during class, and she spoke with a slow, careful Appalachian accent. She was probably the best teacher I've ever had—strict, fair-minded, dedicated to her job. Because of her, when we finally returned to the outside world I was, academically at least, more than prepared to keep up with my peers.
>
> (*Manzanar*: 105)

As we have seen in Chapter 4, teachers reappear with a surprising regularity in the autobiographies of political prisoners who include childhood memories in their life narratives. Bad teachers – those who are racist (e.g. Malcolm X (1964); Ed Husain, 2007; Wataksuki Houston and Houston, 1973) or sexist (e.g. Dworkin 2002), can be the source of longstanding anger, and facilitate considerable antagonism as a retrospectively motivational childhood memory as the cause or basis of radicalization later in life. As Jeanne's story shows, however, 'good' teachers don't have to share, espouse or indeed 'counter' any particular political viewpoint, or any other identity or sentimental attachment in relation to their pupils, but rather simply do their jobs with fairness, professionalism and integrity, treating the children they teach with openness and respect. Even Ed Husain's teacher, whom he credits with introducing him to a certain relationship with 'the text' that he partially credits for leading him to his extremist interpretation of Islam, can ultimately be vindicated by his eventual 'textual' counter-narrative of de-radicalization, which he later constructs in autobiographical form in *The Islamist* (2007). Such micro-narratives about the childhood experiences of education by latterly radicalized autobiographers would suggest that current governmental policies in this area might better be directed towards enhancing the general professionalism and anti-racist agenda in teacher training and in the day-to-day running of schools, rather than expecting teachers and other school staff to identify and 'counter' extremism in their pupils and their families (e.g. Department for Children, Schools and Families, 2008).

Leisure and consumption

In *Farewell to Manzanar*, as in other political prisoner life writings about the family and other social groups noted in previous chapters, leisure pursuits and consumption activities constitute an important site for (re)imagining the radical subject. Among other things, they afford a sense of relief and opportunity for protest for the internees, despite being presented in order to give the inmates a sense of normality and to make their incarceration endurable. One revealing and much-quoted instance is the performances, every weekend at the recreation hall, of dance bands and country and western bands made up of Japanese internees. One of these bands included among its members one of Jeanne's relatives in the camp, her brother-in-law Bill:

> Bill played trumpet and took vocals on Glenn Miller arrangements of such tunes and *In the Mood, String of Pearls*, and *Don't Fence Me In*. He didn't sing *Don't Fence Me In* out of protest, as if trying quietly to mock the authorities. It just happened to be a hit song one year, and they all wanted to be an up-to-date American swing band. They would blast it out into recreation barracks full of bobby-soxed, jitterbugging couples ...
>
> (*Manzanar*: 101–2)

Depending on the context and the motivation, singing or not singing *Don't Fence Me In* was regarded by the inmates as an opportunity for an act of protest, or – alternatively – as a way of being *en mode* with the rest of American popular culture, and indeed doing the work of making life endurable under unbearable circumstances by simply having fun and enjoying themselves as much as was possible. In any case, the ironies of 'blasting out' the song so evocative of the American frontier spirit are multiple in these circumstances.

As can be observed in the life writings of other radicalized political prisoners and highlighted in the previous chapter, children's experiences of consumption as well as school are infused with particular significance by the authors of these family biographies. This is indicative of what Shapiro (2001) terms the 'triumph of consumer capitalism' as a centralizing political orientation in the lives of families mainly via the opportunity that children provide as a specially designated site for adult consumer activity within the family, a reality of modern family life under consumer capitalism which is not always a pleasant or unifying experience:

> Politically, it is a time in which a homology develops between the consumer and citizen subject, as the coding of commodities converges stylistically with the coding of political events. Citizen-subjects and consumers merge into a single target of diverse economic and political media manipulation. Confusing and ambiguous codes evoke or dissimulate danger. And the family, far from being a reassuring unity of collective solidarity and protection, becomes instead a conflictual and susceptible collection that amplifies the symbolic manipulations of economic, political, and bureaucratic agents. Divided against itself, the family is less a collection of characters than it is a set of voices that relay different codes into the family's midst.
>
> (Shapiro, 2001: 19)

In the consumer and risk society, less and less of children's time is spent outside the sequestered spaces constructed and sectioned off for them by (and often for) the satisfaction of the consumer- and security-obsessed market of adult concerns. This contraction of the public and private spaces in which an increasing number of children and their families are made to live is materially and morally undermined by what is essentially the amplified and also increasingly unbounded character of generational lineage in contemporary society. This is evidenced not least is the profusion of the potential types of families (e.g. single, blended and step, etc.) and the geographical dissemination of extended family members. While this profusion of diversity in the family form increases the available opportunities for children (as well as other family members) to actively exercise comparatively high levels of choice in the character and duration of their familial bonds, their own *subjective* roles as children are significantly affected by their greatly augmented roles as the *objects* of family (usually read 'adult') consumption and anxiety. It is not hard to see how, in the proliferating reproduction of generational and consumer capitalism, these very same subjective and objective qualities of childhood can lend themselves to the high value that is placed upon personal choice and private entrepreneurship as decisive factors shaping the constantly shifting and ambiguous moral codes of late modernity, and in this regard the family is certainly not exempt. The disaffection of children and families (however these roles – e.g. 'brother', 'sister', 'mother' – are constituted in the seemingly endless choices provided by contemporary market capitalism) can easily be assuaged by the selective participation or external invitation into alternative moral–political markets. In the Internet and 24-hour-news age, it is the consumer (with a grievance) who is always right, and who can (and should) fight. Children and young people are increasingly aware of, and motivated by, their awareness of their power as a distinctive demographic consumer group with real clout. Within a modern social environment in which they have relatively few other public outlets for expressing and exercising their agency and power, the frustration or channelling of children's activities and identities as consumers is particularly salient to the development of their self-images as socio-political actors, whether in the form of law-abiding citizen or something else.

What emerges from Wakatsuki Houston's narrative of her childhood and family experiences in Manzanar is the agency of children, even in extreme circumstances when their most basic human and civic rights are taken away:

> In such a narrowed world, in order to survive, you learn to contain your rage and your despair, and you try to re-create, as well as you can, your normality, some sense of things continuing. The fact that America had accused us, or excluded us, or imprisoned us, or whatever it might be called, did not change the kind of world we wanted.
>
> (*Manzanar*: 100)

Stories about family fun, anger or disaffection among children and families using the trope of consumption and leisure are common features in political prisoner life writings, providing a narrative 'hook' onto which humorous or humiliating experiences can be related in a way that is understandable to others who have not been in prison, and also makes them more likely to 'speak' to the reading public. In the absence of the voice of the child in legal discourse (McNamee *et al.*, 2005), they also enable the articulation of children's experiences as a political force and politically empowered – even radicalized – agents to emerge.

'Each stone was a mouth ... ': voicing the radicalized childhood

> The *mouth* is the central character in the story outlining the corporeality of (modern) consumption ... not only due to its role as the primal organ of consumption (eating) but also due to its expressive functions, as an organ of speech.
>
> (Falk, 1994: 10, original emphasis)

Jeanne continues throughout her life to reflect on her enforced need to recreate a sense of normality in her childhood and for her family by reiterating her own and fellow detainees' link to American culture, and listing a series of places of worship, consumption and leisure incorporated in the camp that are common to *all* American children and small towns:

> Most of us were born in this country; we had no other models. Those parks and gardens [made by families in the camps] lent it an oriental

character, but in most ways it was a totally equipped American small town, complete with schools, churches, Boy Scouts, beauty parlors, neighborhood gossip, fire and police departments, glee clubs, softball leagues, Abbott and Costello movies, tennis courts, and traveling shows.

(*Manzanar*: 100)

This litany of ordinary small-town aspects with which the camp was 'equipped' is contrasted to the profusion of rock, flower and vegetable gardens made by the detainees during the years of their incarceration. 'People who lived in Owens Valley [a town just outside of the camp] during the war still remember the flowers and lush greenery they could see from the highway as they drove past the main gate' (ibid.: 99). These gardens created by the detainees furnished the camp with a wide variety of fresh fruits and vegetables as well as improving upon their Spartan environment. When the adult Jeanne later returns to the site of the camp with her husband and their children, she remarks how her doubts and fears about seeing Manzanar again brought on something of an existential crisis in her sense of self and the reality of her family's past, making it into something of a 'joke':

When we finally started to talk about making a trip to visit the ruins of the camp, something would inevitably get in the way of our plans. Mainly my own doubts, my fears. I half-suspected that the place did not exist. So few people I met in those years had even heard of it, and those who had knew so little about it, sometimes I imagined I had made the whole thing up, dreamed it. Even among my brothers and sisters, we seldom discussed the internment. If we spoke of it at all, we joked.

(ibid.: 186)

When she eventually returns, she notes how the infrastructure of the camp has almost totally disintegrated, the buildings all gone, leaving only the barest foundations of latrines and irrigation ditches covered by weeds. What still remains intact, however, are the rock gardens constructed by the detainees, not only in Manzanar, but also in the other camp where her father was held prior to their detention as a family:

I had found out that even in North Dakota, when Papa and the other Issei men imprisoned there had free time, they would gather small stones from the plain and spend hours sorting through a dry stream bed looking for the veined or polished rock that somehow pleased the most. It is so characteristically Japanese, the way lives were made more tolerable by gathering loose desert stones and forming with them something enduringly human. These rock gardens had outlived the barracks and the towers and would surely outlive the asphalt road and crusted pipes and shattered slabs of concrete. Each stone was a mouth, speaking for a family, for some man who had beautified his doorstep.

(*Manzanar*: 191)

Jeanne's reference to the ornamental garden stones remaining in the ruins of the camp as 'mouths' expresses the complexities of maintaining her collective identity with the past generations of her (non-American) family, and at the same time retaining her openness to her adopted culture, even as it puts her and her family under unjustified and almost unendurable duress in the name of 'national security'. As Pasi Falk (1994) states, this is manifestly expressed in the moral and (in late modern societies) consumption-based political economy of body, self and culture: 'First, the stronger the cultural Order and the community bonds in which the subject is constituted, the more "open" is the body both to outside intervention ad to a reciprocal relationship with its cultural/social context' (12). So, while in the story about Mama shattering the china, her mouth remains resolutely closed, in this second story about the stones left behind in the rock gardens of Manzanar, the mouths of all its former internees are opened for ever to history, replacing the bodies of the families who occupied those now invisible huts.

The activity of collecting these stones and creating beautiful Japanese rock gardens by the *Issei* men detainees demonstrates the strength of their enforced reliance upon their Japanese cultural roots in the wake of their stigmatization by their fellow Americans. These closing episodes of the book powerfully evoke the pathos, but also the enduring strength, of these families and their access to their distinctive multicultural heritage, both during and long after their period of detention in the various camps. Not only did they not 'make up' these events, they faced them with dignity and inventiveness, even beauty; not only did they survive, but their traditional rock gardens with which they decorated the entrances of the huts outlasted the sentinel towers and fences of the camp. As American citizens who were incarcerated because of their ethnicity, these individuals (if not also their families) persevered more or less intact. What could be more 'American' in the sense of rebellion and resilience than in this manifestation of being 'more Japanese'? And what could be more American about America than ' ... the way it can both undermine you and keep you believing in your own possibilities, pumping you with hope' which is what the millions of Japanese-Americans of this generation learned the hard way (*Manzanar*, 154)?

Tracing a radical line

Thai Jones's *A Radical Line: From the Labor Movement to the Weather Underground, One Family's Century of Conscience* (2004) represents a relatively rare example of the genre of radical life writing: a radical political family memoir. This is a story of a radical family history, traced by the author from his maternal Jewish grandmother's involvement in American Communist politics and his paternal grandfather's punishment as a conscientious objector in the 1910s and 1920s, to his own parents' membership of the notorious Weathermen/Weather Underground in the 1960s and 1970s. His father, Jeffrey, was also a leader of the organization, and his mother Eleanor was a law student and was also active in the group. The Jones family lived 'underground' for several years, during which time they moved around frequently and were known by a number of aliases; this included young Thai (who was named after a Vietnamese National Liberation Front soldier Nguyen Thai, whom his mother Eleanor met at an event in Havana). The narrative concludes with the arrest of his parents by FBI at their family apartment in New York City when Thai (at the time known as Timmy) was 4 years old.

This final event in the narrative is recounted at the start of the book, and takes place on what was otherwise an ordinary day in the family's life in October 1981. The family, father 'John Maynard' (Jeff), mother 'Sally' (Eleanor) and young 'Timmy' (Thai) were relaxing at home together on a Friday night. After receiving a telephone call from an FBI Special Agent, who warned him that the apartment was surrounded and that in 30 seconds there would be a knock at the door by one of his men, 'John' covered the receiver with his hand and said to 'Sally', 'We're busted'. After being told by his mother that 'something really bad is about to happen' but that 'it's going to be ok' (Jones, 2004: 2), there was a battering at the door. When Thai's father opened the door, a 'flood' of police in full riot gear entered, armed with shotguns and M-16s. They searched every room of the apartment, and forced his father to crawl the length of the hallway before then manacling him and laying him on the floor. While his mother argued with the police, young Thai retreated to his bedroom where he briefly considered his options, having retrieved a pair of child's scissors from his desk drawer:

> Bouncing them in my hand and snipping at the air, I considered putting on the cowboy hat and charging into the hallway with scissors blazing to defeat these men who had come to hurt our family. Even then, I knew it was a battle against long odds. But I didn't realize it was a question that many in my family had already faced. They had chosen to fight.

> For me, the decision was easy to make. I returned the scissors and closed the drawer. I went out to the hallway where my father was manacled, skid my small fingers around the cold cuffs into his palm, and stood with him in the corridor holding hands.
> This is my earliest memory.

(ibid.: 2)

Even the boy's first memory is readable into his family's extended and sometimes violent political history as is, just as significantly, what he regards as his own departure from it by deciding not to put on the cowboy hat and wield the scissors, i.e. not to react with violence. It is also narrated very much within the popular culture of American children of the time, whereby the action hero *du jour* who was capable of attacking and fighting off the forces of the state was epitomized by the figure of the cowboy.

Jones proceeds to describe his father Jeffrey's upbringing in the California San Fernando Valley, a childhood vignette that foreshadows the narrative of his own future life and connection to his father, with the precursor of the cowboy hero, the rugged frontier outdoorsman linked in the children's popular imagination of the 1950s with the rebel hero and frontiersman, Davy Crockett:

> Some of the best hours of his life had been spent wandering through the Mojave desert with his YMCA camp friends and, since childhood, he had liked nothing better than to get lost in the wild and then find his way back home again.
>
> (ibid.: 9)

Later, having learned about the explosion in the Greenwich Village town-house of a bomb that was prematurely detonated by other members of the Weather Underground, Jeff is

> upset but not surprised. In the previous months, bombings had spread like an infection. From a localized outbreak in Vietnam, they had been borne by frustration to Laos and Cambodia, India and Algeria, Paris and German, Chile, Argentina and now America. Less than a month earlier, Jeff had been shocked when a bomb killed a police officer in San Francisco. With the accident in New York, it seemed as if the violence was still escalating and, sure enough, four days later, a different group detonated explosives inside three corporate offices in midtown Man-hattan.
>
> (ibid.: 11)

The violence, though shocking (the three people making the Greenwich bomb were killed), is not surprising to Jeff, as recalled by his son Thai. Interestingly, the event of the townhouse bomb – probably the single most well-known event linked to the Weather Underground – is immediately read into a broadly international political narrative of violence and dissent. Death and destruction by a number of political actors on the world stage, and the regrettable nature of violent death suffered by a diversity of victims (including a policeman) are seen as part of an interconnected global whole, within which the Weathermen are just bit players. The implication is that this is simply an outcome of the way things are, a symptom of a world in conflict dominated by violence, and not the fault of the individuals or political organization involved. This is broadly con-sistent with the psychological defence mechanism identified by Taylor and

Quayle (1994), whereby responsibility for terrorist violence is deflected away from the individuals: 'Violent responses are forced by circumstance, by conspiracy, by the State's inaction, but never by deliberate intent; these are the rationalizations of violence from terrorists the world over' (29). Even though neither Thai nor his father were directly involved in the Greenwich Village bombing, the work of averting a sense of shock or moral outrage and dispersing responsibility among international state conflicts is something the author has seemingly learned by way of his family upbringing, despite the fact that he has apparently eschewed a life of political radicalism (violent or otherwise) himself. This means that, though the values and rationales associated with radicalization may be transmitted intergenerationally, they do not necessarily result in political radicalization, let alone terrorist action, although the rationales may still be discernible as an inherited way of making sense of the (family's) radical past and interpreting current events.

Jones's family history is characterized by a number of disjunctions and contradictions in its discursive narrative of a shifting legacy of political radicalism and contingent strategies of violence or non-violence, and inherited memories of gender identities and perceived injustices. In a revealing episode, Thai recounts the emotional farewell between the deeply committed Quaker and First World War conscientious objector Albert (Thai's grandfather) and Albert's father Malcolm: 'Albert gave his father a firm handshake and thought of the words he had spoken a few nights earlier. "I don't believe in one thing you're doing," Malcolm had told him, "but I'll whip the man who calls you a coward"' (Jones, 2004: 69). This is a rather paradoxical farewell from a father to his son who abhors violence. Throughout the war years, there was tension between Malcolm and Albert, and bemusement over Albert's reluctance to fight as a member of the self-professed 'rough-housing Joneses':

> Conversation between Albert and his father was limited to essential topics only, and pacifism was not among them. Malcolm had never understood his son: Why would a strong, healthy American, a rough-housing Jones, have such an abhorrence for fighting?
>
> (Jones, 2004: 72)

When the time came to make a final decision about whether or not to answer the call of the draft board, Albert followed not his family's wishes, but that of another conscientious objector who was sentenced to prison for his beliefs, David Dellinger.

> During the trial, Dellinger and the other defendants made clear their position that 'in order to live in harmony with the will of God,' it was necessary to 'obey our conscience before we obey the State.' Albert felt the same way.
>
> (Jones, 2004: 73)

In other words, part of the family political legacy was a stubborn determination to obey personal political principles based on deeply held and fundamentalist religious belief, even if they contradicted those of the family or indeed the wider community. This would be a 'radical' trait that would according to this family biography transmit down the Jones family line.

Thai's family history dwells upon the experiences of his grandfather Albert, who was named for the King of Belgium who was visiting their home town at the time of his birth, and later consigned to a Civilian Public Service Camp for the duration of the war to work for the Forest Reserve as a punishment for refusing military service (he was not sent to prison, but issued by the draft board – which included doctors and other respected members of the community who had known Albert for the whole of his life – with the rating IV-E 'wrong-headed, incorrigible, hopeless' (ibid: 76)). The chapter devoted almost entirely to Albert records the stigma and humiliation that was continually visited on the camp internees, and the ridicule of the men by locals and the media for their presumed cowardice, effeminacy and treachery. Thai tells the story of Albert's brave and selfless involvement in the attempted rescue of a flight crew following the crash of an Army plane into the side of the mountain on which the camp was situated. Though there were no survivors, Albert and his fellow inmates managed to recover the bodies of the aircrew at great risk to their own safety. For their bravery, they were not exactly met with gratitude by the locals:

> The word got around that the conscientious objectors had gone up the mountain when the bomber crashed. They had found the bodies, the locals said, and robbed them. It was rumored that by the time the army personnel had taken charge of the corpses, all of their wallets were gone. It was partly true. So desperate had been one of the men in sneakers for warm shoes that he had peeled the boots from off a corpse and worn them down the mountainside. Back in the camp, the boots stood at the doorway for a few days, giving off a faint, nauseating smell. Finally, somebody took then into the woods and quietly buried them.
>
> (ibid.: 82)

At this time, Albert and his new bride Millie were also not averse on principle to taking advantage of the spoils of war. In a reference to an encounter with some of the desperate Japanese farmers who were being rounded up and evacuated to internment camps like Manzanar, Thai records proudly how Albert and Millie were able to bag a bargain and purchase a beautiful Plymouth coupé from a Japanese man forced to leave everything behind for only 40 dollars (ibid.: 74). This aside in the Jones's family biography expresses the complex and often competing experiences communicated intertextually in (political) family historiographies, especially during times of conflict.

Jeff, Thai's father and later Weatherman, though very much interested in politics, was very different from his father Albert the conscientious objector. In 1966, Jeff left home in southern California to pursue a career in politics in New York City, starting with a work-study placement at a well-known labour law firm as the launching point of his career. Just one month later, his entire outlook on his future and his participation in politics had changed dramatically:

> Jeff spent his lunch breaks pounding the pavement thinking about the government. Wandering through Battery Park, chewing a hot dog from a vendor, he had decided to become a socialist. With all the troubles in the world, that was the only justifiable thing one could be. Of course, just declaring the fact didn't make it so. He had to live it, and what was the best way of doing that? For now the answer could wait.
>
> When he left work on the afternoon of October 27, 1966, he was becoming a twenty-year-old radical. Walking to the subway station from the law office on Broad Street, he kept himself aloof from the bodies sprinting by him. Earlier he might have seen himself in these ambitious young Wall Street workers, but now he had nothing but disdain for the shallow purpose they had chosen. He stood out from the crowd and not just because he was a blond Californian. He was a subversive element in their midst, a hungry wolf.
>
> (ibid.: 120–1)

This story is revealing, not just because it records the very moment in which his father was radicalized, but because of the plotting devices in the narrative used to represent it. The scene is an urban leisure space (a park) and the action takes place during otherwise unstructured free time from the work schedule (the lunch break), again suggesting the importance of consumption and leisure on the construction of the radicalization narrative. The details as to *why* he made this decision are absent, presumably because they are – from the perspective of the narrator – either obvious or irrelevant. Perhaps more than anything, what comes through in this story is the *momentary* character of this pivotal change in Jeff's sense of self and his life course, from the ambitious legal ingénue to radical 'subversive' and 'hungry wolf'.

How are we to interpret this story, what does it tell us about the reasons behind radicalization and how they are represented and communicated in life stories within radical subcultures transmitted via the family history? In many ways, the account of radicalization contained in this story contradicts what has become the accepted premise in the research literature on radicalization detailed in Chapter 1, i.e. that it is the result of a sometimes long but progressively temporal *process* (e.g. Taylor and Quayle, 1994) that can be reduced to a discrete number of observable stages suitable for prediction and prevention by external bodies or forces or internal states of mind (e.g. Dyer *et al.*, 2007). The 'rationale' implied in this story is however *event-oriented*, and not apparently based on any particular set of externally observable or 'rational' choices through which the actor is coerced or compelled in light of outside influences (the basis of RCT explanations of criminality and criminal behaviour). In the event, there would appear to have been little or no process of rationalization going on at all, but rather something more instantaneous and momentous in the manner of a conversion experience, in which perspectives are fundamentally changed, if not completely reversed.

I am aware that in making this observation, I am in danger of immediately reigniting outdated presumptions or old debates about the implied 'irrationality' of terrorist actors or violent extremists; this is not my intention. As de Figueiredo and Weingast (2001) posit in their review of the overwhelming consensus of argument on this point among terrorism experts, terrorists are neither irrational nor insane. While many terrorism experts (de Figueiredo and Weingast among them) are dismissive of what is generally categorized under the banner of 'emotion' as an insufficient explanatory cause of terrorism, the stories recounted in these family biographies suggest that different kinds of knowledge and rationalities are at work at different times and in a variety of ways, especially at this pivotal early stage, in which the radical identity is formulated and more fully embraced. The instrumental influences of causal elements, such as the inculcation of extreme hatred, provocation of state violence, and the dominance of 'in groups' noted by de Figueiredo and Weingast (2001) are crucial to understanding the macro trends of terrorism; at the same time, it is vital not to conflate 'terrorism' with 'radicalization', nor to reify its formative temporal, subjective or social qualities in a reductive or deterministic process that necessarily results in violence, even where we are trying to uncover the sense-making process that links radicalization with later terrorist action, as in the life stories of individuals like Jeff Jones. As Feldman (2003) indicates in his ethnographical research on paramilitary violence in Northern Ireland, at the micro level, it is clear that a wide variety of overlapping and often competing, if not openly contradictory, narrative stratagems are available to individual actors when it comes to exploring and (re)constructing possible rationales for terrorist or related forms of interpersonal violence. In his research, the highly synchronic nature of these rationalizations is suggestive of the intrinsically localized and situational iterations of socio-political interaction at the community – and often at or involving the family – level that forms the underlying basis of this hermeneutical sense-making process, which can take place (in his experience) during the course of a car journey or on a lunchtime walk. In this significant context, the findings of McKie and Lombard (2005) in their research into families and political violence would seem to be in agreement, foregrounding the ways in which the living and telling of family stories about shifting political differences and consensus provides an important site for the sanctioning of violence within and between families:

> Families can become a conduit for the creation and reinforcement of differences that may be worked out through tensions and violence. At

the same time inter-communal violence creates a cultural context in which the prevalence of violence in families, such as domestic violence, increases. The sanctioning of violence becomes evident between and within families.

(McKie and Lombard, 2005: 169–70)

The story of Jeff's conversion experience immediately introduces a number of new problems for the young man, such as how to be a subversive radical in the context of his new career as a lawyer with political ambitions, and how to handle what was ' … in theory at least, the gap between him and the family back home [which] was wider than ever' (Jones, 2004: 122). This 'gap' opening up between Jeff and his family is not simply a matter of Jeff's radicalization (his father's personal sacrifice in order to put into practice his religiously oriented political beliefs is certainly testimony to this); the difference would seem to pivot on the violent character of his radicalization, which is in stark contrast to that of his father Albert. While this comprises yet another twist in this family's radical history, it is one that from Jeff's point of view was rooted in a particular moment in time; in many respects, this is a reaction against his father's (non-violent) radical past and predominantly directed toward his future life and immanent (if as yet unknown) sense of self.

After rejecting his prospective career as a lawyer and politician, Jeff's next step in becoming a radical on his own terms was to become heavily involved as an organizer and activist in the Student Democratic Society (SDS). He wrote a letter to his father Albert discussing his activities, which Albert (and later Thai) was able to 'read into' the family history of political non-violence:

Reading this letter gave Albert a good chuckle. It sounded almost identical to the work he had done as a member of the pacifism movement of the 1930s. He was impressed. Jeff, so upset by the war, seemed to have learned well the abhorrence of violence that he had tried to teach. If Albert had felt some concern that he was not focusing enough on his education, he could hardly have expressed it without feeling hypocritical. After all, it was he who had taken Jeff to Quaker meeting each Sunday and introduced him to community activism.

(ibid.: 133)

If Albert felt ambivalent about how he had taught by example and raised his son, Jeff's feelings about following his father's example of becoming a conscientious objector and refusing the draft for the Vietnam War were equally fraught. Was it right for Jeff (as Albert had done before him) to take advantage of his status as a recorded CO and university student to refuse the draft, while poor black young men did not have these luxuries and were required to go and fight in Vietnam? Could his conscience allow him to concentrate on pursuing his own university education without feeling he had somehow let down the poor and oppressed? Jeff's experiences of the Vietnam War and the injustices it implied 'at home' (which is precisely where, incidentally, as the popular Weatherman slogan went, they wanted to 'bring the war'), in combination with his admiration for the Vietnamese in bravely fighting a far superior military force coalesced into another dramatic change in his ' … moral compass … he forswore pacifism and determined that at certain times, fighting was the only way' (ibid.: 136). In the wake of the perceived failures of the previous generation of radicals, for Jeff and his generation of radicals, violence was the new pacificism – that is to say, the ethically preferable option to non-violent protest as a more effective mechanism for pursuing social change in the interests of social justice. Hence either victory or death were the only viable outcomes. Unlike other non-violent activists from the civil rights movement, conscientious objectors or some paramilitary groups (such as the PIRA), prison would not be envisioned as having any particular functional or operational role in the advancement of their campaigns, and indeed, for those who ended up in the criminal justice system as opposed to the glorification of martyrdom achieved by death in battle, the realities of prison life came as something of a nasty shock (e.g Stern, 2007).

A very similar family history comprising a tradition of pacifist resistance to what was perceived to be a bellicose state regime during wartime, founded on a radical Protestantism and resulting in the violent radicalization of a member of the younger generation of activists in the 1960s, is presented in Jillian Becker's biography of Ulrike Meinhof contained in her book on the Baader-Meinhof Group/Red Army Faction *Hitler's Children* (1978). Becker's explanatory thesis regarding Meinhof's radicalization is that it was not so much influenced by Marxist ideology or Communist doctrine (in fact, Becker claims that none of the members of the RAF – least of all Meinhof or Baader – were inclined to studying dry political tracts), but rather that Meinhof's religious upbringing in a radical Protestant, middle-class family environment, within a society where the traditional bonds of family life were already fundamentally compromised by the fascist state, inclined her to regard the issue of radicalism as more question of *morality* as opposed to mere politics. Her radicalization therefore marked the unfolding of an emotive and romantic 'love affair' (Becker, 1978: 159) with Communism, which following the breakup of her marriage and culminated with the embracing of violence as 'less and less morally inexcusable' (ibid.: 189). In many respects, this accords with Maldonado's (1993) findings concerning the rise of evangelical Protestantism and its seminal influence on middle-class families as a contributing factor to political radicalism in Latin American countries whose social infrastructures have been severely damaged by decades of violence, conflict, poverty and corruption. Maldonado attributes this to the 'fundamentalist orientation' of an authoritative Christian guide to life, underpinned by literalist interpretations of religious texts combined with the promotion of a strict moral code, a separatist attitude to the public order, and the amenability of eschatological narrative/temporal schemes to serve current political objectives in socio-economic context of violence, chaos and disorder. In the case of the conflict in Bosnia, Bringa (1995, in McKie and Lombard, 2005: 181) also found that the identity markers of religion and ethnicity were key to positioning families and their members against the state in the here and now, followed in order of importance by socio-economic factors and nationality:

> In Bosnia, Bringa (1995) found that even though villagers defined themselves in terms of ethno-religious groups, socioeconomic factors were more significant for inclusion than nationality. In this case, boundaries were physical, localised and also contemporary. For the people their village was the entity to which they all belonged and it was this boundary that united and separated them from the state.
>
> (ibid.: 181)

Zuckerman *et al.* (2007) found in their qualitative survey of political attitudes and decision-making in Germany and Britain that family members strongly influence these processes and practices; in societies that are severely affected by conflict, poverty or war, these family biographies suggest that the influence of religious fundamentalism on family subcultures can have a stronger impact than political ideology (which can manifest itself as an ad hoc contributing factor) on the violent radicalization of members of the younger generation. As noted in Chapter 1, the variable of religion and the nature of its 'causal' influence, if any, is a major concern in the understanding of radicalization. These family biographies suggest a discernible pattern with respect to the influence of fundamentalism, as opposed to religion, in the form of any particular religious tradition (such as but not limited to Islam). We may recall that in *Farewell to Manzanar*, the authors implicitly use Japanese mythical–religious tradition, and explicitly refer to Catholicism (a religion to which the family did not adhere) as discursive resources for narrating this family's biography, and also narrating Jeanne's *non-violent* radicalization as a Japanese-American mother who will pass this down the generations as part of her legacy (and through the book, onto other families and future generations). In contrast, the subcultural praxes relating to fundamentalism – notably literalist interpretation of text, perception of the present moment reconfigured in eschatological time, and overwhelming confidence in individualistic moral codes that are all divorced or exempted from the context of hermeneutic religious tradition – transmitted intergenerationally through families living in societies in crisis, can result in a dramatic rise in *violent* radicalization.

Other influences from the past affected Jeff's turn towards violence. Jeff's status in the SDS increased, and in 1967 he became the regional director for New York City. At the SDS national convention in the summer of 1967, in the wake of record deaths of American soldiers in Vietnam, the nature and intensity of the student protests were escalating and becoming increasingly violent, and were due to conclude with a protest march on the Pentagon. The task of organizing this march pitted Jeff against his father's one-time role model, radical pacifist David Dellinger:

> Everyone who came to see him [Jeff] at the SDS office in Union Square wanted to talk about the upcoming march against the Pentagon. Jeff represented SDS on a steering committee led by David Dellinger. In 1940, Dellinger had inspired Albert by choosing prison over the army. Now he was leading the next generation of activists, but Jeff, at least, was beginning to find Dellinger's way old-fashioned. After years of non-violent protests, the war had only expanded.
> Jeff was exploring another philosophy.
>
> (Jones, 2004: 137)

This encounter by two generations of the Jones family with Dellinger, a radical icon of the twentieth century, demonstrates how the complexities of family loyalties and radical values and how they are developed, negotiated and transmitted across the generations in the context of ongoing political conflict and in real people's lives. That the influence of Dellinger has the opposite effect on the son that it had on the father shows how the dynamics of family relationships resist the simplistic reproductive transmission of cultural or political values from one generation to the next in the same way, even as in this case where the same individual source of inspiration is concerned. As Ed Husain (2007) also relates in his political memoir, it is not at all uncommon for the young generation to rebel against the values and beliefs of their 'old-fashioned' forbears, even when these family members were already activists in the promotion of their beliefs, or else political radicals. Eventually, even the SDS proved too conservative for the young firebrand Jeff, and he, along with his colleagues Bernardine Dohrn, Bill Ayers and the woman who would later become Jeff's wife and Thai's mother, Eleanor Raskin (née Stein) among others left the SDS and relinquished non-violence to form the Weathermen.

It wasn't just along paternal–child lines that this type of rebellion against radical family tradition was taking place, nor were all the arguments based on religious or political ideological beliefs. As mentioned previously, consumerism features in the radicalization narratives of the maternal side of this family too. Thai tells how his mother Eleanor inflamed her own mother's Communist ethos by her shopping habits and dress sense:

> Eleanor and Jonah [her first husband] went to her mother's house at least once a week for dinner and political conversation. Annie, never shy, would express disapproval toward her daughter's wardrobe. When Eleanor insisted on buying a sheared lamb coat from Gimbel's—thigh-length with a zipper running all the way up—Annie was furious. At $200, the coat was way too expensive; worse, it was made from South African sheared lamb.

The thought of her only daughter breaking the apartheid boycott for such a thing was more than Annie could stand. She brought out the family's most deadly insult for the occasion—the 'B' word. But bourgeois or not, Eleanor bought the coat. She had been defying her mother for years.

(Jones, 2004: 148)

In the new radical consumer politics, 'bought' trumps 'bourgeois' every time. Even compared with Jeff's upbringing in a politically radical family, Eleanor was raised in a very politically active and radical household, in which child-rearing provided a crucial opportunity for indoctrination of the new generation. Significantly, this included the communal family meal – yet another example of the symbolic ritual and cultural significance of food and its consumption in resistance cultures (Ellmann, 1993). In this story, food is used by the young Eleanor's father to teach her a lesson about the politics of global capitalism:

Eleanor had learned to crawl, then walk, then march. She was in her mother's picket lines as soon as she could toddle. She had picked up the rudiments of socialism at the dinner table. Arthur, her father, had taken a lamb chop from the platter and placed it on her plate. Everyone in the world wants lamb chops, he said. But some people had no lamb chops while others ate two each night. There were even some greedy people who wanted more lamb chops than they could ever eat. Was it fair that they should acquire so many lamb chops, while others went hungry? No, Eleanor decided, it was not.

(Jones, 2004: 152)

School memories feature in the maternal family history too, functioning as a site where Eleanor as a child was compelled to learn the skills of negotiating between the divergent political realms of mainstream American culture at school and the radical Communism that was the predominant influence on life at home. At the same time, her parents were also obliged to develop the necessary self-protective strategies to be able to continue to live and speak about their political beliefs as they chose at home, managing on a daily basis the sharing and/or leaking of information about their political affiliations to outsiders through sophisticated practices of disclosure. The formal role of indoctrinating the young Eleanor was consigned to long-time family friend Chavy. This arrangement placed the child in some tricky situations with respect to home and school, presenting a number of questions for her parents to answer; it also raises questions about the effectiveness of concentrating on school as a main site for dealing with the 'threat' of radicalization or extremism on behalf of the state, given the sophistication of families to resist disclosing these beliefs, and thereby elide or neutralize any possible reactive influence:

At school, she got a different lesson. One day her teacher taught her that all Communists were bad people. Annie and Arthur said, 'No, that's not true.' In fact, they told her, Annie's friend Chavy was a Communist. Of course, they couldn't tell her that they too belonged to the Party. Chavy's job was to indoctrinate Eleanor to the cause. She brought over a Soviet children's book, *The Story of Zoya and Shura*, which quickly became a favorite in the Stein house.

(ibid.: 152)

But the burden of being the child of a truly committed radical can sometimes be too much to bear, even for the most revolutionary child:

In Brooklyn, as in Washington, there were times when Annie's [Eleanor's mother] commitment was just too much. Vendors at Coney Island sold Confederate flags, and Eleanor was mortified by her mother's insistence on arguing about it with every single shop owner all the way down the boardwalk. Eleanor was closer to her father, who had gone through the ordeal of the witch hunt without losing his sense of fun.

(ibid.: 153–4)

Once again, the crux of the problem of overzealousness or extremism emerges for the child during the course of a family leisure-consumption activity, in this case a visit to Coney Island. All children can be embarrassed by the outspoken or anomalous behaviours of their parents, and this applies to radical as much as to non-radical families, in their associated public interactions with those whom they oppose or from whom they separate themselves for ideological reasons. While this can be offputting for the next generation, the influence of other parental bonds, such as the good humour of her father, can have an attenuating effect. As Max Weber noted, charisma is important in the communication and manifestation of political causes, and this also extends not just to the public at large, but also to intrafamilial social interaction. As we have seen throughout this work, while the pleasure and enjoyment of belonging and bonding have an important role to play in becoming radicalized, humour and fun also play an important part in being and remaining a radicalized actor. This makes bearable what can be a difficult task over an extended period of time, and provides respite from the seriousness and often relentless po-faced nature of daily life in radical subcultures.

At school, Eleanor was editor of the school newspaper, and published her own political poetry:

A heavenly guide for refugee,
The way to freedom
For those escaped from the shackles of slavery,
And martyrdom.

(ibid.: 155)

Eleanor's close relationship to her father – who was called to testify twice before McCarthy's House Un-American Activities Committee but refused to cooperate or 'name names', a man of great integrity who was extraordinarily committed to his radical political principles – strongly influenced Eleanor's radical political activism. His sudden death when she was 15 years old abruptly marked what she regarded as the end of her childhood. Soon after, she would initiate her own political career as an adult, though still as ever in the not always welcome or comfortable shadow of her mother. Her father's legacy as a non-violent radical lawyer and intellectual would continue to be her model:

> The war was escalating in Vietnam, and American students were in upheaval. In some ways, growing up around stories of the 1930s, she had lived her whole life in anticipation of a chance to join such a movement. She wanted to apply to law school at Columbia, the university her father and brother had attended. As a girl, Eleanor had been surrounded by progressive lawyers. She had seen the way they used intellect to further political causes and at the same time earned public notoriety and respect. Even the most radical lawyers had been able to earn a living and avoid serious persecution during the 1950s, when many other activists were out of work and facing prison … .
>
> (ibid.: 163)

This esteem for the law was complicated by her mother's more outrageous forms of activism:

> Soon after law school began, Eleanor went with her mother to the protest at the Pentagon. Annie was as militant as protesters one-third her age; she had had all that extra time to store up hatred for the military. Eleanor watched her mother scale a wire fence and shout wild curses at the building. Eleanor hung back. She was on her way to becoming a lawyer, and her mother's behavior seemed excessive, even unseemly.
>
> (ibid.: 163)

At this point in Eleanor's life, as a young woman she wished first and foremost to consolidate her future through a course of action that emulated her father and brother by becoming a lawyer, not her often unconventionally militant mother, whose behaviour she considered 'unseemly'.[4] Eventually, she would change her attitude, abandon her studies at Columbia and take part in what would be remembered by staff at the university as an especially disruptive protest, which involved taking over campus buildings. As a result, her involvement in these student protests on the campus would prove to be so enduringly bitter in the memories of faculty members that decades later she would be denied re-entrance in order to finish her law degree.

Anarchy and emotivism – even at the level of flouting of codes of politeness and civility – frequently provide expressive influences on these radical subcultures, as in the case of another radical group of the time often allied with the Weathermen, the Motherfuckers:

> The Motherfuckers referred to themselves as 'a street gang with an analysis,' though they seemed to emphasize the street gang part. As for the analysis, a full-page ad in the *Rat* offered an example, 'What is our program? We'll know we've got it if it makes us feel good. Is there any place in the revolution for incoherence? Incoherence is the only place.'
>
> (ibid.: 182)

But, as is often the case with competing radical groups, such influences are embraced on a continually shifting and sliding scale. What can seem 'radical' and 'edgy' at one moment, can be regarded by the same people as distasteful or counter-revolutionary from another perspective or in hindsight. Many women members allied to feminist groups (e.g. Morgan, 1989) found the condoning of violent sexism encapsulated in the name offensive and entirely inappropriate for a supposedly radical group devoted to the task of liberation from the oppressive regimes of patriarchal society. Jeff recalls his father's disdain for such selfish and indulgent motives surrounding the consumption of drugs and rock and roll music, perhaps not a surprising attitude to leisure and consumption-based protest given his puritanical Quaker upbringing. In time, Jeff developed similar disdain for the motives and *modus operandi* of the Yippies, specifically their plan for what would be one of the most notorious events of the 1960s, the riots outside the Chicago Hilton Hotel during the Democratic Party Convention in 1968. It would seem that, in this respect at least, Jeff was very much his Quaker father's son, regardless of what would later prove to be the success of this plan as a public relations coup for the radical left:

> 'Their intention,' he wrote, 'to bring thousands of young people to Chicago during the DNC to groove on rock bands and smoke grass and then to put them up against bayonets—viewing that as a radicalizing experience—seems manipulative at best. The idea would not be bad, were it not for the Illinois National Guard and the Chicago Police.' What he didn't foresee was that the strategy would lead to one of the biggest public relations victories the antiwar movement would ever win.
>
> (Jones, 2004: 185–6)

While these riots may have constituted a successful protest event and an integral part of the historical memory of the international student protests of 1968, it is less clear in hindsight how durably 'radicalizing' it (or indeed the protests of 1968) was (see Becker, 1978). Despite Jeff's misgivings, for some, like his wife Eleanor, 'The business end of a policeman's billy club had been a radicalizing agent' (in Jones, 2004: 193). The immediate demands of violent confrontation with the police, and the need for groups like the Weathermen to issue press releases to an emergent and voracious media (mainly in the form of a 'garbled Marxist doctrine' which would mark the group's 'coming of age' (ibid.: 195)) would henceforth form the major influences on the Weather/men/Underground, over the 'conventional' revolutionary influence of Marxism that was handed down though the generations of traditionally radical families like the Joneses, the Raskins and the Steins. Indeed, an audacious act of 'political yoga' would witness the members of these new radical groups changing tack, no longer seeing themselves as defenders of the interests the oppressed proletariat whose objective was to inspire the masses to revolutionary action as couched in the historical conventions of American radicalism, but instead to identify themselves more fully with the burgeoning and increasingly violent street culture of working-class youth, to whom they look for their inspiration as middle-class activists:

> Weatherman's solution was to show that 'most young people in the US are part of the working class ... Most kids are well aware of what class they are in, even though they may not be very scientific about it. So our analysis assumes from the beginning that youth struggles are, by and large, working-class struggles.' Therefore, the Weathermen weren't college-educated middle-class youths who could rely on their families for financial support. Not at all. They were working-class revolutionaries. Having performed that uncomfortable feat of political yoga, no ideological barriers remained to block the path to Marxist struggle.
>
> (ibid.: 195)

In short, an outcome of generations of political radicalism was to coalesce in the Weather movement, not so much a consolidation not of resistance culture transmitted through the generations via radical family tradition, as a convergence of burgeoning (and highly commodified) youth culture founded on a dual ethos of *violence* and *consumption*. For radical families like the Joneses and the Steins, this comprised a signal reversal of much of their past family values of radicalism, which were expressed primarily through non-violent symbolic protest, altruistic self-denial of class privilege[5] and intellectual debate. The payoff for these mainly young, middle-class radicals? A sense of vitality, potency, individuality, liberation and hedonistic enjoyment, combining to produce above all an overwhelming sense of *agency* in the history of modern politics – i.e. of acting in a way that is ' ... not the subject of coercion or constraint' (Crewe, 2009: 15) or the stultifying norms of their bourgeois origins. By forging new identities as revolutionaries based on emergent cultural forms such as consumerism and youth culture – by for example adapting styles of dress and developing tastes in music, art, literature and sexuality befitting the ethos of a new radicalism decoupled from traditional leftist political doctrine – the radicals of the 1960s generation created new models of political activism based on the politics of identity and individualism that functioned in a much more public, and in many ways more acceptable (to the emergent capitalism that benefited substantially from these new political norms) way compared to the radicalization of their parents' generation (who had to hide their radical views from those around them and (ostensibly) practice a rather stoic form of (material) self-denial). This provided potent mechanisms for attracting and recruiting other disillusioned young people who also felt disempowered and constrained by their (family's) past, if only via the consumption of one or more of a variety of 'alternative' lifestyle symbols that were now on offer. This is how the middle-class members of the elite Weather/men/Underground were able to close the gap created by class difference and make a decisive break with the doctrinal demands of political ideologies like Marxism that were so closely linked with the overtly intellectual and genteelly austere (as opposed to bodily, sexual, hedonistic, performative, excessive, irrational, etc.) radicalism of their parents and earlier generations. For the children of the pre-Second World War radicals, simply continuing the revolutionary struggle was no longer enough; henceforth, the commitment to 'the cause' must be greater and more personally demanding, if not also emotionally challenging, and indeed more excessive in its rewards for the 'self-consummating' individual. It must also be visible to those on the 'outside' (i.e. not just a secret shared among family members) through the participation in and consumption of certain political activities in the public as well as private sphere. It must also result in the more visible manifestation and reciprocal influence of 'internal' or subjective states on political debate, for example in the production and range of emotional qualities consistent with the demands of a more challenging, excessive and subjective political ethos – to 'do' politics by actively pushing oneself beyond the confines of the comfort zones in which one was constrained to live by virtue of their middle-class origins and associated rationalism based on the continuity and progression of class privilege and refinement of associated codes of civility (Elias, 1978–81). Jones thus writes of his mother Eleanor's motivation to join the Weathermen:

> It was not speeches that made Eleanor go with the Weathermen. She went because they were the scariest choice. The group demanded the biggest sacrifices and represented the strongest challenge to the status quo. She felt—and everyone who joined agreed—that with the current state of the world, it would be impossible to do too much. It was normal to want to participate in violence, to fight and be arrested, to leave the comforts of life behind. It was staying in the middle class cocoon that sounded crazy.
>
> (Jones, 2004: 197–8)

Though of course some of the lessons from the past learned at her mother's knee were still of use, not least in relation to this particular use of 'text':

Eleanor put in [a pamphlet called *The Bust Book: What to Do Until the Lawyer Comes*] a lesson that her mother had taught her about how to prepare for a demonstration. 'The New York Times,' she wrote in the chapter on self-defense, 'although not useful for any other purpose, makes a very hard object when rolled up lengthwise and folded in half, and unlike other weapons, is inconspicuous and not incriminating.'

(ibid.: 199)

The handing-down of such knowledge within radical families concerning the alternative uses of ordinary and commonly available objects is also one of the mainstays of prison culture. Here it informs what we see as one of the first efforts in recognizing the likelihood of entering the criminal justice system, if not yet moving beyond the initial event of arrest. The days of identifying with the oppressed from a comfortable distance for middle-class revolutionaries was well and truly over, as far as the Weathermen were concerned: sacrifices had to be made. This had an immediate impact on Eleanor's relationship with her mother, and also contributed to the collapse of her first marriage:

Her relationship with Jonah was ending. He had been arrested at Columbia and was fired from his professor's job at the university in Stony Brook, but Jonah was a writer and a thinker, not a revolutionary. It was possible in America to be a radical and also have a good career, a nice house, a healthy marriage, wealth, and even fame. Many lawyers, authors, doctors, and labor leaders had done it. But Weatherman said this was wrong. These options were not available to the Black Panthers or the Hispanic Young Lords, and they certainly were not possible for the people of Vietnam. A white revolutionary had to be willing to abandon these things, which Weatherman referred to as 'the enemy within.' She had to take to the streets; fling up the cobblestones into barricades, as the students had done in France; pick up the gun, like the blacks were urging in the ghetto, and bring the war home.

(ibid.)

This use of 'the enemy within' trope, as discussed in Chapter 1, is instructive, as it points not to the proximity of 'the Other' construed as deviant or unassimilated co-dweller, but rather to the distracting temptations of middle-class and race privileges, and practices inherited from the previous generation of radicals – and thus of one's own 'home' culture, a part of the self through the extended family biography. The truly revolutionary links that white radicals could make were with their black, Hispanic, French and Vietnamese contemporaries, not with the thinkers, mentors or family members from the past. This refocusing on the struggle of other peoples in the present moment, and the need to foster new identities and resistance cultures from other ethnic and nationalist groups, did not however result in the consolidation of a single revolutionary ethos, nor indeed did it result in a spirit of cooperation among young people. On the contrary, competition was rife between radical groups as to who was most authentically revolutionary, as were splits, purges and infighting within the separate groups. Continuous efforts toward 'self-improvement' via 'criticism-self-criticism' in the process of creating new, radical identities were more often experienced as psychologically disturbing exercises in group bullying and personal abuse (Stern, 2007; Rojas and Rodríguez Calderón, 1971), which took the family practice of what is normally intended to be socialization through constructive criticism or disciplinary practices to excessive levels. What became a well-known risk to psychological well-being represented by these activities, it was argued within these groups, should be matched on the part of the individual recipient by a willingness to risk freedom, life and limb in the pursuit of the collective political aim: '[Fred Hampton] was the twenty-eighth Panther to meet a violent death in the past two years. Black militants were risking their lives to be political. The Weathermen felt they should be doing the same' (Jones, 2004: 207). The political violence that characterized black and urban radicalism translated within the popular culture of the Weathermen into a frenzied party atmosphere of 'free love', drug-taking and symbolic invocation with some of the more chaotic and destructive influences of the time, such as represented by one particularly notorious 'family' – the Manson family – creating a dark and foreboding atmosphere, and driving a politics of terror through the need for confession, self-purgation and absolution:

> At Flint [a meeting of hundreds of Weathermen], there was a feeling of desperation and a need for self-purgation, confession and absolution. ... The ballroom was dark. Blankets, sleeping bags, pillows, and trash were piled into the corners to make room on the floor. The Weathermen slept for an hour each night, and in the days, found time for meetings and work. Eleanor dropped acid for the first time in her life. But Flint was more about dancing. The last night of the War Council ended in frenzy. Weathermen frolicked until morning, with three fingers raised in imitation of the fork that Manson had stuck into the body of one of his victims. 'He made people afraid,' they said, 'that's what we have to do.'
>
> (ibid.: 209)

These hedonistic parties and emulation of urban revolutionary violence modelled on heroic icons from the Black Power movement and the Manson family murders, and the need to make people afraid, would coalesce into the notorious bombing campaign initiated by the Weather Underground:

From the start of 1969 to mid-April 1970, there had been 40,934 bombings, attempted bombings, and bomb threats, leading to forty-three deaths and almost $22 million in damage. Out of this total, 975 had been explosive, as opposed to incendiary, attacks. This meant that an average of two bombs that someone had planned, constructed, and placed had detonated every day for more than a year. Nothing like it had ever been seen before.

(ibid.: 213)

Neither has anything like this been witnessed on American soil since, in terms of the number of attacks and the duration of the bombings, including the terrorist attacks of 9/11. As the campaign continued, the frustration of law enforcement attempts to apprehend the culprits was reflected in a government political response that claimed not just total incomprehension, but a distinct lack of motives on the part of the bombers: 'The old days began to look surprisingly rosy. At least with the Commies, you were dealing with people who had a system. These Weathermen have no historical materialism, no motive at all' (ibid.). These were no usual political opponents with a worked-out doctrine setting out the enmity of the USA and a formal military strategy for defeating the American behemoth, these were the self-proclaimed 'kids' who were 'everywhere,' playing with guns, having sex, taking drugs and causing havoc, as described in one of their many press releases:

'If you want to find us,' they had said, 'this is where we are. In every tribe, commune, dormitory, farmhouse, barracks and townhouse where kids are making love, smoking dope and loading guns.'

(ibid.: 214)

Revealingly, the locations referred to in this press release are those that normally refer to domestic dwellings – places where 'kids' usually live, either with their families or as students or soldiers, prior to becoming independent adults. The implicit reference to this specific life stage is instructive in terms of making sense of the radicalism and radicalization being pursued (and its eventual demise as its 'grown-up' adherents would tire of life in the underground and the intolerable pressures it placed on their own growing families, as in the case of the Joneses). As with most, if not all, revolutionary groups, there were no half-measures in terms of the total sacrifices demanded within a polemical 'us-and-them' view of the world (Taylor and Quayle, 1994); this was a view that would become unrelenting and impracticable as time went on, as these family biographies show.

While the replacement of traditional, dynastic, intergenerational transmission of radicalism through the family may appear to have been eroded, if not replaced, by a convergence of more contemporaneous cultural influences emanating from post-war consumerism and youth culture, it would be an exaggeration to argue that the influence of family practices and values on radicalization have completely disappeared. As argued in the previous chapter, in many ways the new forms of radicalization based on consumption and youth culture are facilitated through the new cultural construction of childhood and family life (not least including the invention of the teenager). Yet despite their efforts to rebel against their parents, influences from past generations of revolutionaries nevertheless continued to exert a seminal influence on these radicalized young people and their emergent radical groups, usually through the (often communal) reading and discussion of radical or revolutionary texts by 'veterans' of other conflicts:

> Training came from the veterans of Third World revolutions. Weathermen watched *The Battle of Algiers* and read guerrilla manuals by Carlos Marighella from Brazil and Amílcar Cabral of Guinea Bissau. In 1971, Random House published the scrapbooks of a woman freedom fighter in *Tania: The Unforgettable Guerrilla*. Tania, who had died with Che Guevara in Bolivia in 1967, became a heroine to Americans, including Patty Hearst who adopted the name as her own after being kidnapped by the Symbionese Liberation Army in the mid-1970s. The original Tania taught the lessons of becoming a new person. 'I was able to practice sustaining a personality image,' she wrote. 'As the days went by, I found it necessary to tell anecdotes of my life and talk about my family problems and my aspirations. It reached the point that I convinced myself I was talking about my real life.'
>
> (ibid.: 220–1)

Though not a practice that is exclusive to families, reading to and with children as a way of inculcating certain cultural values particularly in middle-class families (as noted earlier in the young Eleanor's home) is an established practice, as is the naming of new family members after particularly revered individuals (often relatives from previous generations) as a way of honouring and preserving their memory. In the case of Patty Hearst, referred to above by Thai Jones, Hearst's encouragement by the group to identify with 'Tania' was so intense as to lead her to blur the boundaries between her own memories of family life and those of her revolutionary namesake in her new 'family' collective. These family-based practices are very much a part of the subcultural practices of modern radical groups and mainstays of resistance culture, as indeed are the incorporation (especially notable during this period) of decidedly traditional hegemonic sex roles and gender norms in these groups:

> On Long Island, the writing collective worked at their statement in the mornings over coffee. Jeff distributed the last of the Owsley acid and took Bernardine, Bill, and Eleanor on a wild seashell gathering expedition along the area's Atlantic beaches. On Thanksgiving Day, Eleanor

cooked a Turkey while the boys played touch football in the yard—just
a typical All-Amerikan family.

(ibid.: 229)

This citation of the misspelled 'Amerika' is obviously intended to undercut
the overly saccharine and sexist evocation of traditional American family life,
as most conventionally represented by the observation of this most colonialist
and distinctively American holiday and its traditions associated with the
idealized family. It does little to subvert or allay such cultural identification,
however. As many feminist scholars and political activists have continually
pointed out (e.g. Dworkin, 2000; Davis, 1990; Gillespie, 1994; John, 1997;
Perkins, 2000; Smith, 1974; Vaughan, 1999; Ward, 2006), women have consistently been obliged – if not coerced – to play not just conventional but also
often exaggeratedly idealized gender roles within radical groups, by for
example, being charged with the 'political' work of cooking, cleaning, organizing, communicating, transporting and overseeing such collective or
'family' rituals, all the while maintaining an ostensible sexuality in dress and
presentation and remaining sexually available (often to more than one partner, usually but not always men (Craig, 2002; Stern, 2007; Alpert, 1981;
Rojas and Rodríguez Calderón, 1971)). This is a potent reminder of the
powerful ideological presence and function of the family as a hugely influential and formative model for the development and sustenance of (radical)
political subcultures, and the subsequent impact on the lives of women
through the exaggeration of patriarchal values and other associated cultural
norms even with 'radical' groups.

Thai Jones's family memoir concludes with a story that brings his father
Jeff back into alignment with his own father's values as a political pacifist. In
the absence of a revolution in response to their extensive bombing campaign,
and in the wake of the realities of losing friends to violent conflict and the
pressures of life underground, the attractions of revolutionary violence paled
dramatically. Not only had the Weathermen's campaign failed to 'bring the
war home', the chances of toppling the government were even more remote
than at any time since 1968 when they started out (Jones, 2004: 237). The
transition from 'Smash Monogamy' radicals and underground terrorists to
settled, pacifist married couple and soon to be parents would be a difficult one
for both Jeff and Eleanor, a situation exacerbated for Jeff in part due to his
Communist mother-in-law Annie's arrival on the scene prior to Thai's birth
(representing on Jeff's part anything but an unconventional – even clichéd –
attitude towards his mother-in-law). Annie's attitude was at once disapprov-
ing, protective, judgemental and paternalistic:

Annie had to be polite because her daughter was involved with these
people, but she conversed with them through gritted teeth. Realizing that
the best way to protect Eleanor was to guide the group toward the

nonviolent politics of the mass movement, Annie tried to become mentor to the Weathermen. Perhaps the best way to do this would have been to sooth, not to taunt; to ease, not prod. But that was not how Annie talked politics ... If Jeff said something that sounded particularly naïve, she didn't gently suggest alternatives. She said, 'You couldn't be more wrong' or 'These ideas have been considered and rejected by every revolution in the world.' Jeff's suspicion that she was probably correct hardly helped ease the unpleasantness of being scolded.

(ibid.: 236)

Jeff's performance of youthful rebellion in a 1976 film about the Weathermen entitled *Underground* would also give rise to ambiguous emotions for his father Albert. At Jeff's request, Albert was invited to a private screening of the film. Having not seen his son for five years, he was understandably keen to see him again, if only in the form of an obscured image on screen. However, while he was relieved to see the recognizable figure of his son behind the gauze curtain, Jeff's words were less comforting.

Then there was footage of Jeff from the Democratic convention in 1968. He was standing on a stage with a microphone, promising, 'Someday we're gonna knock those motherfuckers who control this thing right on their ass.' Albert cringed. He hated that word, the M-F word, and had raised his son never to say it. Then, later, another jolt, as Jeff outlined his beliefs. 'The imperialist power will fight as long as it can with the most advanced technological weapons that it has,' he said. 'And I feel that pacifism and non-violence becomes an excuse for not struggling.' There it was, as if he was speaking directly to his father, repudiating everything he had been taught.

(ibid.: 242)

Notwithstanding his bravura, by this time, for Jeff, the allure of life underground was already beginning to dissipate. As in the case of his Thai's namesake Nguyen Thai's family, life for the Jones family had been severely affected by the parents' pursuit of violent politics. Jones concludes the book by revealing that *thai* means 'peace' in Vietnamese. 'Peace and protest, family and politics: it was all in the name' (ibid.: 244). Politics of a radical stripe has obviously suffused, and was reflexively seen to characterize, this family throughout the generations, though the course of this radicalization and radicalism was subject to change and shifting patterns of external forces and individual agency. What we see in the Jones example is that rebellion against the previous generation is characteristic of most if not all families, even radical ones. The transmission of radicalization from one generation to the next can, in practice, mean the rebellion of the younger generation against the older, regardless of their place on the political spectrum. For

Eleanor, even the act of giving birth to Thai ' ... was political, and refusing to take drugs made it wholesome and radical and, most important, different from how her mother had done it' (ibid.: 245), a precious opportunity to rebel against her mother as well as align herself politically.

At the same time, as with all families, the task of constructing a biography of family life and the life histories of the individuals who comprise them are made all the more difficult by being riddled with contradictions and aporia. While it is common for members of the younger generation to act from a passionate belief that they will be different from their predecessors, often they find that they are more like their parents than they ever expected or knew – and such is the situation with Thai Jones's family. All families devise ways and means to deal with the specific demands of their situation, and develop a sense of a mythological family past and indeed a visionary future. For the young Jones family, this included the shifting tides of identity, work and home life on a continuous and frequent basis, in order to facilitate a life underground – a practice that their young son would have to be initiated into somehow, and to have explained to him in a way he could understand (much as Eleanor's father had used the lamb chops to explain socialism to her):

> They sat me down and said, 'Our family is a little different from other families. We use lots of nicknames; sometimes we use one and some-times we use another. Some people only know one of our names and others know all of them.' Two names that I never heard spoken were Jeff and Eleanor. They tried to make it easy for me by sticking with the same sounds. My father was usually Jason, James, John, or Jake. My mother was Sally or Sarah. Somehow I never stopped to wonder at the situation. This was our family, and even if my parents admitted it was 'a little different,' I had nothing to compare it to.
>
> (ibid.: 264)

Most if not all families are familiar with the use of nicknames. What we see here is a very good example of how perfectly ordinary family practices like nicknaming can be transposed within radicalized families as an aide to con-tinuing their activism while at the same time presenting to the world – and to other family members, most importantly the children – how 'normal' they really are, and thereby maintaining the clandestininty of their radicalism. This is an example of the innovative creativity of resistance cultures, in which 'normal' tropes or practices are reinterpreted, albeit with a twist, to conform to the needs of the family in question. Even the literary device of alliteration is used to make the situation easier for a young child like Thai to remember – 'Timmy' sounding a bit like 'Thai'. The nicknames story is brilliant in its simplicity, conforming to a *logos* of radicalization that, as shown in the pre-vious chapter, is often linked by radicalized adults to the knowledge and practices originating in (their) childhood(s) – a logic that even a child can understand. What is perhaps most surprising and revealing about this story is how easily the required tactics of radical fugitives are amendable to the quotidian practices of 'normal' families and children.

Immediately after their arrest, Thai relates how his mother is able to regain a position of negotiation by virtue of her identity as a parent, albeit a negotiating position that relied on her hope that the FBI agent she was dealing with was a parent too:

> When the invaders were satisfied that this was a family apartment and there would be no fighting [arrest], the extreme tension vanished, and Eleanor started negotiating again. She was sitting in a rocking chair, cuddling me on her lap. She started talking to the FBI agent [Wack] about me. She sat face to face with Wack, and all she could think was, 'I hope this man has children of his own.'
>
> (ibid.: 273–4)

Clearly Eleanor considered herself to be a normal, loving mother (as did her son), and hoped that the FBI agent shared these same beliefs concerning the well-being of a vulnerable child who would soon be transferred into his care. While these stories raise questions about how 'deviant' radical families actually are compared to their 'normal' counterparts, given the evident elasticity of ordinary ways of 'doing family' and how they can mask a great diversity of individual practices and values, one important qualification is in order. The task of concealing their clandestine identities and practices as a result of their radicalization (and in the case of the Jones family, extending even to terrorist action) was in all likelihood greatly eased for the Jones by the fact that they were a middle-class, white family headed by a monogamous heterosexual couple. In other words, by being part of the normative 'majority' culture, they were already well placed to successfully mask any 'deviant' aspects of their family life, particularly from the surveillance of school or other agencies with which they would ordinarily expect to come into regular contact. Other families, such as those from ethnic minority backgrounds, from lower classes, same-sex couples or those with disabilities, etc. would probably find the work of maintaining a sufficiently convincing performance of normality a considerably more difficult task – as it often is even for these types of families who are in no way engaged in political extremism. This subsequently casts doubt on the capacity for external agencies (such as schools, doctors or social workers, not to mention the police) to reliably identify (1) what are in fact signs of radicalization in children and their families, and (2) who are the families that present a real and present threat; the latter is a key consideration given the UK Government's agenda on the surveillance of children and their families by their teachers for signs of extremism and radicalization. It also raises questions about the convergence of the child *protection* model and the PREVENT agenda pursued by counter-terrorism forces in the UK. The protection model is based on a perception of children and their families as the *object* of official (usually abstract, legal) gaze, rather than as *subjects* who are active in the construction of their everyday lives and values, and who should be engaged with and listened to in a way that respects their own distinctive family norms (McNamee *et al.*, 2005). In addition, as the growing wealth of research literature on terrorism indicates, *culture* and *context* are both extremely important, and this relates as much to terrorist narratives as it does to any individual family's unique biographies, needs and circumstances. In short, the task of recognizing who is a terrorist threat by identifying which families are involved in radicalization or extremism in many respects exceeds the capacity of external agencies to reliably detect, not least because of the middle-class origins of these families or their individual members, and the subsequent ease with which they (as well as other families who have something to hide) can develop the skills to 'pass' as 'normal'. In practice, it means that this task is as difficult for those working in the field of counter-terrorism as it can be for those working in other areas of child protection.

Conclusion

The use of the sorts of coping strategies developed by the Joneses while living underground, and by the Wakatsukis while living in detention, reiterates the social constructivist theory of 'doing' family, i.e. that families are less about the durability and manifestation of 'the family' as an ideal or institution and more about family as an ongoing series of 'family practices'. Hence family members are not to be regarded as the passive recipients of social structures or functional patterns of family life, but rather actively contribute to how these macro conceptualizations of their family are inherited and shaped according to their own needs in the present, and passed on in story form to future generations. Thus what becomes emphasized is the interpretive and moreover *discursive* nature of family life (e.g. Gubrium and Holstein, 1990) whereby 'family' is construed as an ongoing and interactive process that is contingent upon the mutual understandings of family members and is moreover convergent with the demands of external social life and hence negotiable in nature rather than normatively defined (Finch and Mason, 1993). It is vital for those working in security and counter-terrorism to remember in their interactions with and focus on the family that *every* family engages in such activities – i.e. they develop their own unique take on these types of practices and the (re)production of these kinds of stories for posterity, as a way of preserving their own family identity and legacy in the face of what can at times seem to be the unsympathetic gaze of the outside world, especially the state. It is imperative that certain types of families are not unintentionally stigmatized or suspect on the basis of 'visible' signs that indicate deviation from the 'norm' such as by their religious or ethnic beliefs or the sexual orientation of the parents, etc.

One of the many ironies in Jeff's eventful life is that, due to the fact that he was living underground as a wanted terrorist, he was at one stage compelled to take what is a very dangerous job in order to support his family, from an industry who would hire anybody, as bicycle messenger. When the couple were finally 'busted' by the police, it was not as the result of the ongoing investigation to find them, but rather the serendipitous discovery of radical literature, materials for falsifying identities and rather large sums of money in their apartment, after receiving a tip-off that marijuana plants were growing on the balcony outside of their apartment. In the event, the apprehension of this active underground terrorist 'cell' was not achieved through investigative detective work by counter-terrorism police, but rather by happenstance. This suggests that the focus upon children and families by security forces as a fertile source for identifying and apprehending extremists is unlikely to prove to be particularly useful as an investigative strategy, if only because families such as these (like all families) are already very good at covering their tracks and masking their internal activities, practices and beliefs. This is consistent with the unwritten contract existing between the family and the state.

The UK Government's PREVENT strategy recognizes the need to 'address grievances', 'support individuals who are being targeted and recruited to the cause of violent extremism' and 'increase the resilience of communities', in addition to the techniques designed to 'challenge' and 'disrupt' what are deemed to be unacceptable 'narratives' and extreme points of view. However, the strong implication is that the main focus of concern is on children and their families, with much less evidence of direct scrutiny of teachers and other school and child welfare professionals. If we recall from the previous section the stories told by the likes of Malcolm X and Ed Husain, they suggest that greater attention should be directed specifically at *empowering children* as well as their families (and their teachers) to challenge racism and other extremist views to which they are unfortunately subjected at school by the adults and other children who are also part of the school community (and indeed beyond the school gates). This is not a 'top-down', but very much a 'two-way' approach, the dialogical character of which is arguably counter-indicated by the dominance of the child protection model that tends to view children (and their families) as vulnerable, and lacking agency and understanding of their situation. Similarly, the 'toolkit' should not be limited merely to addressing or promoting simplistic 'counter-narratives' to extremism in classroom debates with children, but should be more proactive in challenging and fighting social exclusion, inequality and injustice in society in general. This means extending the social responsibility agenda both within and beyond schools, which inevitably means providing a forum for the (constructive) *critique* of the state and its constituent institutions (including schools), not simply providing a site for the implementation of its policies designed to monitor and control children and their families, or interpreting any anti-government sentiment voiced by children and/or their families as inherently 'dangerous'.

The rise of radicalization in recent years marks a significant development in policy-making in the areas of counter-terrorism and security. Now widely considered to be a 'driver' of terrorist action, radicalization represents a rich target for legislative and law enforcement agencies that seek to deal with the threat of terrorism and other risks to national security under the aegis of crime prevention, as opposed to holy war. Its resistance to definition and hence analysis, in addition to its highly relativistic, diverse and subjective character, however, makes radicalization a difficult concept to regulate for these very rationalistic if not bureaucratic purposes. As we have seen throughout the course of this study, Fraihi's (2008: 135) initial reference to the 'willingness' and 'conviction' of the individual's involved in radicalization is clearly justified. The kind of 'deep' and 'serious' changes that they often seek to affect at the social level are reflected in the deeply felt subjective and interpersonal realms of their own lives, incorporating areas of life that have historically been deemed to be 'private' and thus beyond (or at the fringes of) the reach of the state, incorporating childhood, gender, sexuality and the family. Counter-terrorism strategists have sought out the empirically observable and verifiable 'causes', 'profiles' or 'processes' that readily conform to the existing power mechanisms of the state (e.g. military, law enforcement or both); coming to terms with radicalization as a more deeply interpersonal, affective and messy phenomenon could help to make more substantial and less destructive advances on this front. One way of doing this is to develop existing agencies and structures within or contingent to the state to facilitate a greater and more reciprocally participative commitment to human rights, social justice and the rule of law in the areas of racial and gender equality, education, children and families, as well as other areas such as housing and employment. As the stories recounted in these pages suggest, greater attention to these aspects of the lives of citizens everywhere could yield greater benefits as preventative measures than the alternative reactive and punitive or bellicose solutions to the problem of extremism and terrorism. It is important that radicalization is recognized for what it is: a mechanism for seeking and occasionally affecting social change that is contingent on a cultural view of the individual agent, whether acting alone or as part of a more organized collective. As moderns, we fear as well as rely on the emergence of this often challenging and traumatic phenomenon as a way of testing and sometimes changing attitudes or systems deemed to be unacceptable or obsolete – whether for better or worse.

Notes

I What is radicalization? From the civil society to the enemy within

1 By focusing their attention on the problem of 'violent' radicalization, the European Union is more precise and careful in its use of language, which is advisable in what can easily become heated debates. However, as Žižek (2008b) insists, such qualification can be counter-indicative, as it can obscure the tendency for governments or political elites to focus on the 'subjective' violence of assault, murder and terror carried out by 'radicals', and not considering, let alone critiquing, the 'symbolic' and 'systematic' forms of violence embedded in language and social systems that are themselves implied in the manifestation of radicalization. Similarly, as others such as Darby and MacGinty (2003) suggest, analysis of conflict strongly indicates that there is a false dichotomy between pivotal issues, such as violence and non-violence, and war and peace. Quoting Zartman (1997 in Darby and MacGinty, 2003), they argue that it is these very asymmetries of power, with respect to the contested appropriation of political rhetoric, that are fundamentally characteristic of internal conflict; it is only when these perspectives become more equitable, dialogical and reciprocal – accounting for manifold forms of 'violence' on both sides – that peace processes can be said to have begun. This study will therefore not be exclusively limited to consideration of 'violent' radicalization, though it will concentrate on this as a priority concern.
2 The Hague Programme takes a typically holistic view of the problem of radicalization, linking it from the outset to other relevant issues on the subject of 'freedom, justice and security', including fundamental rights and citizenship, migration, border patrol, asylum, intelligence sharing, organized crime, the congruence of criminal and civil justice among EU members, and other such topics.
3 It is worth mentioning that, despite the comparative dearth of textual examples, throughout his work, Erving Goffman (1963) regarded biographies and the recovery of auto/biographical narratives to be of seminal importance to the study of stigma generally, and to physical disability in particular.
4 Coincidentally, Curcio (2005) singles out radio advertisements as being reported by detainees at Guantánamo Bay as instrumental in their recruitment into jihadi groups.
5 Indeed, depending on the latest terrorist atrocity, attention to global or domestic terrorism is apt to change dramatically and swiftly, notwithstanding that, in the contemporary global geopolitical environment, the distinction between the two is arguably not at all clear-cut.

6 The term 'individualistic' is used here to denote a tendency towards methodological individualism, ' ... the claim that social phenomena must be explained by showing how they result from individual actions, which in turn must be explained through reference to the intentional states that motivate the individual actors' (Heath, 2005), a perspective implicitly adopted by American law enforcement and policy-makers. This contrasts to other approaches focused on the radicalization of individuals, as for example denoted by the French scholar Olivier Roy (2008).

2 Using auto/biographical methodologies to analyze radicalization

1 The PREVENT strand of UK counter-terrorism policy is, if anything, even higher in profile in the latest strategy document, known as CONTEST2 (Home Office, 2009), which emphasizes the cultural aspects of radicalization that are, as the report's authors admit, currently inadequately understood.

2 Just how RCT can help explain terrorism (or perhaps more precisely the process orientation that leads up to it from the individual perspective, which we may closely identify with radicalization) is addressed by Horgan in his book *The Psychology of Terrorism* (2005). Very briefly, RCT is a criminological theory that is derived from economics, succeeding behaviouralism as a major theoretical influence throughout the social sciences (and beyond) in the 1980s. Simply put, according to RCT, individual offenders commit crimes because they think it will be more beneficial for them to do so than not to do so. It assumes that offenders are much like other individuals in that they make decisions based on their own free will and rationality. Apart from this, it has little interest in the individual offender, focusing instead on the offence. Much of RCT's attraction is due to its pragmatism and strong adherence to common sense, and also its rather narrow focus – for instance, it is not necessary to consider causes beyond the thought processes that influence individual actors, such as structural or social inequalities, e.g. unemployment, poor housing, poverty, etc. Despite its huge influence upon crime prevention policy (particularly situational crime prevention), it has not been without its critics. It ignores contexts such as history, subjective motives, intent, social pressures, gender, ethnicity and other interpretive elements of crime that are arguably of major significance in understanding violent radicalization, and thereby encourages government policy that ignores the broader social conditions that give rise to crime. It has also been criticized for its tendency to target certain kinds of crimes (e.g. street crime, theft, vehicle crime and property crime) and ignore others (domestic violence, crimes against children, corporate crime and state crime) echoing concerns about violent radicalization and terrorism raise. In practice, it encourages privatization in the arena of crime prevention, and the concentration on risk. It has been criticized for being a *post hoc* response – for instance, CCTV kicks in after crimes have already been committed, offering little by way of pre-empting or preventing crime – which is a salient issue in relation to current demands by policy-makers and law enforcement concerning radicalization.

3 Interestingly, the CONTEST2 UK national strategy document is, with respect to its bibliographic citations, heavily reliant upon journalistic sources as an evidence base. The implicitly self-referential nature of citations as presented in CONTEST2 could be problematic, given that many security correspondents derive their information from 'off the record' remarks originating from unidentified sources in the security services, which implies a circular evidential base with no real accountability or transparency. Given the serious issues arising from the US governmental report presented to the UN, which set out the case that Saddam Hussein possessed

weapons of mass destruction (WMD) in the run up to the Iraq War, the provenance of such cited evidence is paramount, not least in light of the potential seriousness of the consequences with respect to decision-making on policy and action. While there are clearly tensions here with respect to the possible exposure of intelligence information and/or sources conventions regarding the provision of evidence via bibliographic citation and referencing within such documents disseminated in the public domain for the purposes of justification should nevertheless be reassessed; in addition, a range of 'open source' data – such as these auto/biographies – should be included, as should their contingent methods of analysis.

4 Examples of biographical or life narrative methods in criminological research are provided by Carlen (1985), Maruna (2001), Goffman (1968, 1963), Shaw [1930] (1966), Morgan (1999), Nellis (2002), Wilson and McCabe (2002), and (with reference to new methodologies) Walker (1987) and Goodey (2000). In terrorism studies, examples include Hegghammer (2006), Kay (2005), Sageman (2004). With the exception of Shaw, Morgan, Goffman, Nellis and Wilson and McCabe, the overwhelming majority of existing examples in the research literature focus on 'life narrative' in the form of oral histories, using mainly interview data, rather than writing. As the theoretical and methodological issues raised in this chapter attest, analysis of written auto/biographies gives rise to a number of distinctive concerns and approaches.

5 There have been recent claims in the media regarding the link between paedophiles and terrorists in the consumption of pornographic images of children and the purported use of child pornography websites for the exchange of encrypted data and communication (Kerbaj and Kennedy, 2008; Kerbaj et al., 2008).

6 This can be illustrated by the following example: people go to church on Sunday to worship God; the *social* function of this activity is to enhance social unity, not to please an omnipotent being (the intentional or subjective aim).

7 Examples of the pathological presence of excessively high levels of altruistic suicide are the emergence of so-called suicide 'epidemics' among teenagers in and around the Welsh village of Bridgend in recent years. An example of excessively low levels of altruistic suicide would be represented by the unwillingness of rescue or medical staff to risk their own lives by trying to save or care for others who are in danger.

8 See Pedahzur et al. 2003 on the analysis of suicide bombers in terms of Durkheim's typology.

9 Following Liz Stanley, the term 'auto/biography' is used to refer to both biography and autobiography and also ' … as it disrupts conventional taxonomies of life writing, disputing its divisions of self/other, public/private, and immediacy/memory. Relatedly, '"the auto/biographical I" signals the active inquiring presence of sociologists in constructing, rather than discovering, knowledge' (Stanley 1993: 41).

10 Many experts and non-experts alike with an interest in radicalization and terrorism will know, for example, of the prominence of Sayyid Qtub's prison autobiography *Milestones* (2006), but relatively few will have actually read it – not least because, if media stories are to be believed, the possession of such 'terrorist' materials could turn out to be very problematic for the individual concerned should the security services and/or law enforcement decide to take such a view.

11 I am indebted to Paul Dearey for this observation.

12 As Ioan Davies notes, this particular 'genre' of prison writing is of particular significance, since 'much of the influential literature of Judeo-Christian civilization was composed under conditions of incarceration or involuntary exile' (Davies, 1990: 3).

3 'There are so many roots … ': sex, sexuality, gender and the body in political prisoner radicalization narratives

1 The usage of the two designations 'north of Ireland' and 'Northern Ireland' throughout this chapter is deliberate and is intended to reflect two main concerns: first, to recognize the disagreements over how this territory as a political space is named and who has the power to decide this as part of an ongoing nationalist struggle, resisting as much as possible the adoption of one or the other term as decisive and thereby putatively aligning myself with either side. Hence for the most part the designation Northern Ireland is used when it is quoted or referenced by other sources or alternatively denotes the state institutions (usually penal institutions) constructed and operated within that specific jurisdiction (as distinct from the prison system in the Irish Republic, Great Britain or elsewhere). Second, and in many ways more importantly, this use of language is meant to acknowledge that the playing out of this specific conflict has taken place throughout the centuries well beyond what are now the internationally recognized national borders of Northern Ireland as a nation state, and to attempt to incorporate the experiences, suffering, and agency of individuals and communities along the so-called border regions, especially counties Louth, Monaghan, Donegal, Cavan and Leitrim, as well as other parts of the UK and Europe.

2 The 'criticism-self-criticism' sessions were a practice adopted by the Weathermen (later the Weather Underground Organization (WUO) in deference to its women members) from the Chinese Communist Party, and were developed and relied upon by the group perhaps more than any other radical organization of the time as a way of instilling a sense of collectivity as well as manipulation and control of individuals (Berger, 2007). While the purported intention, as described by Stern [1975] (2007), was to rid Weathermen of their selfish and anti-revolutionary sentiments, in actuality it was more of a cult-like practice for breaking down individual members' resistance to group thinking, and instilling a sense of dependency through lack of self-confidence and paranoia. Though the practice receded as a matter of necessity after the group went underground, it became more entrenched, frequent and intense in the group's development over time. These sessions were often unannounced and could last hours (or even days) at a time. While in some instances they consisted of individuals 'confessing' to their anti-revolutionary or unWeatherly faults, according to Stern's account, it was more common for them to consist of attacks by a gang of members upon an individual singled out for censure (often, in her recollection, directed at her, despite what she claims were her notable displays of bravery in the field of battle with riot police). Male chauvinism was a frequent topic of critique by women members of the men, but the male leadership seemed to take little notice (Berger, 2007). Another major topic was monogamy, as the leadership exercised a nearly obsessive interest in uncovering instances in which couples were forming and 'smashing' these nascent bonds of exclusivity within the group.

3 Also published under the title *Violent Delights*.

4 I refer here to Alpert's claim that her one-time confidant, the feminist activist and poet Robin Morgan, strongly implied (falsely, according to Alpert) to others in the radical feminist movement that she and Alpert were lovers, in order to prove, according to Alpert, her own feminist credentials by having had a lesbian relationship with a woman living underground.

5 Reage's *Story of O* is similarly cited by Alpert (1981) as a primary text that influenced the radicalization, terrorist militancy and violent sexual proclivities of her boyfriend Sam Melville.

6 The same could be said for radical women beyond the confines of the conflict in Northern Ireland, as in the case of, for example, the controversy and ambiguity surrounding Angela Davis's relationship with George Jackson, official claims about its role in her radicalization and involvement in a criminal trial, and indeed her highly successful efforts to conceal her lesbianism throughout her autobiography against these highly contentious and potentially life-threatening backgrounds (at one point she faced the real possibility of being sentenced to the death penalty as a result of this presumed connection with Jackson).

7 It is counter-intuitive to call it the 'blanket protest' (which the male Irish Republican prisoners preferred to 'dirty protest') as the women prisoners were allowed to wear their own (unwashed) clothes and hence were not compelled to wrap themselves in the prison issue blanket that gave this particular form of protest its name in the Maze Prison (once again, prioritizing the experience of the men).

8 Ellmann (1993) also notes the symbolic analogousness of force-feeding with rape as an assertion of power on the body.

9 To appreciate the meaning of 'anti-altruism' as it is used by Gaukroger (1995) – as opposed to the blatantly antisocial disposition of misanthropy – it is instructive to refer briefly to the definition of altruism adopted by the philosopher Thomas Nagel (1970). According to Nagel, 'Altruism itself depends on a recognition of the reality of other persons, and on the equivalent capacity to regard oneself as merely one individual among many' (1970: 3). In contrast, the development of cultural individualism reflected in auto/biography during the interim between the counter-reformation in seventeenth-century France (Gaukroger, 1995) and the nineteenth-century industrial revolution in Britain (Danahay, 1993) evidences this capacity to withhold such a recognition of the reality of other persons, and to resist the need to recognize oneself as one among many, but rather to insist on one's own supremacy as the focal point for the many around 'the one'. This is epitomized in Danahay's idiomatic description of the paradigm male autobiographical subject as embodying 'a community of one' (1993), i.e. the fullest possible identification of society with a certain kind of individual, one who is bourgeois, white and male. The resistance of this species of the autobiographical subject to the social collective in any other sense than as the first among equals is clearly detectable in the autobiographies of the many 'worthy' men written during the nineteenth century in Britain, with figures such as Samuel Taylor Coleridge, Thomas de Quincey, William Hazlitt, Charles Lamb, William Wordsworth, Matthew Arnold, Edmund Gosse and John Stuart Mill among the many exemplars of the type. These are men who used writing in general, and autobiographical writing in particular, to celebrate their 'genius' as a consummate expression of the naturalness of their singular personalities and social superiority as gendered subjects occupying an already privileged political and economic position in society (DeNora, 1995; Battersby, 1989). As Abbott (1982) writes, 'This is what made the "Chinaman of Konigsberg" (Kant) say: "Genius makes it own rules." Even European philosophers have taken notice that most of what we take for knowledge is nothing but bias and prejudice' (1982: 168).

10 The halo effect of the auto/biographical 'I' helped ensure that their privileged social positions were reciprocally enhanced by the very act of reproducing their 'lives', which were for some time generally received by an appreciative and ever more eager public market. The convergence in this type of autobiographical writing of the great male writer as 'great man' or 'genius' with the patriarchal society of the nineteenth century and the increased rationalization of economic market forces exposes the deep cultural interconnections between autobiography, patriarchy and industrial capitalism, and indeed the challenge to it by women and others, often in the auto/biographical format. In this context, 'genius' as the preserve of masculine

subjectivity emerged as a hybrid invention of the exercise of political and economic power combined with a good marketing strategy enhanced by the 'life' as text. The canonical nineteenth-century masculine autobiographical subject hence represents a dual cultural phenomenon, maintaining its grip on the public imagination through the exercise of a kind of 'intellectual imperialism' within an existing political and economic power structure suited to the needs of such a colonial social order (DeNora, 1995), and at the same time guaranteeing its ideological dominance within a patriarchal social framework through the systematic appropriation of the products of feminine intellect and creativity (Battersby, 1989). It is significant that Sands found himself more drawn to this type of patriarchal, imperial, masculine subject than to the 'other' subjectivities represented by women and ethnic resistance literature (whether in auto/biographical or other forms).

4 'I felt myself turning cold like the bottle of Coke': children, childhood and 'the child' in political prisoner life writing

1 With respect to the current study, the relevance of sociological concepts such as anomie in relation to childhood and familial experience are potentially considerable, not least given the ambivalence encapsulated in the meaning of anomie, which relates at once to a condition whereby the individual lacks the control of social regulation and is susceptible to the motivational influences (as evidenced by subsequent action) of internal feelings of despair and pessimism (Gane, 1993: 25).

> Tiryakian wants from Durkheim a conception of anomie as a condition and not as a social force, for as far as the latter is concerned Durkheim is explicit: it is a force of rejection, despair, pessimism, irrationalism, mysticism, i.e., is deeply reactionary. Tiryakian half acknowledges this by referring to Durkheim's use of the term to describe the wave of terrorism in Europe in the 1890s.
> (Gane, 1993: 25).

2 It is useful to recall here Spierenburg's (2008) empirical study of the general trends of interpersonal violence, which have been in steady decline throughout modernity – with the exception of the steep rise in serious interpersonal violence in the private and domestic sphere among intimates (mainly enacted by men against women and children). Hence it is important to note that families can be implicated in the transmission of extremism and radicalization (and therefore implicated in the manifestation of terrorist violence) at the same time that it is vital to acknowledge that they and their members are also susceptible to being victims of violent conflict and suffering. It is important therefore to resist the temptation to reify the family (or childhood or youth) in terms of their interests or cultural practices, or to conflate them with a tendency to *do* (as opposed to be subject to) violence, be it interpersonal violence or violence against the state.

3 The rhetorical use of children, childhood and other vulnerable populations is demonstrated, for example, by the repeated and rhetorical use of stories about their suffering and violent deaths contained in the statements of Dr Ayman a Zawahiri and Osama bin Laden: 'Because you have killed ... we must kill. Your innocents are not less innocent than ours' (Bin Laden, 2005: xix).

4 Brocklehurst (2006) cites, among others, the example of the powerful symbolic function afforded by idealized notions of childhood and parenting in Nazi Germany as a way of legitimating the violent and oppressive structures of the state.

5 The 'responsibilisation thesis' (Garland, 2001) in criminology refers to the incremental devolution of responsibility for crime prevention and social control from central government onto local communities. O'Malley (2001, 2006) assigns the origins and growth of responsibilization in response to crime to socio-economic changes linked to the rise of neoliberalism and a range of changes to contemporary crime control, whereby an 'elective affinity' is established between two parallel sets of practices and/or ideas, which are bound by an analogous rationality and which as a consequence are mutually reinforcing. Hence, the reliance on 'responsibilization' in crime control policy (e.g. the UK Government's PREVENT strategy) is frequently accompanied by the presence of predictive, RCT models that seek causality and focus on prevention; the (gradual) prioritization of deterrence in punitive responses over rehabilitation or welfare; and the rise of cost-effectiveness and consumerism in the rhetoric of crime control (Newburn, 2007).

6 'Weatherman' was originally adapted from a Bob Dylan song lyric, 'You don't need a weatherman to know which way the wind blows'. As a result of criticism for its sexist connotations, and indeed the latterly adopted strategy for covert action by members who were 'underground', the group's title was later changed to the 'Weather Underground'.

7 The main focus in this chapter will be on the influential role of leisure and consumption on the radicalized/izing individual. It is also worth noting that leisure and consumption provide a central touchstone for the identification of the targets of terrorist actions – e.g. the concentration on sport in the cases of the capture and murder of Israeli athletes by Palestinian terrorists at the 1972 Berlin Olympics and the terrorist attack on the Sri Lankan cricket team in March 2009, and the terrorist attacks on nightclubs in Bali in 2004 and London in 2007. Sport is also identified as a way of countering radicalization and extremism by encouraging social interaction, tolerance and community cohesion: 'Sport and particularly football is powerful in providing a tool which can be used to help break down barriers amongst young people who have a common interest in playing and/or watching football' (Wheeler, 2008: 18). These examples highlight the concentration of terrorist ideologies and mentalities on the personal and subjective experience of consumption and leisure by individuals afforded by western cultures, in addition to the structural mechanisms of global capitalism represented by attacks on financial and state institutions (e.g. the attacks on the World Trade Center and the Pentagon, and US military installations and embassies).

8 The relative absence of experiences of prejudice and the acceptance of individuals from the 'other' side as experienced by children and young people in Northern Ireland (at least prior to their entry into the adult world of formal employment) is consistent with research on community divisions along sectarian lines carried out by a number of researchers and summarized by McKie and Lombard: 'Studies on the segregation of Northern Ireland (McGrellis, 2004 pg 4) have indicated that it tends to be when young people start work or leave home that they first have sustained contact with people from religious or ethnic backgrounds different to their own; it is then that the boundaries are transgressed. As Connolly and Healy (2003) noted, children may be accepting of an individual who was of a different religion to them, but this did not sway their opinion of the community from where that individual came' (McKie and Lombard, 2005: 182).

9 These types of exercises are not uncommon in the life writings of radical authors, see for example Susan Stern's descriptions of 'criticism-self-criticism' sessions regularly

carried out by the Weathermen (2007). Such psychological exercises, as Stern notes, are designed to break down the existing sense of self and replace it with a more strongly committed, consciously aware and collectively oriented radical personality structure. Such practices relating to self-construction and memory-mining were designed by radical groups to break down 'normal' or previously accepted self-images that were endorsed by society at large, and replace them with more narrowly focused and 'truthful' versions of self modelled on radical group values and consistent with ideological political aims.

10 The psychoanalyst D. W. Winnicott argued that children use consumer objects as stand-ins for the mother in her absence (in Schudson, 1998).

11 We may also add to this the contribution of children to the manufacture of a very special type of handmade consumer good that is typically treasured by adults for whom these items are made and given, whether it be a simple drawing or something more unusual or elaborate.

12 According to the *Oxford Companion to Philosophy* (Honderich, 2005), logos is defined as

> A Greek word, of great breadth of meaning, primarily signifying the context of philosophical discussion the rational, intelligible principle. Structure, or order which pervades something, or the source of that order, or giving an account of that order. The cognate verb *legein* means 'say', 'tell', 'count' ... Aristotle, in his *Nicomachean Ethics*, makes use of a distinction between the part of the soul which originates a logos (our reason) and the part which obeys or is guided by a logos (or emotions). The idea of a generative intelligence (*logos spermatikos*) is a profound metaphysical notion in Neoplatonic and Christian discussion.
>
> (Honderich, 2005: 545)

5 Is radicalization a family affair? A tale of two families

1 An interesting cultural development in the publication of life histories relating to seminal historical events of the twentieth century – notably the internment of Japanese-Americans – is the proliferation of these texts in the genre of children's literature, as opposed the more common and popular genre of (adult) auto-biography (e.g. Jerry Stanley's *I Am an American: A True Story of Japanese Internment* (1998), Leni Donlan's *How Did This Happen Here?* (2007); George W. Chilcoat and Michael O. Tunnel's *Children of Topaz* (1996)). It is arguable that this choice of genre is based on the pedagogical rationale behind producing these stories in public in the form of books intended mainly to be used in schools, thereby enabling the writers to 'save face' by resisting the sometimes salacious and populist association with the 'misery memoir' represented by a number of bestselling auto-biographies by adults about their damaged childhoods.

2 In his research into class and crime in black American auto/biography written during the first half of the 'long' twentieth century, Anthony S. Foy (2008) emphasizes the significance of disclosure as a special consideration in autobiography written by black authors, particularly the disclosure or even acknowledgement of past criminality within the wider political discourses underpinning black auto/biography. This gives rise to a number of tensions and complexities in enunciating the black auto/biographical subject and his or her intimate relationships, and to the acts of reading and writing, not least because so much of black auto/biography in

the twentieth century relates directly or indirectly to the emergence of the auto/biographical subject from episodes concerning some sort of 'trouble', encapsulated in acts of 'criminal' resistance (e.g. Malcolm X), protest (e.g. Rosa Parks) or some other such difficulties with the law (e.g. Angela Davis). In black American life writing from the late nineteenth to the mid-twentieth centuries (circa 1965), the driving force behind the use of this contested form of discourse – which is so closely linked to the ideology of the individual celebrated as normatively white, privileged, 'western' and male – was closely associated with what has come to be known as 'racial uplift', i.e. life writing for the purposes of recovering the respectable hard-working and socially aspirational black subject and advancing the cause of black people collectively (e.g. Booker T. Washington's *Up From Slavery* (1996), and the life writings of and about George Washington Carver), often narrated within the moral superiority of the family led by the virtuous black woman as 'pillar of society' (Craig, 2002). The problem arises with respect to the disclosure of 'criminal' pasts (or even presents) within the lives (and family histories) of black people and others, especially those who are or have been actively engaged in political resistance – the anxiety is that relating these stories is likely to impede the advancement and frustrate the 'uplift' of black people (or other ethnic or 'race' groups) by implicitly reiterating the disreputability and implicit criminality of their members as represented in these texts and interpreted by the specific and general readership to which these texts would inevitably be exposed.

3 Gilman refers in this article to the production of a prize-winning comic produced in the manga style by the Japanese artist Osamu Tezuka 'Also Tell Adolf', which recounts the Holocaust from the Japanese point of view. The highly controversial and emotive use of the humorous and visual medium of comics is notable, not least in the recent incidents surrounding the Danish cartoons depicting the Prophet.

4 The use of such 'unseemly' behaviour as a form of radical activism has been an issue of debate since at least the time of the suffragettes. A current example is afforded by the members of the environmentalist group Plane Stupid, which uses many such 'anti-social' but relatively harmless tactics – epitomized by the throwing of green custard by a middle-class, educated young woman member, Leila Deen, into the face of the British peer Labour Transport Secretary Lord Peter Mandelson – to draw public attention to their cause. While it is interesting and suggestive that Deen directly references the protests of the suffragettes as influences on her chosen form of radical activism, the effectiveness of such protest actions in the achievement of stated political goals is as yet unclear. However, in the modern, media-dominated age, they seem to be very effective as a way of raising the public profile of specific issues.

5 In place of class privilege, 'skin privilege' would take priority, and would (according to the life writings of the women members or associates of radical groups like the Weathermen) often take the form of interracial heterosexual relationships, whereby it became the ideal practice for radical and middle-class white women to become pregnant by black men to whom they were not married (Morgan, 1989).

Bibliography

Abbas, T. (2007a) 'Introduction: Islamic Political Radicalism in Western Europe,' in Abbas, T. (ed.) *Islamic Political Radicalism: A European Perspective*. Edinburgh: Edinburgh University Press, 3–14.

—— (2007b) 'Ethno-Religious Identities and Islamic Political Radicalism in the UK: A Case Study'. *Journal of Muslim Minority Affairs*, 27(3), 429–42.

Abbott, J. H. (1982) *In the Belly of the Beast: Letters from Prison*. New York: Vintage Books.

Abuza, Z. (2006) 'Education and Radicalization: Jemaah Islamiyah Recruitment in Southeast Asia', in Forest, J. J. F. (ed.) *The Making of a Terrorist: Recruitment, Training, and Root Causes*. Westport, CT and London: Praeger Security International, 66–83.

Adams, G. (1994) *Falls memories: A Belfast Life*. Lanham, MD: Roberts Rinehart Publishers.

—— [1996] (2001) *Before the Dawn: An Autobiography*. Dingle, County Kerry, Ireland: Brandon.

Adekson, A. O. (2004) *The 'Civil Society' Problematique: Deconstructing Civility and Southern Nigeria's Ethnic Radicalization*. New York: Routledge.

Almeida, J. L. T. D. and Schramm, F. R. (1999) 'Paradigm Shift, Metamorphosis of Medical Ethics, and the Rise of Bioethics'. *Cadernos de Saúde Pública*, 15(Sup. 1), 15–25.

Alpert, J. (1981) *Growing Up Underground*. New York: William Morrow and Company, Inc.

Alston, L. (1992) 'Children as Chattel', in West, E. and Petrick, P. (Eds.) *Small Worlds*. Lawrence, KA: University Press of Kansas, 208–31.

Anderson, L. (2001) *Autobiography: The New Critical Idiom*. London and New York: Routledge.

Andrews, M., Day Schlater, S., Squire, C. and Treacher, A. (eds.) (2000) *Lines of Narrative: Psychosocial Perspectives*. London and New York: Routledge.

Arendt, H. (1993) 'Nightmare and Flight', in Kohn, J. (ed.) *Hannah Arendt: Essays in Understanding 1930–1954*. New York: Harcourt Brace.

Aretxaga, B. (1997) *Shattering Silence: Women, Nationalism and Political Subjectivity in Northern Ireland*. Princeton, NJ: Princeton University Press.

Ariès, P. (1962) *Centuries of Childhood*. New York: Vintage.

Arif, Z. (2007) 'Radicalisation is Often Too Subtle to Spot', *Nursing Standard*, 26–7.

Atkinson, J. M. (1982) *Discovering Suicide: Studies in the Social Organization of Sudden Death*. London: Macmillan.

Atran, S. (2003) 'Genesis of Suicide Terrorism'. *Science*, 299(5612), 1534–39.

Awan, A. N. (2007a) 'Radicalization on the Internet? The Virtual Propagation of Jihadist Media and its Effects'. *RUSI Journal*, 152(3), 76 – 81.

—— (2007b) 'Virtual Jihadist Media and the Ummah as Transnational Audience: Function, Legitimacy, and Radicalising Efficacy'. *European Journal of Cultural Studies*, 10(Special Issue, no. 3), 389–408.

—— (undated) 'The Virtual Propagation of Jihadist Media and its Effects').

Baldick, C. (1996) *Criticism and Literary Theory 1890 to the Present*. London and New York: Longman.

—— (2001) 'Science Fiction'. *Oxford Concise Dictionary of Literary Terms*. Oxford, Oxford: University Press.

Bataille, G. (2006) *Literature and Evil* (Hamilton, A. Trans.) London and New York: Marion Boyars.

Battersby, C. (1989) *Gender and Genius: Towards a Feminist Aesthetics*. London: Women's Press.

—— (1998) *The Phenomenal Woman: Feminist Metaphysics and the Patterns of Identity*. Cambridge: Polity Press.

Baumeister, R. F. (1986) *Identity: Cultural Change and the Struggle for the Self*. New York and Oxford: Oxford University Press.

Beck, U. (1992) *Risk Society: Towards a New Modernity*. (Ritter, M. Trans.) London: Sage.

Becker, J. (1978) *Hitler's Children*. London: Panther Granada Publishing.

Begg, M. (2007) *Enemy Combatant: A British Muslim's Journey to Guantanamo and Back*. London: Free Press.

Bell, E. (1985) 'Telling One's Story: Women's Journals Then and Now', in Hoffmann, L. and Culley, M. (eds.) *Women's Personal Narratives: Essays in Criticism and Pedagogy*. New York: Modern Language Association), 167–76.

Benard, C. (ed.) (2005) 'A Future for the Young: Options for Helping Middle Eastern Youth Escape the Trap of Radicalization' [working paper *WR-354*]. New York: RAND Corporation.

Bennington, G. and Derrida, J. (1999) *Jacques Derrida*. Chicago: University of Chicago Press.

Bensmaïa, R. (1999) 'Postcolonial Nations: Political or Poetic Allegories? (on Tahar Djaout's *L'invention du désert*).' *Research in African Literatures*, 30(3), 151–63.

Benton, T. (1993) *Natural Relations: Ecology, Animal Rights and Social Justice*. London: Verso.

Berger, M. S. (2007) 'Radicalisation in International Perspective: How Successful is Democratisation in Countering Radicalisation?', in National Coordinator for Counter Terrorism (ed.) *Radicalisation in Broader Perspective*. Breda: Broese and Peereboom, 14– 21.

Bhatia, A. (2008) 'The Discourses of Terrorism'. *Journal of Pragmatics*, Vol. 41, issue 2. February 2009. 279–89.

Biggar, N. (2003) *Burying the Past: Making Peace and Doing Justice after Civil Conflict*. Washington, DC: Georgetown University Press.

Bin Laden, O. (2005) *Messages to the World: The Statements of Osama Bin Laden*. London and New York: Verso.

Bjorgo, T. and Horgan, J. (eds.) (2008) *Leaving Terrorism Behind: Individual and Collective Disengagement*. London: Routledge.

Blears, H. (2008) 'Preventing Violent Extremism: The Government's Approach', paper presented at A Policy Exchange seminar led by Rt. Hon. Hazel Blears MP, Secretary of State for Communities and Local Government, London, 17 July).

Bobbitt, P. (2008) *Terror and Consent: The Wars for the Twenty-First Century*. London: Allen Lane).

Brée, G. (1988) 'Autogynography', in J. Olney (ed.) *Studies in Autobiography*. New York: Oxford University Press).

Brocklehurst, H. (2006) *Who's Afraid of the Children? Children, Conflict and International Relations*. Aldershot: Ashgate).

Brown, C. (2008) 'Gender-Role Implications on Same-Sex Intimate Partner Abuse' *Journal of Family Violence*, 23(6), 457–62.

——(2006) Speech at RUSI concerning key policy perspectives UK national security, Banqueting House, Whitehall, RUSI, Westminster, London, 13 February 2006).

Brown, K. (2008) 'The Promise and Perils of Women's Participation in UK Mosques: The Impact of Securitisation Agendas on Identity, Gender and Community'. *British Journal of Politics and International Relations*, 10(3), 472–91.

Brown, M. P. (2000) *Closet Space: Geographies of Metaphor from the Body to the Globe* (London and New York: Routledge).

Browne, A. and Williams, K. R. (1993) 'Gender, Intimacy, and Lethal Violence: Trends from 1976 through 1987'. *Gender Society*, 7(1), 78–98.

Bruss, E. W. (1976) *Autobiographical Acts: The changing Situation of a Literary Genre.*, (Baltimore, Johns Hopkins University Press).

Bryman, A. (1996) *Quantity and Quality in Social Research* (London: Unwin Hyman).

Burke, L. K. and Follingstad, D. R. (1999) 'Violence in Lesbian and Gay Relationships: Theory, Prevalence, and Correlational Factors'. *Clinical Psychology Review*, 19(5), 487–512.

Bush, G. W. (2002) *The National Security Strategy for the United States of America*. Report for the White House (Washington, DC).

Butler, J. (1999) *Subjects of Desire: Hegelian Reflections in Twentieth-Century France* (New York: Columbia University Press).

Campbell, C. (1998) 'Consuming Goods and the Good of Consuming', in D. A. Crocker and T. Linden (eds.) *Ethics of Consumption: The Good life, Justice and Global Stewardship*. (Lanham, MD: Rowman and Littlefield), 139–54).

Card, C. (2002) *The Atrocity Paradigm: A Theory of Evil*, (Oxford: Oxford University Press).

Carey, H. F. (2007) 'Troublemakers or Peacemakers? Youth and Post-Accord Peace Building'. *Political Science Quarterly*, 122, 355–7.

Carlen, P. (1985) *Criminal Women: Some Autobiographical Accounts* (Cambridge: Polity Press).

Carnochan, W. B. (1995) The Literature of Confinement, in N. Morris and D. J. Rothman (eds.) *The Oxford History of the Prison: The Practice of Punishment in Western Society*. (Oxford and New York: Oxford University Press), 381–406.

Castells, M. (2000) *The Rise of the Network Society*. (Oxford: Blackwell).

Chakrabarti, A. (2005) 'The Moral Psychology of Revenge'. *Journal of Human Values*, 11(1), 31–6.

Chan, S. (2005) *Out of Evil: New International Politics and Old Doctrines of War*. London: I.B. Taurus and Company Ltd.

Chauvin, L. O. (1998) 'University in Peru Sheds 'Tragic Legacy' of Rebel Ties as it Struggles to Rebuild'. *Chronicle of Higher Education*, 44(44), A33).

Chilcoat, G. W. and Tunnel, M. O. (1996) *The Children of Topaz: The Story of a Japanese-American Internment Camp: Based on a Classroom Diary* (New York: Holiday House).

Cockburn, A. (2000) 'The Radicalization of James Woolsey'. *New York Times Magazine*, 149(51458), 26).

Cohen, S. (1980) *Folk Devils and Moral Panics: The Creation of Mods and Rockers*, (Oxford: Robertson).

—— (1985) *Visions of Social Control: Crime, Punishment and Classification*, (Cambridge: Polity).

—— (1987) *Folk Devils and Moral Panics: The Creation of Mods and Rockers* (Oxford: Basil Blackwell).

Cohen, S. and Taylor, L. (1990) 'Time and the Long-Term Prisoner', in J. Hassard (ed.) *The Sociology of Time* (London: MacMillan), 178–87.

Collier-Thomas, B. and Franklin, V. P. (eds.) (2001) *Sisters in the Struggle: African American Women in the Civil Rights-Black Power Movement* (New York: New York University Press).

Collins, F. (1999) 'The Use of Traditional Storytelling in Education to the Learning of Literacy Skills'. *Early Child Development and Care*, 152(1): 77–108.

Collins, P. H. (1990) *Black Feminist Thought: Knowledge, Consciousness, and the Politics of Empowerment* (New York: Routledge).

Commission to the European Parliament and the Council (2005) *Communication from the Commission to the European Parliament and the Council Concerning Terrorist Recruitment: Addressing the Factors Contributing to Violent Radicalisation*. Brussels: Publications Office of the European Union).

Connolly, P. and Healy, J. (2003) 'The Development of Children's Attitudes Towards "The Troubles" in Northern Ireland', in O. Hargie and D. Dickson (eds.) *Researching the Troubles: Social Science Perspectives on the Northern Ireland Conflict*. Edinburgh and London: Mainstream Publishing).

Coogan, T. P. [1971] (2000) *The IRA* (London: Harper Collins Publishers).

—— (1980) *On the Blanket: The H-Block Story* (Dublin: Ward River Press).

Coolsaet, R. (ed.) (2008) *Jihadi Terrorism and the Radicalisation Challenge in Europe* (Aldershot: Ashgate).

Corcoran, M. (2006) *Out of Order: The Political Imprisonment of Women in Northern Ireland 1972–1998* (Cullompton: Willan Publishing).

Corsaro, W. A. (2005) *The Sociology of Childhood*, second edition (Thousand Oaks, CA, London and New Delhi: Pine Forge Press).

Council of the European Union (2007) '*The EU Strategy for Combating Radicalisation and Recruitment – Implementation Report*' Report for Council of the European Union (EU: Brussels).

Couser, G. T. (1997) *Recovering Bodies: Illness, Disability and Life Writing* (Madison, WI: University of Wisconsin Press).

Craig, M. L. (2002) *Ain't I a Beauty Queen? Black Women, Beauty and the Politics of Race* (Oxford: Oxford University Press).

Crawley, E. and Crawley, P. (2007) 'Culture, Performance and Disorder and the Communicative Quality Of Prison Violence', in Byrne, J. and Taxman, F. (eds.) *Prison Violence and Prison Culture*. (Boston, MA: Allyn and Bacon).

Crenshaw, M. (2004). 'Terrorism', in N. J. Smelser and P. B. Baltes (eds.) *International Encyclopedia of the Social and Behavioural Sciences'*. (Amsterdam: Elsevier Ltd), 15604–6.

—— (2008) '"New" Versus "Old" Terrorism: A Critical Appraisal', In R. Coolsaet (ed.) *Jihadi Terrorism and The Radicalisation Challenge in Europe'* Farnham, Surrey: Ashgate), 25–38.

Crewe, D. (2009) 'Will to Self-Consummation, and Will To Crime: A Study in Criminal Motivation', in R. Lippens and D. Crewe (eds.) *Existentialist criminology* (London and New York: Routledge-Cavendish), 12–50.

Croft, S. (2006) *Culture, Crisis and America's War on Terror* (Cambridge: Cambridge University Press).

Curcio, S. (2005) 'The Dark Side of Jihad: How Young Men Detained At Guantanamo Assess Their Experiences'. in C. Benard (ed.) *A Future for the Young: Options for Helping Middle Eastern Youth Escape the Trap of Radicalization.*

Currie, E. (2002) *Diaries 1978–1992* (London: Little Brown and Company).

Dallos, R. (1997) 'Constructing Family Life: Family Belief Systems', in J. Muncie, M. Wetherell, M. Langan, R. Dallos and A. Cochrane (eds.) *Understanding the Family*, second edition (London, Thousand Oaks, CA, and New Delhi: Sage Publications).

Daly, N. (2005) 'Nationalism, Imperialism and Identity in Late Victorian Culture: Civil and Military Worlds by Steve Attridge' [review]. *Victorian Studies*, 47(2), 305–7.

Danahay, M. A. (1993) *A Community of One: Masculine Autobiography and Autonomy in Nineteenth-Century Britain* (New York: SUNY Press).

Daniel. M. (1994) 'Biography as a Cultural Discipline' in M. Daniel and L. Embree (eds.) *Phenomenology of the Cultural Disciplines* (Dordrecht, Boston and London: Kluwer Academic Publishers).

Darby, J. and MacGinty, R. (2003) 'Coming out of Violence: A Comparative Study of Peace Processes', in O. Hargie and D. Dickson (eds.) *Researching the Troubles: Social Science Perspectives on the Northern Ireland Conflict* (Edinburgh and London: Mainstream Publishing).

D'Arcy, M. (1981) *Tell Them Everything: A Sojourn in the Prison of Her Majesty Queen Elizabeth II at Ard Macha (Armagh)* (London: Pluto Press).

Davies, C. A. (1999) *Reflexive Ethnography: A Guide to Researching Selves and Others* (London: Routledge).

Davies, I. (1990) *Writers in Prison* (Oxford: Blackwell Publishers).

Davis, A. [1974] (1990) *An Autobiography* (London: Women's Press).

De Figueiredo Jr, R. J. P. and Weingast, B. R. (2001) 'Vicious Cycles: Endogenous Political Extremism and Political Violence', (http://faculty.haas.berkeley.edu/rui/m13.04.pdf [accessed 6 July 2009]).

De Man, P. (1984) *Rhetoric of Romanticism* (New York: Columbia University Press).

De Mause, L. (ed.) (1974) *The History of Childhood* (London: Souvenir Press).

De Mesquita, E. B. and Dickson, E. S. (2007) 'The Propaganda of the Deed: Terrorism, Counterterrorism and Mobilization'. *American Journal of Political Science*, 51(2), 364–81.

De Mijolla-Mellor, S. (2006) 'Sublimation', in Mijolla, A. D. (ed.) *International Dictionary of Psychoanalysis* (online). Gale Cengage, 2005 (http://www.enotes.com/psychoanalysis-encyclopedia).

De Schweinitz, R. (2005) 'The "Shame of America": African-American Civil Rights and the Politics of Childhood', in Goddard, J., McNamee, S., James, A. and James, A. (eds.) *The Politics of Childhood: International Perspectives, Contemporary Developments* (Basingstoke: Palgrave Macmillan), 50–70.

Dearey, M. (2005) *Life in the Pen: Subject Representation in Political Prisoner Auto/Biography, 1963–1983* (York: University of York).

—— (2006) 'Soledad Sister: On the Absence of Angela Davis from Current Historiographies of the Black Power Movement' *a/b: Autobiography Studies*, 21(2), 222–46.

—— (2007) 'The Irish Wordsworth? A Criminological Analysis of the Prison Life Writings of Bobby Sands', in Sparkes, A. (ed.) *Auto/biography Yearbook* (Oxford: Clio Publishing, 1–21).

Defoe, D. [1719] (1985) *Robinson Crusoe* (London: Penguin Classics).

Delion, P. (2006) 'Death Instinct (Thanatos)', in Mijolla, A. D. (ed.) *International Dictionary of Psychoanalysis* [Online]. Gale Cengage, 2005. Available at eNotes. com (http://www.enotes.com/psychoanalysis-encyclopediadeath-instinct-thanatos [accessed 23 January 2009]).

DeNora, T. (1995) *Beethoven and the Construction of Genius: Musical Politics in Vienna 1792–1803* (Berkeley, CA: University of California Press).

Denzin, N. (1989) *Interpretive Biography* (Newbury Park: Sage).

Department for Children, Schools and Families (2008a) 'Learning Together to Be Safe: A Toolkit to Help Schools Contribute to the Prevention of Violent Extremism' (Annesley, Nottinghamshire: DCSF Publications).

——(2008b) 'Schools to Play Key Role in Preventing Violent Extremism'. Press notice 2008/0223 (London: Department for Children, Families and Schools, www.dcsf.gov. uk/pns/DisplayPN.cgi?pn_id = 2008_0223 [accessed 13 October 2008]).

Derrida, J. (1985) *Otobiography: The Ear of the Other* (Lincoln and London: University of Nebraska Press).

——(1986) *Memoires for Paul de Man*, (Lindsay, C., Culler, J., Cadava, E. and Kamuf, P. Trans.) (New York: Columbia University Press).

Diani, M. and Forno, F. (2003) Italy, in Rootes, C. (ed.) *Environmental Protest in Western Europe* (Oxford: Oxford University Press), 135–65.

Dilthey, W. (1976) *Selected Writings*. (Rickman, H. P. Trans.) (Cambridge: Cambridge University Press).

Dittmer, J. (1994) *Local People: The Struggle for Civil Rights in Mississippi*, (Urbana, IL: University of Illinois Press).

Donlan, L. (2007) *How Did This Happen Here?: Japanese Internment Camps*, (Mankato, MN: Raintree).

Durana, J. (2008) 'Review of Who's Afraid of the Children? Children, Conflict and International Relations by Helen Brocklehurst'. *Political Studies Review*, 6(1), 115–16.

Durkheim, E. (1938) *The Rules of Sociological Method* (Glencoe, IL: Free Press).

——(1952) *Suicide: A Study in Sociology* (London: Routledge and Kegan Paul).

——(1960) *The Division of Labour in Society* (Glencoe, IL: Free Press).

Durodie, B. (2004) 'Cultural Influences on Resilience and Security'. *Homeland Security and Resilience Monitor*, 3(7), 4–6.

——(2006) 'Cultural Precursors and Psychological Consequences of Contemporary Western Responses to Acts of Terror', in Fitzduff, M. and Stout, C. E. (eds.) *The Psychology of Resolving Global Conflicts* (Westport, CT: Praeger Press), 307–26.

Durodie, B. (2006) 'We Are the Enemies Within'. *The Times Higher Education Supplement*, 22 September 2006. (www.timeshighereducation.co.uk/story.asp?sectioncode = 26and storycode = 205528 [accessed 29 July 2008]).

Dworkin, A. (2000) *Scapegoat: The Jews, Israel and Women's Liberation* (New York: Free Press).

Dwyer, C. (2008) 'Political Prisoners', in Jewkes, Y. and Bennett, J. (eds.) *Dictionary of Prisons and Punishment* (Cullompton, Devon: Willan Publishing), 204–6.

Dyer, C., Mccoy, R. E., Rodriguez, J. and Van Duyn, D. N. (2007) 'Countering Violent Islamic Extremism: A Community Responsibility'. *FBI Law Enforcement Bulletin*, 76(12), 3.

Dyson, M. E. (1995) *Making Malcolm: The Myth and Meaning of Malcolm X* (New York: Oxford University Press).

Eager, P. W. (2008) *From Freedom Fighters to Terrorists: Women and Political Violence* (Aldershot: Ashgate Publishing, Ltd).

Eagleton, T. (2005) *Holy Terror* (Oxford and New York: Oxford University Press).

Edgell, S. and Duke, V. (1986) 'Radicalism, Radicalization and Recession: Britain in the 1980s'. *British Journal of Sociology*, 37(4), 479–512.

Edwards, D. B. (1993) 'Summoning Muslims: Print, Politics and Religious Ideology in Afghanistan'. *Journal of Asian Studies*, 52(3), 609.

Edwards, R. (2002) 'Violence Against Women and Crime Prevention'. Paper presented at Expanding Our Horizons: Understanding the Complexities of Violence Against Women, Meaning, Cultures, Difference Conference. University of Sydney, Australia, 18–22 February 2002 (www.austdvclearinghouse.unsw.edu.au/Conference%20papers/Exp-horiz/Edwards.pdf [accessed 25 November 2008]).

Elam, D. (1994) *Feminism and Deconstruction: Ms. En Abyme* (London and New York: Routledge).

Elias, N. (1978–81) *The Civilizing Process.* (Jephcott, E. Trans.) (Oxford: Blackwell).

Ellmann, M. (1993) *The Hunger Artists: Starving, Writing and Imprisonment* (Cambridge, MA: Harvard University Press).

Ellner, S. (2005) 'Revolutionary and Non-Revolutionary Paths of Radical Populism: Directions of the Chavista Movement in Venezuela'. *Science and Society*, 69(2), 160–90.

Enders, W., Sandler, T., Keith, H. and Todd, S. (1995) 'Terrorism: Theory and Applications'. *Handbook of Defense Economics*, vol. 1 (Amsterdam: Elsevier), 213–49.

Ericson, R. V. and Haggerty, K. D. (1997) *Policing the Risk Society* (Oxford: Clarendon Press).

Evans, M. (1998) *Missing Persons: The Impossibility of Auto/Biography* (London: Routledge).

Falk, P. (1994) *The Consuming Body* (London and Thousand Oaks, CA: Sage Publications).

Fanon, F. (1968) *Black Skin, White Masks* (London: MacGibbon and Kee).

Farrall, S. (2009) '"We Just Live Day-to-Day": A Case Study of Life After Release Following Wrongful Conviction', in Lippens, R. and Crewe, D. (eds.) *Existential Criminology* (London: Routledge-Cavendish), 169–96.

Feeley, M. M. and Simon, J. (1992) 'The New Penology: Notes on the Emerging Strategy of Corrections and Its Implications'. *Criminology*, 30(4), 449–74.

Feldman, A. (1991) *Formations of Violence: The Narrative of the Body and Political Terror in Northern Ireland.* (Chicago, IL: University of Chicago Press).

——(2003) 'Political Terror and the Technologies of Memory: Excuse, Sacrifice and Actuarial Violence'. *Radical History Review*, winter (85), 58–73.

Felski, R. (1989) *Beyond Feminist Aesthetics: Feminist Literature and Social Change* (New York: Hutchinson Radius).

Ferguson, K. E. (1993) *The Man Question: Visions of Subjectivity in Feminist Theory.* (Berkeley, CA and Oxford: University of California Press).

Finch, J. and Mason, J. (1993) *Negotiating Family Responsibilities* (London: Routledge).

Finley, C. (1998) *Art of Japan* (Minneapolis, MN: Lerner Publications).

First, R. [1965] (1988) *117 days: An Account of Confinement and Interrogation Under the South African Ninety-Day Detention Law* (London: Bloomsbury).

Forest, J. J. F. (ed.) (2005) *The New Children of Terror.* (Westport, CT: Praeger Security International).

Forman, J. [1972] (1985) *The Making of Black Revolutionaries* (Seattle: University of Washington Press).

Foucault, M. (1977) *Discipline and Punish: The Birth of the Prison* (London: Allen Lane).

Foucault, M., Khalfa, J. and Murphy, J. (2006) *History of Madness*, second edition. (Murphy, J. Trans.) (London: Routledge).

Foucault, M. and Martin, L. (eds.) (1998) *Technologies of the Self: A Seminar with Michel Foucault* (Amherst: University of Massachusetts Press).

Foy, A. S. (2008) 'Police and Thieves: Class, Crime and African-American Autobiography', paper presented at Crime and Cultures: Figuring Criminality in Literature, Media and Film, Portsmouth, University of Portsmouth, 14–16 July.

Fraihi, T. (2008) '(De-)Escalating Radicalisation: The Debate within Muslim and Immigrant Communities,' in Coolsaet, R. (ed.) *Jihadi Terrorism and the Radicalisation Challenge in Europe* (Aldershot: Ashgate), 131–8.

Franklin, B. [1791] (1964) *The Autobiography of Benjamin Franklin* (New Haven, CT: Yale University Press).

Franklin, H. B. (1978) *The Victim as Criminal and Artist: Literature from the American Prison* (New York: Oxford University Press).

——(ed.) (1998) *Prison Writing in 20th Century America* (London: Penguin).

Friedan, B. [1963] (1992) *The Feminine Mystique.* (Harmondsworth: Penguin).

Friedman, J. and Lash, S. (eds.) (1992) *Modernity and Identity* Oxford: Blackwell).

Gagnier, R. (1991) *Subjectivities* (New York: Oxford University Press).

Gagnier, R. [1990] (1998) 'The Literary Standard, Working-Class Autobiography and Gender', in Smith, S. and Watson, J. (eds.) *Women, Autobiography, Theory: A Reader* (Madison, WI and London: University of Wisconsin Press).

Gamage, S. (1994) 'Radicalisation of the Tamil Middle Class and Ethnic Violence in Sri Lanka'. *Journal of Contemporary Asia*, 24(2), 161.

Gane, M. (1992) *The Radical Sociology of Durkheim and Mauss* (London: Routledge).

——(1993) *Harmless Lovers? Gender, Theory and Personal Relationships* (London and New York: Routledge).

——(2003) *French Social Theory* (London and Thousand Oaks, CA: Sage Publications).

Gane, N. (2006) 'Speed Up or Slow Down? Social Theory in the Information Age'. *Information, Communication and Society*, 9(20–38).

Garland, D. (2001) *The Culture of Control: Crime and Social Order in Contemporary Society* (Oxford: Clarendon).

Gartenstein-Ross, D. (2007) *My Year Inside Radical Islam: A Memoir* (New York: Jeremy P. Tarcher).

Gaukroger, S. (1995) *Descartes: An Intellectual Biography* (Oxford: Clarendon Press).

Gerges, F. A. (2005) *The Far Enemy: Why Jihad Went Global* (Cambridge: Cambridge University Press).

Gibney, M., Howard-Hassmann, R. E., Coicaud, J.-M. and Steiner, N. (eds.) (2008) *The Age of Apology: Facing Up to the Past* (Philadelphia, PA: University of Pennsylvania Press).

Giddens, A. (1990) *The Consequences of Modernity* (Stanford, CA: Stanford University Press).

——(1991) *Modernity and Self-Identity: Self and Society in the Late Modern Age* (Cambridge: Polity Press/Blackwell Publishers).

——(1992) *The Transformation of Intimacy: Sexuality, Love and Eroticism in Modern Societies* (Cambridge: Polity Press).

——(1999) 'Family'. Reith Lecturers 4 (London: BBC).

Giddens, A. and Pierson, C. (1998) *Conversations with Anthony Giddens: Making Sense of Modernity* (Stanford, CA: Stanford University Press).

Gillespie, U. (1994) *Women in Struggle* (www.holysmoke.org/fem/fem0514.htm [accessed 29 July 2008]).

Gilman, S. L. (2000) 'Is Life Beautiful? Can the Shoah be Funny? Some Thoughts on Recent and Older Films'. *Critical Inquiry*, 26(2), 279–308.

Gilmore, L. (1994) *Autobiographics: A Feminist Theory of Women's Self-representation.* (Ithaca, NY: Cornell University Press).

——(2001) *The Limits of Autobiography: Trauma and Testimony* (Ithaca, NY: Cornell University Press).

Gilroy, P. (1993) *The Black Atlantic: Modernity and Double Consciousness* (London: Verso).

Githens-Mazer, J. (2008) 'Islamic Radicalisation Among North Africans in Britain'. *British Journal of Politics and International Relations*, 10(3), 550–70.

Goddard, J. (2005) 'Future Directions for the Study of Childhood', in Goddard, J., McNamee, S., James, A. and James, A. (eds.) *The Politics of Childhood: International Perspectives, Contemporary Developments* (Basingstoke: Palgrave Macmillan), 263–71.

Goffman, E. (1963) *Stigma: Notes on the Management of Spoilt Identity* (New York: Simon and Schuster).

——(1968) *Asylums: Essays on the Social Situation of Mental Patients and Other Inmates* (Harmondsworth: Penguin).

——[1961] (1972) *Encounters: Two Studies in the Sociology of Interaction* (London: Allen Lane).

Goodey, J. O. (2000) 'Biographical Lessons for Criminology'. *Theoretical Criminology*, 4(4), 473–98.

Graebner, W. (2008) *Patty's Got a Gun: Patricia Hearst in 1970s America* (Chicago, IL: University of Chicago Press).

Graham, S. (2002) *Shoot to Kill* (London: Blake Publishing Ltd).

Grebesallassie, T. (2003) 'Commentary: Internationalism and Post-September 11 Activism' *Social Justice*, 30(2), 133.

Groch, S. (2001) 'Free Spaces: Creating Oppositional Consciousness in the Disability Rights Movement,' in Mansbridge, J. and Morris, A. (eds.) *Oppositional Consciousness: The Subjective Roots of Social Protest* (Chicago, IL: University of Chicago Press), 65–98.

Groves, J. M. (1999) 'Animal Rights: History and Scope of a Radical Social Movement [review]'. *Contemporary Sociology*, 28(3), 347–48.

Gruen, M. (2006) 'Innovative Recruitment and Indoctrination Tactics by Extremists: Video Games, Hip-Hop and the World Wide Web', in Forest, J. J. F. (ed.) *The Making of a Terrorist: Recruitment, Training, and Root Causes* (Westport, CT and London: Praeger Security International), 11–22.

Gubrium, J. and Holstein, J. (1990) *What is Family?* (Palo Alto, CA: Mayfield Publishing Company).

Guither, H. D. (1998) *Animal Rights: History and Scope of a Radical Social Movement* (Carbondale, IL: Southern Illinois University Press).

Gusdorf, G. [1956] (1980) 'Conditions and Limits of Autobiography', in Olney, J. (ed.) *Autobiography: Essays Theoretical and Critical.* (Princeton, NJ: Princeton University Press).

Gustafson, D. L. (2007) 'White on Whiteness: Becoming Radicalized about Race'. *Nursing Inquiry*, 14(2), 153–61.

Haase, D. (ed.) (2004) *Fairytales and Feminism* (Detroit, MI: Wayne State University Press).

Hajer, M. A. (1995) *The Politics of Environmental Discourse: Ecological Modernization and the Policy Process* (Oxford: Oxford University Press).

Hanawalt, B. A. (1993) *Growing Up in Medieval London: The Experience of Childhood in History* (Oxford: Oxford University Press).

Hannah, G., Clutterbuck, L. and Rubin, J. (2008) *Radicalization or Rehabilitation: Understanding the Challenge of Extremist and Radicalized Prisoners.* Report for RAND Europe (Cambridge: RAND).

Hargie, O. and Dickson, D. (2003) 'Putting it All Together: Central Themes from Researching the Troubles', in Hargie, O. and Dickson, D. (eds.) *Researching the Troubles: Social Science Perspectives on the Northern Ireland Conflict* (Edinburgh and London: Mainstream Publishing).

Harlow, B. (1987) *Resistance Literature* (New York and London: Methuen).

—— (1992) *Barred: Women, Writing and Political Detention* (Hanover and London: Wesleyan University Press).

—— (2002) 'Redlined Africa: Ruth First's *Barrel of a Gun*'. *Biography*, 25(1), 151–70.

Healy, L. M. (2001) *International Social Work: Professional Action in an Independent World* (New York: Oxford University Press USA).

Hearst, P. C. and Moscow, W. A. [1982] (1988) *Patty Hearst: Her Own Story* [originally published as Every Secret Thing] (London: Corgi/Avon).

Heath, J., [2005] (2009) 'Methodological Individualism'. *Stanford Encyclopedia of Philosophy* (http://plato.stanford.edu/entries/methodological-individualism [accessed 6 July 2009]).

Heelas, P., Lash, S. and Morris, P. (1996) *Detraditionalisation: Critical Reflections on Authority and Identity* (Cambridge, MA: Blackwell).

Hegel, G. W. F. (1977) *The Phenomenology of Spirit.* (Miller, A. V. Trans.) (Oxford: Oxford University Press).

Hegghammer, T. (2006) 'Terrorist Recruitment and Radicalization in Saudi Arabia'. *Middle East Policy*, 12(4), 39–60.

Heidensohn, F. (2002) 'Gender and Crime', in Maguire, M., Morgan, R. and Reiner, R. (eds.) *The Oxford Handbook of Criminology*, third edition (Oxford: Oxford University Press), 491–530.

Heller, Agnes (1992) 'Death of the Subject?', in Levine, G. (ed.) *Constructions of the Self* (New Brunswick, NJ: Rutgers University Press).

Hier, S. P. (2008) 'Thinking Beyond Moral Panic: Risk, Responsibility and the Politics of Moralization'. *Theoretical Criminology*, 12(2), 173–90.

Hill, M. (2003) '"Challenging the State We're In": The Feminist Seventies in "Troubled" Northern Ireland,' in Graham, H., Neilson, A. and Robertson, E. (eds.) *The Feminist Seventies Web Book* (York: Raw Nerve Books).

Hobbs, D. and Dunnighan, C. (1998) 'Global Organised Crime: Context and Pretext', in Ruggiero, V., Taylor, I. R. and South, N. (eds.) *The New European Criminology: Crime and Social Order in Europe* (London: Routledge, 289–303).

Hodge, J. (2000) 'Kierkegaard's Writing Machines: Epistemology of the Demon', in Banham, G. and Blake, C. (eds.) *Evil Spirits: Nihilism and the Fate of Modernity.* (Manchester and New York: Manchester University Press), 22–39.

Hoffman, B. (2006) *Inside Terrorism*, revised and expanded edition. (New York: Columbia University Press).

Holroyd, M. (2002) *Works on Paper: The Craft of Biography and Autobiography.* (London: Little, Brown and Company).

Holyoake, D. (2007) 'All Spheres of Public Life are Open to Threat'. *Nursing Standard*, 21(48), 27.

Home Office (2009) 'Pursue, Prevent, Protect, Prepare: The United Kingdom's Strategy for Countering International Terrorism [CONTEST2]' (London: HM Government, RIPA).

Honderich, T. (ed.) [1995] (2005) *Oxford Companion to Philosophy*, new edition (Oxford: Oxford University Press).

Horgan, J. (2005) 'Psychological Factors Related to Disengaging from Terrorism: Some Preliminary Assumptions and Assertions', in Benard, C. (ed.) *A Future for the Young: Options for Helping Middle Eastern Youth Escape the Trap of Radicalization.*

Horowitz, D. (1998) *Betty Friedan and the Making of the Feminine Mystique: The American Left, the Cold War and Modern Feminism* (Amherst, MA: University of Massachusetts Press).

Husain, E. (2007) *The Islamist: Why I Joined Radical Islam in Britain, What I Saw Inside and Why I Left* (London: Penguin Books).

Inwood, M. J. (2005) 'Enlightenment', in Honderich, T. (ed.) *Oxford Companion to Philosophy*, new edition (Oxford: Oxford University Press), 252–3.

Ismail, N. H. (2008) 'Kinship and Radicalisation Process in Jamaah Islamiyah's Transnational Terrorist Organisation', in Coolsaet, R. (ed.) *Jihadi Terrorism and the Radicalisation Challenge in Europe* (Aldershot: Ashgate), 55–68.

Jamieson, L. [1988] (2002) *Intimacy: Personal Relationships in Modern Societies* (Cambridge: Polity Press).

Jason, H. (2007) 'Who's Afraid of Children? Children, Conflict and International Relations by Helen Brocklehurst' [book review]. *Children and Society*, 21(4), 323–4.

Jelinek, E. C. (1980) *Women's Autobiography: Essays in Criticism* (Bloomington, IN: Indiana University Press).

Jenkins, B. M. (2007) *Building an Army of Believers: Jihadist Radicalization and Recruitment* (Report for RAND Corporation Santa Monica, CA).

Jervis, R. (2003) 'Understanding The Bush Doctrine'. Political Science Quarterly. Fall 2003. vol 118. no. 3. pg 365–388.

Joannou, M. (1995) '"She Who Would Be Politically Free Herself Must Strike the Blow": Suffragette Autobiography and Suffragette Militancy', in Swindells, J. (ed.) *The Uses of Autobiography* (London and Bristol: Taylor & Francis), 31–44.

John, A. V. (1997) 'Men, Manners and Militancy: Literary Men and Women's Suffrage', in John, A. V. and Eustance, C. (eds.) *The Men's Share? Masculinities, Male Support and Women's Suffrage in Britain, 1890–1920*, (London and New York: Routledge), 88–109.

John, A. V. (2003) '"Behind the Locked Door": Evelyn Sharp, Suffragette and Rebel Journalist'. *Women's History Review*, 12(1), 5–13.

Jones, G. S. (2005) 'An End to Poverty: The French Revolution and the Promise of a World Beyond Want'. *Historical Research*, 78(200), 193–207.

Jones, S. S. (2001) *Durkheim Reconsidered* (Cambridge: Polity).

Jones, T. (2004) *A Radical Line: From the Labor Movement to the Weather Underground, One Family's Century of Conscience* (New York: Free Press).

Judovitz, D. (1988) *Subjectivity and Representation in Descartes: The Origins of Modernity* (Cambridge: Cambridge University Press).

Kadar, M. (ed.) (1992) *Essays on Life Writing: From Genre to Critical Practice.* (Toronto: University of Toronto Press).

Kant, I. (1960) *Religion within the Limits of Reason Alone* (T. T. M. G. A. H. Hudson, Trans.) (New York: Harper & Row).

Kapcia, A. (2005) 'Educational Revolution and Revolutionary Morality in Cuba: The "New Man", Youth and the New "Battle" of Ideas'. *Journal of Moral Education*, 34(4), 399–412.

Kay, S. (2005) 'Hoop Dreams', in Benard, C. (ed.) *A Future for the Young: Options for Helping Middle Eastern Youth Escape the Trap of Radicalization. September 22–23, 2005.*

Kelly, J. (2008) 'Neo-Nazi Had Child Abuse Images' (BBC News Online).

Kerbaj, R. and Kennedy, D. (2008) 'Link Between Child Porn and Muslim Terrorists Discovered in Police Raids, Paedophile Websites are Being Used to Pass Information Between Terrorists' (*Times Online*), 17 October.

Kerbaj, R., Kennedy, D., Owen, R. and Keeley, G. (2008) 'Dangerous and Depraved: Paedophiles Unite with Terrorists Online' (*Times Online*), 17 October.

Kinzie, J. D. (1989) 'Therapeutic Approaches to Traumatized Cambodian Refugees'. *Journal of Traumatic Stress*, 2(1), 75–91.

Koopman, C. (1997) 'Political Psychology as a Lens for Viewing Traumatic Events'. *Political Psychology*, 18(4), 831–47.

Kristeva, J. (1982) *Powers of Horror: An Essay on Abjection* (New York: Columbia University Press).

——(1984) *Revolution in Poetic Language* (New York: Columbia University Press).

Laclau, E. and Mouffe, C. (1985) *Hegemony and Socialist Strategy: Towards a Radical Democratic Politics* (London: Verso).

Landi, M. and Colucci, D. (2008) 'Rational and Boundedly Rational Behavior in a Binary Choice Sender–Receiver Game'. *Journal of Conflict Resolution*, 52(5), 665–86.

Lareau, A. (2003) *Unequal Childhoods: Class, Race, and Family Life* (Berkeley and Los Angeles, CA: University of California Press).

Lejeune, P. (1971) *L'Autobiographie en France* (Paris: A. Colin).

——[1973] (1982) 'The Autobiographical Contract', in Todorov, T. (ed.) *French Literary Theory Today*. (Cambridge: Cambridge University Press).

Linebaugh, P. (1993) *The London Hanged: Crime and Civil Society in the Eighteenth Century* (London: Penguin).

Little, A. (2009) *Give a Boy a Gun: One Man's Journey from Killing to Peace-Making*. (London: Darton, Longman and Todd Ltd).

Lorde, A. [1970] (1982) *Chosen Poems Old and New* (London: W.W. Norton and Company Limited).

Lubbers, R. (2007) 'Radicalisation', in National Coordinator for Counter Terrorism (Nctb) (ed.) *Radicalisation in Broader Perspective* (Breda: Broese and Peereboom), 11–13.

Luxemburg, R. (1946) *Letters from prison*, (E. A. C. Paul, Trans.) (London: Socialist Book Centre Ltd).

Lyons, D. (2006) *Theorizing Surveillance: The Panopticon and Beyond* (Cullompton, Devon: Willan Publishing).

Mabogunje, A. L. (2000) 'Institutional Radicalization, The State, and the Development Process in Africa. *Proceedings of the National Academy of Sciences of the United States of America*, 97(25), 14007.

Macfarlane, A. (1986) 'Introduction to the Study of Kinship and Marriage' (www.alanmacfarlane.com/kin/kin1_1.html).

Mairs, N. (1997) 'Introduction,' in *Recovering bodies: Illness, disability, and life writing* (Madison, WI: University of Wisconsin Press), ix–xiii.

Maldonado, J. E. (1993) 'Building "Fundamentalism" From the Family in Latin America', in Marty, M. E. and Appleby, R. S. (eds.) *Fundamentalisms and Society: Reclaiming the Sciences, the Family and Education* (Chicago, IL: University of Chicago Press), 214–39.

Mallan, K. and Stephens, J. (2002) 'Love's Coming (Out): Sexualising the Space of Desire'. *Media and Culture*, 5, 6(November), 1–6.

Mansbridge, J. (2001a) 'The Making of Oppositional Consciousness', in Mansbridge, J. and Morris, A. (eds.) *Oppositional Consciousness: The Subjective Roots of Social Protest* (Chicago, IL: University of Chicago Press), 1–19.

Mansbridge, J. (2001b) 'Complicating Oppositional Consciousness', in Mansbridge, J. and Morris, A. (eds.) *Oppositional Consciousness: The Subjective Roots of Social Protest* (Chicago, IL and London: University of Chicago Press), 238–64.

Mansbridge, J. and Morris, A. (eds.) (2001) *Oppositional Consciousness: The Subjective Roots of Social Protest*. (Chicago, IL: University of Chicago Press).

Marcus, Laura (1994) *Auto/biographical Discourses: Theory, Criticism, Practice* (Manchester and New York: University of Manchester Press).

Markel, L. C. M. W. (2006–7) 'The Making of a Terrorist: Recruitment, Training and Root Causes' [book review]. *Parameters*, winter, 129–34.

Marty, M. E. and Appleby, R. S. (eds.) (1993) *Fundamentalism and Society: Reclaiming the Sciences, the Family and Education* (Chicago, IL: and London: University of Chicago Press).

Maruna, S. (2001) *Making Good: How Ex-Convicts Reform and Re-Build their Lives* (Washington, DC: American Psychological Association).

Marx, K. [1867] (1972) *Capital: A Critique of Political Economy* (London: Lawrence and Wishart).

Mascush, M. (1997) *Origins of the Individualist Self: Autobiographical Practice and Self-Identity in England, 1591–1791* (Cambridge: Polity Press).

Mason, M. (1999) *Environmental Democracy* (London: Earthscan Publications Ltd).

Mason, M. G. (1980) 'The Other Voice: Autobiographies by Women Writers,' in Olney, J. (ed.) *Autobiography: Essays Theoretical and Critical* (Princeton, NJ: Princeton University Press).

McAdam, D., Mccarthy, J. D. and Zald, M. N. (eds.) (1996) *Comparative Perspectives on Social Movements: Political Opportunities, Mobilising Structures and Cultural Framings* (Cambridge and New York: Cambridge University Press).

McEvoy-Levy, S. (ed.) (2006) *Troublemakers or Peacemakers? Youth and Post-Accord Peacebuilding* (Notre Dame, IN: University of Notre Dame Press).

McGuire, M. (1973) *To Take Arms: A Year in the Provisional IRA* (London: Macmillan).

McIntyre, A. (1981) *After Virtue: A study in Moral Theory* (London: Duckworth).

McKie, L. and Lombard, N. (2005) 'Violence and Families: Boundaries, Memories and Identities', in Mckie, L. and Cunningham-Burley, S. (eds.) *Families in Society: Boundaries and Relationships* (Bristol: Policy Press), 169–84.

McNamee, S., James, A. and James, A. (2005) 'Family Law and the Construction of Childhood in England and Wales', in Goddard, J., McNamee, S., James, A. and James, A. (eds.) *The Politics of Childhood: International Perspectives, Contemporary Developments* (Basingstoke: Palgrave Macmillan), 226–44.

McNay, L. (2000) *Gender and Agency: Reconfiguring the Subject in Feminist and Social Theory* (Cambridge: Polity Press).

Merton, R. (1988) 'Some Thoughts on the Concept of Sociological Autobiography', in Riley, M. W. (ed.) *Sociological Lives* (Newbury Park: Sage).

Middleton, J. (1998) *Convictions: A Woman Political Prisoner Remembers.* (Randburg, South Africa: Ravan Press).

Middleton, S. (1987). 'Schooling and Radicalisation: Life Histories of New Zealand Feminist Teachers'. *British Journal of Sociology of Education*, 8(2), 169.

Miller, N. K. (1994) 'Representing Others: Gender and the Subjects of Autobiography". *Differences*, 6, 1–27.

Miller, N. K. [1985] (1995) 'Changing the Subject: Authorship, Writing and the Reader', in Burke, S. (ed.) *Authorship: From Plato to the Postmodern, a Reader* (Edinburgh: University of Edinburgh Press).

Millett, K. (1994) *The Politics of Cruelty: An Essay on the Literature of Political Imprisonment.* (London: Viking Press).

Mills, C. W. [1959] (1970) *The Sociological Imagination* (Harmondsworth: Penguin).

Milton-Edwards, B. (2005) *Islamic Fundamentalism since 1945* (London and New York: Routledge).

Misztal, B. A. (2003a) 'Collective Memory in a Global Age: Learning How and What to Remember', paper presented at the Collective Memory and Collective Knowledge in a Global Age – An Interdisciplinary Workshop, London, 17–18 June 2007).

——(2003b) *Theories of Social Remembering.* (Maidenhead: McGraw-Hill International).

Moonman, E. (2005) *Learning to Live in the Violent Society* (Bloomington, IN: AuthorHouse).

Morgan, R. (1989) *The Demon Lover: On the Sexuality of Terrorism* (New York and London, W.W. Norton and Company).

Morgan, S. (1999) 'Prison Lives: Critical Issues in Reading Prisoner Autobiography'. *Howard Journal*, 38(3), 328–40.

Mostern, K. (1999) *Autobiography and Black Identity Politics: Racialization in Twentieth-Century America* (Cambridge: Cambridge University Press).

Munthe, T. (2005) 'Terrorism: Not Who But Why?' *RUSI Journal*, 150(4), 8–12.

Murray, P. (1996) 'In Search of Honey-Voiced Sappho'. *TLS*, 4854, 11.

Myers, S. L. (2003) 'Death Toll Rises as Bombings Escalate Chechnya's War'. *New York Times*, 152(52564), 4.

Nagel, T. (1970) *The Possibility of Altruism* (Oxford: Clarendon Press).

Namias, J. (1993) *White Captives: Gender and Ethnicity on the American Frontier.* (Chapel Hill, NC: University of North Carolina Press).

Nardoccio, E. (ed.) (1997) *Readers Response to Literature: The Empirical Dimension* (Berlin and New York: Mouton de Gruyter).

Nasaw, D. (1985) *Children of the City* (New York: Anchor).

Nasstrom, K. L. (2003) 'Sisters In The Struggle: African American Women in the Civil Rights-Black Power Movement'. *Journal of Southern History*, 69(4), 981–2.

National Coordinator for Counter Terrorism (NCTb) (2007) 'Radicalisation in Broader Perspective' (Broese and Peereboom: Breda).

Nead, L. (1992) *The Female Nude: Art, Obscenity, and Sexuality* (London: Routledge).

Neier, A. (2005) 'Confining Dissent: The Political Prison', in Morris, N. and Rothman, D. J. (eds.) *Oxford History of the Prison: The Practice of Punishment in Western Society* (Oxford and New York: Oxford University Press), 350–80.

Nellis, M. (2002) 'Prose and Cons: Offender Auto/Biographies, Penal Reform and Probation Training'. *Howard Journal*, 41(5), 434–68.

Nesser, P. (2005) 'Profiles of Jihadist Terrorists in Europe', 'In A Future for the Young: Options for Helping Middle Eastern Youth Escape the Trap of Radicalization [working paper WR-354]'. (New York: RAND Corporation), 31–49.

Neumann, P. R. (2008) 'Forward', in Neumann, P. R., Stoil, J. and Esfandiary, D. (eds.) *Perspectives on Radicalisation and Political Violence: Papers from the First International Conference on Radicalisation and Political Violence* (London: International Centre for the Study of Radicalisation and Political Violence).

Neumann, P. R., Stoil, J. and Esfandiary, D. (eds.) (2008) 'Perspectives on Radicalisation and Political Violence: Papers from the First International Conference on Radicalisation and Political Violence.' (London: International Centre for the Study of Radicalisation and Political Violence).

Newburn, T. (2007) *Criminology* (Cullompton, Devon: Willan Publishing).

Nielsen, J. S. (2007) 'The Discourse of "Terrorism" Between Violence, Justice and International Order', in Abbas, T. (ed.) *Islamic Political Radicalism: A European Perspective* (Edinburgh: Edinburgh University Press), 15–24.

Nussbaum, F. (1989) *The Autobiographical Subject*, second edition (Baltimore, MD: John Hopkins University Press).

Obaid-Chinoy, S. (2007) 'Terrorism and Children'. *Countering the Terrorist Mentality: eJournal USA Foreign Policy Agenda*, May (US Department of State).

O'Hearn, D. (2006) *Bobby Sands: Nothing but an Unfinished Song* (London: Pluto Press).

O'Keefe, T. (2006) 'Menstrual Blood as a Weapon of Resistance'. *International Feminist Journal of Politics*, 8(4), 535–6.

O'Keeffe, A. (2006) 'Planet Saved? Why the Green Movement is Taking to the Streets' [cover story]. *New Statesman*, 135(4817), 12–15.

Olney, J. (ed.) (1980) *Autobiography: Essays Theoretical and Critical* (Princeton, NJ: Princeton University Press).

Olujic, M. B. (1998) 'Children in Extremely Difficult Circumstances: War and its Aftermath in Croatia', in Scheper-Hughes, N. and Sargent, C. (eds.) *Small Wars: The Cultural Politics of Childhood* (Berkeley, CA and London: University of California Press), 318–30.

O'Malley, P. (2001) 'Policing Crime Risks in the Neo-Liberal Era', in Stenson, K. and Sullivan, R. (eds.) *Risk and Justice: The Politics of Crime Control in Neo-Liberal Democracies.* (Cullompton, Devon: Willan Publishing).

——(2006) 'Criminology and Risk', in Mythen, G. and Walklate, S. (eds.) *Beyond the Risk Society: Critical Reflections on Risk and Human Security* (Maidenhead: Open University Press).

Opie, I. and Opie, P. (eds.) (1997) *Oxford Dictionary of Nursery Rhymes* (Oxford: Oxford University Press).

Palmer, S. H. (1972) *The Violent Society* (Lanham, MD: Rowman and Littlefield).

Parr, S. (1992) 'Everyday Reading and Writing Practices of Normal Adults: Implications for Aphasia Assessment'. *Aphasiology*, 6(3), 273–83.

Patton, J. O. (2004) 'African American Women, Civil Rights and Black Power'. *Journal of African American History*, 89(3), 262–5.

Payne, C. M. (1996) *I've Got the Light of Freedom: The Organizing Tradition and the Mississippi Freedom Struggle* (Berkeley, CA: University of California Press).

Pedahzur, A. and Perliger, A. (2006) 'The Making of Suicide Bombers: A Comparative Perspective', in Forest, J. J. F. (ed.) *The Making of a Terrorist: Recruitment, Training and Root Causes* (Westport, CT and London: Praeger Security International), 151–64.

Pedahzur, A., Perliger, A. and Weinberg, L. (2003) 'Altruism and Fatalism: The Characteristics of Palestinian Suicide Terrorists'. *Deviant Behavior*, 24(4), 405–23.

Pei, M. (2003) 'The Paradoxes of American Nationalism'. *Foreign Policy*, 136, 30–7.

Perkins, M. V. (2000) *Autobiography as Activism: Three Black Women of the Sixties* (Jackson, MS: University of Mississippi Press).

Plummer, K. (1995) *Telling Sexual Stories: Power, Change and Social Worlds* (London: Routledge).

——(2001) *Documents of Life 2: An Invitation to Critical Humanism* (London: Sage).

Pollock, L. A. (1983) *Forgotten Children: Parent-Child Relations from 1500 to 1900–* (Cambridge: Cambridge University Press).

Potter, J. (1996) *Representing Reality: Discourse, Rhetoric and Social Construction.* (London and Thousand Oaks, CA: Sage Publications).

Qutb, S. (2006) *Milestones* (New Delhi: Islamic Book Service).

RAND (2007) 'The Radicalization of Diasporas and Terrorism: A Joint Conference by the RAND Corporation and the Center for Security Studies, Zurich', in Hoffman, B., Rosenau, W., Curiel, A. J. and Zimmermann, D. (eds.), (RAND Corporation).

Rasmussen, L. M. (2009) 'Is Laughter the Best Medicine After All? The Use of Humor in Breast Cancer Memoirs by Meredith Norton and Tania Katan', paper presented at the 'The Work of Life-Writing' conference, London, 26–28 May 2009.

Rauch, J. (2007) 'Activists as Interpretive Communities: Rituals of Consumption and Interaction in an Alternative Media Audience'. *Media Culture Society*, 29(6), 994–1013.

Rayson, A. (1999) 'Beneath the Mask: Autobiographies of Japanese American Women', in: Brownley, M. W. and Kimmich A. B. (eds.) *Women and Autobiography*. Lanham, MA: Rowman and Littlefield Publishers, 131–47.

Reage, P. (1976) *Story of O.* London: Corgi.

Reed, A. (2009) 'Revisiting RD Laing: The Role of Nurture'. *Mental Health Practice*, 12(6), 16–19.

Regan, T. (2004) *The Case for Animal Rights* (Berkeley, CA: University of California Press).

Ricœur, P. (1994) *Oneself as Another* (Chicago, IL: University of Chicago Press).

Ritchie, J. and Lewis, J. (2003) *Qualitative Research Practice: A Guide for Social Science Students and Researchers* (London: Sage).

Roberts, B. (2002) *Biographical Research* (Buckingham: Open University Press).

Rojas, M. and Rodríguez Calderón, M. (1971) *Tania: The Unforgettable Guerrilla* (New York: Random House).

Rootes, C. (2003) 'The Transformation of Environmental Activism: An Introduction, in Rootes, C. (ed.) *Environmental Protest in Western Europe*' (Oxford: Oxford University Press), 1–19.

Roy, O., (2008) 'Radicalisation and De-radicalisation', in Neumann, P. R., Stoil, J. and Esfandiary, D. (eds.) 'Perspectives on Radicalisation and Political Violence: Papers from the First International Conference on Radicalisation and Political Violence' (London: International Centre for the Study of Radicalisation and Political Violence), 8–14.

Rucht, D. and Roose, J. (2003) 'Germany', in C. Rootes (ed.) *Environmental Protest in Western Europe* (Oxford: Oxford University Press), 80–108.

Rugh, A. B. (1993) 'Reshaping Personal Relations in Egypt', in Marty, M. E. and Appleby, R. S. (eds.) *Fundamentalism and Society: Reclaiming the Sciences, the Family and Education* (Chicago, IL and London: University of Chicago Press), 151–80.

Saadawi, N. E. (1983) *Memoirs from the Women's Prison* (M. Booth, Trans.) (Berkeley, CA: University of California Press).

Sageman, M. (2004) *Understanding Terror Networks* (Philadelphia, PA: University of Pennsylvania Press).

Said, E. W. [1981] (1997) *Covering Islam: How the Media and the Experts Determine How We See the Rest of the World* (London: Vintage).

Sands, B. (1983) *One Day in My Life* (Cork and Dublin: Mercier Press).

——(1998) *Writings from Prison* (Cork: Mercier Press).

Sandywell, B. (1996) *Logological Investigations*, vols 1–3. (London: Routledge).

——(2004) 'The Myth of Everyday Life: Toward a Heterology of the Ordinary'. *Cultural Studies*, 18(2–3), 160–80.

Sarachild, K. (1978) Consciousness-Raising: A Radical Weapon (http://scriptorium.lib.duke.edu/wlm/fem/sarachild.html [accessed 26 February 2008]).

Sayigh, Y. (2008) 'Negotiations and Peace Processes', paper presented at the Perspectives on Radicalisation and Political Violence: Papers from the First International Conference on Radicalisation and Political Violence, London, 17–18 January 2008.

Schinkel, W. (2009) 'Biaphobia, State Violence and the Definition of Violence', in Lippens, R. and Crewe, D. (eds.) *Existentialist Criminology* (London: Routledge-Cavendish), 70–93.

Schmid, A. P. and Jongman, A. J. (2005) *Political Terrorism: A New Guide to Actors, Authors, Concepts, Data Bases, Theories and Literature* (New Brunswick, NJ: Transaction Publishers).

Schor, J. B. (2004) *Born to Buy* (New York: Scribner).

Schudson, M. (1998) 'Delectable Materialism: Second Thoughts on Consumer Culture', in Crocker, D. A. and Linden, T. (eds.) *Ethics of Consumption: The Good Life, Justice and Global Stewardship* (Lanham, MD: Rowman and Littlefield), 249–68.

Scott, A. L. W. R. (2009) *Give a Boy a Gun* (London: Darton, Longman and Todd).

Seippel, Å. (2001) 'From Mobilization to Institutionalization? The Case of Norwegian Environmentalism'. *Acta Sociologica*, 44(2), 123–37.

Seiter, E. (1995) *Sold Separately: Children and Parents in Consumer Culture* (Chapel Hill, NC: Rutgers University Press).

Serge, V. (2002) *Memoirs of a Revolutionary* (P. Sedgwick, Trans.) (Iowa City: University of Iowa Press).

Shakespeare, T. (ed.) (1998) *The Disability Reader: Social Science Perspectives.* (London: Continuum).

Shamgar-Handelman, L. (1994) 'To Whom Does Childhood Belong?' in Qvortrup, J., Bardy, M., Sgritta, G. and Wintersberger, H. (eds.) *Childhood Matters: Social Theory, Practice, Politics* (Aldershot: Avebury), 249–65.

Shapiro, M. J. (2001) *For Moral Ambiguity: National Culture and the Politics of the Family* (Minneapolis, MN and London: University of Minnesota Press).

Shaw, C. R. (1931) *The Natural History of a Delinquent Career* (Chicago, IL: University of Chicago Press).

——[1930] (1966) *The Jack Roller: A Delinquent Boy's Own Story* (Chicago, IL University of Chicago Press).

Shaw, C. R., McKay, H. D., McDonald, J. F., Beirne, P., Thomas, W. I., Anderson, N. and Thrasher, F. M. [1923–42] (2005) *Chicago School Criminology: Brothers in Crime* (London: Taylor & Francis).

Silber, I. F. (1995) 'Space, Fields, Boundaries: The Rise of Spatial Metaphors in Contemporary Sociological Theory'. *Social Research*, 62(2), 323–55.

Silber, M. D. and Bhatt, A. (2007) *Radicalization in the West: The Homegrown Threat* (Report for New York City Police Department, New York).

Silverman, D. (2005) *Interpreting Qualitative Data: Methods for Analysing Talk, Text and Interaction*, second edition (London: Sage).

Singer, P. (2005) 'The New Children of Terror', in Forest, J. J. F. (ed.) *The Making of a Terrorist: Recruitment, Training and Root Causes*, vol. I. (Westport, CT: Praeger Security International), 105–19.

Smith, D. E. (1974) 'Women's Perspective as a Radical Critique of Sociology'. *Sociological Inquiry*, 44(1), 7–13.

Smith, S. and Watson, J. (eds.) (1998) *Women, Autobiography, Theory: A Reader* (Madison, WI and London: University of Wisconsin Press).

Solzhenitsyn, A. (1963) *One Day in the Life of Ivan Denisovich* (Harmondsworth: Penguin Books).

Sontag, S. (1983) *The Susan Sontag Reader* (London: Penguin).

Spacks, P. M. (1988) 'Female Rhetorics', in Benstock, S. (ed.) *The Private Self: Theory and Practice of Women's Autobiographical Writings* (Chapel Hill, NC: University of North Carolina Press).

Spengemann, W. C. (1980) *The Forms of Autobiography: Episodes in the History of a Literary Genre* (New Haven, CT: Yale University Press).

Spierenburg, P. (2008) *A History of Murder: Personal Violence in Europe from the Middle Ages to the Present* (Cambridge: Polity).

Stanley, J. (1998) *I am an American: A True Story of Japanese Internment* (New York: Scholastic).

Stanley, L. (1992) *The Auto/Biographical I* (Manchester: University of Manchester Press).

——(1993) On Auto/Biography in Sociology. *Sociology*, 27(1), 41–52.

Stanton, D. C. [1984] (1998) 'Autogynography: Is the Subject Different?', in Smith, S. and Watson, J. (eds.) *Women Autobiography, Theory: A Reader* (Madison, WI and London: University of Wisconsin Press).

Starrett, S. N. (1996) 'Critical Relations in Hegel: Woman, Family and the Divine', in Mills, P. J. (ed.) *Feminist Interpretations of Hegel* (University Park, PA: Pennsylvania State University Press), 253–74.

Steedman, C. K. (1986) *Landscape for a Good Woman: A Story of Two Lives* (New Brunswick, NJ: Rutgers University Press).

Steedman, C. K. (1992) *Past Tenses: Essays on Writing, Autobiography and History.* (London: Rivers Oram Press).

Steedman, C. K. (1995) *Strange Dislocations: Childhood and the Idea of Human Interiority 1780–1930* (London: Virago).

Stern, N. (2007) *The Economics of Climate Change: The Stern Review.* Report for Cabinet Office, HM Treasury (Cambridge: Cambridge University Press).

Stern, S. [1975] (2007) *With the Weathermen: The Personal Journey of a Revolutionary Woman* (New York: Rutgers University Press).

Sturrock, J. (1993) *The Language of Autobiography: Studies in the First Person Singular* (Cambridge: Cambridge University Press).

Suleman, S. (2009) 'Things Do Change' (Calderdale Council (UK)).

Sutton, J. (2003) *Draft Review of Dennis des Chene, Spirits and Clocks: Machine and Organism in Descartes* (Ithaca, NY and London: Cornell University Press, 2001, *www.phil.mq.edu.au/staff/jsutton/SpiritsandClocks.htm*).

Swindells, J. (ed.) (1995) *The Uses of Autobiography* (London: Taylor & Francis).

Sykes, G. (1958) *The Society of Captives* (Princeton, NJ: Princeton University Press).

Taylor, M. and Quayle, E. (1994) *Terrorist Lives* (London and Washington, DC: Brassey's).

Thomas, W. I. and Znaniecki, F. [1918] (1984) *The Polish Peasant in Europe and America* (Urbana and Chicago, IL: University of Illinois Press).

Tobin, E. H. (1985) 'War and the Working Class: The Case of Dusseldorf 1914–18'. *Central European History*, 18(3/4), 257.

Todorov, T. (1990) *Genres in Discourse* (Cambridge: Cambridge University Press).

Tosh, J. (1997) 'The Making of Masculinities: The Middle Class in Late Nineteenth-Century Britain', in John, A. V. and Eustance, C. (eds.) *The Men's Share? Masculinities, Male Support and Women's Suffrage in Britain, 1890–1920* (London and New York: Routledge), 38–61.

Maududi, Sayyid Abdula'la (1998) 'Towards Understanding Islam' Ahmad, K. (ed.) (Markfield, Leicestershire: Islamic Foundation, www.al-islamforall.org/litre/eng-litre/Undislam.htm [accessed 28 December 2007]).

Trnka, J. (2003) 'The West German Red Army Faction and its Appropriation of Latin American Urban Guerrilla Struggles', in Giles, S. and Oergel, M. (eds.) *Counter-Cultures in Germany and Central Europe* (Oxford and Bern: Peter Lang), 315–32.

Tyson, T. B. (1998) 'Robert F. Williams, "Black Power", and the Roots of the African-American Freedom Struggle'. *Journal of American History*, 85(2), 540–71.

UN Committee on the Rights of the Child (CRC) 'Consideration of Reports Submitted by States Parties Under Article 44 of the Convention: Convention on the Rights of the Child: Concluding Observations: United Kingdom of Great Britain and Northern Ireland', 20 October 2008, CRC/C/GBR/CO/4 (www.unhcr.org/refworld/docid/4906d1d72.html [accessed 21 July 2009]).

Unicef (2007) *Report Card 7 – Child Poverty in Perspective: An Overview of Child Well-Being in Rich Countries* (Report for Unicef, Florence).

Vahed, G. (2001) 'Race or Class? Community and Conflict Amongst Indian Municipal Employees in Durban, 1914–49'. *Journal of Southern African Studies*, 27(1), 105–25.

Valente, J. (1994) 'The Myth of Sovereignty: Gender in the Literature of Irish Nationalism'. *ELH*, 61(1), 189–210.

Vaughan, T. A. (1999) 'Shattering Silence: Women, Nationalism and Political Subjectivity in Northern Ireland' [book review]. *American Ethnologist*, 26(3), 781–2.

Videla, N. P. (2006) 'It Cuts Both Ways: Workers, Management and the Construction of a "Community of Fate" On the Shop Floor in a Mexican Garment Factory'. *Social Forces*, 84(4), 2099–120.

Voglis, P. (2002) *Becoming a Subject: Political Prisoners during the Greek Civil War* (New York and Oxford: Berghahn Books).

Wakatsuki Houston, J. and Houston, J. D. (1973) *Farewell to Manzanar* (New York and London: Bantam Books).

Walker, N. (1987) *Crime and Criminology: A Critical Introduction* (Oxford and New York: Oxford University Press).

Ward, S. (2006) 'The Third World Women's Alliance: Black Feminist Radicalism and Black Power Politics', in Joseph, P. E. (ed.) *Black Power Movement: Rethinking the Civil Rights-Black Power Era* (Oxford: Routledge).

Washington, B. T. [1901] (1996) *Up from Slavery* (Mineola, NY: Dover Publications Inc).

Watson, A. M. S. (2006) 'Children and International Relations: A New Site of Knowledge?' *Review of International Studies*, 32(2), 237–50.

Weber, M. [1930] (1992) The Protestant Ethic and the Spirit of Capitalism (Parsons, T. T., Trans.) (London and New York: Routledge).

Weekes, K. (2006) '"Other" Autobiographies: Automythography as Alternative Memoir', paper presented at the Fourth International Conference on New Directions in the Humanities, University of Carthage, Tunis, Tunisia, 3–6 July.

Weeks, J. [1986] (2003) *Sexuality*, second edition (London and New York: Routledge).

Weimann, G., 2006. 'Terrorist Dot Com: Using the Internet for Terrorist Recruitment and Mobilization', *in* J. J. F. Forest (ed.) *The Making of a Terrorist: Recruitment, Training, and Root Causes* (Westport, CT: and London: Praeger Security International), 53–64.

Weintraub, K. J. (1978) *The Value of the Individual: Self and Circumstance in Auto-biography* (Chicago, IL: University of Chicago Press).

West, E. (1992) 'Children on the Plains Frontier', in West, E. and Petrick, P. (Eds) *Small Worlds* (Lawrence, KS: University Press of Kansas), 26–41.

Whalen, L. (2007) *Contemporary Irish Republican Prison Writing: Writing and Resistance* (New York: Palgrave Macmillan).

Wheatley, F. (2007) 'Withdraw from Iraq and Root Out Radicals'. *Nursing Standard*, 21(28), 26.

Wheeler, R. (2008) 'What Works in Yorkshire and the Humber: A Guide to Projects which Help Reduce the Threat and Influence of Violent Extremism'. IN G. O. F. Y. A. T. Humber (ed.).

White, R. W. (1993) *Provisional Irish Republicans: An Oral and Interpretive History*, (London: Greenwood Press).

Wiggins, D. (1985) 'The Play of Slave Children in the Plantation Communities of the Old South, 1820–60', in Hiner, N. and Hawes, J. (eds.) *Growing up in America: Children in Historical Perspective* (Urbana, IL: University of Illinois Press), 173–92.

Wilde, O. (1999) *De Profundis, the Ballad of Reading Gaol and Other Writings* (Ware, Hertfordshire: Wordsworth Editions Publishers).

Wilson, D. and Mccabe, S. (2002) 'How HMP Grendon "Works" in the Words of Those Undergoing Therapy'. *Howard Journal*, 41(3), 279–91.

Winders, J. A. (1999) 'Writing Like a Man (?): Descartes, Science and Madness', in Bordo S. (ed.) *Feminist Interpretations of René Descartes* (University Park, PA: Pennsylvania State University Press), 114–40.

Woelfel, J., Woelfel, J., Gillham, J. and Mcphail, T. (1974) 'Political Radicalization as a Communication Process'. *Communication Research*, 1(3), 243–63.

Wolfreys, J. J. (ed.) (1999) *Literary Theories: A Reader and Guide* (Edinburgh: Edinburgh University Press).

Wonmo, D. (1987) 'University Students in South Korean Politics: Patterns of Radicalization in the 1980s'. *Journal of International Affairs*, 40(2), 233.

Wooffitt, R. (1992) *Telling Tales of the Unexpected: The Organisation of Factual Discourse* (Hemel Hempstead: Harvester Wheatsheaf).

X, M. and Haley, A. (1964) *The Autobiography of Malcolm X* (London: Penguin).

Young, A. (1996) *Imagining Crime: Textual Outlaws and Criminal Conversations* (London: Sage Publications).

Young, J. (2007) *The Vertigo of Late Modernity* (London: Sage Publications).

Zandberg, E. (2006) 'Critical Laughter: Humor, Popular Culture and Israeli Holocaust Commemoration'. *Media Culture Society*, 28(4), 561–79.

Žižek, S. (1998) *Cogito and the Unconscious* (Durham, NC: Duke University Press).

——(2008a) *For They Know Not What They Do: Enjoyment as a Political Factor*, second edition (London and New York: Verso).

——(2008b) *Violence: Six Sideways Reflections* (London: Profile Books).

Zuckerman, A. S., Dasovic, J. and Fitzgerald, J. (2007) *Partisan Families: The Social Logic of Bounded Partisanship in Germany and Britain* (Cambridge: Cambridge University Press).

Index

For Product Safety Concerns and Information please contact our EU
representative GPSR@taylorandfrancis.com
Taylor & Francis Verlag GmbH, Kaufingerstraße 24, 80331 München, Germany